COMPUTER GRAPHICS FOR DESIGNERS & ARTISTS

Isaac Victor Kerlow
& Judson Rosebush

VNR VAN NOSTRAND REINHOLD COMPANY
_____ New York

Library of Congress Catalog Card Number 85-15061
ISBN 0-442-24712-5

Printed in the United States of America

Van Nostrand Reinhold Company Inc.
115 Fifth Avenue
New York, New York 10003

Van Nostrand Reinhold Company Limited
Molly Millars Lane
Wokingham, Berkshire RG11 2PY, England

Van Nostrand Reinhold
480 La Trobe Street
Melbourne, Victoria 3000, Australia

Macmillan of Canada
Division of Canada Publishing Corporation
164 Commander Boulevard
Agincourt, Ontario M1S 3C7, Canada

16 15 14 13 12 11 10 9 8 7 6 5 4 3 2 1

**Library of Congress Cataloging-in-
Publication Data**

Kerlow, Isaac, 1958–
  Computer graphics for designers and artists.

  Bibliography: p.
  Includes index.
  1. Computer graphics. I. Rosebush, Judson.
II. Title.
T385.K47 1986   006.6'0247   85-15061
ISBN 0-442-24712-5

ACKNOWLEDGMENTS iv
INTRODUCTION v

SECTION I
Understanding the Computer 1

CHAPTER 1
Basic Concepts of Computer Graphics 3

CHAPTER 2
Hardware and Software 27

CHAPTER 3
Peripheral Devices 53

CHAPTER 4
Interfacing with the System 83

SECTION II
Visual Language 107

CHAPTER 5
Color and Black-and-White 109

CHAPTER 6
Two-dimensional Imaging Processes 125

CHAPTER 7
Three-dimensional Modeling 157

SECTION III
Applications in Design 201

CHAPTER 8
Two-dimensional Media Applications 205

CHAPTER 9
Two-dimensional Interactive Systems 235

CHAPTER 10
**Three-dimensional Media:
The Production of Material Goods** 263

CONCLUSION 283
BIBLIOGRAPHY 284
INDEX 293

ACKNOWLEDGMENTS

Books evolve through the efforts of many people. As active participants in the fields of commercial computer graphics production and design, hundreds of interactions over the years with friends, co-workers, clients, students, teachers, and the press have helped shape our attitudes and concepts.

For the actual production of this book, we wish to thank our editors, Dorothy Spencer, for her detailed suggestions and criticism, David Sachs, for his comments on the outline, and Donna Rossler, for her careful editing and her patience. Our clerical and research staff included Elaine Goodman, Ted Panken, and Gail Goldstein. For the line drawings we thank Patrice Bolté, Shane Kelly, Peter Morrison, and Mark Sudell. Those who provided pictures are credited throughout.

Finally we wish to thank our parents and our families, especially Linda Marchand and Christine Shostack.

INTRODUCTION

The decreasing price of computers, the proliferation of efficient programs, and the design of better systems have facilitated the incorporation of computer technology into design and fine arts; computer-based visual creation is a phenomenon that is currently changing the way we produce images. Graphic designers and artists, students and professionals, must therefore recognize the new possibilities that computers offer for more diverse, more efficiently executed, and more elaborate designs. This text describes, in nontechnical terms, the functions and limitations of computers in the creation of images and objects.

The merging of print, film, and broadcasting, the birth of communication channels, such as videotex and video games, and sophisticated systems with methods for generating and assembling images on a computer have revolutionized our visual environment. Systems alone, however, cannot produce effective designs at the touch of a button. Computer technology can only routinize some production and design tasks; the basic design challenges—style, functionality, and quality—must be effected by skilled professionals. Customers place new demands on designers as a result of more sophisticated graphics techniques, while designers are rewarded with new creative possibilities, new challenges, and an expanding market. Innovative artists can produce graphics that are as precise as vision, yet can simulate fantastical images, limited only by the imagination.

This text is intended as a reference tool designed to address questions that arise in the course of a career in graphics, not as a guide for programming computer graphics. This is reflected in the organization of the book, which is divided into three sections, made up of ten chapters. The first section contains background material and basic terminology, which are essential for mastering the more complex graphic procedures included in the second section. The third section describes specific applications. Definitions throughout the book appear in boldface italic and are included in the index. Figures are sequentially numbered within each chapter. A bibliography is included, with select bibliographic references scattered throughout the text.

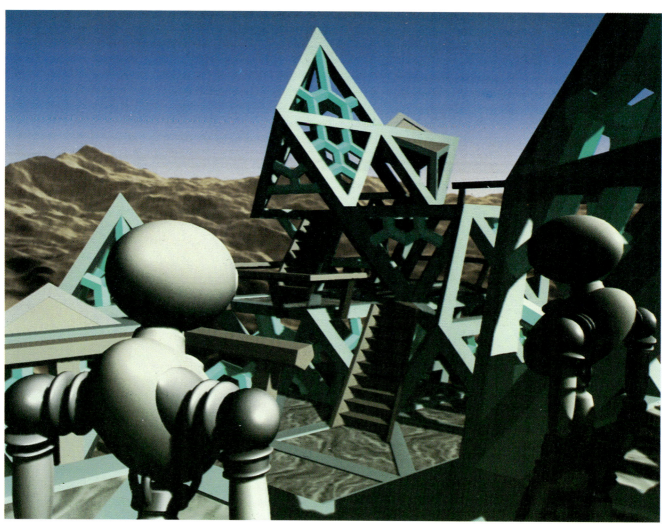

I-0. Mondo Condo by Ned Greene. Courtesy of New York Institute of Technology,
Computer Graphics Lab.

| 1 | 2 | 3 | 4 | | | | | | |

SECTION I

UNDERSTANDING THE COMPUTER

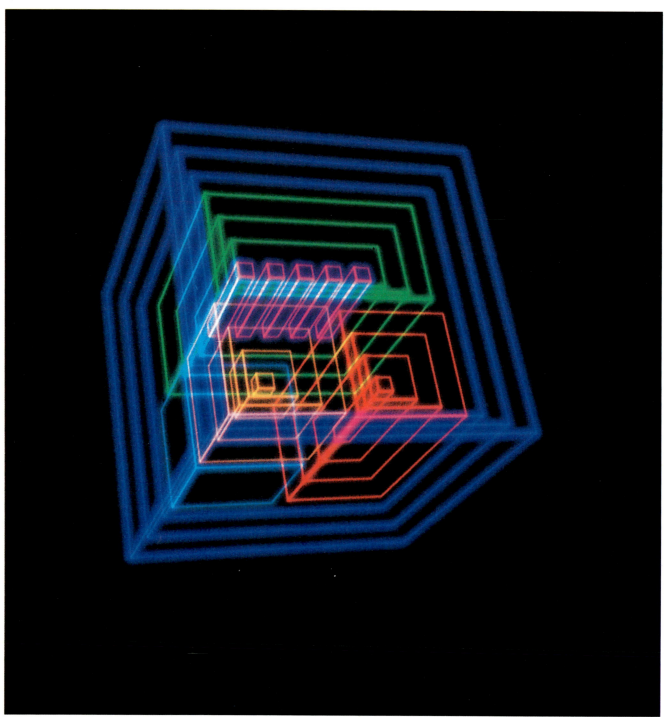

1-0. Hierarchically organized
data structures. (Courtesy
of Digital Effects Inc.)

1

BASIC CONCEPTS OF COMPUTER GRAPHICS

BITS, BYTES, AND WORDS
DATATYPE: NUMBERS AND CODES
DATA AND PROGRAMS
DATA STRUCTURES
DIMENSIONALITY AND COORDINATE SYSTEMS
CONTINUOUS AND DISCRETE
CONVERSIONS, HYBRID FORMS, AND ZELS
ANALOG AND DIGITAL
ALIASING

RELATED READING

Bradbeer, Robin, Peter DeBono, and Peter Laurie. *The Beginner's Guide to Computers.* Reading, MA: Addison-Wesley, 1982.

Greenberg, Donald, Aaron Marcus, Allan H. Schmidt, and Vernon Gorter. *The Computer Image: Applications of Computer Graphics.* Reading, MA: Addison-Wesley, 1982.

Jankel, Annabel, and Rocky Morton. *Creative Computer Graphics.* Cambridge, England: Cambridge University Press, 1984.

Laurie, Peter. *The Joy of Computers.* Boston: Little, Brown & Company, 1983.

McCarthy, John. "Information." *Scientific American* (September 1966).

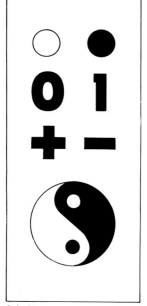

1-1. Bits can represent one of two states: void, ether; +, −; 0, 1; yin, yang.

□
A BIT

▭
A BYTE

▭
A 16-BIT WORD

▭
A 32-BIT WORD

1-2. A bit, a byte, a two-byte word, and a four-byte word.

The principles of computing explained at the beginning of this chapter are general—not limited to computer graphics—but understanding and mastering them are essential for attaining computer graphics literacy. These basic principles are therefore followed by more specialized graphics information (fig. I-0).

The introductory concepts needed for the development of computer graphics applications include numbers and codes; data structures; dimensionality, particularly that of two- and three-dimensional spaces; and the representation of multidimensional objects. Continuous and discrete methodologies are introduced, along with the basic building blocks of graphics—points, lines, planes, pixels, volumes, and voxels. The chapter concludes with a discussion of analog and digital techniques, including an explanation of the mechanics of digitizing, analog and digital conversions, and aliasing. A thorough mastery of the terms and definitions found in this chapter will facilitate understanding of the rest of this book.

BITS, BYTES, AND WORDS

A **bit** is the quantum, indivisible, unit of information, the result of a choice between two alternatives in logic or numbers. The two states of the bit correspond to the differentiation of the ether from the void, yin from yang, male from female, zero from one, and positive from negative electrical charges (fig. 1-1). Bits in a computer are used to control information as well as to represent information.

Memory in a computer is made possible by organizing bits into fixed-length strings or modular units. One of the two modular units used is the **byte,** a string of eight bits that can represent a number from 0 to 255, or a code (for example, a letter, numeral, or punctuation mark). The other modular unit is the **word,** which has a length defined by the hardware of the machine; typically it is a byte or some even multiple of bytes. Thus a word in a sixteen-bit machine contains two bytes, and a double word (or a single thirty-two-bit word) would contain four bytes (fig. 1-2).

A **kilobyte** (KB) is 1,024 bytes. The number 1,024 is the value of two raised to the tenth power. Calling 1,024 a kilobyte is a bastardization of the metric term for one thousand, but should not be confused with the third power of ten. A **megabyte** is 1,024 kilobytes, two raised to the power of twenty, or 1,048,576 bytes.

DATATYPE: NUMBERS AND CODES

Words and bytes can store numbers, letters, and even program instructions. In general, these can be organized into two major catagories or **datatypes**—numbers and codes.

Numbers are used to count. **Integer numbers,** 36 for example, are whole and indivisible. **Floating point numbers,** 98.64, for example, denote continuously varying quantities and have a decimal point.

Codes are used to represent objects or concepts—letters, suits of cards, or model numbers—and are usually organized into tables. Figure 1-3 illustrates a code table for suits of cards, and figure 1-4 a code table for letters.

In a computer, numbers are counted with bits and are called **binary numbers,** because only two digits (0, 1) are used. Integer binary numbers are counted just like decimal numbers and employ a system of positional notation with zeros (fig. 1-5). Positive and negative values may be indicated by the left-most bit. Decimal numbers (numbers with a decimal point) may be represented in the binary system as well. Binary numbers, like decimal numbers, can be added, subtracted, multiplied, and divided, and generally function like other numbers.

Codes must not be mistaken for numbers. The number *1* can be added, but the alphanumeric code for 1 is merely a symbol. For example, the number *5* is expressed as 00000101 in binary; the character *5* is expressed as 00110101.

RELATED READING

Anderson, Allan Ross, ed. *Minds and Machines.* Englewood Cliffs, NJ: Prentice-Hall, 1964.

Feigenbaum, Edward A., and Pamela McCorduck. *The Fifth Generation.* Reading, MA: Addison-Wesley, 1983.

Frates, Jeffrey, and William Moldrup. *Computers and Life.* Englewood Cliffs, NJ: Prentice-Hall, 1982.

Hofstadter, Douglas R. *Godel, Escher, Bach.* New York: Basic Books, 1979.

Hofstadter, Douglas R., and Daniel C. Dennett. *The Mind's I.* New York: Basic Books, 1981.

McCorduck, Pamela. *Machines Who Think.* San Francisco: W. H. Freeman and Co., 1979.

Minsky, Marvin. "Artificial Intelligence." *Scientific American* (September 1966).

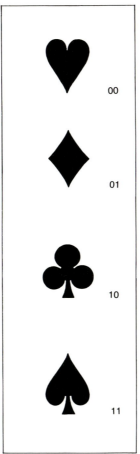

0	0011	0000
1	0011	0001
2	0011	0010
3	0011	0011
4	0011	0100
5	0011	0101
6	0011	0110
R	0101	0010
S	0101	0011
T	0101	0100
U	0101	0100
V	0101	0110
W	0101	0111
X	0101	1000

1-3. Code table for suits of cards.

1-4. Fragment of the ASCII code table.

RELATED READING

Booth, Kellogg S. *Tutorial: Computer Graphics.* Long Beach, CA: IEEE Computer Society, 1979.

Foley, James D., and Andries Van Dam. *Fundamentals of Interactive Computer Graphics.* Reading, MA: Addison-Wesley, 1982.

Freeman, H., ed. *Tutorial and Selected Readings in Interactive Computer Graphics.* Long Beach, CA: IEEE Computer Society, 1980.

Newman, William M., and Robert F. Sproull. *Principles of Computer Graphics.* 2d ed. New York: McGraw-Hill, 1979.

Decimal	Binary
0	000
1	001
2	010
3	011
4	100
5	**101**
6	110
7	111

$$1 \times 2^2 \quad 0 \times 2^1 \quad 1 \times 2^0$$

$$4 + 0 + 1 = 5$$

1-5. Binary and decimal numbers.

DATA AND PROGRAMS

Bits, or binary media, are the common elements for representing data as well as logic instructions. **Data** is the information provided for a problem; for example, in 4 + 5, the *4* and the *5* are data. In general, data refers to organized information and not to process. Numbers, letters and symbols, colors, pictures, buildings, and animation can all be stored in a computer system and are represented by numbers and codes. Data can denote material things, like a package, as well as abstract nonmaterial things, like pork belly futures.

Computers not only manage information but store, organize, and manage processes as well. Processes are executed with a **program,** a well-defined series of steps that yield a singular result. A program may be a simple function like plus ($+$) or minus ($-$) or a complicated one like "expand the contrast ratio in the photograph of the fireman."

Numerous processes in computer graphics can be expressed as programs (fig. 1-6). Two-dimensional graphic processes include freehand drawing, color mixing, making a negative, contrast expansion, and block pixing. Three-dimensional processes include perspective drawing, determining visible surfaces, texturing, and shading. Processes also exist for analyzing three-dimensional designs, controlling milling machines that fabricate parts, assembling parts, controlling factories, and auditing operations. Some processes even analyze other processes and seek to optimize the performance of a system—metaprocesses, so to speak.

When using a computer both data and programs are represented notationally. In an addition problem

$$4 + 5$$

the computer stores both the data (4, 5) and the process ($+$) internally as bits. The numbers are represented as binary numbers—100, 101—and the function $+$ is represented as an instruction or operation code. Here is a simple table:

$$00 \quad +$$
$$01 \quad -$$
$$10 \quad \times$$
$$11 \quad \div$$

The entire addition problem reads 10000101. Binary codes are also used for logical functions (not, and, or), test conditions (greater than, less than, equal to), branches, and instructions that receive and transmit data to peripherals and memory.

DATA STRUCTURES

Data is organized as a sequence of bits, bytes, or words that are in turn organized into increasingly complex forms such as matrices, records, and hierarchies.

Words in a computer are organized in memory as a numbered list starting with the word zero and continuing through the word for the highest number in the machine (fig. 1-7). The **address**, or index, of the word is its position in this numbered sequence, where it can be found if one wants to retrieve data from or add data to that specific location. Note that the content of a word is different from its address.

Users of computers, both graphic artists and programmers, seldom reference a word by its specific address, though this is possible. A word is typically referenced by a **variable name,** an English language mnemonic that the computer converts to the internal storage address. Thus, words referenced by names are called variables, because the contents of the word can vary, that is, the string of bits that make up the word can be modified by an artist or a programmer.

The computer has two primary instructions for dealing with variables in memory. The first is an operation called **read,** which locates the contents of a variable; its complementary operation is called **write,** which stores a value at the variable location. These commands extract information from and store information into a

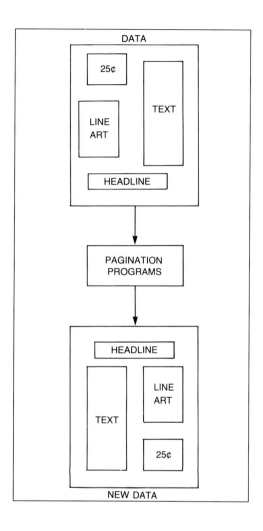

1-6. The process of designing a page is contained in a program.

1-7. Memory organization, where each location has an address and a value.

Decimal		Binary	
Address	Value	Address	Value
0	36	000	00100100
1	38	001	00100110
2	24	010	00011000
3	47	011	00101111
4	50	100	00110010
5	12	101	00001100
6	45	110	00101101
7	20	111	00010100

```
Instruction                 Variable Name
and Result                  and Contents


WRITE A 30              A    ( 30 )

WRITE B 21             B    ( 21 )

WRITE C 10             C    ( 10 )


WRITE 15 INTO A        A    ( 15 )

READ A                 B    ( 21 )

15                     C    ( 10 )


WRITE (A+B) INTO C     A    ( 15 )

READ C                 B    ( 21 )

36                     C    ( 36 )
```

1-8. Variable names permit us to read, modify, and write the contents of the computer's memory using Englishlike words.

Columns

		1	2	3	4	5	6	7
	1	2	76	32	12	64	38	31
	2	92	20	39	13	28	3	89
Rows 3		37	56	42	51	2	49	78
	4	71	43	15	58	7	80	11
	5	16	43	72	35	95	27	44

MATRIX D

1-9. The shape of this matrix of numbers is 5 × 7, or the number of rows by the number of columns. The matrix can have a single variable name, and each individual element is addressed by row and column: READ D[3,4] reads the contents of the address where the third column intersects the fourth row (15).

computer memory (fig. 1-8).

Variables in a computer are not necessarily single numbers and can be constructed with two- and three-dimensional addressing schemes. Often data is stored in a *matrix*—a well-organized collection of numbers (fig. 1-9). Each individual value in the matrix has a row and column address. The number of rows and columns when expressed as a relation (for instance, 5 × 7) is known as the *shape* of the matrix.

In addition to being stored as matrices, data may be stored as *records*, where each record is a row in a table that may contain several different data items or attributes (fig. 1-10). Data may also be organized as *trees*, which allow records, matrices, and single words to be hierarchically structured (fig. 1-11). *Relational* data structures permit information to be organized in a network fashion, so it can be accessed in a variety of ways (fig. 1-12).

Matrices, records, and networks are different ways to build *data bases*. These organized collections of information are compiled so that individual pieces of information can be retrieved by searching and sorting its attributes.

Images and objects as well as nongraphic data, such as accounting information, schedules, and descriptive textual information, are all stored in data bases. They can relate graphic data, like the representation of a bolt, to nongraphic data, such as its part number.

DIMENSIONALITY AND COORDINATE SYSTEMS

A close relationship exists between the ability to structure data and to create graphics. By definition graphics is a two-dimensional activity, though it involves other dimensions as well. For example, letters are an ingenious way of representing a one-dimensional sequence of phonetic symbols as unique two-dimensional patterns. Pictures also use perspective projections to represent volumes with three

Country	Capital	Population	Latitude	Longitude	Area (km²)	Map
Thailand	Bangkok	34,152,100	13.45 N	100.31 E	514,000	
France	Paris	51,000,000	48.52 N	2.20 E	543,998	
Mexico	Mexico City	55,000,000	19.24 N	99.09 W	1,972,544	
Hungary	Budapest	10,428,000	47.30 N	19.05 E	93,032	
Indonesia	Djakarta	119,252,000	6.05 S	106.48 E	2,000,000	

1-10. This example depicts a data set of geographic information, including a table of countries and their capitals (alphanumeric data), population (numerical data), and a contour plot of the country (pictorial data). It might also contain abstract dimensions and relationships like the per capita annual earnings. It is often used to search for attributes—for example, how many of the countries have capitals in the northern hemisphere with a population greater than one million?

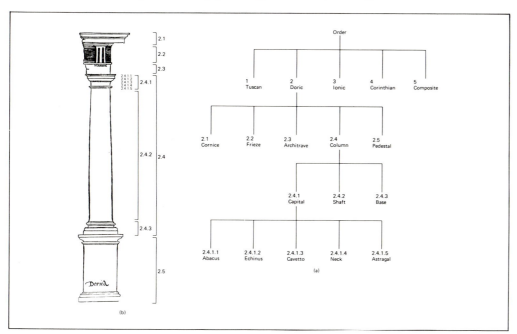

1-11. Tree-structured data base showing hierarchy of the Doric column. (Reprinted, by permission, from Mitchell, *Computer Aided Architectural Design*, 140.)

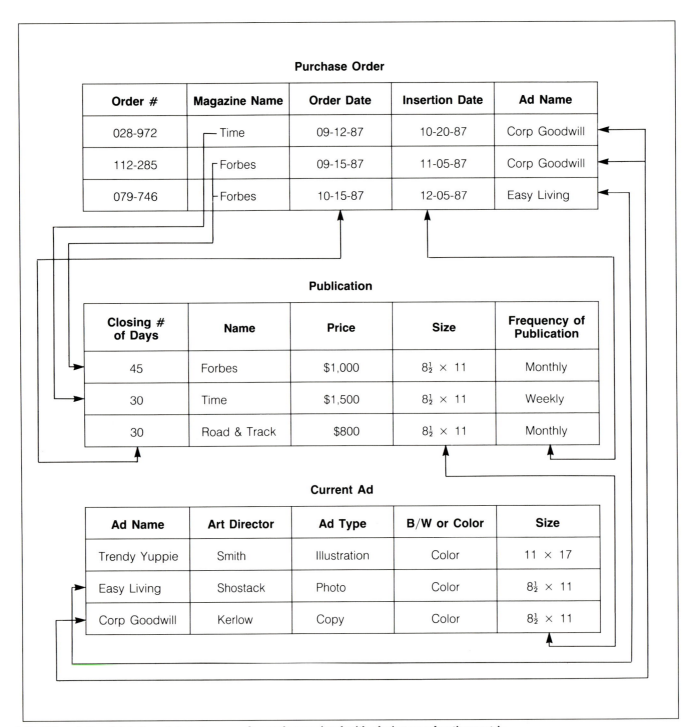

Purchase Order

Order #	Magazine Name	Order Date	Insertion Date	Ad Name
028-972	Time	09-12-87	10-20-87	Corp Goodwill
112-285	Forbes	09-15-87	11-05-87	Corp Goodwill
079-746	Forbes	10-15-87	12-05-87	Easy Living

Publication

Closing # of Days	Name	Price	Size	Frequency of Publication
45	Forbes	$1,000	$8\frac{1}{2} \times 11$	Monthly
30	Time	$1,500	$8\frac{1}{2} \times 11$	Weekly
30	Road & Track	$800	$8\frac{1}{2} \times 11$	Monthly

Current Ad

Ad Name	Art Director	Ad Type	B/W or Color	Size
Trendy Yuppie	Smith	Illustration	Color	11×17
Easy Living	Shostack	Photo	Color	$8\frac{1}{2} \times 11$
Corp Goodwill	Kerlow	Copy	Color	$8\frac{1}{2} \times 11$

1-12. This relational data base integrates several records associated with placing an advertisement in a magazine and might be used by a purchaser in an ad agency. The ad order specifies the work requested; the publication record contains data about the individual publications; and the ad description covers the ad itself.

dimensions, and sequences of pictures may involve time, the fourth dimension.

Spatial dimensions progress from the most primitive element, the **point,** a dimensionless entity. A point extended in one direction becomes a one-dimensional **line,** or an axis. A line extended along a second axis forms a **plane,** a two-dimensional surface. A plane extended along an axis perpendicular to it forms a **volume,** which has three dimensions. A volume enters the fourth dimension by incorporating **time,** which is not a spatial dimension but is orthogonal, or at right angles to volume and permits different spatial relationships to be expressed, such as in moving images for film and animation (fig. 1-13).

Computer graphics systems fuse text (one dimension), pictures (two dimensions), volumetric representations (three dimensions), and time (four dimensions) into a common binary representation. In other words, a two-dimensional blueprint and the corresponding three-dimensional object are simply different manifestations of the same data base.

The model for the two-dimensional working area of computer graphics was developed centuries ago by the mathematician and philosopher René Descartes and is called the *Cartesian coordinate system.* **Cartesian coordinates** numerically represent a two-dimensional area with width and length, say the surface of a piece of paper, by defining two mutually perpendicular axes that meet at an origin. The horizontal axis is called the *X axis* and the vertical axis is called the *Y axis.* Each axis has a scale that has a value of zero at the origin and that extends in both directions with positive and negative numbers (fig. 1-14). The scales are typically linear so that the distances between numbers are constant; scales can also be logarithmic, where distances between numbers are not constant. A location on a two-dimensional area is defined by the X and Y coordinates of that location and therefore by two numbers.

Two-dimensional spaces are not always defined with four quadrants and a central

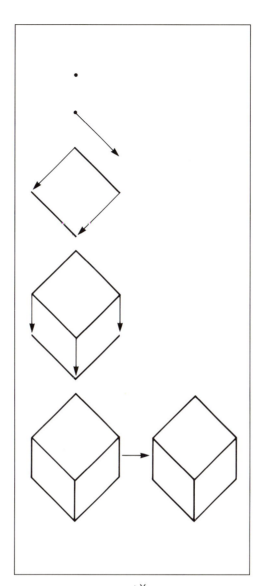

1-13. Point, line, plane, volume, time progression.

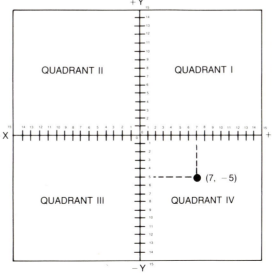

1-14. Two-dimensional Cartesian coordinate system has X and Y axes with linear scales extending in the positive and negative directions from the origin.

1-15. The origin may be placed at any of four positions in a single quadrant.

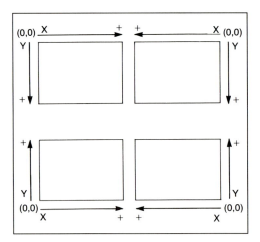

1-16. Three-dimensional coordinate system, with X, Y, and Z axes.

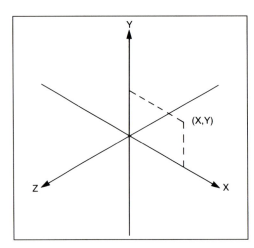

origin; sometimes only one quadrant is used, with the origin located in one of the four corners, and the direction of the positive axes different in each (fig. 1-15).

A three-dimensional space is represented by three mutually perpendicular axes intersecting at an origin. The positive X axis points right, the Y axis up, and the Z axis toward the viewer. The axes have scales, and a location in three-dimensional space is defined by the XYZ triplet of coordinates (fig. 1-16).

It is also possible to have a coordinate system in which the positive Z axis points away from the viewer, the positive X axis points left, or the positive Y axis points down. Indeed, it is possible to configure eight different axis orientations (fig. 1-17). It is imperative to know what orientation is being used in order to navigate successfully. This book follows the convention that the positive X points right, Y up, and Z toward the viewer.

Coordinate systems also exist that permit a location to be specified by an angular position instead of by one that is XY. **Polar coordinates** are two-dimensional areas with an origin at the center, and they define locations in terms of a magnitude and an angle (fig. 1-18). **Spherical coordinates** are the corresponding three-dimensional spaces, specifying a point either in terms

1-17. Eight variations of the three-dimensional axis system.

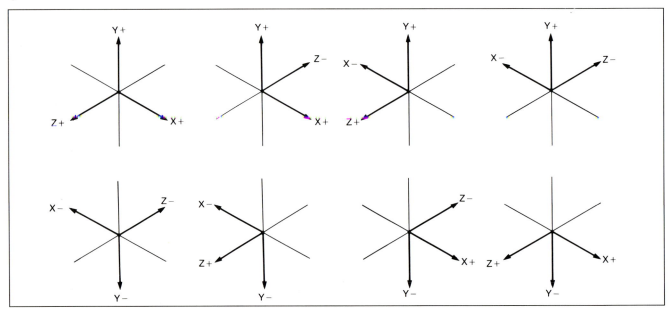

of two magnitudes and an angle, or one magnitude and two angles (fig. 1-19). These systems are often preferred in situations that involve a field of view from the standpoint of an observer.

Two-dimensional images can represent three-dimensional spaces. Photographs, for instance, can imply space, but the implication is illusory and should not be confused with space itself. After all, a photograph looked at from the side is perceived as a line and has no actual spatial volume. A three-dimensional space cannot exist in two dimensions, but a two-dimensional area can exist in three dimensions.

Sometimes two-dimensional graphics includes the concept of **priority,** that is, things on top of each other, as in cell animation, where a two-dimensional character is drawn on clear acetate and opaques a two-dimensional background (fig. 1-20). Priority systems are sometimes called *2½ dimensional.*

Two-dimensional structures that occur in a series, such as the pages of a book, may also be thought about in the aggregate as a three-dimensional structure. That is, a book is a one-dimensional serial array of two-dimensional areas.

Methodologies exist to convert three dimensions to two dimensions—**perspective**—and to convert two dimensions to three dimensions—**reconstruction.** The perspective calculation takes points in three-dimensional space and collapses them as points on a two-dimensional plane; in humans perspective is a calculation made by the lens of the eye. Reconstruction works by comparing points in two or more pictures so that a point in three-dimensional space can be determined; in humans reconstruction is a calculation made by the brain. Computer techniques for both processes are discussed in chapters 6 and 7.

CONTINUOUS AND DISCRETE

We have already noted that numbers can be expressed either as integers or

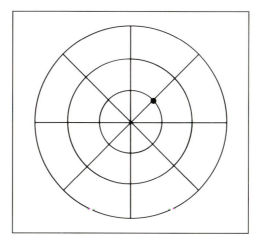

1-18. The polar coordinates of the point are located at a 45-degree angle and a radius of 100 units.

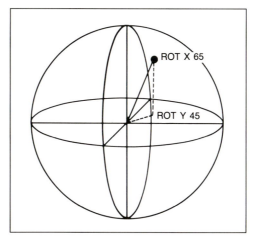

1-19. The spherical coordinates of the point are located at an angle of 45 degrees around the vertical axes, 65 degrees around the Z axes, with a radius of 7/10.

1-20. Priority or two-and-a-half-dimensional systems. (Courtesy of Activision.)

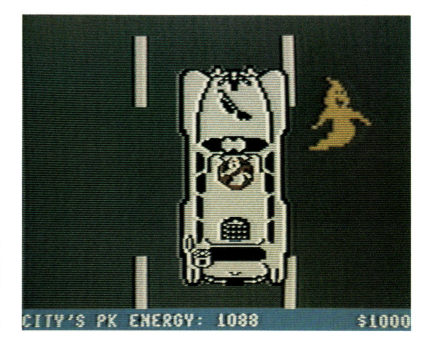

CITY'S PK ENERGY: 1088 $1000

floating point numbers. Computer graphics employs either integer or floating point numbers depending on whether the data being measured is discrete or continuous. *Discrete* data occurs in distinct units. Individuals, playing cards, and letters of the alphabet must all be represented by discrete data, as they cannot be divided and still retain their identity. Likewise, the pages of this book come in integer whole numbers and are not counted in fractional units.

Data is *continuous* if the axis or dimension that is measured has no apparent indivisible unit from which it is composed. Examples abound in our space-time-matter environment, such as weight, length, and temperature as well as an intelligence quotient or a readability index; no matter how precise the scale of measurement, a finer resolution always exists.

The continuous/discrete dichotomy applies to graphics as well as to Cartesian spaces. Both incorporate an origin, axes, and equal-interval scales. If the Cartesian space is floating point and continuous, then a location is expressed as a decimal number and called a *point,* which is an XY number pair. If the Cartesian space is discrete, a location is expressed using a pair of integers and is called a *pixel* (fig. 1-21). Pixels cannot be fractional.

The distinction between point (line) and pixel representations is analogous to the distinction between line copy and halftones in traditional graphics. Logos, diagrams, and type—objects with sharp edges and no continuous tone—are best represented as line copy, while photographs, paintings, and shaded color areas (benday) are best represented using continuous tone methods. Of course, it is possible to represent logos, type, and rules using halftone methods and to represent photographs using line copy techniques, but this crossover seldom improves visibility and is not recommended except to achieve a particular artistic effect.

Many aspects of computer graphics can be either discretely or continuously represented—time and color for example. Pixels and points are everyday tools that illustrate the fundamental differences between the two.

1-21. Continuous and discrete Cartesian areas. Points are best thought of as locations on a plane that are recorded at a precision useful to the task at hand. Points specify a location, but do not have an area. They are often used to define objects—entities that have an identity distinct from the area, or environment, in which they exist. Pixels, because they are discrete whole numbers, represent a minute area of a two-dimensional image, similar to each square on a piece of graph paper. A pixel representation is a description of a two-dimensional image, and each pixel is individually accessible. It is the collection or matrix of pixels that compose an image.

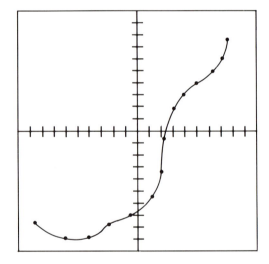

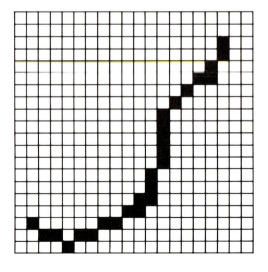

Pixels: Two-dimensional Discrete Images

A *pixel* is the basic quantum unit of an image (fig. 1-22). Pixels are discrete, modular units often organized in a rectangular matrix akin to a piece of graph paper. Each pixel corresponds to one square on the graph paper and is addressed with an integer X and Y value. The value of each pixel represents the intensity value for that area of the image. The entire matrix of pixels is called a *bitmap.* Pixel matrices have a long tradition in the graphic arts, including needlepoint, the halftone, and weaving.

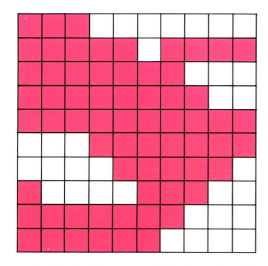

1	1	1	0	0	0	0	0	0	0
1	1	1	1	1	0	1	1	1	1
1	1	1	1	1	1	1	0	0	0
1	1	1	1	1	1	1	1	0	0
1	1	1	1	1	1	1	1	1	1
0	0	0	1	1	1	1	1	1	1
0	0	0	0	1	1	1	1	1	0
1	0	0	0	0	1	1	1	0	0
1	1	1	1	1	1	1	0	0	0
1	1	1	1	1	1	0	0	0	0

1-22. An enlarged section of a digitized image shows the grid of pixels with its corresponding numerical values. An individual pixel is the quantum unit of an image.

A simple bitmap or **bitplane** is only one bit deep and stores either a zero or a one in each pixel location and can represent black or white. Characters and symbols are often represented as pixel patterns in the shape of the letter.

The **spatial resolution** of a bitmap is the number of pixels used to represent the image from top to bottom and from right to left. Typical resolutions range from 5 × 7 dot matrices for characters to bitmaps of 1,000 pixels square and larger for images. The **aspect ratio** of a bitmap image is equal to the number of horizontal pixels divided by the number of vertical pixels (fig. 1-23).

The **intensity resolution** or **dynamic range** is a function of how many bits are used to store each pixel. Computers process images the same way they process all information, as numbers; thus the value of each pixel is represented by a number within a range or scale. Should there be two bitplanes where each pixel has two bits, four numerical possibilities exist. If there are three bitplanes, then there are eight possibilities (fig. 1-24). If there are eight bitplanes of memory, then each pixel is one byte and could have a value 0, 1, 2, 3, up to 255. The luminance value or intensity of a pixel is often stored in one byte of computer memory using binary integer numbers. A value of zero might specify black and a value of 255 white, with values between representing shades of gray (fig. 1-25).

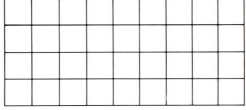

5 / 4   1.25:1 ASPECT RATIO

9 / 4   2.25:1 ASPECT RATIO

1-23. Aspect ratios are the width divided by the height of an image.

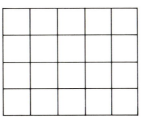
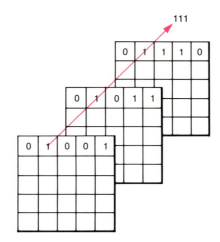

1-24. A pixel in a three-level bitmap can have any of eight intensity or color values. The value of the pixel is determined by reading in sequence the value from each one of the three levels. Eight values can be represented with a three-bit-long number: 000, 001, 010, 011, 100, 101, 110, and 111.

1-25. Pixels can specify intensity values in the image. The numbers (right) express a decimal pixel value, which is the number formed by the binary values from eight bitplanes. The decimal values are expressed as gray levels in the final image (left).

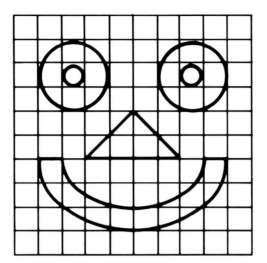

60	95	60			60	95	60	
95	20	95			95	20	95	
60	95	60			60	95	60	
			50	50				
		50	100	100	50			
95	5					5	95	
45	85	20			20	85	40	
	20	85	100	100	85	20		

1-26. Triangular pixel grids.

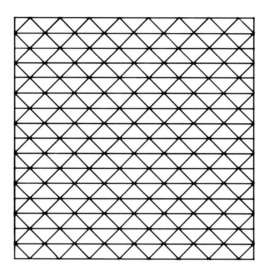

1-27. Rectangular pixels. Each pixel has an aspect ratio of 1.5:1, and the aspect ratio of the image is 2:1.

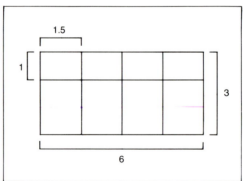

Pixels do not have to be arranged in rectilinear grids; they are sometimes organized into triangular grids (fig. 1-26), whereby each pixel touches three adjacent pixels rather than four. Pixels may also be rectangular instead of square, and in these situations the aspect ratio of the image is not equal to the aspect ratio of the bitmap (fig. 1-27).

Pixels and bitmaps may be represented by a stadium full of people with placards or with computer hardware. Computers store bitmaps in memory, where they can be simultaneously addressed by the central processing unit (CPU) and by a video processor, which displays the image on a raster television monitor.

Points, Lines, Planes: Two-dimensional Continuous Graphics

As indicated before, the differences between points and pixels stem from their continuous and discrete origins. Whereas a pixel represents an area, a point represents a location in a Cartesian environment. Points may be used to compose more complex objects.

On a plane, a point has two addresses, and two points define a straight line, also called a ***vector.*** The orientation of the line on the plane is called its ***slope.*** A more complex line can be described with several points (fig. 1-28). The term *vector graphics* has come generically to mean computer graphics defined by lines. A ***polygon*** is a closed shape formed by lines. The shapes may be simple—a square or circle—or they may be more complicated—the letter S or the contour of Australia (fig. 1-29). The simplest polygon is made of three points—a triangle—but the number of sides a polygon can have is unlimited. The corner points of a polygon are called ***vertices,*** and the sides, ***edges.***

Voxels: Three-dimensional Discrete Volumes

Three-dimensional graphics can employ both continuous and discrete methods. A point in three dimensions is still called a *point;* the discrete quantity of three-dimensional volume is the ***voxel,*** a microscopic cube, a quantum unit of volume (fig. 1-30) in a three-dimensional lattice of space. Voxels do not represent a square area or a grid of reflected light values; rather, they represent volume. A matrix of voxels is three dimensional and represents the densities of matter that occupy the space.

Voxels are digitized using density scanners, such as a Computer-Aided Tomography (CAT) scan. The scan is made as a series of discrete sections or contours, and although individual CAT scan sections might look like images, their source is not reflected light values but tissue densities (fig. 1-31).

Polyhedra: Three-dimensional Continuous Solids

Points can be three dimensional, and lines, planes, and polygons can exist in three-dimensional spatial environments, such as the volumetric world around us. Three-dimensional environments can also contain ***polyhedra***—volumetric solid objects such as a cube, sphere, or ship (fig. 1-32); each face is a facet.

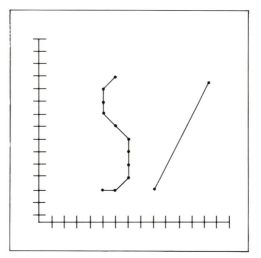

1-28. A vector is defined by two points. Many short vectors are needed to make smooth curves. The individual points, or vertices, that make up an object are often listed in sequence, with the assumption that a connecting line will be drawn between them. The list for the line is: 9, 3; 13, 12 and for the curve: 5, 3; 6, 3; 7, 4; 7, 5; 7, 6; 7, 7; 6, 8; 5, 9; 5, 10; 5, 11; 6, 12.

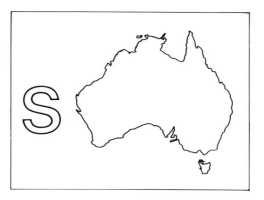

1-29. Polygons are closed shapes defined by lines.

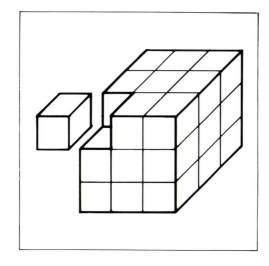

1-30. Voxels are discrete quantum units of volume.

1-31. A cross section of a human body recorded by a CAT scanner (A). A three-dimensional density of this section of the volume is represented by assigning different intensity values to the different tissue densities (B). (Courtesy of General Electric Company.)

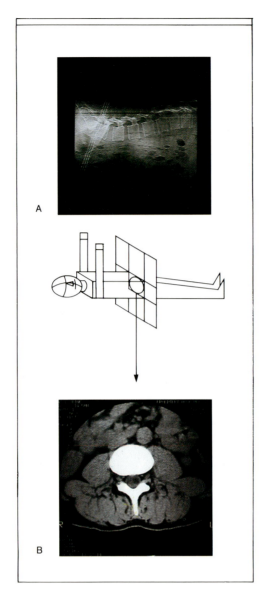

A

B

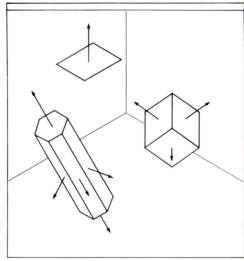

1-33. Normals indicate how a polygon is angled in space and can be thought of as rays perpendicular to the surface.

A point, line, or polygon in three-dimensional space has three spatial coordinates. All the points in a polygon lie flat on a two-dimensional plane, but they reside in a three-dimensional space. The orientation of a surface is described by a **normal,** which is the direction it is facing. A normal is specified by three numbers that indicate a line drawn perpendicular from the face of a surface (fig. 1-33). A normal is not a coordinate or position but a direction, an orientation.

Three-dimensional solid objects are defined several ways in a computer. Polyhedra may be constructed as surfaces, where a polygon, or a network of polygons, describes the surface. The simplest polyhedron, composed of four points, is the tetrahedron. Solid objects may be regular shapes in which the surfaces are bounded planes, such as a cube bounded by squares, or they may be objects whose surfaces are curvilinear, such as a sphere constructed as a mesh of polygons (fig. 1-34). Solid objects may also be mathematically defined, so that the surface of a sphere is a mathematical equation and not a series of facets. Obviously voxels can be converted to polyhedra too. We will use the term *solid models* to refer to three-dimensional solid objects in general, regardless of how they are constructed.

1-32. Three-dimensional objects defined by vertices.

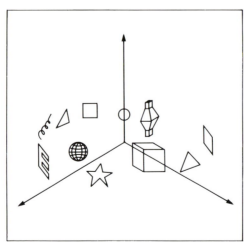

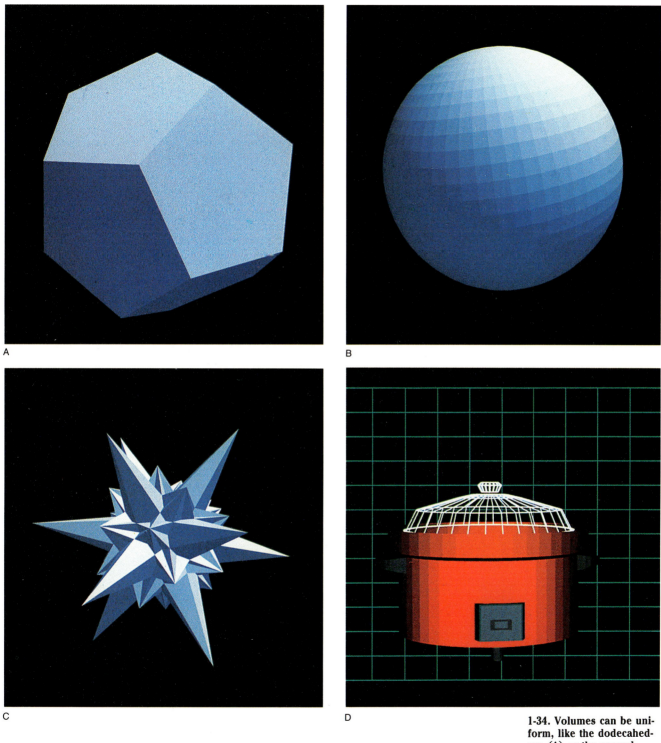

A

B

C

D

1-34. Volumes can be uniform, like the dodecahedron (A) or the second stellation of the icosahedron (C), mathematical like a sphere (B), or irregular like the crockpot (D). (Courtesy of Digital Effects Inc.)

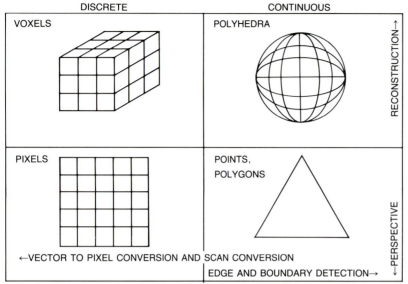

DISCRETE | CONTINUOUS

VOXELS | POLYHEDRA

←RECONSTRUCTION→

PIXELS | POINTS, POLYGONS

PERSPECTIVE↓

←VECTOR TO PIXEL CONVERSION AND SCAN CONVERSION

EDGE AND BOUNDARY DETECTION→

1-35. Cross reference table of two-dimensional/three-dimensional and discrete/continuous. *Rasterization* is a technique that converts lines to pixels. Techniques that convert contours of pixels into lines are called *edge detectors*. Procedures that convert polygon representations into pixel area representations are called *scan conversions*. And techniques that identify areas of pixels that have a uniform value and convert them to polygons are called *boundary detectors*.

1-36. Zels are discrete numbers in a two-dimensional bitmap that store three-dimensional or depth information. In this case the depth values, or Z elements, express the distance between an object and the image plane. Two depth values are shown.

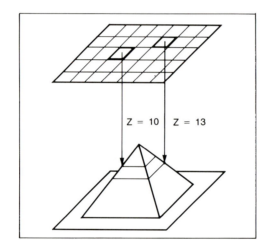

Z = 10   Z = 13

1-37. An analog signal represents continuous information.

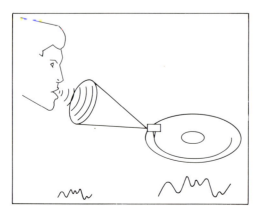

CONVERSIONS, HYBRID FORMS, AND ZELS

A graphic cross-reference table (fig. 1-35) summarizes the two-dimensional/ three-dimensional and discrete/continuous distinctions discussed in this section. In practice the distinctions are not always clear-cut; hybrid forms such as the *zel,* which will be discussed shortly, can also be used. Conversions between the different representations are also frequently performed, although the results are often unsatisfactory. For example, a point can be approximated by a pixel, and a pixel by a point. A line can be approximated by a collection of pixels, and a collection of pixels can be converted into a line. Polygons can be approximated by areas of pixels, and areas of pixels can be converted to polygon outlines. These conversions are detailed in chapter 6.

Typical of the hybrid possibilities are **zels,** a method of storing three-dimensional information in two-dimensional bitplanes by using bitplanes to store a matrix of depth values—Z distances from the image plane to a three-dimensional surface or object located in the space behind it (fig. 1-36). Zels are similar to pixels in that they are discrete representations, but are different in that pixels represent luminance at each point in the image, whereas zels represent depth.

ANALOG AND DIGITAL

Analog and digital aspects of computer technology are the keys to understanding operations related to the creation of images. Computers use numbers to represent our world, which is made up of objects that can be counted with whole numbers as well as those that continuously vary and do not exist in discrete quantities, such as the height or weight of a person.

Analog media propagate messages as continuous signals; for example, in voice communications the medium of air pressure is continuously modulated by the muscles of the throat; and in photography, the intensity of light determines the outcome of chemical reactions. Analog media record the varying analog signals in nature by mechanically or electrically converting it to a different physical representation. A phonograph recording is a good example, because it essentially freezes the signal into matter (fig. 1-37).

A **digital medium** represents the continuously varying signal as a sequence of numbers. Such numbers can be whole or fractional and represent the changes in the amplitude or intensity of the signal.

Measurement (Digitizing): Sampling and Quantization

In order to convert a continuous analog variable into a number, it is necessary to sample and quantify. Both of these concepts are concerned with resolution—the number of samples made and the number of steps for each sample.

A **sample** is a measurement made at a particular instant in space and time, according to a specified procedure. In graphics each pixel represents one sample of the image area. The pixel matrix divides the image area into a uniform two-dimensional grid. The number of pixels across a line or down a column corresponds to the number of samples and represents the spatial resolution to which the picture has been sampled. The more lines or columns, the more pixels, the bigger the sample, and the finer the spatial resolution.

The second step in digitizing is **quantization,** which gives each sample a numerical value (fig. 1-38). This requires that the continuously varying quantity be measured with a defined precision or scale. In other words, a continuous variable is represented using a number with a certain precision, or number of decimal places. All real number measurements are approximations since it is not possible to measure exactly, only to measure to some resolution (fig. 1-39). The resolution of the quantization is the precision of the measurement along the axis of the variable itself. For example, a yardstick might resolve ⅛ inch; the resolution of a good

PHOTOGRAPH

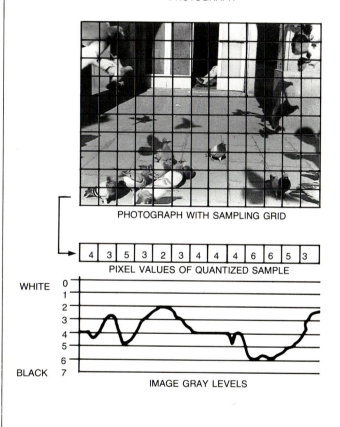

PHOTOGRAPH WITH SAMPLING GRID

| 4 | 3 | 5 | 3 | 2 | 3 | 4 | 4 | 4 | 6 | 6 | 5 | 3 |

PIXEL VALUES OF QUANTIZED SAMPLE

IMAGE GRAY LEVELS

1-38. The photograph depicts continuously varying light intensities with two spatial axes, X and Y. A grid of a specific resolution, here 10 × 13 squares, is overlaid and indicates where samples of the intensities will be taken. The number of squares in X and Y is the spatial resolution of the sample in X and Y. Each square is then quantized by determining the numerical magnitude of each sample on a brightness scale. In the drawing, the intensities of only the last row are represented as an intensity curve, with brighter luminance at the top. The numerical measurements, or digits, are listed at the bottom. In a computer system these numbers would be stored in bitplane memory as pixels.

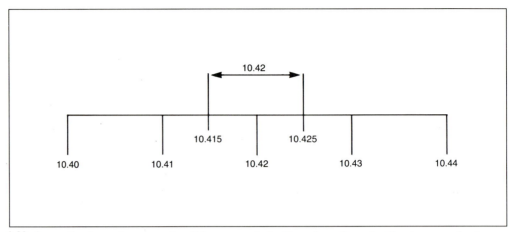

1-39. A quantized sample, even when it is represented with real numbers, implies an approximate value that lies within a range of values. In the illustration the value of 10.42 implies a continuous variable 10.415 < 10.425. Because the resolution of the quantization is fixed, it is also possible to think of the real number 10.42 as 1042 hundredths, a whole number, but remember that measurement involves an approximation, whereas counting with whole numbers does not.

1-40. To quantify or digitize a halftone, the diameter of each dot could be measured with a ruler. This measurement could then be written down at the corresponding location on a piece of graph paper.

6	6	6	2	1
4	1	3	4	6
4	2	1	5	7
3	5	1	2	3
1	2	1	3	5

foot ruler might be ¹⁄₆₄ inch. Quantization requires that you approach the continuous variable (what it is you are going to measure with yardstick in hand) with the understanding that although the resolution of the continuous variable is infinite, you are going to measure at some accuracy, say eight units to one inch. The resolution of the quantization should not be confused with the spatial resolution, which is the number of samples along the size or area of the medium. The accuracy of measuring tools have practical limits, and, of course, integers and real numbers are subject to reading and recording errors made both by humans and machines.

Analog and Digital Conversions

Analog signals, like the grooves in a phonograph, consist of a continuous modulating signal; digital signals consist of discrete samples quantized into numbers. Most graphics media involve a combination of both techniques. Motion picture film, for example, records time discretely in a sequence of frames, but each image is a continuous photograph. Data that is discrete is not necessarily digital. The suits of playing cards are discrete, but not digital, unless they are represented with numerical codes. A halftone, seen on the front page of virtually any newspaper, represents an image as an orderly (discrete) sample of pixel dots, but the diameters and areas of the dots vary continuously and are analog (fig. 1-40).

All **analog to digital conversions (ADC)** involve transforming what is often a real world quantity into a numerical representation. It is a process that involves measurement (sampling and quantization) at a specific resolution.

If you point a light meter at a subject, look at the dial, and write down an exposure, you have digitized the light reading—an analog continuous quantity existing in nature is converted into a numerical representation. The light is continuous, and the movement of the needle on the dial is continuous, but the scale is read at a precision of about an f-stop and recorded as a number.

Machines can do this quite fast and are able to measure each pixel in an image. A video digitizer uses a television camera pointed at the subject. The camera sends out a waveform consisting of a series of discrete scan lines. Each scan line is an analog waveform; the amplitude of the wave indicates the relative brightness of the picture at that particular area. The waveform is sampled several hundred times for each line by an ADC circuit that converts the voltage into a binary number, then transmits the stream of binary numbers to the memory of the CPU.

The number of subdivisions in the sample is the resolution of the luminance. The number of samples across each line is the spatial resolution in the X axis, whereas the spatial resolution of the Y axis is the number of lines. Video is both an analog and a discrete medium; intensity across a scan line is analog, but scan lines (and frames) are discrete, and latently digital.

Digital to analog conversions (DAC) convert digital representations to continuous waveforms. High resolution is important if digital data is to appear continuous. For example, a pentagon with a discrete number of straight sides can approximate a circle. An octagon is a better approximation, and a centagon (100 sides) is better still (fig. 1-41).

ALIASING

A common problem encountered in measurement is **aliasing,** the loss of information resulting from insufficient or poorly integrated samples. In graphics aliasing occurs in both spatial and temporal dimensions. **Temporal aliasing** is concerned with the integration of the exposure over time; **spatial aliasing** is concerned with the integration of exposure over area.

The mechanics of the motion picture camera illustrate temporal aliasing. When shooting a frame of film the sample does not represent an instantaneous event in time, but rather an interval the length of which is determined by the shutter speed (the time that the shutter is open). In motion pictures, because the film needs some time to advance, the exposure time must be less than the frame rate; this will cause some action to be **blanked** or to go unrecorded (fig. 1-42). Short exposure times leave most of the sample interval blanked and thus are highly aliased, producing sharp images with little blur of motion. Longer exposure times record more motion; the resulting individual frames are blurred, but they appear smoother and more realistic when viewed in motion.

The amount of aliasing in a sample is inversely proportional to how integrated it is; if the exposure is completely integrated it has minimal aliasing. By and large aliasing is undesirable, because, like objects under a strobe light, the visual image produced may be incorrect, as when the spokes of wagon wheels appear to be going

1-41. The better the resolution of the discrete approximation, the more continuous the circle appears.

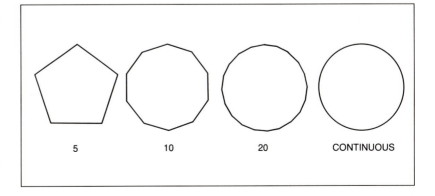

5   10   20   CONTINUOUS

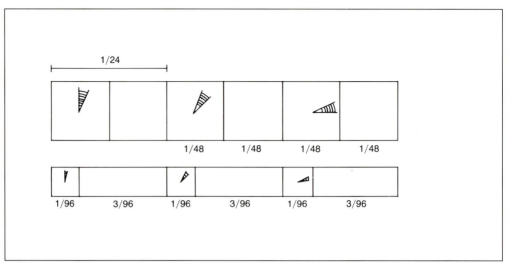

1-42. A camera is recording twenty-four frames (samples) per second. If the shutter is open for one-half of the cycle, the film records the continuously moving world as a 1/48-of-a-second-long time-elapsed exposure blur. It then records nothing for the next 1/48 of a second, which results in temporal aliasing. If the sample is even shorter, say 1/96 of a second, the picture is less blurred, but only represents about 1/5 of the event—4/5 of the event would never have been recorded.

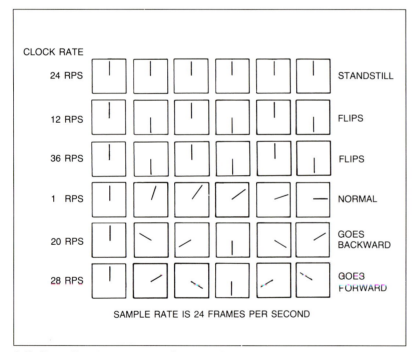

1-43. Recording the movement of wagon wheels with short exposures produces temporal aliasing. The wheels might be rotating at a speed that positions them on a sequence of frames where their rotational continuity differs from their actual continuity, causing them to appear to be standing still, chattering, or going backward. As the wheels change speed, the illusion changes.

backward in movies (fig. 1-43).

When each pixel is sampled so that the measurement does not incorporate information about its total area, spatial aliasing results. This is particularly prevalent in sampling techniques that only measure the intensity of a point in the center of the pixel (fig. 1-44). A **moiré pattern,** an irregular, wavy finish on a fabric, results from interference between patterns at two different spatial frequencies. This will result when a tweed clothing pattern is printed, because there is interference between the halftone screen and the pattern.

Aliasing affects computer-generated pictures as well, particularly those created on low-resolution displays and in animation. The most common spatial aliasing effects encountered in computer-generated images are the **jaggies**—jagged lines that represent diagonals or curves. These are reduced (but not eliminated) by increasing spatial resolution. Proper solutions require computing and displaying the integrated value of each pixel area (fig. 1-45).

Understanding aliasing is a way to better understand, control, and direct graphic arts media, whether these are computerized and digital, or traditional.

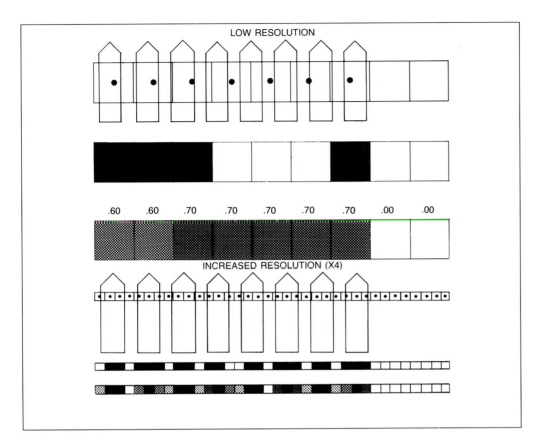

LOW RESOLUTION

.60 .60 .70 .70 .70 .70 .70 .00 .00

INCREASED RESOLUTION (X4)

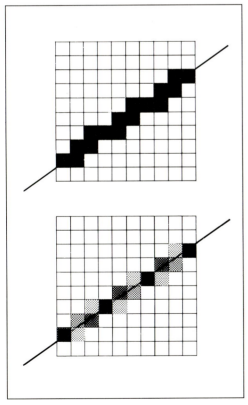

1-44. If, when digitizing a black picket fence on a white background, the image of each black picket is slightly smaller than the width of a pixel, then point sampling would produce a spatially aliased picture in which most pixels would be black, a few would be white, and the continuity of the fence would be lost. Increasing the sample resolution improves, but does not solve the problem. A proper solution requires that the exposure of the entire area of each pixel must be integrated and digitized, not point sampled as in figure 1-38. Digitization produces a gray blur that represents the average contents of each pixel in the image. The blur does not have the precision of the original, because the sample resolution is too coarse to capture every detail, but the sample is anatomically complete.

1-45. A common technique for improving the definition of a line uses gray levels in proportion to the area of the grid occupied by the sampled line.

2-0. Hardware repair manuals can be implemented in software. The manual shown is interactive, guiding the user through a sequence of repair steps. (Courtesy of Steven Feiner and Brown University.)

2

HARDWARE
AND
SOFTWARE

HARDWARE: THE BASIC ELEMENTS
SOFTWARE
LANGUAGES
DISTRIBUTED PROCESSING AND
COMPUTER NETWORKS

RELATED READING

Boraiko, Allen A. "The Chip." *National Geographic* (October 1982): 421–57.

Evans, David C. "Computer Logic and Memory." *Scientific American* (September 1966).

Holton, William C. "The Large Scale Integration of Microelectronic Circuits." *Scientific American* (September 1977).

Mayo, John S. "The Role of Microelectronics in Communications." *Scientific American* (September 1977).

Toong, Hoo-Min D. "Microprocessors." *Scientific American* (September 1977).

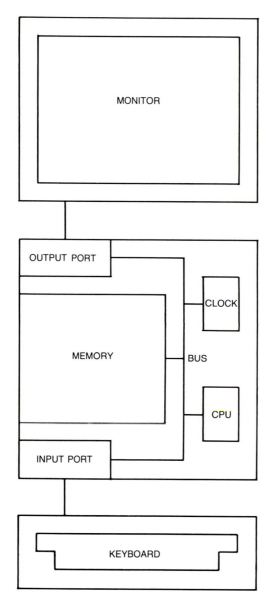

2-1. A block diagram of a computer system.

Hardware in computer systems is the physical configuration of a machine, its steel and silicon. *Software* is a series of commands written in an unambiguous language, for example, a program. The hardware executes the program; the program governs the performance of hardware. Notations as diverse as music, arithmetic, word processing, typesetting, graphics, and robot control are processed by the computer. A computer is therefore similar to any device that is used to compose and execute a sequence of events.

Hardware in a computer system is changed by disassembling and reassembling the machine. Software is changed by rewriting the program, which causes the computer to perform a different task. Software is an erector set for logic and is much easier to change than the physical configuration of the computer. A player piano can execute many programs written in a single kind of notation, but it cannot perform other tasks, because its mechanism is fixed. A computer, limited only by its software and its user's invention, can perform innumerable tasks. Computerized media, which combine data and reprogrammability, like clay, can be added to, subtracted from, and reshaped indefinitely. Computers are tools, never substitutes for the imagination.

HARDWARE: THE BASIC ELEMENTS

All computers, regardless of their size or purpose, share a similar basic structure and perform similar functions. The term *hardware* refers to all the physical components in general, including the hardwired circuits inside the machine.

A computer has five basic components: the bus, clock, central processing unit (CPU), memory, and ports (fig. 2-1).

The Bus

A *bus* is a collection of wires that electronically connects all the parts of a computer and has as many wires as the machine word size has bits. If a bus is sixteen bits wide, sixteen parallel wires connect the processor, memory, and peripherals; a single sixteen-bit word may be simultaneously transferred across the bus.

The bus transfers data of all types. For example, when a CPU is programmed to retrieve information from memory, it sends an address via the bus to memory. The memory then returns, through the bus, the data contained in the address specified. Instructions are transferred by way of the bus as is data going to and from the ports to the CPU.

The Clock

In a computer, time is treated discretely and controlled by a *clock*—a device that produces electrical pulses, zeros and ones, at a regular rate. The CPU is driven by the clock, so at each clock pulse an event occurs: transferring bus data, loading a register, decoding an instruction. The number of clock cycles needed to execute an instruction differs according to the instruction that is to be decoded and executed; the speed of the clock is almost always faster than that of executing instructions.

The Central Processing Unit

The *central processing unit (CPU)* is the switching and operations center of the computer. By executing the instructions that constitute programs, the CPU controls the entire system, including the handling and processing of data (fig. 2-2). The CPU consists of registers, a program counter, and the *arithmetic and logic unit (ALU),* the hardware that actually performs the computations. In large computers the CPU consists of one or more circuit boards. In small computers the CPU is usually contained on a single microprocessor chip, which is mounted on a circuit board and plugged into the bus.

The CPU operates by fetching an instruction word from memory and loading it into an *instruction register.* This register, like memory, has an address and can store one word, but, unlike memory, its contents flow into the logical circuits

of the machine, which decode the contents and cause the ALU to perform an action, such as adding two memory words and placing the result in a third word or a data register. *Status registers* display test and error conditions, such as dividing by zero. Another component of the ALU is the *program counter,* which indicates to the CPU where the program is stored.

CPUs can be cataloged according to their clock speed (number of instructions processed per second), the width of the registers, the width of the bus, the number of registers, and the complexity of the particular set of instructions. All of these factors affect the performance of a system.

A computer with thirty-two–bit registers, as opposed to a computer with sixteen-bit registers, can operate on larger numbers and address more memory. More registers provide flexibility and if the clock speeds are the same, a CPU with a wider bus can

2-2. Microphotograph of a 68000 CPU. The electrical circuitry includes registers, counters, and arithmetic/logic unit circuits that interpret the software and perform an operation. The CPU links software to hardware. (Courtesy of Signetics Corp.)

move more data faster. Some machine instructions can cause hardware to perform floating point arithmetic in the ALU, causing execution to be faster than on machines that simulate floating point arithmetic in software. Specialized graphics applications, such as trigonometric functions, complex arithmetic, analytical geometry, and image processing may also be supported as part of the hardware. These variables make it difficult to compare the performance of CPUs. For example the Motorola 68000 microprocessor has thirty-two–bit registers but a sixteen-bit bus: two fetches are required to load each register. The chip runs significantly faster than a competitor chip, the Intel 8086, with sixteen-bit registers and a sixteen-bit bus. It would seem that the 68000 is superior. Neither chip handles floating point, but a coprocessor, the 8087, complements the 8086 in this regard, and when using floating point, the 8086/8087 is faster. Thus, the performance of the chip is determined by the instructions that make up a program.

Memory

Memory is the section of the computer where information is stored. All information is represented with binary digits, including instructions, programs, text, images, and numerical data.

Information encoded in a binary form is stored as a sequence of words, each with an address. Through the bus the CPU can fetch, or read, the contents of a word at a certain address and direct or write it to another location. The CPU can also move data between memory and its own registers, as well as between memory and **ports** (input and output channels).

Main memory is a high-speed memory that is addressed directly by the CPU and may be read and written in any order. In the first computers, main memory was made out of magnetic rings or cores. The term *core memory* now refers to this active working space, though today core is actually made up of semiconductor chips.

Main memory serves as an "erasable blackboard," a working memory space that is loaded with a program and the data that is to be manipulated. The program is loaded by copying a program from a peripheral memory across the bus into main memory. The computer then executes the instructions that constitute the program (fig. 2-3). Memory that can be read and written in any order is called **random access memory (RAM).** In fact, the semiconductor chips used for this memory are commonly called *RAM.* **Sequential memory** must be read in a particular order.

Main memory is not always writable. Memory that is fixed and can only be read is called **read only memory (ROM).** ROM is typically part of the address space of the CPU, but its contents are fixed. ROM is often used to store the information required for the computer to work properly—instructions for loading a program and performing self-test diagnostics and the dot matrix patterns of the character generators are typical examples.

Any program or data can be "etched" or "burned" into ROM. This is done by some manufacturers to distribute software, including languages like BASIC and video game programs. ROM ensures that a user cannot erase or modify certain critical programs and is thus a protection against human programming errors and hardware failure.

Like RAM, ROM is made up of semiconductor chips on the CPU board or on a memory board and is connected to the bus. ROM is sometimes created and dis-

2-3. The CPU loads main memory by transferring a copy of a program on a peripheral disk into main memory.

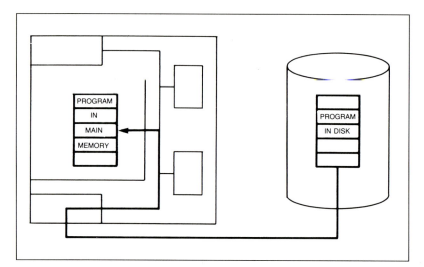

PROGRAM
IN
MAIN
MEMORY

PROGRAM
IN DISK

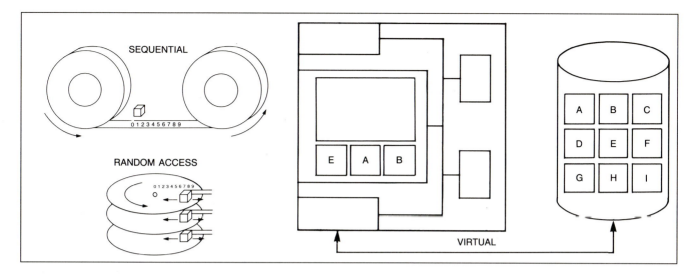

tributed in switchable plug-in cartridges. Since different ROM can be plugged into the hardware, and its contents are software, it has aspects of both hardware and software and is therefore sometimes called *firmware.*

Peripheral memory is memory that is not addressed directly by the computer and is connected to the bus by a port. The computer accesses it by dispatching a device name or number and a file name onto the bus. Another processor, located within the peripheral memory, resolves the storage address within the memory system and then returns the requested data to the CPU via the bus.

Early peripheral memory units stored information on punched paper tape or cards. Today peripheral memory is usually stored on magnetic tape, drums, or disks, either rigid or floppy (fig. 2-4). Because of the extra address calculations as well as the mechanical parts in the disk drives, access to information on disks takes longer than access to information stored in the main memory. The advantages of peripheral memory are that large amounts of information can be stored cheaply, and that the memory is nonvolatile, that is, it does not vanish when power is turned off.

Disk peripheral memories are random access memories and have individual bytes that can be read or written, although they may also be write protected. Tape peripheral memory is a long string of data

that is read or written in sequence; tapes do not provide random access.

Another type of memory is virtual memory. Virtual refers to processes and components whose functions are simulated by the computer. For example, ***virtual memory*** is like main memory in that it is addressed directly by the CPU, but it does not physically exist inside the main memory (core). The virtual memory is stored in peripheral memory, but the programs and data in execution are stored in main memory as needed and are moved back and forth from peripheral memory. This allows a program to operate in an environment where there is not enough main memory to make full use of the addressing space of the CPU.

In addition to regular disk and tape peripherals, specialized peripheral memories are used to store images. These include the videodisc, frame buffer, and display list memory. The ***videodisc*** uses a laser to read bits and has a very large storage capacity. Videodiscs can be read and write or read only. Depending on the configuration, data on the videodisc may be input to the CPU via the bus, or directed to a video monitor (fig. 2-5).

A ***frame buffer*** is specialized memory for storing bitmaps and displaying them on a screen. A frame buffer memory is organized as a pixel matrix and is dual ported: an individual pixel can be read or written by a computer through one port,

2-4. Sequential, random, and virtual memories. A tape must be read and written sequentially, but a disk can be randomly accessed. Virtual memory operates as if it were part of main memory, but is actually stored on a peripheral device and organized in pages (here, A through I). Pages used by the program are moved into main memory when needed (here, E, A, B).

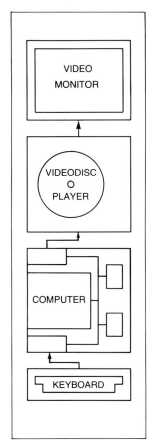

2-5. The CPU outputs addresses to the videodisc, often in the form of frame or page numbers. The disk then returns either programs, text, or images to the CPU, or outputs text or images to a video monitor. The disk controller may contain a microprocessor that interprets the commands from the master computer and uses them to control the machine.

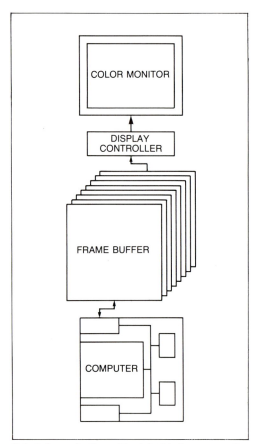

2-6. A frame buffer with eight bitplanes can display 2^8 or 256 intensity levels. The numerical values written by the computer into the frame control the intensity of the video signal.

while a display controller continually reads the contents of the frame buffer through a second port and converts the pixels into a video signal. This can be viewed on a color video monitor (fig. 2-6).

Frame buffer memory is composed of one or more bitplanes with the binary value of each pixel stored in the successive layers. Thus as more bitplanes are added to the frame buffer, more intensity levels can be displayed. The number of intensity levels is equal to two raised to the power of the number of bitplanes.

A *display list memory* is another specialized memory designed for storing lists of numbers, typically points and polygons. Display list memories also provide ways to organize tree-structured hierarchies of objects, define colors and surface properties, and specify compound actions, for example a walking robot.

Like frame buffers, display list memories are dual ported: one port allows the memory to be read or written by the CPU; the second port allows the memory to be read by a display controller, which continually reads the contents of the memory and displays the output onto a monitor as lines or solid objects (fig. 2-7).

Display list memories and frame buffer memories complement each other—frame

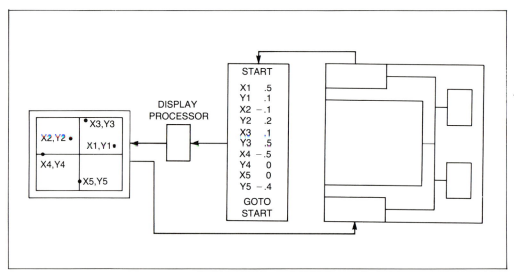

2-7. Display list memories consist of an input port, the memory itself, and an output port, which is connected to a display processor. The user directs the CPU to move points using an input peripheral. When the CPU changes a value in display list memory—for example, makes the value of −.4 equal to −.8—the object on the screen changes.

buffer memory is image oriented and stores pixels, whereas display list memory is object oriented and stores points. Both memories allow a graphic artist to manipulate the objects on the screen while looking at them in real time. The CPU captures the artist's commands as input, and then writes or modifies the contents of the memory accordingly. As these contents are changed the corresponding image on the screen changes. This is discussed in more detail in chapter 3.

Ports and Peripherals

The CPU is a switching device that retrieves and stores information from and into the ALC, the memory, and the peripherals. Peripherals include not only memory but also input and output devices such as keyboards, alphanumeric displays, and graphics devices. (Peripherals are explored in detail in chapter 3.)

A computer connects to a peripheral via a *port,* typically a hardware board of interface circuitry that is attached both to the bus and the peripheral. All input and output of the computer is performed through the ports, also called channels because of their communicative nature. Ports can connect standard hardware to different computers and can also connect several computers.

Ports may be serial or parallel. A *serial port* receives a word from the bus, stores it, and then transmits a sequence of bits, one after another, to the peripheral on a single wire. A *parallel port* simultaneously passes the word to the peripheral on many wires—as many wires as there are bits in the word (fig. 2-8). Although ports run at different speeds, parallel ports run faster.

Ports, like memory locations, have addresses. A CPU passes information to a port first by transmitting the port address on the bus and then by transmitting the data itself. Whereas a memory cell simply holds data, the port hardware reformats the data into signals that the peripheral, such as a printer or terminal, can act on. Ports can be read as well as written and, like memory locations, can have variable names, also called *unit names.*

SOFTWARE

Software comprises the formal procedures used to accomplish a task as well as the data these procedures evaluate. Examples of software in the broad sense include computer programs and system documentation, the paper-and-

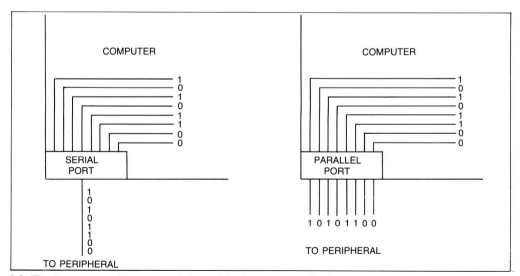

2-8. The drawing, a enlargement of figure 2-1, shows a port. The bus is depicted with eight parallel lines. The serial port converts a simultaneous transmission to a sequential transmission on one wire; the parallel port maintains the simultaneous aspect of the transmission, but requires eight wires.

RELATED READING

Denning, Peter J., and Robert L. Brown. "Operating Systems." *Scientific American* (September 1984).

Kay, Alan. "Computer Software." *Scientific American* (September 1984).

Knuth, Donald E. "Algorithms." *Scientific American* (April 1977): 63–80.

Strachey, Christopher. "Systems Analysis and Programming." *Scientific American* (September 1966).

Van Dam, Andries. "Computer Software for Graphics." *Scientific American* (September 1984).

Wirth, Niklaus. "Data Structures and Algorithms." *Scientific American* (September 1984).

```
1. N ← 5 6 7 8                      A list of
                                    numbers

2. PRINT SHAPE N                    Print the
                                    shape of the
                                    list
          4                         (the number of
                                    numbers)

3. BEGIN FUNCTION SUM

4. RESULT ← 0                       Initialize RE-
                                    SULT variable

5. I ← 0                            Initialize a
                                    loop counter
                                    variable

6.     BEGIN LOOP

7.     I ← I + 1                    Increment in-
                                    dex counter

8. RESULT ← RESULT + N(I)           RESULT is as-
                                    signed a value
                                    equal to its
                                    current value
                                    plus N(I),
                                    where (I) is
                                    an index into
                                    N

9. IF I < SHAPE N THEN BEGIN LOOP   If the value
                                    of I is less
                                    than the shape
                                    of N, then go
                                    to BEGIN LOOP
                                    and repeat the
                                    operation

10. END LOOP

11. PRINT RESULT                    Print final
        26                          result

12. END FUNCTION SUM
Execution analysis prior to line 8 executing:
N           5678  5678  5678  5678  5678
shape N        4     4     4     4     4
I (loop)       0     1     2     3     4
RESULT         0     5    11    18    26
```

2-9. Program to calculate the sum of a group of numbers.

pencil method of long division, and media products like books and movies.

Machine executable software dates as far back as the early 1800s, when the Jacquard loom was developed using punched cards to guide the thread when weaving complex patterns. The term itself is quite modern; software now contains the coded instructions that were previously built into hard-wired circuits. In a computer only the most basic functions are part of its hardware, which is capable of executing a primitive yet complete logic set. The software is a coded sequence of instructions that specify what logical operations the computer hardware should perform. Logic is thus not limited by mechanics.

Programs

A *program* is an organized sequence of instructions that defines a function not existing on the computer itself. For example, a computer with an addition but with no multiplication instruction can be programmed to multiply simply by using successive additions.

A program organizes the flow of control information in a series of notational commands. It is a means by which a process is defined; programs follow a script that has alternate routes and conclusions. A properly composed program can be referred to by a single name or a symbol and can have its own *arguments,* variables that it evaluates to determine a result. Some programs, like the arithmetic functions $+$, $-$, $\times$, and $\div$, are usually implemented as primitive machine language instructions and are executed in hardware. More complicated programs or functions, like the sum of a group of numbers, are constructed using primitive functions (fig. 2-9). These higher-level programs, like primitive functions, may also have arguments and can, in turn, be used by even higher-level procedures.

$$N \leftarrow 5\ 6\ 7\ 8$$

SUM N

26

In fact, the program will calculate the sum of any list of numbers, for example:

$$A \leftarrow 1\ 2\ 3\ 4\ 5$$

$$\text{SUM A}$$

$$15$$

The sum divided by the **shape,** or the quantity of numbers, is the average. This can be composed into a single new function called *Average:* (SUM N) ÷ (SHAPE N). If we wanted an average of N, we could just type: AVERAGE N. The computer would respond as if the entire text had been entered and print 6.5, the answer.

A program is said to **call,** or use, a more primitive procedure, and a program that is called is said to be **invoked.** Invoked programs are sometimes referred to as *subprograms,* or *subroutines,* and many different programs might call the same subprogram (fig. 2-10)—subroutines can call other routines, and so on. Programs and subroutines are also referred to as *functions* or *procedures.*

A **language** is a set of procedures with a consistent syntax and is used to communicate directions to a computer as well as to represent numbers. Languages are to programs what musical notation is to musical compositions. Programming languages, as in the above SUM and AVERAGE functions, use elements of human, mathematics, and design languages.

An **algorithm** is the essence of a program, the step-by-step instructions that define a process and generate a specific result in a finite number of steps. A program is the implementation of an algorithm in a computer language. Executing a program involves reading arguments, following a series of steps, determining a result, and terminating (fig. 2-11).

Not all sequences of instructions on a computer form an algorithm. A process that repeatedly adds one then subtracts one to a variable is not an algorithm, because it will go on computing until it is externally terminated. A programmer would say the program has gotten "hung up" and that it had to be "aborted."

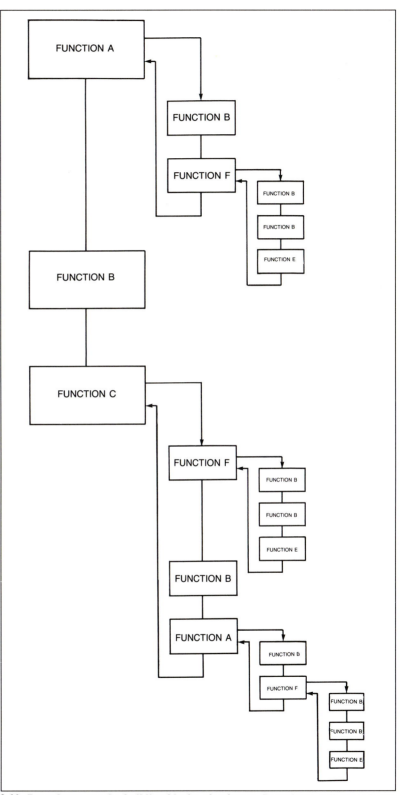

2-10. Procedures are the building blocks of software. Procedures call procedures and are in turn called by other procedures.

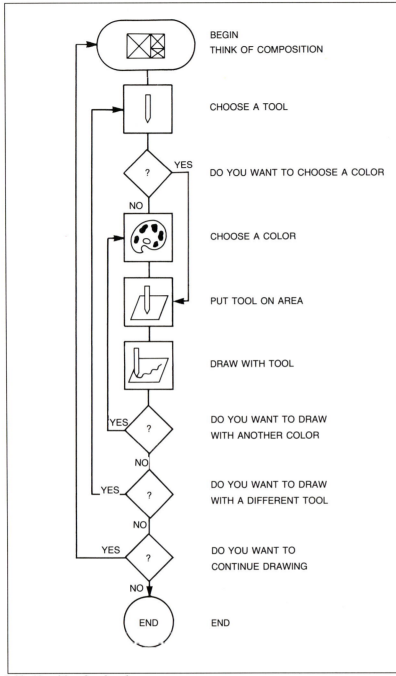

BEGIN
THINK OF COMPOSITION

CHOOSE A TOOL

DO YOU WANT TO CHOOSE A COLOR — YES

NO

CHOOSE A COLOR

PUT TOOL ON AREA

DRAW WITH TOOL

DO YOU WANT TO DRAW WITH ANOTHER COLOR — YES

NO

DO YOU WANT TO DRAW WITH A DIFFERENT TOOL — YES

NO

DO YOU WANT TO CONTINUE DRAWING — YES

NO

END

2-11. Algorithm for drawing a scene.

Another such sequence is a program that writes its results back into the same memory locations that store its instructions, thus destroying itself and its ability to conclude the task in the process. The programmer would say that the program "crashed," probably because it executed its results as if they were instructions.

Most of the paper-and-pencil methods we employ for solving problems arithmetically are algorithms. Long division, for example, is an orderly procedure composed of even more fundamental arithmetic functions, particularly multiple subtractions and a test to determine the end. The procedure by which long division is executed on a computer is similar to the pen-and-paper method (fig. 2-12).

Algorithms are solution strategies that are independent of particular processes. Many different algorithms can often be implemented to solve the same problem. Mathematicians have long sought new algorithmic formations to reduce the number of operations required to solve a problem. For example, our function SUM works by adding together a series of numbers. To add together the first one hundred numbers, $1 + 2 + 3$ and so on to 100, would require one hundred separate additions. At the end of the eighteenth century, a German schoolboy, Carl Friedrich Gauss, was given this task as a homework assignment. He observed that to solve the problem it was only necessary to multiply the number of numbers by a number one greater (101) and divide by two.

$$N \leftarrow 100$$

$$N \times (N + 1) \div 2$$

$$5050$$

Gauss reduced an algorithm requiring one hundred steps to an algorithm that required three steps—one addition, one multiplication, and one division. The algorithm remains the same when adding the first one million numbers.

Gauss did this not by employing more hardware but by using the hardware in an economical way. Intuition led him to manipulate algebraic symbols, which repre-

The problem is symbolically represented thus: 76/3. The traditional precomputer hardware used to solve the problem includes two lines and places for two arguments—the divisor and the dividend—and a result.

$$\overline{\underset{)}{\text{(result)}}}$$

A space below allows room for the calculation and an open space at the right allows work space if results are to include a decimal point. An integer solution, like the one below, will produce a remainder. Long division is composed of multiple subtractions and a test to determine the end.

Step 1.   Draw the box and insert the numbers.

$$3\overline{)76}$$

Step 2.   Identify the first (next) digit of the dividend. This will be a test number. Write it below.

$$3\overline{)76}$$
$$7$$

Step 3.   Determine the number of times the divisor can be subtracted from the test number.   Write this number above the horizontal line. Write the total amount subtracted below.

$$\overset{2}{3\overline{)76}}$$
$$7$$
$$6$$

Step 4.   Subtract and write the result below.

$$\overset{2}{3\overline{)76}}$$
$$7$$
$$\underline{6}$$
$$1$$

Step 5.   Is there another digit to drop in the dividend? If so go to step 2. If not go to endstep.

$\overset{25}{3\overline{)76}}$	repeat step 3
7	
$\underline{6}$	
16	repeat step 2
$\underline{15}$	repeat step 3
1	repeat step 4
	repeat test 5; go to endstep

Endstep. Write R beside remainder.

$$\overset{25}{3\overline{)76}}$$
$$7$$
$$\underline{6}$$
$$16$$
$$\underline{15}$$
$$1\ R$$

2-12. Long division algorithm.

2-13. The operating system supports applications programs and provides a way for them to communicate with files, data bases, and systems utilities.

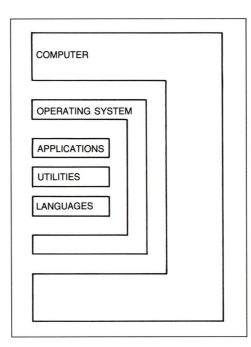

COMPUTER

OPERATING SYSTEM

APPLICATIONS

UTILITIES

LANGUAGES

2-14. A single-user system.

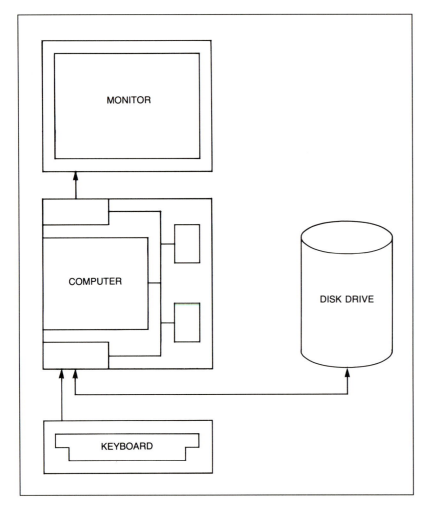

MONITOR

COMPUTER

DISK DRIVE

KEYBOARD

sented the primitive arithmetic processes. The proof of the new algorithm was not only in testing it against the known method and getting identical results, but in the ability to symbolically translate the initial algorithm into an improved one using a series of successive substitutions, or a proof.

The *operating system* (OS) is a special program designed to schedule and manage other programs and to manage the flow of operations in the computer. You might think of the operating system as an algorithm for running a machine; it is the framework for the creative tool. OS lets you run different languages, such as BASIC or Pascal, as well as utilities, application programs and file managers, and data-base systems.

Utilities programs perform a restricted set of operations. These are often basic system-oriented tasks required by the operating system and by users, including file managers, librarians, sort and merge procedures, backups, archives, maintenance and diagnostic routines. Communications, not only between the user and the machine, but between peripherals and the machine, are also handled by utility programs (fig. 2-13), as are tasks like job scheduling, loading programs from the disk into core memory, monitoring the flow of program execution, spooling output until it can be printed, error tracking, and logging usage information.

Application programs usually focus on specialized areas of use, including word processors, paint systems, electronic mail, and spread sheets.

Operating systems are accessible to either one or many users. In a *single user system* only one person can use the system, and has access to all the system files (fig. 2-14). A *multiuser system* is structured to support several users or tasks simultaneously, each with his or her own application program and files. An OS utility manages core memory and assures that application programs do not interfere with each other. Another OS procedure determines how the resources are shared among the users, another lets users control who can access their files.

Single or multiuser systems can function in interactive or batch mode. **_Interactive_** systems allow an artist to create and modify images in real time. If, however, the image is a complex one, the computer may not be able to calculate interactively the image display.

An OS, just like a language, often has an **_interactive command interpreter,_** which responds to a user's input, either typed on a keyboard or selected from a menu. A command interpreter, discussed in detail in chapter 4, employs a languagelike syntax similar to a programming language.

In multiuser systems, interactivity is supported by a process called **_time-sharing,_** which allows several users access to the CPU resources (fig. 2-15). It is assumed that the time-sharing users do not require the full service of the CPU, so each gets to use it a fraction of the time, which should be sufficient for the CPU to evaluate the user's input and produce results without delay.

Batch processes are collections of transactions processed as single units, and need not communicate with the user during execution (fig. 2-16). Batch computations are not constrained to situations where

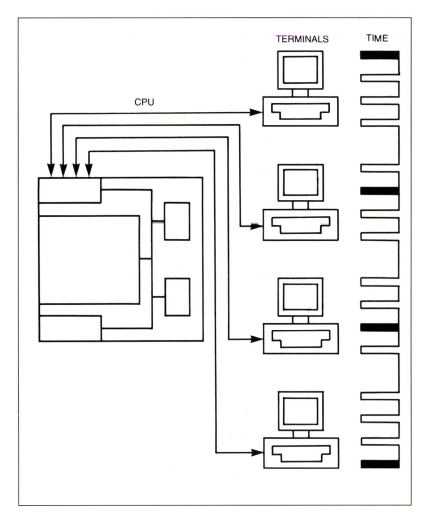

2-15. A multiuser time-sharing system divides memory and time among different users, so each has access to the processor for a fraction of the time. Here, four users each get about one quarter of the memory and are able to use the CPU one quarter of the time.

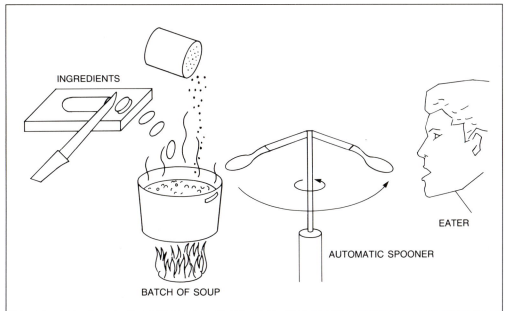

2-16. Making soup is a _batch_ process: you make up a whole bowl of soup and eat it one spoonful at a time.

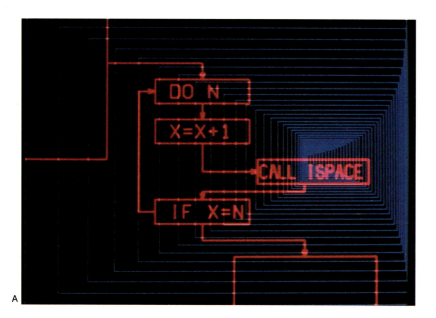

A

B

2-17. Image A was generated with a program—a compositional technique. Image B was produced with an interactive paint system—an improvisational technique. (Image A provided by Judson Rosebush. Image B courtesy of New England Technology Group. Image by Tom Christopher.)

processing must be done in real time; therefore more complex imagery can be calculated. These processes work by aggregating related operations and then executing them as a unit. For example, in motion picture production an entire roll of film is shot, then developed and edited, and finally screened. The production process would be very different if each frame had to be individually shot, developed, edited, and screened.

Batch and interactive technologies parallel compositional and improvisational techniques. Composing is command oriented and literal. Improvisation is interactive and nonliteral (fig. 2-17).

LANGUAGES

A computer programming language is a standardized notation that defines operations between arguments. Different languages have different syntaxes, or grammar rules, for the composition of statements as well as for performing different operations. Languages include machine languages, assemblers, high-level languages, and special-purpose graphics languages.

The syntax of a language may be rich or sparse. A typesetting language, for example, operates on textual data, letters and words, and may have commands for font, height, line width, leading, and weight. This set of commands is finite and includes processes that have already been defined in the language program. Sometimes a language provides more than one way of doing something; sometimes a task is inaccessible. For example, if a particular typesetting language lacks an upside-down command, you cannot set type upside down. The feature can be added to the language (by a systems programmer), augmenting the fundamental program and creating the extra command in the typesetting language.

A language is ideally more than a collection of related functions and should include syntax for variable names, assignments, arithmetic, if-then scenarios, and iterative operations.

Machine Language

The interface between software and hardware is the binary machine instruction word that, when loaded into an instruction register, is decoded in a precise and exact way.

An *instruction word* contains an opcode and an operand. The *opcode* specifies functionality, such as $+$, $-$, $\times$, or $\div$, and is represented by a binary code. The *operand* is the data, the numbers or characters that will make up the arguments of the function.

A group of instruction words, or an instruction set, make up the *machine language* and define the functionality of the basic machine. Each computer has its own instruction set that is decoded by the computer circuitry. A machine language for one brand of computer usually cannot run on another.

Assembly Language

Machine language is the only language that the central processor can act on. When computers were first invented all programs had to be written in machine language. *Assembly language* was then invented to make programming easier by using mnemonic instructions that translate to opcodes; decimal numbers and alphanumeric variable names are converted to binary digits and assembled into binary addresses (fig. 2-18).

The assembly language is converted into machine language by a program called the *assembler* (fig. 2-19). As you can see, assemblers optimize the programming resources tremendously with virtually no resources wasted. Nonetheless, programming in assembly language remains a tedious, time-consuming process. For that reason even more English-like languages have been developed. Although these languages do not execute as quickly, they are easier and faster to write.

Compilers and Interpreters

Languages, like assembly languages, have to be converted into machine language to run. Programs that convert commands into machine code can be either compilers or interpreters. A *compiler* is a program that translates an entire source program, written in a high-level programming language, into machine code and then saves it as a binary file, which can then be loaded and executed. In this sense the assembler just described is a compiler. A statement in assembly language typically represents a single primitive machine instruction; a statement in a high-level language typically represents several machine instructions. The process of compiling, loading, and executing is one method of processing information in batches. Here the first step is to convert all the high-level statements into machine instructions, then to load the instructions, and then run them. The strategy is basically the same as the assembler depicted in figure 2-19.

An *interpreter,* on the other hand, reads each command, determines its intent, and then calls a preexisting machine language subroutine to execute that action. Interpreters run interactively, often in time-sharing environments. The interpreter itself is a program, as is the information it reads and processes. The interactive mode gives the user access to the program while it is running, so it can respond in real time to the user's commands (fig. 2-20).

Compilers and interpreters each have their purposes and advantages. The interpreter is immediate, but compiled programs run faster, because the high-level language is translated to machine code only once. In an interpreter the program is translated every time it is run.

High-level Programming Languages

The first high-level languages (HLL) were invented in the 1950s. FORTRAN and COBOL, two early entries, eliminated any references to the CPU's registers, incorporated a simple way of passing data to and from subprograms, and permitted data to be represented as arrays of two or more dimensions or as sequential character records. FORTRAN was first used in science, COBOL in business.

Symbolic HLL	Assembly Language	Machine Language
NOT 1	NOT 1	1000 000000000001
3 + 4	PLUS 3,4	0000 000011000100

2-18. Table shows corresponding instructions for NOT and PLUS written in a symbolic high-level language, an assembly language, and machine code. All contain an opcode and an operand(s). An assembler program converts the assembly language to machine language. An instruction can be *monadic,* having one oper- and, or *dyadic,* a function with two operands. An example of monadic function is "NOT 1": *NOT* is the opcode, *1* is the operand, and *0* is the result. An instruction with two operands is *PLUS,* where + is the opcode, *3* and *4* are the operands, and *7* is the result.

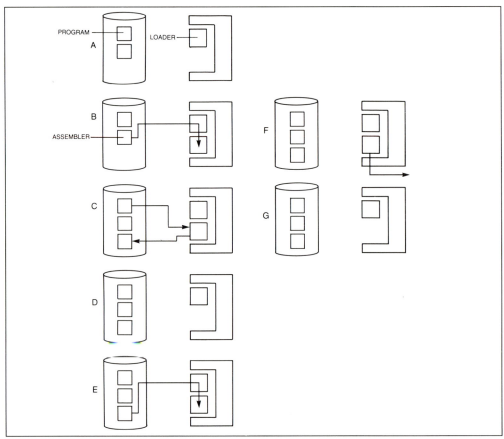

2-19. Assembly language instructions are first composed as a file of text (A). A program called the *assembler* is loaded into main memory (B). The assembler reads the alphanumeric files of assembly language statements, then translates them into a file of binary machine language instructions that are saved on peripheral mem- ory (C). The function of the assembler program is finished and is erased from main memory (D). A program called the *loader* now retrieves the newly created binary machine language file into main memory (E) and the computer exe- cutes it (F). The system is then ready to execute the next task (G).

Thousands of programming languages are available today; some even have dialects. Programming languages are both general purpose, like FORTRAN, and special purpose, like Synthavision, a language to simplify the creation and manipulation of three-dimensional graphic animation.

High-level languages are **portable,** that is, compilers and interpreters for common high-level languages can be written to translate the language into the machine language of many different CPUs, from microprocessors to mainframes (fig. 2-21).

High-level languages are written in lower-level languages, often assemblers, and very-high-level languages (VHLL), such as a paint system, are written in high-level languages. Indeed, an artist or designer working on a system might be three or more levels above the machine language. It is helpful to know the level of language you are communicating at. This is less important, however, than knowing how to communicate using that particular notational language.

The most relevant high-level languages have been designed for a variety of applications, including graphics, but no one language has been adopted as the standard for the computer industry. Indeed, general-purpose languages are very useful in writing special-purpose tools. Special-purpose graphic languages also exist and are discussed later in the chapter (fig. 2-22).

FORTRAN (Formula Translation) was developed in the late 1950s by an IBM research team headed by John Backus. It became the first portable language and is still widely used for scientific and mathematical applications.

ALGOL (Algorithmic Language) was developed by European and American scientists led by Alan J. Perlis and Nicholas Wirth between 1958 and 1960. ALGOL was the first language to recognize the use of a formal notation for syntax and was used by academics to publish algorithms. Its concepts and structural design have influenced other languages.

COBOL (Common Business Oriented Language) was created by a team headed by Joseph Wegstein and A. Eugene Smith.

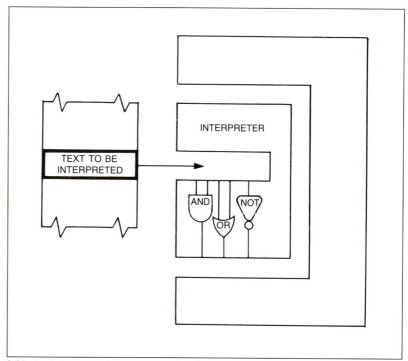

2-20. An interpreter is a program that has been previously written and converted into an executable file of binary machine language instructions. Once this program is loaded into main memory, it operates by evaluating an input file one statement at a time, and then executing an interpreter code, calculating the result. The input file is either interactively typed on the keyboard or read from a disk.

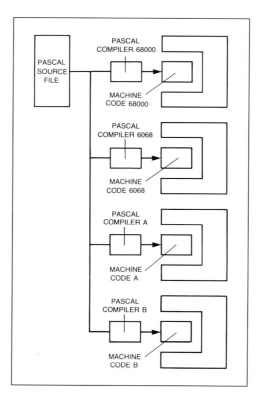

2-21. Programs written in high-level programming languages are *portable,* because they can be compiled, or translated, into the machine code of different CPUs. In this example a single Pascal file is processed by different compilers that generate their own machine language instructions.

<table>
<tr><td valign="top">

APL

```
Delta
R ← RECT CENTX, CENTY,
  WIDTH, HEIGHT
R[1;1] ← CENTX -
  (WIDTH/2)
R[1;2] ← CENTY -
  (HEIGHT/2)
R[2;1] ← R[1;1]
R[2;2] ← CENTY +
  (HEIGHT/2)
R[3;1] ← CENTX -
  (WIDTH/2)
R[3;2] ← R[2;2]
R[4;1 2] ← R[1;1], R[2;3]
delta
```

</td><td valign="top">

Logo

```
TO BOX
REPEAT 4 (FD 50 RT 90)
END
```

</td></tr>
<tr><td valign="top">

Pascal

```
PROGRAM SQUARE;
  USES TURTLEGRAPHICS;
  VAR SIDE: INTEGER;
BEGIN
  INITTURTLE;
  PENCOLOR (BLUE)
  FOR SIDE:= 1 TO 4 DO
    BEGIN
      MOVE (50)
      TURN (90)
    END
END.
```

</td><td valign="top">

FORTRAN

```
SUBROUTINE RECT (CENTX,
CENTY, WIDTH, HEIGHT, XA,
YA, N)
DIMENSION XA(4), YA(4)
XA (1) = CENTX - (WIDTH/2)
YA (1) = CENTY - (HEIGHT/2)
XA (2) = XA (1)
YA (2) = CENTY + (HEIGHT/2)
XA (3) = CENTX - (WIDTH/2)
YA (3) = YA(2)
XA (4) = XA(1)
YA (4) = YA(3)
N=4
RETURN
END
```

</td></tr>
<tr><td valign="top">

BASIC

```
10 HGR:HCOLOR=3
20 X=50 : Y=70
30 HPLOT X,Y TO X+20,
Y TO X+20,Y+20 TO X,Y+20
TO X,Y
60 END
```

</td><td valign="top">

CALD

(A high-level graphics language. Stores a rectangle at address 8001 with a center at 4.2, 3.1, and 2 units wide by 5.1 units high.)

```
RECT 8001 4.2 3.1 2.0 5.1
```

</td></tr>
</table>

2-22. Making a rectangle in six different programming languages.

Its design was heavily influenced by Grace Hopper's FLOWMATIC language. The team's efforts were directed toward producing a business language with simple English commands, aimed at making entries to journals and then posting them.

LISP (List Processor) was designed by John McCarthy while working at MIT's Artificial Intelligence Project in 1958–1960. LISP allows a programmer to construct logical assertions and is widely used for artificial-intelligence projects and for symbolic mathematical work.

BASIC (Beginners All Purpose Symbolic Instruction Code) was developed in 1967 by John Kemeny and Thomas E. Kurtz of Dartmouth College. BASIC was implemented in an interactive environment on a time-sharing system and used teletype terminals. It was the first interpretive language and was designed to simplify the computing process, serving users with backgrounds in fields other than science. It has an INPUT statement that allows data to be entered from the terminal during program execution. BASIC uses simple commands and has become the most popular microcomputer language.

Pascal (named for the French mathematician Blaise Pascal) was developed by a team headed by Nicholas Wirth and introduced in 1971. It is a language rich in control structures and is used in universities, because it encourages the production of clear, well-structured programs. Pascal retains the style of ALGOL, but incorporates the modern features of simplicity and generality.

The **C** language in conjunction with the **Unix** operating system was developed in the 1970s by Dennis Ritchie at Bell Laboratories. It is a structured programming language that creates complex programs from simple elements and executes these quickly. Unix is widely used as a portable operating system.

APL (A Programming Language) is an interpretive language developed at IBM by Kenneth E. Iverson in the 1960s as an interactive teaching tool for algebra. APL uses a unique character set and permits primitive functions to execute parallel operations on arrays without having to specify iterative loops.

The **Logo** programming language was developed during the 1970s by a group headed by Seymour Papert in the Artificial Intelligence Laboratory at MIT. Logo is a language learned easily by beginners and was developed to make computers accessible to children. It is an interactive (interpreted) language, incorporating procedural definitions that allow Logo users to create computer images by commanding a goal-oriented drawing "turtle."

Ada (named for British mathematician Lady Lovelace) was commissioned in 1980 by the Department of Defense as their official language. It is oriented toward batch or time-sharing systems and has provisions for coordinating several computers working concurrently on the same task.

Graphic (Visual) Languages

Graphics software can be used to produce images such as graphs, charts, and realistic three-dimensional images. Some languages have been designed exclusively to create and manipulate images and three-dimensional environments. These programs are designed to equip a user with the equivalent of an elaborate repertoire of graphic and visual representation techniques. Often the mathematical and algebraic statements needed to create or manipulate an image are programmed in a high-level language and are invoked with a single command in a graphics language (fig. 2-23).

Graphics software is designed to be used as a creative tool and should provide the artist and designer with batch or interactive commands, a compact language suited to express visual operations, and high-level language capabilities.

The optimal graphics language should express different visual operations and provide users with quick feedback on their actions. It should be easy to learn, demand little memorization, and conform to the user's methods of working. The interaction techniques should be sophisticated and include textual as well as graphic commands.

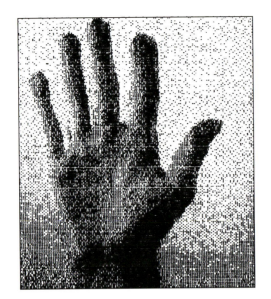

LOAD PICTURE

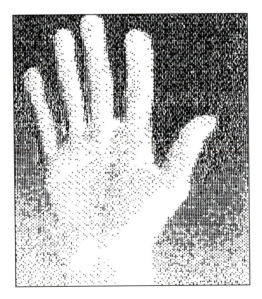

NEGATIVE PICTURE

Function Line (X1, Y1, X2, Y2)

Function Arc (X, Y, BEG, END, RADIUS)

2-25. Functions for drawing a line and an arc between two points.

Graphics software should be portable, or adaptable to different computers. It should also be *device independent,* or able to interface with various graphic peripherals. Thus a graphics subroutine library provides a standardized, portable interface between applications programs and graphics peripherals by isolating device dependent routines, which are commands unique to a specific model of a peripheral, from the body of the subroutine library, which contains only device independent subroutines. Because the device dependent routines constitute a small portion of the system, they are written anew for each physical display (fig. 2-24). Another feature is *device intelligence,* where software detects the capabilities of hardware, performing only necessary calculations and letting the hardware do more of the work.

Three techniques have emerged for the creation, manipulation, and display of visual images: subroutine libraries, preprocessors, and complete languages. *Subroutine libraries* are collections of functions that can be used with and called by a preexisting high-level language, thereby retaining the full repertoire of the high-level language. Examples of subroutine libraries include the ACM Core System for vector graphics and the Graphics Kernel System (GKS) for raster graphics. These packages define basic drawing interfaces such as a routine to draw a line between two points (fig. 2-25). Subroutine packages support basic two- and three-dimensional geometric operations, perspective, and the drawing of text, lines, and areas of color.

A *graphics preprocessor* is an extension of the compiler and permits the syntax of an existing language to be augmented by new (graphics) commands. It works by recognizing and incorporating extensions to the language. The preprocessor program is executed prior to the interpreter or compiler, and its output, which combines native language commands with expanded commands, is passed to the high-level language compiler and compiled normally (fig. 2-26). The advantage of this technique is that it uses a graphics language that fully incorporates

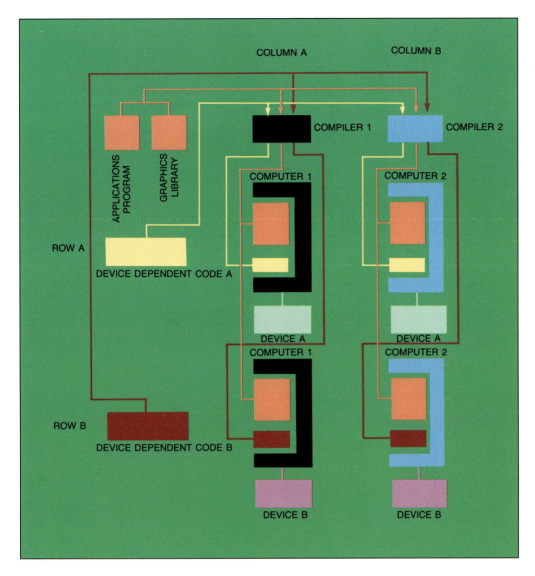

COLUMN A COLUMN B

COMPILER 1 COMPILER 2

APPLICATIONS PROGRAM

GRAPHICS LIBRARY

COMPUTER 1 COMPUTER 2

ROW A

DEVICE DEPENDENT CODE A

DEVICE A DEVICE A

COMPUTER 1 COMPUTER 2

ROW B

DEVICE DEPENDENT CODE B

DEVICE B DEVICE B

2-24. Four permutations of device-independent and device-dependent graphics software are illustrated in this drawing: two pairs of computers, each with its own compiler (columns A and B), and two pairs of graphic peripherals (rows A and B). Each peripheral is driven by each type of computer. One common applications program and the device-independent routines contained in the graphics subroutine library (top left) are shared by all systems. The device-dependent code is shared only by peripherals of the same type and is compiled with different compilers.

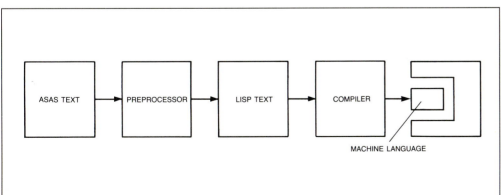

ASAS TEXT → PREPROCESSOR → LISP TEXT → COMPILER → MACHINE LANGUAGE

2-26. The Actor/Scriptor Animation System (ASAS) is an animation language that is an extension of LISP and includes the full programming features of the structured parent language. The original ASAS animation notation (mixed with some LISP) at the left is expanded into LISP by the preprocessor, creating a file that is then either interpreted or compiled (LISP can do either) to produce animated images.

an existing high-level language as well as new commands.

A *complete programming language* with syntax to express logic, store and manipulate variables, and create graphics is yet another approach to developing, manipulating, and displaying visual images. Complete programming languages are often interpreters and can be controlled by graphic menus (fig. 2-27) as well as by text (fig. 2-28). Complete programming languages exist for creating two-dimensional as well as three-dimensional graphics, but unless they are extremely comprehensive they will have limited command and logical structures compared to high-level languages.

The role of the computer in society began with a monolithic central computer surrounded by a plotter, disk drives, memory, and terminals and managed by a set of professionals, who focused on cramming work through a finite resource.

With the advent of the microprocessor and the personal computer it became possible for laboratories, offices, and individuals to acquire their own machines. These personal computers are not as comprehensive as the mainframes, but provide the single user with many options.

2-27. Graphic languages controlled by menus combine commands selected by touching a menu with an ability to draw interactively. The menu and image illustrate changing line widths, changing colors, and solid versus broken lines. (Courtesy of Digital Effects Inc.)

Distributed processing is the connection of a personal computer to a mainframe (or to another computer) so that the computing is spread between at least two CPUs (fig. 2-29). The combination is a truly synergistic marriage; the user is able to locate data in the highly centralized system of the mainframe, bring it into his or her domain, manipulate and analyze the data, and return results to the centralized processor. The centralized processor can still do what it always did—large batch processing and supporting a network of time-sharing users. The difference is that the time-sharing users are not calculating on the mainframe; they are mostly computing on their own machines

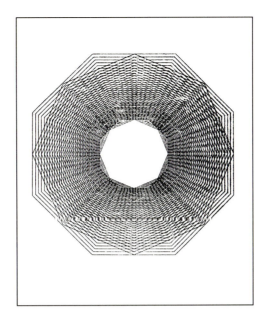

2-28. This program written in CALD (an extinct graphic language) first defines two octagons, then starts a loop that sizes and draws them thirty-six times. (Provided by Judson Rosebush.)

```
        C                                              DATA CARDS FOLLOW . . .
        C                                              OCTAGONS
        C                                              PROGRAM IN CALD
        ERASE1000                                      CLEAR STACK
        ERASE2000                                      CLEAR STACK
        ERASE3000                                      CLEAR STACK
        ERASE4000                                      CLEAR STACK
        C                                              MAKE 1ST OCTAGON
        SETCV1001   4.5     0.88    7.50    0.88       CARD 1, 1ST OCTAGON
        EXPAR1001   9.62    3.0     9.62    6.0        CARD 2, 1ST OCTAGON
        EXPAR1001   7.5     8.12    4.50    8.12       CARD 3, 1ST OCTAGON
        EXPAR1001   2.38    6.00    2.38    3.00       CARD 4, 1ST OCTAGON
        EXPAR1001   4.50    0.88    4.50    0.88       CARD 5, 1ST OCTAGON
        C                                              MAKE 2ED OCTAGON
        SETCV3001   6.00    0.88    8.54    1.96       CARD 1, 2ED OCTAGON
        EXPAR3001   9.62    4.50    8.54    7.04       CARD 2, 2ED OCTAGON
        EXPAR3001   6.00    8.12    3.46    7.04       CARD 3, 2ED OCTAGON
        EXPAR3001   2.38    4.50    3.46    1.96       CARD 4, 2ED OCTAGON
        EXPAR3001   6.00    0.88    6.00    0.88       CARD 5, 2ED OCTAGON
        DO          36.                                BEGIN LOOP
        SIZE 1000   6.00    4.50    -.97    -.97       MAKE OCTAGON SMALLER
        SIZE 3000   6.00    4.50    -.97    -.97       MAKE OCTAGON SMALLER
        DRAW 1000                                      DRAW IT
        DRAW 3000                                      DRAW IT
        LOOP                                           END LOOP
        FRAME       15.                                FRAME ADVANCE
        STOP                                           END OF DATA CARDS . . .

        B75813
```

2-29. Networks and broad-
casting; distributed and
centralized processing.

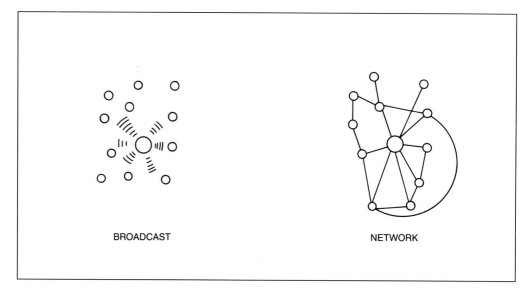

BROADCAST   NETWORK

and using the mainframe as an intelligent switching machine.

The roles of the centralized mainframe computer and the telephone network are merging. A **network** is a switching system that routes messages from one end user to another. Mail and telephones are classic examples—systems with many end users, where each end user can communicate with any other end user. The purpose of the network is to pass the information freely and cost-effectively.

Broadcasting, unlike a network, implies a single, one-way source with many receivers. Broadcasting originated with the printing press and expanded with the invention of movable type and the commercialization of radio and television. There is no requisite that print, radio, or television be broadcasting media—indeed, two-way ham radios and televisions are as old as the mimeograph machine. Broadcasting and mass media are cultural phenomena and are more a product of social organization and nation-building strategies than products of technology.

The mainframe computer, with its centralized repository of information and its master control program, incorporates broadcasting as well as time-sharing features. The computer is an efficient switching exchange, and the conversion by the telephone company of its switching exchanges into computers provides a basis for an internationally distributed processing network. Each citizen can calculate his or her own information, share data and programs, and even publish the results.

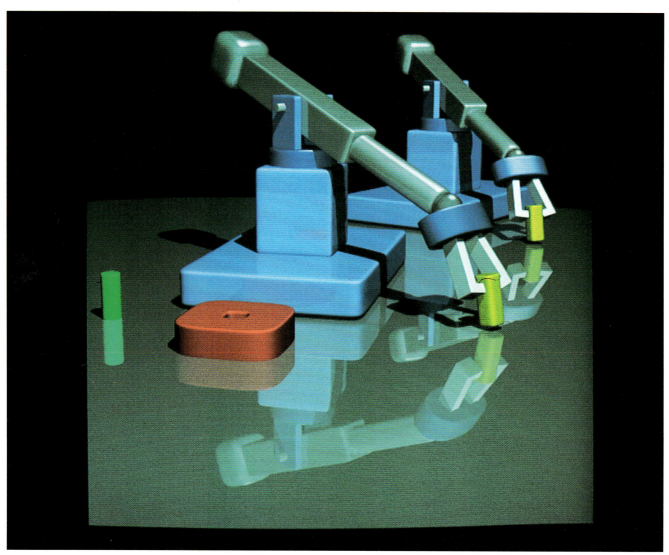

3-0. Computer synthesized robot arm allows the workings of a real device to be previewed. (Courtesy of Raster Technologies.)

3

PERIPHERAL DEVICES

TOPOLOGIES OF PERIPHERALS
ZERO-DIMENSIONAL PERIPHERALS
ONE-DIMENSIONAL PERIPHERALS
TWO-DIMENSIONAL PERIPHERALS
THREE-DIMENSIONAL PERIPHERALS

When we design a building or create an image with a computer-based system, we communicate with the computer through peripherals. Blueprints or instructions are submitted through input peripherals and results (numbers, images, objects) are received from output peripherals. Peripherals include any device that is connected to the computer bus and that the CPU can read or write. Examples include keyboards and printers, the cathode ray tube (CRT) monitor and cameras, tablets, plotters, mice, mechanical equipment, and memories. Peripherals can also be virtual; that is, they may be simulated in software without physically existing.

TOPOLOGIES OF PERIPHERALS

Peripherals can be classified by resolution as well as by dimensionality, point/pixel, input/output, and hard copy/soft copy (fig. 3-1). *Resolution* is a common criterion for classifying input and output peripherals, because all peripherals operate at some spatial, luminance, and often temporal resolution. The luminance resolution is the number of gray levels or colors; the spatial resolution is the number of dots on a screen; the temporal resolution is the number of frames or points the system can display or record per second.

Dimensionality

One way of classifying a peripheral is by the number of dimensions it recognizes or moves. In this regard a peripheral may be zero, one, two, or three dimensional. Zero-dimensional peripherals are switches; they can either be on or off. One-dimensional peripherals let the user communicate with the computer using one-dimensional media, particularly written and spoken language. One-dimensional inputs/outputs include the microphone/speaker, the keyboard/printer and the shaft encoder/stepping motor. (These are all described in more detail below.) Two-dimensional peripherals let the user communicate with the computer using two-dimensional (graphic) media and involve the representation of areas. Two-dimensional inputs/outputs include the tablet/plotter and the television camera/monitor. Three-dimensional peripherals let the user communicate with the computer using three-dimensional media. Three-dimensional inputs include feelers, which sense volumetric objects; outputs include robot arms.

Linked to peripheral dimensionality is the *number of degrees of freedom* of a peripheral, that is, the number of ways it can move (fig. 3-2). The number of degrees of freedom is not necessarily equal to the spatial dimensions of the media the peripheral governs. For example, although a plotter makes two-dimensional images, it has three degrees of freedom: the horizontal and vertical movement of the pen, plus an added degree of freedom that moves the pen up and down. A multijointed robot arm may similarly have many degrees of freedom, even though it only moves in three-dimensional space.

A related concept is that of *constraints.* A constraint is a restriction on movement. For example, a human elbow cannot bend in every direction.

Point/Pixel; Line/Area

Lines (made with points) are simple visual elements that represent the basic features—geometry—of an image. Areas (made with pixels) represent other visual elements, such as color, shading, and texture. Lines traditionally have been created with drawing tools, including the pencil, ink pen, ruler, and compass. Continuous tone renderings are created using tools such as paintbrushes, airbrushes, and cameras.

The mechanical art distinction between line art and continuous tone is paralleled in computer graphics. Lines and shapes are drawn on the computer by connecting a sequence of real points with straight lines called *vectors.* Conversely, areas are defined using a discrete matrix of pixels, which often include intensity values.

Examples of vector devices include

0D

Input	Output
Button	Solenoid

1D

Input	Output
Microphone	Speaker
Keyboard or OCR	Printer
Paper and	Paper and
magnetic tape	magnetic tape
Shaft encoder	Stepping motor

2D

POINT

Input	Output
Mouse	HARD COPY
Trackball	Plotter
Joystick	
Tablet	SOFT COPY
Touch screen	Refresh CRT
Light pen	Storage tube
	COM

PIXEL

Input	Output
Drum scanners	HARD COPY
Flying spot	Drum plotter
Television camera	Ink jet plotter
	Dot matrix printer
	Thermographic plotter
	Electrostatic plotter
	SOFT COPY
	Video raster CRT

3D

POINT

Input	Output
Sonic digitizers	Laser sculpting tools
Radars and sonars	Robot arms
Laser measuring tools	Multiplex holograms
Photogrammetry	
Gimbled joints	

ZEL

Input	Output
Raster pantograph	Vibrating displays
Raster radars	NC machine tools

VOXEL

Input	Output
CAT scanners	Laminations

3-1. A classification of peripherals.

3-2. A robot arm with six degrees of freedom, indicated by arrows.

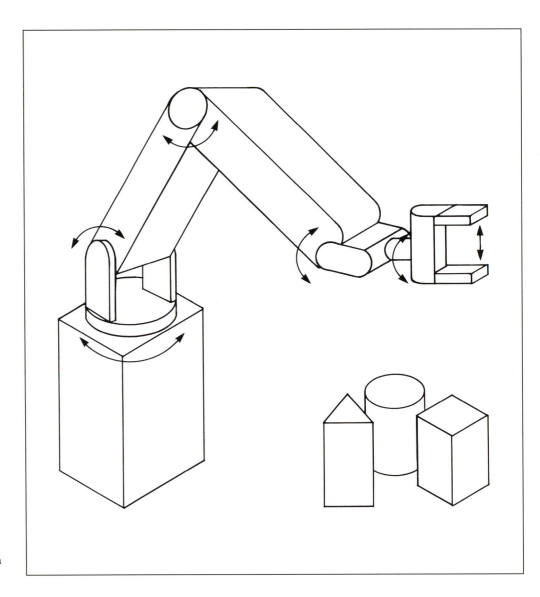

3-3. Input/output—user point of view. An artist uses a computer graphics work station, inputs information through a keyboard and mouse, and views the output of the program on a video monitor.

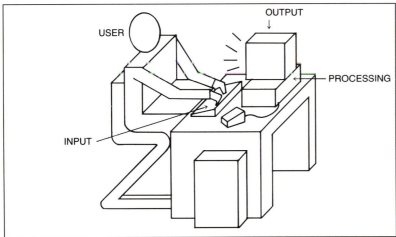

plotters and certain kinds of CRT displays. Pixel displays include dot matrix printers and raster CRT devices, such as a television monitor.

Vector graphics can be approximated on a pixel display, and vice versa, just as type can be screened or a photograph can be displayed as line copy. But interchanging these techniques usually does not produce the best results.

Input/Output (I/O)

Input encompasses the devices and processes for entering information into a computer, and *output* encompasses the devices that convey the results of calculations to users (fig. 3-3). Input peripherals include the keyboard, microphone, and television camera. Output devices include the line printer, the speaker, and visual displays (fig. 3-4). Although it appears at first glance that some peripherals, for example a teletype, perform both input and output functions, a closer examination reveals two distinct processes; the keyboard on the teletype is the input mechanism and the striker is the output.

Hard Copy/Soft Copy

Output peripherals can also be distinguished by the images they display: **hard copy** peripherals produce tangible matter, such as film, prints, and phonograph records; **soft copy** peripherals produce intangible images, such as television monitor displays, which are visible only as long as the display stays on. In the most primitive sense, both hard and soft copy enable a user to *see* results, but only soft copy can be *interactive*—that is, modified more or less immediately. This ability to edit in real time creates what appears to be both an input and output medium (fig. 3-5).

Media produced by a computer often involves hard *and* soft copy. Film itself is hard copy but when projected, the image produced is soft copy. Conversely, film from a computer may be created by exposing it to a soft copy CRT display. Text may be input via a keyboard, displayed and edited on a soft copy CRT, and output using strikers, photographic exposures, or lead cast type (very hard copy).

Soft copy can be distributed faster and easier than hard copy, as soft copy decentralizes the production process by moving information in soft copy form physically closer to the audience. National news magazines and papers, for instance, may be composed, edited, and distributed on soft copy to regional (hard copy) printing centers. Editors, designers, and makeup people work interactively and remotely to construct and preview the paper; the strategy reduces delivery cost and extends the deadline.

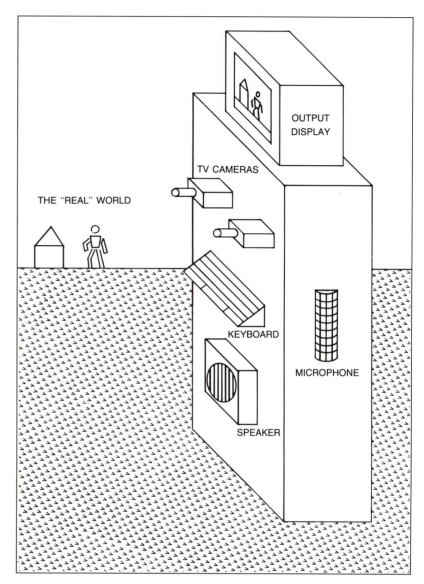

3-4. Input/output—computer point of view. The input channels are the "senses" of the computer. Shown here are a keyboard, two digitizing cameras, and a microphone. The output includes a speaker and a visual display.

3-5. Visual creation can be interactive using soft copy displays. (Courtesy of Artronics, Inc.)

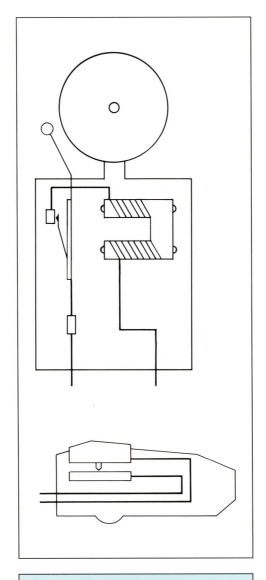

ZERO-DIMENSIONAL PERIPHERALS (SWITCHES)

The simplest peripherals are devices that have no scale and therefore no dimension, but have two states, on and off. Zero-dimensional devices are not inherently graphic but are used in graphic as well as in three-dimensional applications.

An example of a switch input peripheral is a *button* on a mouse used to, say, flip back and forth between a drawing and a textual mode. An example of an output device is a *solenoid*—a mechanical shaft that is slid back and forth using electric pulses. Solenoids are used to move a pen up and down in a plotter (fig. 3-6). In robotics zero-dimensional devices include contact switches that enable a robot to "sense" a surface, and electromagnets, which allow it to adhere to and lift metals.

ONE-DIMENSIONAL PERIPHERALS (SPEECH AND TEXT)

Linear peripherals represent written and spoken language, one-dimensional sequential media. They also relate to controls and measurements that involve a single axis—a thermometer or a volume control, for example.

Examples of linear, one-dimensional, inputs include microphones, keyboards, optical character readers, paper and magnetic tape and cards, shaft encoders, and potentiometers, another name for knobs and slide scales. Examples of linear outputs include speakers, printers and character displays, paper and magnetic tape and cards, stepping motors and dials (fig. 3-7).

Alphanumeric Text Entry

Alphanumeric data, numbers and text, may be entered into the computer orally, with optical character recognition (OCR), and with keyboard entry. Spoken language systems are very primitive, but vocabulary capabilities are increasing.

Computer peripherals that digitize and synthesize speech employ a *microphone,* an ADC to convert the waveform to a serial string of samples, and a DAC and *speaker* for creating speech. Words and letters—written language—are input via the keyboard and output via a printer in any one of its multiple forms, such as a typewriter, teletype, or CRT display (fig. 3-8).

OCR technologies are well advanced and include readers for magnetic ink, bar codes, multiple-choice forms, standard printed text in a multitude of fonts, and longhand (fig. 3-9). OCR allows whole pages to be entered at once.

A *keyboard* is another efficient input device. The familiar alphanumeric layout

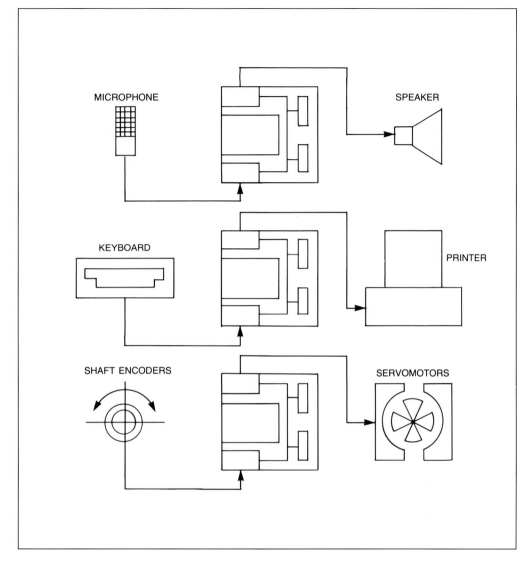

MICROPHONE

SPEAKER

KEYBOARD

PRINTER

SHAFT ENCODERS

SERVOMOTORS

3-7. Input/output pairs of one-dimensional peripherals: microphone and speaker handle spoken words; keyboards and printers handle text. Mechanical connections include shaft encoders and servomotors.

is called a QWERTY keyboard after the keys on the top row (fig. 3-10). In addition to keys for letters and numbers, most keyboards include keys for formatting commands, including tabs, line feed, carriage return, and backspace. Another feature is the case key for creating upper- and lowercase letters. Case keys often attach different meanings to the set of punctuation keys.

Function keys are programmable and can represent a sequence of letters, numbers, or commands. These are used by word-processing programs, for example, to insert and delete letters.

Keyboards can be real or virtual and shaped for a specific purpose—music,

ballet, and a variety of alphabets, for instance (fig. 3-11).

Alphanumeric Text Output

Printers and *CRT* displays are designed to display text as hard and soft copy. Hard copy technologies include *impact strikers* with ink ribbons, such as those in typewriters, and *dot matrix character printers,* where a letter is represented as a small pixel array (fig. 3-12).

The dot matrix letters are usually slightly coarser and harder to read than striker-made letters, unless they are produced at high resolution. When dealing with visual presentations, choosing an output device is important for creating clear images.

3-8. Digitized audio is stored (A) and played back as speech (B), or converted to text (C). It can also be modified or executed as a command (D) or converted back into speech (E).

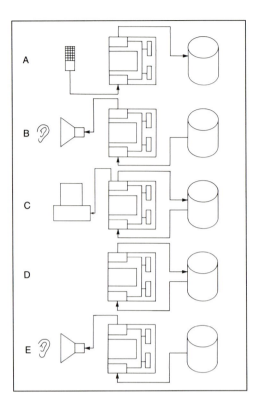

3-9. OCRs accept a variety of input. The most sophisticated systems scan text, recognizing individual letterforms and storing them as character codes.

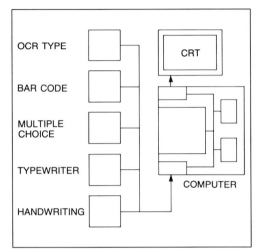

3-10. QWERTY keyboard.

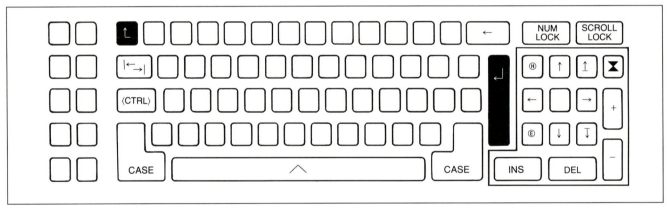

3-11. Music keyboard. (Courtesy of Sight and Sound Music Software, Inc.)

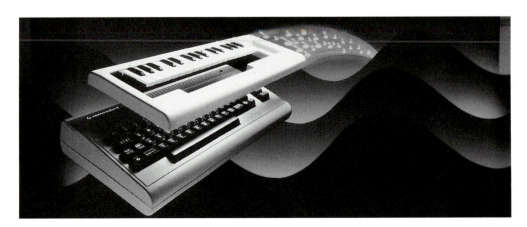

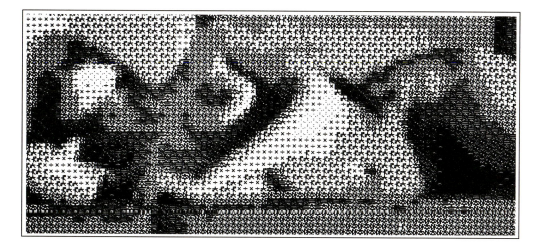

3-12. Striker type is continuous; dot matrix type is made of discrete pixels.

3-13. Dot matrix fonts can be loaded with graphic elements and intensity maps. Although the output images are still character oriented, they have the strong visual texture of computer-generated imagery. (Courtesy of Ken Knowlton.)

Dot matrix fonts are reprogrammable; different fonts can be defined in software as bitmaps. Some character printers allow the dot matrix to be programmed with special-purpose characters or intensity values (fig. 3-13). Programmable dot matrix fonts are often character-oriented displays and have spaces between the individual letters and lines; these should not be confused with the more general-purpose dot matrix printer, which will be discussed in the graphics peripheral section. Halftones can also be approximated on impact printers using normal alphabetic characters, striking over them to create a range of intensities (fig. 3-14).

Shaft Encoders and Stepping Motors

Shaft encoders and stepping motors provide a way to sense and control a rotary shaft, such as a drill. A **shaft encoder** converts a rotary angle to a number and a **stepping motor** converts a number to a physical rotary angle. Shaft encoders are used in photographic systems to record the positions of a camera on a pan-and-tilt tripod head as it is operated by a cameraman (fig. 3-15). The data can then be output to a complementary camera head where the pan and tilt are controlled by steppers. Thus a scene can first be shot

3-14. A striker graphic is composed of alphanumeric characters. Striker graphics were one of the first methods for creating images with computers. (Courtesy of Spatial Data Systems, Inc., a DBA Systems Company.)

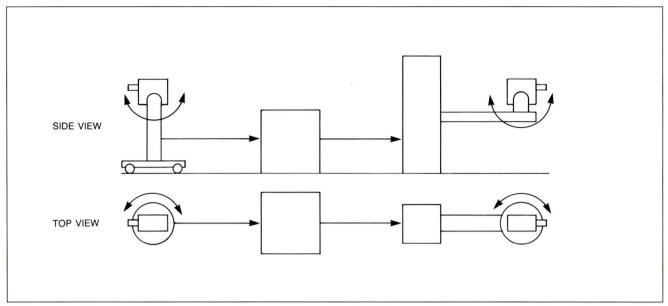

SIDE VIEW

TOP VIEW

3-15. This camera system records and replays the actions of a camera. On the left, a hand-controlled camera may be tilted or panned. Shaft encoders for the tilt and pan record the angular directions and transmit them to the CPU, where they are saved. The CPU then transmits the same positions to a camera that is mechanically controlled by stepping motors; this replays the scene. In practice, the moving camera and replay camera might be the same. Furthermore, additional degrees of freedom may be incorporated in the rig, such as the ability to raise and lower the camera and to move it forward and backward.

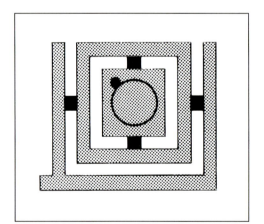

3-16. A three-axis rotating gimballed platen. The square in the middle contains the artwork or model that is manipulated by rotating the parts of the gimballed mount. The sequence of rotations can be changed only by modifying the hardware.

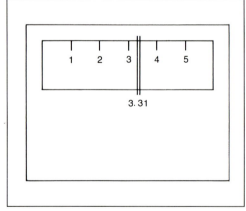

3-17. A combined virtual potentiometer and dial. The operator positions the selector line by moving the mouse that controls the cursor. The insert shows the exact monitored value; should line and monitor deviate, an alarm will sound.

by hand and the camera can then repeat the move independently; or the move could be programmed on the computer.

Stepping motors are widely used in photographic systems, not only for controlling cameras, but for controlling a repertoire of machinery designed to position artwork, models, and lights. Steppers can also control a ***platen,*** a table for holding and moving artwork (fig. 3-16). Motion-controlled cameras and platens are used together to photograph flat artwork and three-dimensional models as well as to perform multiple exposure and time-lapse photography, such as slit scan and streaking, described in chapter 8.

Potentiometers and Dials

A ***potentiometer*** is a continuously changing one-dimensional input peripheral. A potentiometer might consist of a knob or slider that is moved by hand and controls, say, the position of an object on a screen. Virtual, soft copy, sliders are controlled with a cursor or touch screen. Physical or virtual, they represent one-dimensional scalar input variables. Their output companions, ***dials,*** can be either physical meters, like a VU meter, or virtual dials, which are only displayed on the CRT (fig. 3-17).

TWO-DIMENSIONAL PERIPHERALS (GRAPHICS)

Two-dimensional input/output devices include devices that are point, or positionally, oriented and devices that are pixel oriented. Point devices locate inputs and outputs on a continuous plane; pixel devices represent each and every cell on a plane. Examples of point input devices include the mouse, trackball, joystick, tablet, touch screen, and light pen. Examples of point output devices include the plotter, the refresh vector CRT, and the storage tube.

Pixel input devices include the laser drum scanner and video camera. The laser drum film plotter, the ink jet and dot matrix plotter, electrostatic plotters, and video CRT

3-18. A mouse. (Courtesy of Apple Computer, Inc.)

raster displays are pixel output devices. In some sense, line printers used to display images (rather than text) fall into this category as well.

As we have suggested before, point devices can approximate pixel representations and pixel devices can approximate point representations. The two kinds of graphics are distinct, however—point graphics depict continuous real numbers whereas pixel graphics depict discrete integer numbers. The internal representation for the two kinds of data are different, but even point devices are eventually digitized at some resolution.

Point Input Peripherals

The ***mouse*** owes its name to its shape, a small rounded plastic box connected to the computer by a long cable (fig. 3-18). The mouse usually represents and controls the cursor on the screen. A rotating ball on the bottom of the mouse allows it to roll on a smooth surface. The X and Y rotation of the ball allows the computer to locate the mouse at all times. One or several buttons can be pressed on the mouse to execute or choose an operation from a screen menu, or to create and transform images in an interactive fashion. A ***trackball*** is basically an upside-down mouse with a sphere that is rotated by the palm of the hand.

Joysticks (fig. 3-19) are versatile, as they can be pivoted in two dimensions. Some may also be twisted and may contain push-button switches for additional degrees of freedom. The widespread use of joysticks in aviation and in video games demonstrates how useful they are in interactive environments.

The **graphics tablet,** or **digitizing tablet,** is an electronic drawing pad. It contains a two-dimensional grid of sensors that record the location of an electronic stylus or pen, which is held like a regular drawing tool and moved over the tablet (fig. 3-20). The pen does not draw visible lines on the tablet; rather the grid senses the position of the pen and the computer generates a corresponding image on a screen. Usually the stylus contains a push-button microswitch that closes by pushing down on the pen; some styli can sense pressure as well.

The **touch sensitive screen** is similar to a graphics tablet in that it is a positional sensor. It is different, because the touching device does not need to be connected to the computer; a user's finger works well.

Touch screens are fabricated on the surfaces of CRTs and can be programmed to respond in synchronicity with the image displayed (fig. 3-21). Touch screens close the loop of interactive soft copy, because they provide the facility to manipulate the image by touching it.

The pressure-oriented touch sensitive screen consists of a transparent screen overlay that contains a grid of micro-switches. The switches, activated by touch, are captured by the CPU. Another way of detecting touch is with an acoustically sensitive screen that uses two long microphones mounted along two of its sides and two long speakers mounted on sides opposite the microphones. An object can be located when it interrupts the flow of sound between a speaker and a microphone.

The **light pen,** similar to a touch screen in that it interacts with a CRT screen directly, provides a way to draw and view the results immediately (fig. 3-22). A light pen may also be used to point at the screen and interactively select operations from a menu. The light pen does not emit light but senses and times the light coming from the screen to determine what object is being drawn at that instant.

Point Output Peripherals

Plotters produce hard copy by drawing continuous lines with pens onto paper or another drawing material (fig. 3-23). Flatbed plotters move pens in both directions across a fixed sheet of paper. Drum plotters produce drawings on media fixed to a rotating cylinder. The pen moves along one axis of the drawing, while the cylinder rotates along the other axis. Some plotters actually draw circles and arcs, but most approximate curves with straight lines.

A plotter can also be equipped with a light instead of a pen and be operated in a black room to expose lines onto photographic film. Colored lines can be drawn by adding filters.

Refresh vector CRT displays draw lines between points on the screen by deflecting an electron beam. The beam can be repositioned while it is turned off or it

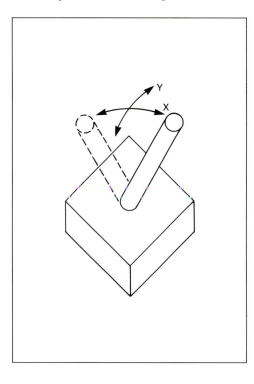

3-19. A joystick can be moved in at least two directions. A joystick with a button performs the same functions as a mouse.

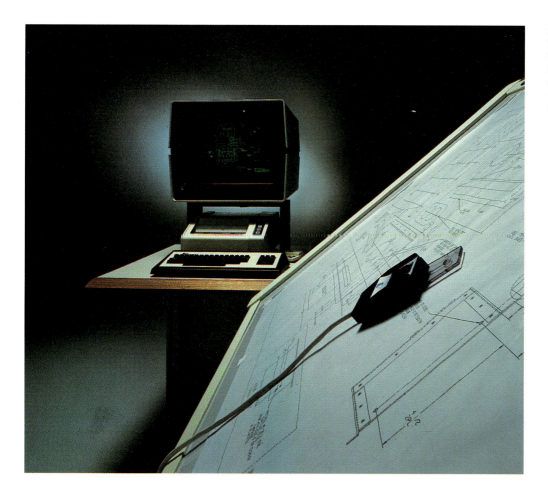

3-20. A graphics tablet can be used to trace and digitize blueprints and drawings and comes with a pen or a crosshair digitizer. (Courtesy of Computervision Corp.)

can draw a line when it is moved to another point while turned on. It is similar to a plotter with a light, except that the light or beam is moved electronically (fig. 3-24).

Refresh vector CRTs allow images to be interactively changed. Because the light emitted by the phosphors on the face of the tube decays right after it is hit by the beam, the entire picture must be *refreshed,* or redrawn, many times per second. The image can be redrawn in the same place, or repositioned and redrawn, giving the appearance of a moving image (see fig. 2-7).

Vector displays can only draw with lines and should not be confused with television raster displays, described in more detail later in the chapter. Vector displays are usually monochromatic, but some have colored lines. They also can be commanded to draw in a pseudoraster style

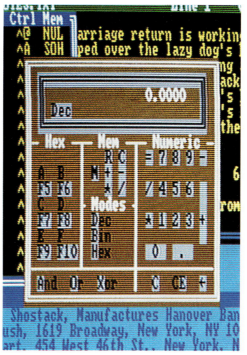

3-21. An interactive virtual calculator can be operated as if it were built out of matter and sitting on a desk. Each button is touch sensitive and changes color when selected. The selected value appears on the numerical readout.

3-22. A light pen is similar to a touch-sensitive screen in that it allows the user to interact with the image directly. (Courtesy of Koala Technologies Corp.)

3-23. Flatbed pen plotter and diagram. The position of the pen is controlled by two stepping motors, one that moves in the X and the other in the Y direction. A solonoid moves the pen up and down. (Color plot courtesy of Mark Wilson. © 1983 by Mark Wilson.)

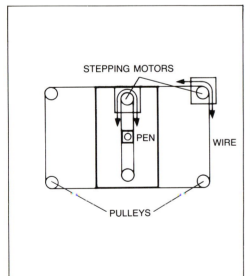

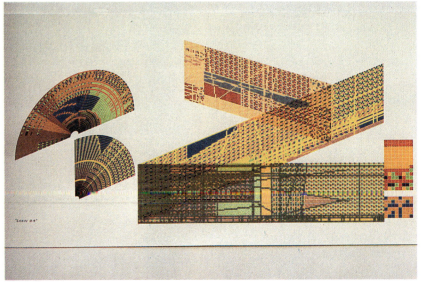

by simulating solid areas with a series of parallel lines.

The ***direct view storage tube*** is a CRT that can display vectors without refreshing them. The technology is cheap but not interactive. The image is stored as a distribution of charges on the inside surface of the screen, written once, and is changed by flashing the screen and drawing a new image.

The film produced by a camera that photographs an image displayed on a CRT is another hard copy output device. ***Computer output microfilm (COM)*** units include a high-precision CRT, color filters, and a camera driven directly by the computer (fig. 3-25). The camera is shutterless and housed in a lighttight box. Exposures take from a few seconds to a few minutes, depending on the number of vectors to be drawn.

Pixel Input Peripherals

Images can be digitized by attaching them to a rotary drum and scanning them as rows of pixels. Transparencies are scanned by shining a laser through them onto a light meter; reflectant art is illuminated and scanned by a light meter (fig. 3-26). Laser scanners have high resolution, twenty-five microns or forty lines per millimeter, and can match photographic and printing resolutions.

Flat (or ***flying spot***) ***scanners*** work by holding the art stationary (a frame of a motion picture, for example) and scanning it with a raster of light generated on a CRT. A light meter behind the film records the exposure (fig. 3-27).

Television cameras equipped with video digitizers may input both still and action pictures. Video consists of raster-quantized horizontal scan lines refreshed at a fixed interval. Each raster line is digitized and stored in a frame buffer. Resolutions for digitizing cameras include broadcast standard video (about 640 × 480 pixels), as well as higher and lower resolutions (fig. 3-28). Digitized video is usually stored on disks or in frame buffers, where it is also displayed.

Pixel Output Peripherals

Drum plotters are used in much the same way as drum scanners. Instead of mounting a transparency on the drum, photographic film is mounted and exposed with the same laser beam. The resolution

3-25. The illustration depicts the logical and physical conversion of digital data to film. The process begins with pictures stored on a disk, read by a CPU, and output to the computer output microfilm (COM) unit. The COM unit converts the digital data into analog form and displays it on a high-resolution black-and-white CRT. Light rays pass through a color filter wheel and are focused by a lens onto the film plane in the camera.

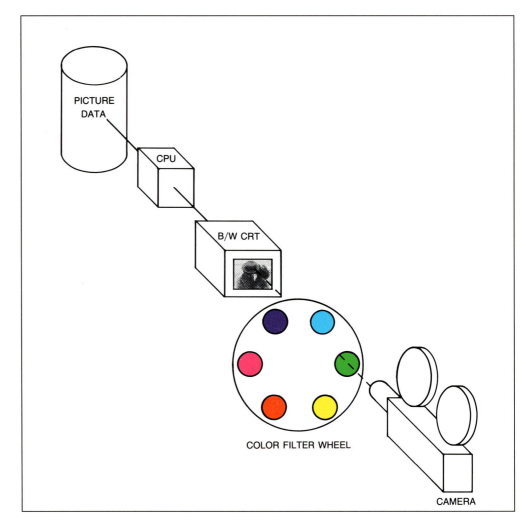

3-26. A color transparency is fastened to a drum scanner—a spinning clear-glass rotating drum. A laser attached to a lead screw is slowly translated along the cylinder while the drum is spinning, so the distance transversed during each revolution is one scan line. A light meter in the center of the drum measures the amount of transmitted light. These values are digitized and stored in magnetic memory as an X, Y matrix corresponding to the original image.

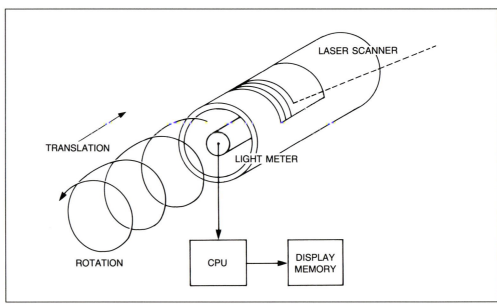

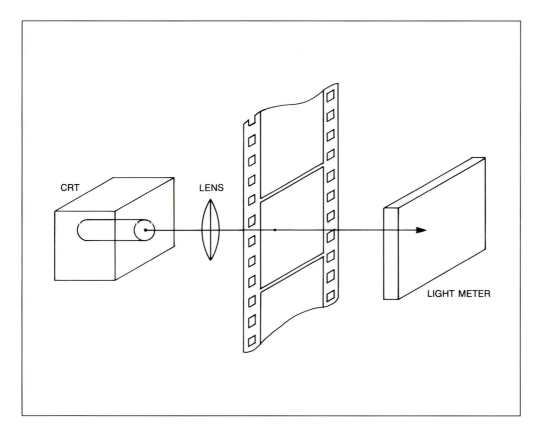

CRT

LENS

LIGHT METER

3-27. A flying spot scanner is like a drum scanner, except the artwork is held steady while a beam of light is moved across it. An exposure meter behind the transparent film records the intensity and transmits the value to a computer where it is stored. A computer also synchronizes the position of the beam and the values recorded.

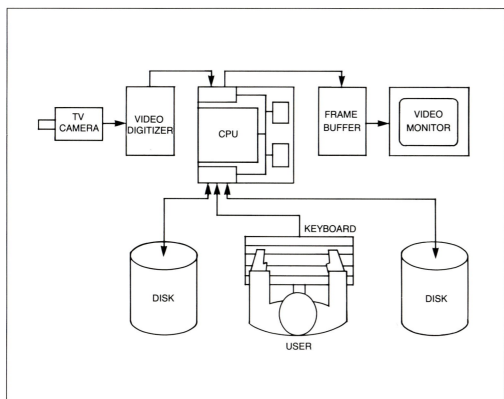

TV CAMERA

VIDEO DIGITIZER

CPU

FRAME BUFFER

VIDEO MONITOR

DISK

KEYBOARD

DISK

USER

3-28. The interface between computer graphics and video is bidirectional (input/output). The drawing shows an integrated system with a user controlling the computer via a keyboard at its center. The computer contains a television camera and video digitizer to capture images and a frame buffer and a video monitor to output the images. Images can either be stored on a disk for later display or can be immediately output.

3-29. The color separations used to make the plates that printed this image were produced by a laser plotter and calculated directly by the computer. This is quantitatively different from recording the computer-generated image onto photographic film (for instance, 35 mm slides) and then color separating it. (Courtesy of Judson Rosebush and Collier Graphic Co.)

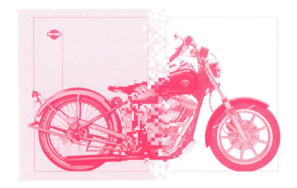

is adequate to etch lines and dot patterns onto film. The output is either color or high-contrast black-and-white film as large as 40 × 60 inches, suitable for offset plate making. Color output is produced by making color separations and then printing with process color (fig. 3-29).

COM units can also draw pixel/scan line data onto 35 mm to 8 × 10-inch full-color film at resolutions between 1,000 and 8,000 square pixels. Medium-resolution COM units offer practical price solutions in the 500 to 2,000 square pixel range, and output onto 35 mm film or 8 × 10-inch instant film.

Hard copy technology is rapidly evolving, especially in the area of high-resolution color. The **ink jet plotter** produces color hard copy directly by spraying a thin stream of ink onto paper. The three colors of ink are the subtractive primaries, cyan, yellow, and magenta. On rotary drum units the ink jets, like the laser, move slowly along a track from one end of the drum to the other, creating a raster image on paper (fig. 3-30).

Dot matrix printers generate text and images with a series of dots. These printers can produce black-and-white or color images. Black-and-white printers, unlike halftone printing screens in which the dot size can vary, use a constant dot size and simulate gray levels by increasing or decreasing the number of dots. The dot matrix printer strikes an inked ribbon against paper much like a typewriter, but instead of using individual strikers it uses a head with rows and columns of pins (fig. 3-31).

Color dot matrix printers work in much the same way; they produce multiple colors by mixing the pixels displayed in a small rectangular area (fig. 3-32). Many of these displays are inexpensive, low resolution, and designed for personal computers. Like dot matrix displays in general, they can incorporate both text and images.

Thermographic printers require several passes, as do the color dot matrix printers, using multicolored ribbons to create a color image. The pigment is transferred by heat contact from the ribbon to a special, very smooth, paper (fig. 3-33).

3-30. Color ink-jet printer output. The output paper is attached to a spinning drum and three ink jets—typically cyan, yellow and magenta—slowly translate down the cylinder and spray ink. (Courtesy of Applicon.)

Electrostatic plotters create an image by first depositing a negative electrostatic charge on the paper with a row of very fine electrical contacts, then flowing positively charged black toner onto the paper so the particles of toner adhere to the paper where the charges were deposited (fig. 3-34). A variation on this xerographic technique employs a laser beam that scans a rotating drum and deposits an electrostatic charge on it, according to the black and white values of the image. Dry toner adheres to the drum where there is a charge and is then transferred to blank paper and fixed with heat. The process works for black-and-white as well as for color output.

Finally, **alphanumeric printers** (and CRTs) can also be used as low-resolution graphic output devices, as illustrated in figures 3-13 and 3-14.

The **video raster display,** such as a television, is a widely used CRT that produces an image in a sequential, line-by-line, order with a predetermined time base, as implied by a raster (fig. 3-35). Unlike a vector CRT, the electron beam of a raster display cannot follow a random path to describe an image, but writes the image as a series of pixels.

A black-and-white raster display uses one electron gun and one type of phosphor coating on the back of the screen for producing images. A color raster display uses three electron guns and three phosphor coatings for red, green, and blue.

3-31. A black-and-white dot matrix picture approximates gray values by increasing the quantity of printed pixels. (Provided by Isaac V. Kerlow.)

3-32. Color dot matrix printers are affordable devices for medium-resolution hard copy. (Courtesy of Lauretta Jones.)

Raster CRTs are connected to computers by *frame buffer memory* (see fig. 2-6), which stores the contents of all the pixels in a frame, as opposed to vector CRTs, which use *display lists*. Actually, modern display list machines sometimes use raster CRT technology and use a frame buffer as well as a display list.

Photographic hard copy of soft copy displays can be made by shooting directly from the screen and yield excellent results if enough care is taken during the recording process—many of the images in this book have been obtained this way. The camera must be mounted on a solid tripod and be perfectly aligned (horizontally and vertically) to the screen. All the lights in the room should be turned off to avoid light reflections on the screen. The controls of the monitor should be adjusted to optimize the image quality. The light reading should be accurate and a series of test exposures should precede the final shots. The test shots should include a ***step wedge***—at least eight levels of gray or color—to assist in evaluation. It is obvious that a good lens and film will produce the best results; a low ASA film offers a very fine grain and good color balance. Exposure times should be under $\frac{1}{8}$ of a second to avoid the flicker that comes when the screen is refreshed every $\frac{1}{60}$ of a second. Finally, the camera should be activated with a timer to avoid vibrations.

A variety of technologies exist and many are being developed that produce flat-panel solid state raster or pixel displays. Existing technologies include liquid crystals, light emitting diodes, and plasma panels. Respectable black-and-white displays exist, and color units are just coming out of the research lab. Like CRTs, solid state displays interface to the computer via a frame buffer. Solid state touch sensitivity displays of arbitrary size and resolution are advantageous, because they are thin and are therefore easily positioned.

THREE-DIMENSIONAL PERIPHERALS (SPATIAL)

Three-dimensional input and output concerns designers of packages and products and requires a thorough understanding of two-dimensional graphics as well, since three-dimensional objects are often digitized as two or more flat graphics.

Positional three-dimensional I/O is very similar to two-dimensional I/O. In two dimensions a point marks a location in an area, and in three dimensions a point marks a location on a solid, or in space. Positional three-dimensional I/O is used to enter shapes of objects when their boundaries can best be described with corners, or with points that can be used to define edges, surfaces, and solids in space. Examples of positional input devices include three-dimensional stylus digitizers, radars, and shaft encoder systems. Positional output devices include machine tools, intersecting laser beams, and robot arms.

Discrete three-dimensional I/O has several variants, including zel and voxel representations. Examples of discrete zel input

3-33. Thermographic hard copy requires special paper, but produces rich full color. (Courtesy of Seiko Instruments, Graphics Devices and Systems Division.)

3-34. Electrostatic plotters work much like a Xerox copier and come in color and black-and-white models. (Courtesy of Versatec, a Xerox Company, Santa Clara, CA.)

3-35. The video raster display outputs images as a series of horizontal lines starting from the top of the screen. The electron gun can modulate light intensity and can be turned on and off.

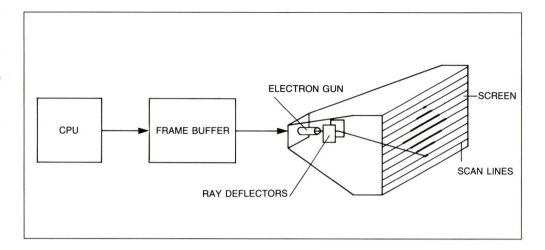

devices include the raster pantograph and sideways looking radars. Zel outputs include machine tools that can reproduce the shape of the original in a new material. The CAT scan peripheral is one example of a voxel input device. The closest thing to a voxel output is a specialized replicator not quite up to Star Trek standards.

Hard copy three-dimensional output is used in product manufacturing, even though the design is usually manipulated on two-dimensional soft copy. Virtual three-dimensional outputs include two-view photographs and holograms, an emerging three-dimensional soft copy. Displays that have color, are touch sensitive, and are tactile will have revolutionary consequences.

Three-dimensional Point Input Peripherals

Three-dimensional digitizers sense points in space or on solid objects and capture a set of XYZ numerical coordinates. These digitizers locate surface points and corners on existing physical models, using a digitizing pen that is sensitive in three dimensions (fig. 3-36). Several technologies are used, including magnetic transducers and sonic sensing.

A *radar* is a three-dimensional point-positioning peripheral that uses electromagnetic waves that travel through the air, hit an object, and return; *sonar* works similarly with acoustics. Both peripherals produce waves that hit the object and bounce back to one or more antennae. Simple triangulation methods, trigonometric calculations, when applied to the radar signals, determine the XYZ location of the object (fig. 3-37).

Point radars are used to locate large objects in large spaces, such as all aircraft or satellites in a sector of space. Radars coupled with interactive soft copy displays are the oldest computer graphics peripherals. Closely allied to radar are *laser measuring* tools, which are widely used in surveying and geological analyses. These tools work by measuring the time it takes light to travel between a transmitter and receiver.

A wide variety of *photogrammetric* techniques exist that analyze two or more images and reconstruct three-dimensional data of objects depicted. These techniques can produce point or zel data depending on the methods used and are discussed in more detail in chapters 6 and 7.

Sensors with *gimbaled joints* (shaft encoders) are also used to determine the location of points in space by measuring the angularity of the articulation. Shaft encoders can be used to determine the positions of equipment and to record human motion, such as the positions of a dancer's joints (fig. 3-38).

Three-dimensional Point Output Peripherals

Three-dimensional *laser sculpting tools* consist of two lasers mounted at right angles to each other, each with two degrees of freedom; one moves on X and Y, the other on Y and Z (fig. 3-39). The space contains three-dimensional photoresist, a volume of light-sensitive material similar, except for the number of dimensions, to photographic paper. Neither laser alone has sufficient energy to expose the resist, but the two beams, when they meet, provide enough light. The exposed resist is then photographically processed, and the result is a three-dimensional transparent solid medium with darkened three-dimensional points.

Laser sculpting tools can also be used in the raster mode and produce continuous-tone three-dimensional photoresist displays. The results are three-dimensional blocks of lucite with the density information represented as intensity.

Complementary to volumetric sensors are **robot arms,** volumetric positioners or devices that can mark a position in three-dimensional space. Gimbaled tables are used along with robotlike arms that

reach out and position a tool (fig. 3-40). A machine tool is often positioned at a point to complete a specific task, such as drilling or boring into metal. Many of these applications are discussed in chapter 10.

Holography is a medium that can record virtual images in three dimensions; holographic techniques can be used for point or voxel data. One technique employs **multiplex holograms,** which use a sequence of computer-generated perspective views to make a virtual, monochromatic, three-dimensional image (fig. 3-41).

Zel Input Peripherals

A **raster pantograph** measures the depth of an object as a series of sections, parallel contours that describe the perimeter of the object at equal intervals (fig. 3-42). Mechanical pantographs sense the object with contact feelers; light systems use profile outlines. The output of a pantograph is a matrix of zels. Pantographs, like zels, can digitize with orthogonal or polar coordinates. They measure objects

3-37. A radar can locate objects in three-dimensional space and represent them on a flat display.

3-36. Three-dimensional point and normal digitizing. Some three-dimensional digitizers are able to digitize the spatial XYZ coordinates of the point as well as the direction the stylus is pointing, or its normal. The measurement has six degrees of freedom: three degrees of spatial freedom and three degrees of freedom to show direction. (Courtesy of Polhemus Navigational Sciences Division, McDonnel Douglas Electronics Company.)

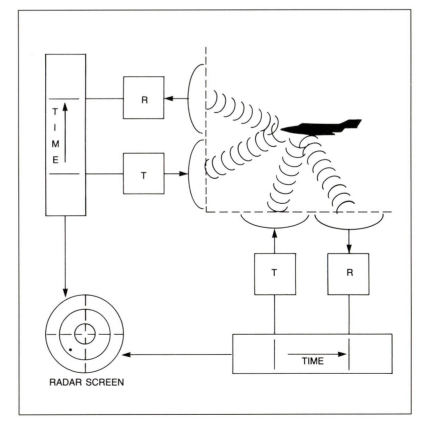

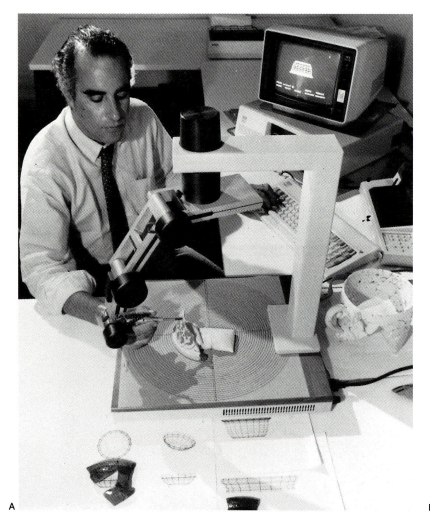

A

B

3-38. Both these three-dimensional digitizers use shaft encoders. In A, the encoders allow the point on the end of the arm to be accurately tracked. In B, a model is wearing a flexible body brace with angular shaft encoders that measure the amount of rotation in each joint.

as a series of sections. This process is subject to many of the problems that arise when images are rasterized, such as aliasing. Another problem is that most raster pantographs cannot detect overhangs (fig. 3-43).

Raster radars and *ultrasound* scan a focused beam across a volume of space and store the amount of time it takes for each electrical pixel to go out and bounce back, essentially producing a bitmap of zels, or distances, as a result. Raster radars are well suited for digitizing terrain (fig. 3-44); ultrasound effectively digitizes human tissue.

Zel Output Peripherals

Zel output represents the contours of an image. *Vibrating mirror* displays that incorporate depth physically modulate the plane of an image in correspondence with the depth of a point (fig. 3-45). Conceptually such displays may be point or raster displays, and the user does not require glasses to see three-dimensional images.

Point as well as zel descriptions can be used to control a machine tool, such as a milling machine, by a process known as *numerical control (NC).* NC tools are widely used in the metal machining and toolmaking industries for prototypes as well as for mass production. NC tools include lathes, milling machines, and special cutting and assembly units (fig. 3-46). Indeed, the entire factory is a computer peripheral.

The *depth-cutting milling machine,* the output complement of the raster pantograph, is essentially an X, Y, and Z plotter

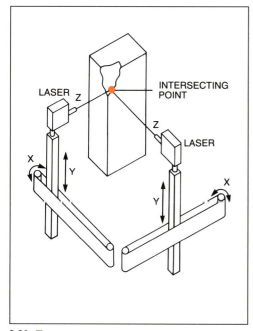

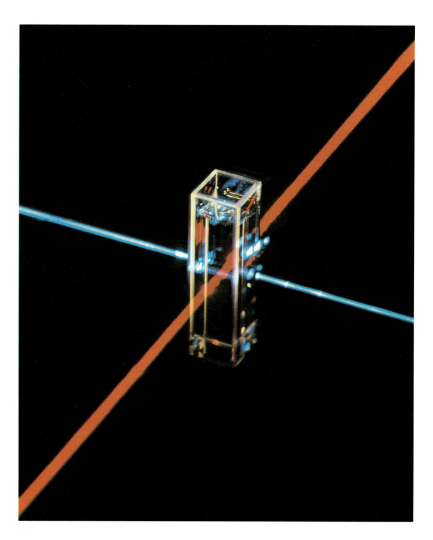

3-39. Two computer-controlled intersecting laser beams can be used to sculpt three-dimensional photoresists. The energy levels must be adjusted so the laser can expose the material only at the intersection points. The laser guns can be translated in two dimensions, so any position in the three-dimensional model can be exposed. (Courtesy of Robert E. Schwerzel/Batelle Columbus Laboratories.)

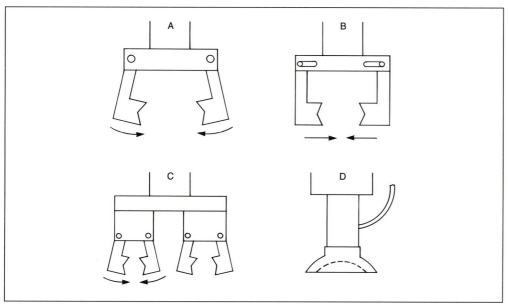

3-40. Computer-controlled mechanical devices include robot arms and even entire assembly lines. Shown here are different types of grippers, each used for a different application: A is a pivoting claw; in B the sides slide horizontally; C contains a double gripper; and D operates with suction.

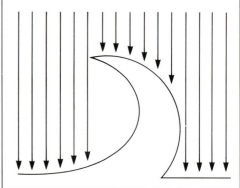

3-43. Objects with overhangs present problems in pantograph digitizing.

3-41. Direct simulation of holograms using computer graphics is in the experimental stage, but the *multiplex hologram,* made using a sequence of images, is a useful method for displaying synthetic three-dimensional environments. (Courtesy of Holo/CAD.)

3-42. A raster pantograph is a volumetric extension of the raster television digitizer and measures material goods as a series of sections of zels.

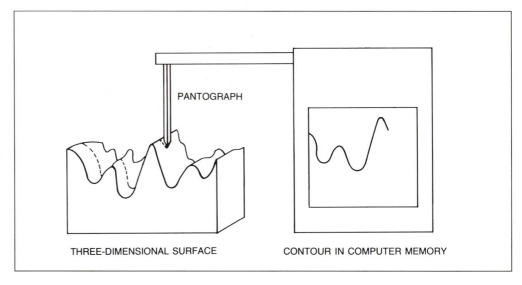

PANTOGRAPH

THREE-DIMENSIONAL SURFACE

CONTOUR IN COMPUTER MEMORY

3-44. A sideways-looking radar is essentially an electronic raster pantograph. Again depth, not luminance, is measured.

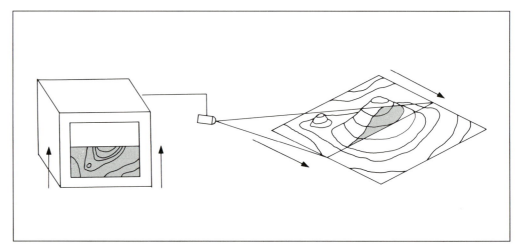

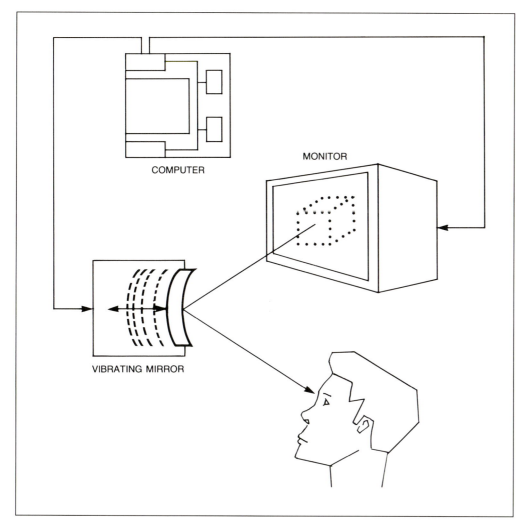

3-45. A volumetric display is synchronized with an oscillating mirror that vibrates in and out at a fixed frequency. Points, lines, and areas are all quantized and stored as zels. The zels are sorted by depth and then displayed at the exact time the mirror is at the corresponding depth.

COMPUTER

MONITOR

VIBRATING MIRROR

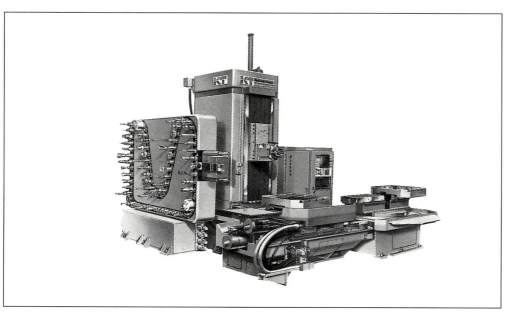

3-46. A numerically controlled tool may actually mount its own work, select a grinding or machine tool, and perform an operation. (Courtesy of Kearney & Trecker Corp.)

with a grinding tool instead of a pen, reproducing the surface of the object in matter (fig. 3-47). Milling machines also exist that cut around a polar axis and correspond to data bases of polar coordinate zels.

Voxel Input Peripherals

Computer aided tomography (CAT) scan peripherals use X rays to measure the density of three-dimensional volumes. The X rays are fired from different angles, and the views are computationally integrated to produce a three-dimensional matrix, the densities of the interior material, which are stored as a three-dimensional matrix of voxels. A single plane of this matrix looks like a cross section of the object and resembles a photographic image (see figs. 1-31 and 6-1); however, the data does not represent luminance or distance, but the density of matter.

Other technologies use tomography to detect radiation from several angles, but instead of firing X rays, they measure radiation emitted by radioactive isotopes that are ingested by the body and determine their location. Newer technologies called *nuclear magnetic resonance* (NMR) are able to pinpoint individual atoms.

Voxel Output Peripherals

While three-dimensional peripheral technologies allow us to describe, transmit, and duplicate the shape, color, and surface orientation of three-dimensional objects, voxels can represent matter. All that is needed is a CAT or NMR scanner able to accurately sample at the atomic level, a three-dimensional memory buffer to store the voxels, each containing the atomic numbers, and an output device with a supply of matter (or the equivalent energy) to scan the product back out. This must be done quickly in order to teleport living matter, which is in motion.

Nature handles this copying problem not with a voxel solution but with a procedural description, particularly the DNA amino acid code used to assemble proteins. High-resolution volumetric input and output is still way beyond our capabilities.

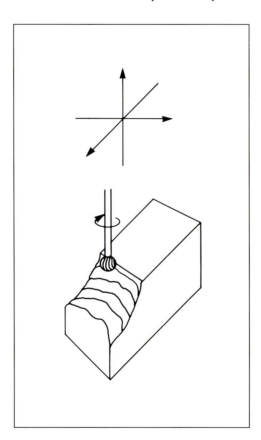

3-47. The depth-cutting milling machine positions a special grinding machine tool at an X, Y coordinate and cuts down to a certain depth. The depth cut is analogous to the value stored in the zel. It is the complement of the raster pantograph and the three-dimensional version of a television monitor.

4-0. Designers sometimes mimic traditional imaging procedures with computer interfaces. (Plug People courtesy of Joe Pasquale and Digital Effects Inc.)

INTERFACING
WITH
THE SYSTEM

INTERACTION SOFTWARE
PROPERTIES OF DIALOGUE
PRODUCING COMPUTER GRAPHICS
INTERFACE DESIGN CONSIDERATIONS

RELATED READING

Cakir, A. D., D. J. Hart, and T. F. M. Stewart. *Visual Display Terminal.* New York: John Wiley & Sons, 1980.

Diffrient, Niels, Alvin R. Tilley, Joan C. Bardagjy, and David Harman. *Humanscale.* Cambridge, MA: MIT Press, 1981.

Martin, J. *Design of Man-Computer Dialogues.* Englewood Cliffs, NJ: Prentice-Hall, 1973.

Woodson, W. E. *Human Factors Design Handbook.* New York: McGraw-Hill, 1981.

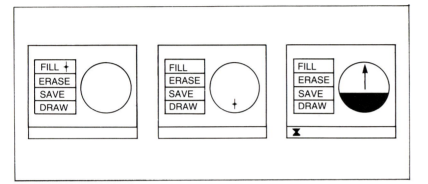

The *interface* between the user and the computer system—that part of the system that the user tactilely and semantically controls—is the focus of this chapter. In an automobile the interface devices include the steering wheel, gas pedal, and brake; in a computer graphics system these include keyboards, tablets, and buttons, as well as virtual representations on a screen.

INTERACTION SOFTWARE

We have already discussed a variety of interaction devices, such as tablets, light pens, and mice; now we turn our attention to *interaction software,* or how peripherals and screens are employed to create computer graphics. Interaction software has a wide range of applications, including, but certainly not limited to, graphics.

Interaction software procedures evaluate input from peripherals, such as keyboards,

4-1. Graphic and text cursors are used for input and output operations. A wait symbol appears at the lower left of screen and indicates that the cursor is unavailable while the process is taking place.

4-2. The cursor is used to select (pick) a function from the menu (A). It is then moved into the drawing area, picked (B), and moved, while in picked position, to draw a line. Relaxed (C), the cursor is moved to another selection and picked.

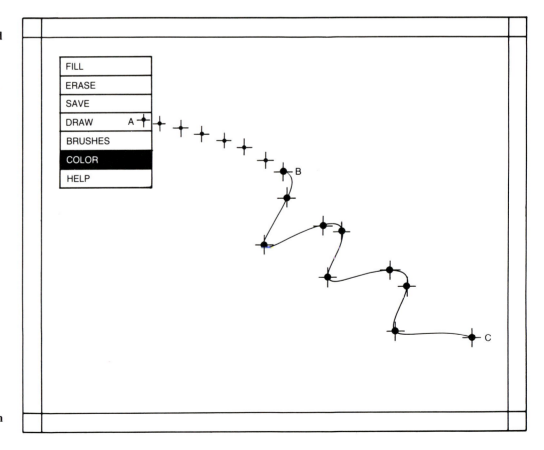

tablets, or mice, and produce output on graphic or textual displays. The operations of a computer can be very basic or highly specialized and are continually evolving. A unique characteristic of interaction software is that reprogramming can alter the interface quickly and easily. This facilitates changes in style and the evolution of the basic semantics in the man-machine dialogue.

The Cursor

Basic interaction tools are likely to remain constant despite the computer industry's rapid changes; these provide the foundation for the more sophisticated tools that are being and will be built. The *cursor,* a symbol on the screen used for pointing, selecting, drawing, and display, is probably the most basic software tool. The cursor indicates either where an input shall occur, or where the next information will be displayed.

The cursor may either be *pointed*—positioned or moved about without affecting the data that has already been entered—or *picked*—in which case the position indicated on the screen is entered as data into the system, effecting a process (fig. 4-1). The position selected might correspond to a command or to data, much as a pocket calculator is "picked" when the buttons are depressed. The position might also indicate a graphic action, where to position a point, line, or figure, for example (fig. 4-2).

In addition to pointing and picking, a cursor may also be either in the input or output mode. It is in *input* when the user, or artist, has it under his or her control and is pointing or picking. The cursor is in *output* when the computer is controlling and positioning it. During this time the user is "locked out," and the system alone can control the display. The artist and the system cannot control the cursor at the same time.

When text is input cursors indicate the position of the next character, and when it is output they indicate where the next character will be displayed. Like graphic cursors, text cursors also have position

and pick (enter) modes (fig. 4-3).

The user can control the cursor with mice, pens on tablets, cursor keys (fig. 4-4), and even three-dimensional wands used for positioning; a button on a mouse, a pressure sensitive end on a stylus, or a special keyboard key are used for the pick.

In the input mode the cursors can take many forms, from crosshairs to rectangular cells of pixels that form a letter or a shape. A cursor may be a point if the screen is continuous space, and one or more pixels if the screen is discrete (fig. 4-5). In the output mode a cursor either displays text or an image or displays a *wait* symbol (fig. 4-6), indicating that the computer is still processing. The wait (or ready) symbol is best implemented as a separate indicator, often at the bottom of the display, that is on when the system is performing calculations and off when the system is awaiting input. The two states of the cursor should be differentiated visually, although sometimes the cursor and ready are the

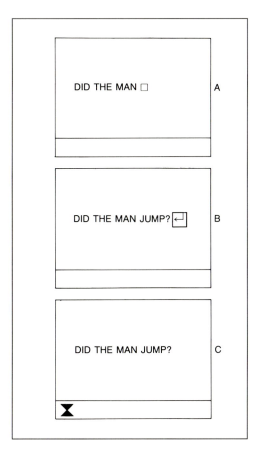

4-3. The cursor is advanced letter by letter as the user inputs text (A). When a query is entered into the system (B), the wait symbol appears as the computer finds the right answer (C).

4-6. The wait symbol is displayed when the CPU is processing information. The only user entry the system will accept in this mode is break, which interrupts processing and returns control to the user.

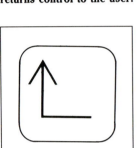

4-7. Break symbol.

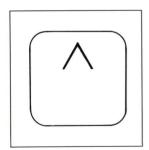

4-8. Space symbol.

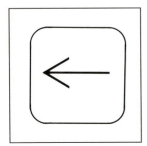

4-9. Backspace symbol.

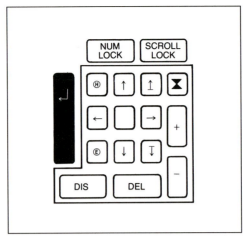

4-4. The four arrow keys move the cursor left, right, up, and down. The enter key picks the position and sends it into the program as input. Holding a cursor key down longer can make the cursor move faster in the direction of the arrow. The cursor has two degrees of freedom in location and one degree of freedom in picking.

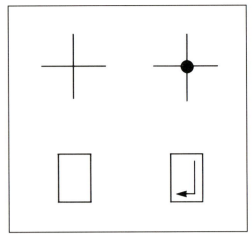

4-5. The symbolic conventions used in this text for cursor representations: a crosshair indicates that the cursor is available to accept entry; and a crosshair with a dot indicates that it is in the picked mode. A text cursor as a blank box indicates that text can be input and as a box with an arrow indicates that information has been entered.

same symbol—the two states are differentiated by slow and fast blinking.

Most applications provide a way for the user to stop the computer processing and to cancel output. This is called **break** (fig. 4-7) and is usually executed by a special key that, when pushed, interrupts the process and returns control to the user.

When handling text, the cursor may be subject to additional rules. Because the keyboard has evolved from a typewriter, it still contains some vestiges. *Wait,* for example, on a hard copy terminal is often indicated mechanically, perhaps by a light, or by the position of the printer head. *Space* (fig. 4-8) and *backspace* (fig. 4-9) are similar to cursor control keys, but the backspace key often deletes text. Other common keys include *insert* and *delete* keys, which allow simple editing, and keys for *tabs* and *case* (fig. 4-10).

The *enter* key is often confused with the *carriage return* from which it evolved. Early computers were line entry oriented like linotypes, and the line was terminated with carriage return, which advanced a line feed, returned the carriage, and performed the enter; that is, activated the process (fig. 4-11). A carriage return and a line feed are actually specifications for

formatting text. *Enter* submits input to the CPU.

Dialogue

A **dialogue** is an interaction, constrained by rules, between a user and a machine. It is made up of a **prompt,** a textual or iconographic message issued by the CPU that requires some response from the operator or artist, and the **response,** also known as the user entry (fig. 4-12). The input prompt is followed by a validation and a selection of potential actions or procedures (fig. 4-13); the user's response may involve picking or text entry. The **validation** indicates whether the response is a valid word, a meaningful number, or in the right position. The computer program validates the user's input, comparing it to predefined tables of valid choices, or checks numerical boundaries (fig. 4-14). If this response is valid, the computer executes a procedure associated with the response. If the response is invalid, or meaningless, the system issues an **error message,** advising the user of the mistake, assisting if possible, and reprompting for response.

A prompt should also have an **escape,** or a way to sidestep the question without

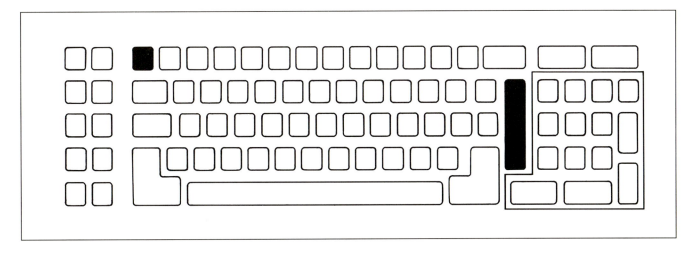

GREETINGS, ARE YOU DR, CHANDLER?

ANSWER YES OR NO PLEASE: NO ☐

4-10. The user's choices in response to a cursor or prompt include valid numbers or text followed by enter, or escape, which releases the user to the next higher level.

4-11. Enter is not line feed/carriage return. In this example, a user's response to a prompt has been typed in but not entered. The cursor remains at the end of the line for the next character input. Will it be a space, another letter, or an enter? Until the enter key is pressed, the computer cannot respond. The entry can therefore be edited before it is submitted.

	Prompt	Response
1	YOUR NAME PLEASE?	HORACE WILLIAMS
2	HELLO MR, WILLIAMS, YOUR PASSWORD?	NMS924
3	DO YOU WANT CASH, DEPOSIT, OR BYE?	CASH
4	HOW MUCH?	$50,00
5	DONE, YOUR BALANCE IS $768,00	
6	DO YOU WANT CASH, DEPOSIT, OR BYE?	BYE
7	YOUR NAME?	

4-12. A dialogue interaction at a money machine contains numbered prompts and responses. Line one validates a response ("Horace Williams") and formats it into the next question, which validates the password. Question three requires one of two table selections for a response, and question four validates the response against the balance and the limit of cash in the machine. After dispensing cash, the machine displays data from memory (line five) and reprompts. Transaction is terminated with BYE, and system prompts for and awaits next user.

Properties of Individual Prompts	Prompt #3	Prompt #4

Input Datatype
   Binary Toggle
   Numerical
   Text
	Text	Numerical

Text of Prompt	DO YOU WANT CASH, DEPOSIT, OR BYE?	HOW MUCH?

Validation Table or Range
   if Boolean, 0 or 1
   if Numerical, Either a Table of Permitted Numbers or a Mini-
     mum and Maximum Value
   if Text, a Table of Proper Choices
	TEXT:
	  CASH
	  DEPOSIT
	  BYE
		NUMERICAL:
		  0 ≤ BALANCE
		  AND 0 ≤ CASH
		  IN MONEY
		  MACHINE

Procedure Table
   List of Procedures to Execute
     upon Proper Responses
	GOTO PROMPT #4
	GOTO PROMPT #4
	GOTO PROMPT #7
		ACTIVATE MONEY MACHINE AND OUTPUT MONEY
		GOTO PROMPT #5

Escape Procedure to Return to if User Exits	GOTO PROMPT #1	GOTO PROMPT #3
Default Value Predefined Selection	BYE	0
Error Message	INVALID RESPONSE TRY AGAIN	TOO MUCH MONEY REQUESTED

4-13. Properties of a prompt. The second and third columns correspond to and illustrate prompts 3 and 4 of figure 4-12.

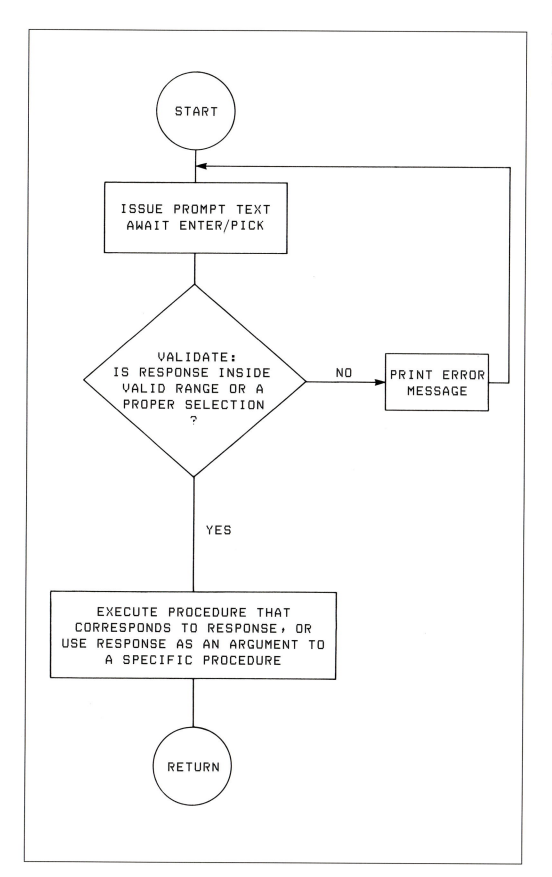

START

ISSUE PROMPT TEXT
AWAIT ENTER/PICK

VALIDATE:
IS RESPONSE INSIDE
VALID RANGE OR A
PROPER SELECTION
?

NO → PRINT ERROR MESSAGE

YES

EXECUTE PROCEDURE THAT
CORRESPONDS TO RESPONSE, OR
USE RESPONSE AS AN ARGUMENT TO
A SPECIFIC PROCEDURE

RETURN

4-15. Motions can be recognized as commands. For example, gesture recognition software accepts a circular movement of the cursor as a request for help. In a similar way, a quick vertical stroke might generate an escape command. A right stroke will remove text information from the screen, and a left stroke will bring it back.

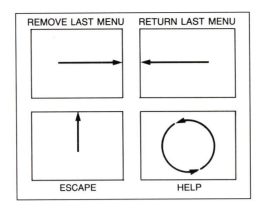

REMOVE LAST MENU RETURN LAST MENU

ESCAPE HELP

4-16. A menu of drawing modules; buttons may be represented with iconographic or alphanumeric labels.

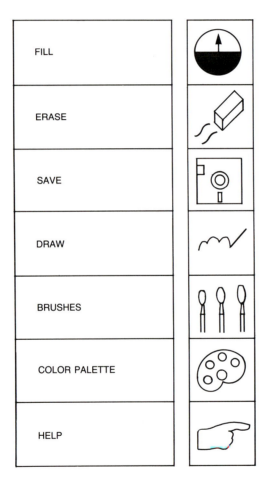

FILL

ERASE

SAVE

DRAW

BRUSHES

COLOR PALETTE

HELP

4-17. Toggles that are found in a graphic system allow an artist to make selections.

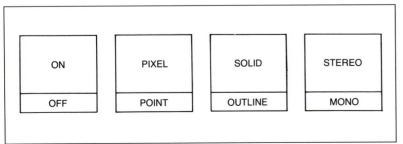

ON	PIXEL	SOLID	STEREO
OFF	POINT	OUTLINE	MONO

answering it, by returning to the procedure (prompt) that invoked the prompt in question. Escape is sometimes activated by a special key, or special symbols entered into the response, such as a space followed by a carriage return. Escape is executed during user control, whereas break interrupts the machine's process.

Virtual Buttons, Toggles, Sliders, Menus, and Active Areas

Dialogue can take many forms, from interactive systems that contain screens that look and respond like real instruments to programming languages that employ text. When implemented gesturally, certain movements of the cursor are associated with certain meanings (fig. 4-15); the software distinguishes the gesture and activates the appropriate procedure. When implemented visually, dialogue manifests as virtual buttons, toggles, and sliders.

Buttons are used to select from a table of choices (fig. 4-16). When a button is selected, the button usually changes color or its graphics change. A *toggle* is a button that lets a user choose between two modes, for example, on and off (fig. 4-17).

Sliders are potentiometers (rheostats) that control range, like volume on an audio system or line width in a graphics system. Sliders appear as either dials or linears (fig. 4-18) and allow an artist to control graphic variables. They may be range bounded, that is, have minimum and maximum values, or they may be differential, which allows you to adjust them relative to a particular setting.

A *menu* is a list of options or prompts; often a collection of buttons, toggles, and sliders can be used together in any order and for some common purpose (fig. 4-19). The graphic artist chooses an option by positioning the cursor over his or her selection and picking. The system then executes the procedure, for example, a color change, or the filling in of a polygon. The user can also choose to have the system display still other menus with even more choices, or to make certain areas of the screen respond to the cursor in special ways.

An *active area* is a portion of the screen that responds to a user's control of the cursor for drawing, painting, and other graphic operations (fig. 4-20). An active area, unlike a button or slider, can be composed and modified by the graphic artist.

Windows and Ports

Menus and active areas can often be repositioned and resized on the screen, which is a process popularly called *window/port management*. A *port* is the position and size of a viewing area on the screen, and a *window* is the position and scale of what is displayed in the port (fig. 4-21).

A window/port manager has its own buttons, so it can be repositioned and sized on the screen and so its contents may be perused. *Scrolling*—the controlled vertical or horizontal movement of data inside the window, or the horizontal or vertical repositioning of the port—is accomplished using the cursor keys, and a toggle button called a *scroll lock* determines whether the window or port is being scrolled.

Zooming—making the window data larger or smaller—is not often implemented on character-oriented displays, which cannot zoom type. The text and graphics displayed in windows are often formatted into *pages,* a series of flat areas much like the pages of a book (fig. 4-22). Films,

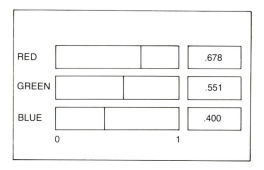

4-18. Three sliders for red, green, and blue are graphically displayed as horizontal windows. Moving the cursor left or right on the scale mixes the colors. The digital readouts to the right display the numerical values where the slider has been positioned by the cursor.

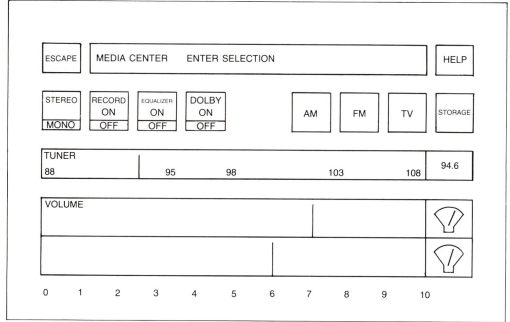

4-19. Buttons, toggles, and sliders comprise this virtual media center. A button implies a single choice from a series of mutually exclusive alternatives, here AM radio, FM radio, TV, or storage systems for sound and pictures (photographs, videotapes, and so on). Toggles have two states, and either one state or the other is active. In fact, several toggles may be active for a given situation. Toggles on the media console include the *record on/record off, equalization on/off,* and *stereo/monoaural.* All toggle possibilities work with each button selection. Sliders are used to adjust the tuning scale and volume controls. They also contain readouts; the channel tuner displays the frequency of the channel being tuned, and the VU meters show the volume of the actual sound.

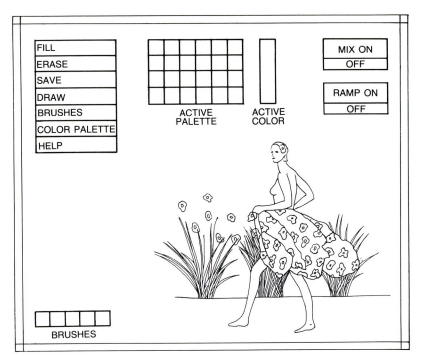

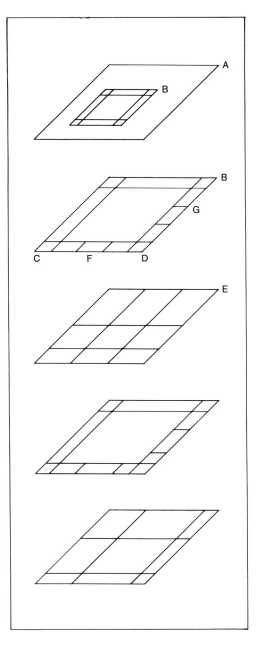

4-20. Paint box with active area outlined depicts a sequence of operations in a graphic arts paint system. First the graphic artist selects the color palette button. The system responds by displaying the color palette in the top of the active area. Next, the graphic artist selects a color, which the system displays in the active color box. The artist returns to the menu and selects the brush button. The system responds with the brush menu seen in the lower part of the screen. He or she then selects a brush. Next, a draw mode is selected, and the artist moves the cursor to the active drawing area and draws a shape.

4-21. On a screen (for example, a color television set), made of glass and pixels (A), a *port* is the area designated for displaying the image (B). The port may be as big as the screen or as small as a few pixels. The port has four degrees of freedom that are controlled by touching the two lower corners of the border (C), allowing the port to be repositioned in X and Y by picking the lower left control and moving the cursor; the port moves with the cursor until pick is released. The control in the lower right (D) scales the port and allows it to be dragged larger or smaller. The port and its controls affect only the screen position and size of a viewing area, and not what is in it. The contents of the port are planes of pictorial or textual data, illustrated below (E). The window is the framing or cropping directions of the data that are viewed and has four degrees of freedom—the X and Y position and the X and Y scale. The controls for the window are located on the port border and are slid up and down to scroll the contents (F) and widened or narrowed to control the enlargement (G). The lower pair of drawings illustrates how these controls are manipulated to make the window bigger and center it; the port controls are unchanged. This process is much the same as that of sizing and cropping pictures.

videos, magazines, and books all have pages; a page may or may not fit on the whole screen; conversely, many pages can be displayed on a single screen, using multiple ports (see fig. 8-31).

Pulldown menus and ports provide a way to graphically overlay menus (fig. 4-23). The new port, or application menu, is pushed on top of ports already displayed on the screen, used and then removed, or popped, when finished. A menu is called up, or pushed, by selecting a button, and it is exited or popped, with an escape. The hierarchy of overlaid menus corresponds to the structure of the procedures in the system (fig. 4-24).

Virtual Applications

A menu is often graphically styled to depict a virtual two-dimensional representation of the application it performs. For example, a pocket calculator, telephone dial, control panel, or keyboard is represented on a CRT and used interactively.

Virtual keyboards can simulate the familiar QWERTY keyboard, or they may assign arbitrary meanings to individual keys (fig. 4-25). It takes a longer time to enter information on a virtual keyboard, but this may be quicker than switching back and forth to a physical keyboard when only a few letters are needed, like a file name.

Virtual applications also simulate many processes in graphic design including word processing, typesetting, layout, drawing, and makeup, as well as applications as diverse as music composition, circuit design, and dance. Many of these applications involve customized menus, window management, and active areas.

Text Manipulation

Word processing allows a user to format text and to combine *text*—letters, numbers, and punctuation—with *formatting commands,* which shape and manipulate the text to form lines, columns, and pages.

A simple word processor can do everything a typewriter can do, as well as change, insert, delete, and rearrange letters, words, paragraphs, sections, and chapters. More sophisticated software will indent, center, format tabular data, justify, number pages, and index (fig. 4-26). At their most sophisticated they become typesetters with a selection of point sizes, faces, and proportional letter spacing. Format commands also control colors and case. On interactive video displays they allow a user to make letters or words blink or to display them in reverse video, that is, in negative—a black letter surrounded by a white box.

Forms entry is an interactive textual

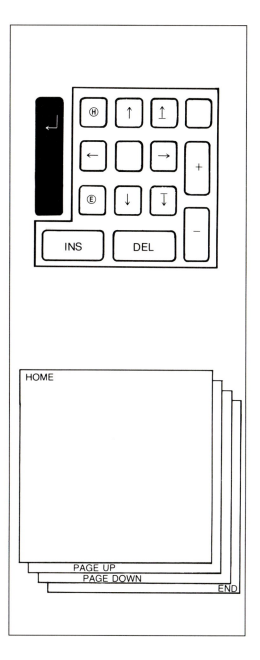

method that displays multiple prompts on the screen and provides spaces for responses (fig. 4-27). The user is able to respond to prompts, review the entire form, then enter it. With this method a user gains perspective on his or her work; especially when different entries are related, mistakes in a single answer are more likely to stand out given this broader view.

Forms entry systems, in addition to performing individual prompt validations, also perform *transaction validations,*

4-22. HOME positions the cursor at the beginning of a page, END at the end of it. PGUP goes back one page, PGDW advances a page. Once on a page, the cursor is positioned with the cursor keys.

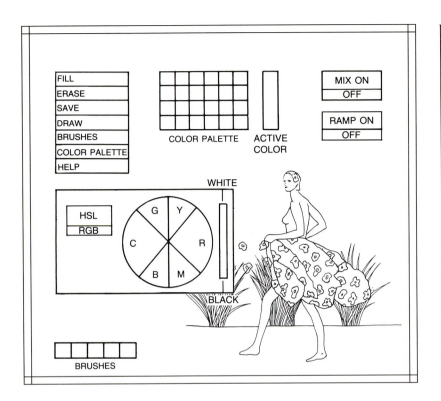

4-23. Selecting the mix color mode *pushes* a color mix menu onto the screen. Toggling from HSL in the mix color menu will bring up the RGB menu. Escape *pops* the mix menu off the screen.

which ensure internal consistencies among groups of prompts, for example, that a state and zip code correspond. Fields that fail to validate are reprompted, and the user corrects the erroneous responses, then reenters.

PROPERTIES OF DIALOGUE

When using a computer graphics system for the first time, communications must be presented in detail. Once a working dialogue is established, shortcuts are employed—abbreviations and acronyms, default behaviors, and gestures that signify an entire sequence of commands.

Communications can be expressed using a languagelike syntax, such as "enlarge that picture 133 percent," or they can be graphically expressed by touching the screen and sliding the picture into position. In textual, aural, gestural, or graphic communications, expressions are bound by rules of syntax and the limitations of the machine.

Command language interpreters are interaction systems that involve a collection

4-24. The selection made in figure 4-23 from the point of view of the system structure parallels the graphic presentation.

MAIN MENU
PAINT
WORD PROCESSING
MEDIA CENTER
END

PAINT MENU
FILL
ERASE
SAVE
DRAW
BRUSH
PALETTE
HELP

PALETTE MENU
COLOR SELECT
MIX
RAMP
RETURN

MIX MENU
HSL
RGB
RETURN

HSL MENU
HUE
SATURATION
LUMINANCE
RETURN

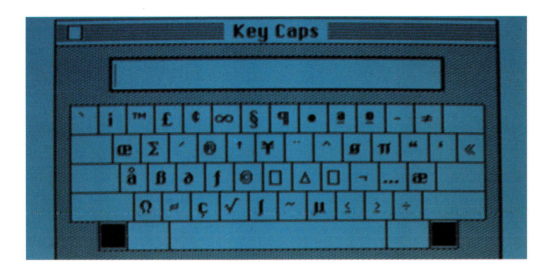

of standardized prompts with a consistent syntax. These interpreters are widely used and examples include operating systems like UNIX or CP/M, languages like BASIC or APL, and virtually all interactive graphics systems. Command language interpreters have a variety of features that enable a user to select predefined **defaults** (responses to prompts), **truncate** responses (type only a few letters of a command), cancel selections, backspace, **backup** (undo what was just done), and **type ahead** (respond to the next prompt before it appears).

Many command language interpreters provide a way for a user to proceed if an error message appears. Still others will avoid prompts when they are unnecessary; almost all allow a user to configure his or her own system; for example, how long a cursor has to be pressed to detect a pick.

Indirect command files are interactive sequences that can be recorded or composed and replayed; they essentially enable a user to write a program, and like programs, indirect command files can be given parameters, or arguments. Thus indirect command files are one way to routinize redundant tasks and define graphic templates—for example, a standard business graph format developed for many applications (fig. 8-33). The designer creates and modifies the template, and the graphs produced maintain all the constraints

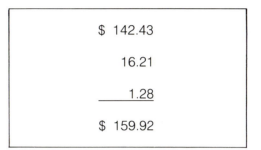

4-26. Formatting command ('$', F6.2) prints a $ followed by six columns of numerical information, containing a decimal point and two decimal places.

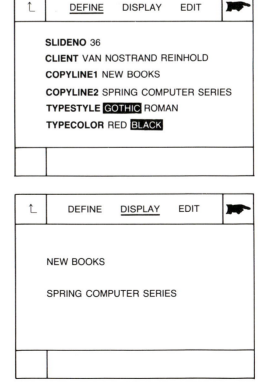

4-27. In this forms entry template for making up word slides, the system positions the cursor at the first input field, here SLIDE#, and the user enters a valid response. The cursor advances to CLIENT, COPYLINE1, and COPYLINE2, with the user entering the appropriate information for each of these fields. At the prompt TYPESTYLE and TYPECOLOR the system allows two choices for each, and the user selects between them by moving the cursor right (or left) using the cursor control keys. The entire form is submitted to the system by pressing ENTER. Moving the cursor to DISPLAY and entering causes the formatted text to appear. Adjustments are made by moving the cursor to EDIT and entering; the filled-in form reappears and the user can edit the entries, enter, and redisplay them. The space to the right of the hourglass displays error messages.

and navigating the system. You generally invoke lower-level environments by issuing commands, either via words or buttons, and exit an environment using an escape.

Good systems harmonize the stylistic design of prompt behavior throughout a system, even between environments. This requires a clear definition of the prompt parameters, plus consistent implementation. Command language interpreters should facilitate the way in which both experienced and inexperienced users operate the system. Redundant systems are easier to learn, but the experienced user wants shortcuts like type ahead and truncated response. A well-designed system should let you do both. A system should be simple and have features that will not get in the way. But the system should not be too simple, since graphic artists seem to quickly want to devise their own shortcuts; and you should not underestimate your own ability or that of your staff to develop more sophisticated commands, or to escalate the demands upon the services a system provides. Finally, a system should be fun to use, efficient, and should foster creativity.

PRODUCING AND DIRECTING COMPUTER GRAPHICS

In computer graphics, as in graphic arts in general, a designer may directly or indirectly manipulate a system. The former situation is typical when an artist works on a system, the latter is more common in commercial production.

Management Systems

Much of what the designer, producer, director, and art director do involves managing information, budgeting, scheduling, and contracting work. A *data-base system,* which includes files of names and addresses, budgets, schedules, and rate cards, is one tool available to the art director. Data bases can include photographs, drawings, and moving pictures in addition to alphanumeric material.

A data base is often designed for a par-

4-28. A particular computing environment is usually invoked by a higher-level environment and may in turn call lower-level environments.

chosen by the designer. The unchanging parameters, such as the font, the chart type, and the layout for these formats would be built into the indirect command file; whereas the parameters that are always unique, such as the actual data to be plotted, would be passed as parameters to the indirect command file at the time the picture was to be made.

A particular command language interpreter, like any other computing language or procedure, is part of a *computing environment,* a conceptual location with constant syntax and language (fig. 4-28). Different environments often employ different syntax, but all, including command language interpreters, procedures, and menus, have a beginning—a place they start when invoked—as well as an end, often activated by escape. Knowing what environment is active as well as knowing how to make the transition between environments is essential for using computers

ticular purpose. A casting director, for instance, can compile a list of actors and actresses, and then search the system for only those who fulfill a set of criteria (see fig. 9-6). A video camera is used to capture data and the pictures are then indexed according to specific parameters. Once selected, the pictures are displayed along with the textual information.

Budgeting systems can use preformatted spread sheets (discussed in more detail in chapter 9). Often the spread sheet is tailored to a specific activity, such as the American Independent Commercial Producers' live-action budget form. *Production scheduling and monitoring systems* track schedules, manage a staff's time, and analyze the fastest ways to do things. Production variables, such as the hours expended and costs, can be graphically plotted, as can more abstract concepts like readability, visibility, or the percent of pictures in a publication.

Computer systems are not significantly different from systems in general. The introduction of a computer into an established organization may represent a radical change in the way information is stored and retrieved, but it does not modify the basic management process. Even in computer facilities salaries constitute the greatest expense and individuals are the most important part of an operation. Their basic skills, knowledge, experience, and creativity determine the success of the organization. Computer systems are not substitutes for human creativity, initiative, or style, but facilitate the expression of these.

Conversions from traditional to electronic media will be fraught with anxiety until workers and managers understand that the value of good retouchers, for example, is their ability to select and position the appropriate color; they need not put color on a brush and touch it to a photograph. These creative acts can be executed after one has enough experience to smooth a wrinkle, or accelerate the flow of a line. The goal is to make the picture read more clearly, which is a skill that is completely transferable to electronic media.

Contracting with Production Units

When considering computer graphics as a solution to a particular design problem, it is best to begin by simply and specifically describing your needs to members of a production unit. If the production unit's personnel say that they cannot execute your designs the way they are drawn, perhaps they can adapt your designs and propose a better solution. Alternate sources of supply should be considered if an absolute requirement cannot be realized.

Contracting for computer graphic production begins with a producer (or client) issuing a request for a quotation, which consists of a drawing or storyboard and a written description of the work to be performed.

The production unit responds with a quotation, which includes a written description of the solution, a timetable, and a price. The producer evaluates the quotation, negotiates the fine points, and issues a purchase order before the production unit begins work. This work is reviewed by the client at predefined intervals and approved before the production unit completes it to spec and delivers it along with an invoice (fig. 4-29).

The *contract* defines the terms of sale and conditions of production; in fact, this can actually be the quotation or purchase order, or even a letter of agreement. This document includes a written description, the number of pieces or the running time, the delivery medium, delivery date, price, terms of payment, and point of delivery. It may also contain credits, rights of resale, and additional conditions (fig. 4-30).

The *written description* provides a clear, technical description of the production. It might describe the visual contents—"a picture showing a three-dimensional robot juggling three colored balls; the robot is inside a house." The written description should indicate whether the design is to be rendered as a pixel image or a vector image, whether the image is described in a two-dimensional or three-dimensional environment, and how the image is to be rendered. If the image depicts a three-dimensional environment, the

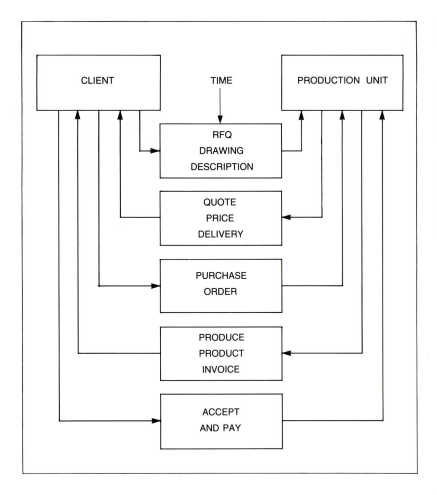

```
┌──────────────────────────────────────────────────────────┐
│  ┌──────────────┐     TIME      ┌──────────────────┐      │
│  │    CLIENT    │               │ PRODUCTION UNIT  │      │
│  └──────────────┘               └──────────────────┘      │
│         ┌──────────────────┐                              │
│         │       RFQ        │                              │
│         │     DRAWING      │                              │
│         │   DESCRIPTION    │                              │
│         └──────────────────┘                              │
│         ┌──────────────────┐                              │
│         │      QUOTE       │                              │
│         │      PRICE       │                              │
│         │    DELIVERY      │                              │
│         └──────────────────┘                              │
│         ┌──────────────────┐                              │
│         │    PURCHASE      │                              │
│         │     ORDER        │                              │
│         └──────────────────┘                              │
│         ┌──────────────────┐                              │
│         │    PRODUCE       │                              │
│         │    PRODUCT       │                              │
│         │    INVOICE       │                              │
│         └──────────────────┘                              │
│         ┌──────────────────┐                              │
│         │    ACCEPT        │                              │
│         │    AND PAY       │                              │
│         └──────────────────┘                              │
└──────────────────────────────────────────────────────────┘
```

4-29. Interactions between a client and production unit in contracting computer graphics.

description should say if shading or lighting are to be used. If the image is wire frame, the description should indicate if hidden lines are to be removed. Descriptions may even include the number of points or polygons used in a picture, the resolution of the image, and its finished size.

Written descriptions often reference storyboards, drawings, and blueprints, but no computer graphic is going to look exactly like a hand-drawn illustration. Clarifications between sketches and desired results are essential to avoid misunderstandings.

The number of pieces should be expressed as a count: "thirteen slides, two copies each for a total of twenty-six slides," for instance. Running times are best expressed in seconds and could include the number of frames per second that are being delivered. "Twos," for example, means each frame is repeated twice, and has half

the production value of "ones," where every frame is unique.

The delivery medium might specify 35 mm or 16 mm film, ¾-inch or 1-inch videotape, 35 mm slides, 4 × 5-inch color transparencies, color separation sets, paper plots, ink jet color plots, or even images in digital form, such as a floppy disk.

A fixed price is a firm bid to do the entire job. Quantity price depends on the number of pieces and the length or running time. Cost-plus-markup pricing specifies that price is equal to the costs of raw materials and services, plus a fixed markup.

Terms dictate when money is paid and how much is paid at each time. Terms might specify one-half in advance and one-half cash on delivery, or 100 percent net thirty days. Contracts spread out over long periods of time often specify monthly payments tied to performance milestones.

The ***point of delivery,*** or F.O.B., specifies the point of delivery, usually the manufacturing site of the production unit. The issue involved is who pays for shipping and sales taxes—these together can account for as much as 10 percent of the cost.

Often clients request that the production unit alter the images in one way or another. The unit pays if the changes are modifications and within the domain of the contract, and the client pays if the changes are revisions, which alter the intent of the original description. There is a fine line distinguishing a modification from a revision, and it is only when both parties are sensitive to each other's economic and visual needs that an acceptable solution can be reached.

Rules of Thumb

Production takes time. Graphic artists at work stations take time. Indecision, committees, rather than an individual, giving and receiving directions, and the "let's hurry up and wait" scenario waste time and money. Lack of direction, lack of planning, and indecision are often as responsible for cost overruns and late deliveries as are technical malfunctions, artistic misunderstandings, and the simple

QUOTATION

FROM:

QUOTATION NO. _____

TO _____   QUOTATION DATE _____

_____   YOUR INQUIRY NO. _____

_____   QUOTE VALID FOR _____ DAYS

QUANTITY	UNITS	DESCRIPTION	UNIT PRICE	AMOUNT

TERMS	F.O.B.	ESTIMATED SHIPPING DATE	DELIVERY MEDIUM

PROVIDED BY CLIENT _____

_____

Submitted
by _____

Accepted
by _____

4-30. Quotation or contract.

grind of production. Poor planning is not easily remedied in the production stage.

A few rule-of-thumb statistics, mostly applying to animation, involving cost and time are useful. The *production time ratio* is the relationship between the wall-clock time required to design and produce a product, and the running time of the finished work. The *production cost ratio* is the average cost of producing a single frame or page (cost/frame). The *CPU time ratio* is the ratio between the computing or console time to produce a product, and its actual screen running time.

In practical terms, it is not unusual to spend two to three weeks and $10,000 to $25,000 making a five-second logo, six weeks and $30,000 to $100,000 to make a thirty-second or one-minute commercial, and three years and $5 million to $15 million to make a ninety-minute movie. Smaller units of work cost more because the costs of data bases cannot be amortized. It may be wise to begin a project with a price in mind and try to design with that price as a constraint, as computer graphics, like anything else, have a wide price range.

The size of the data base (doubling the size of the data base, for instance, more than doubles the complexity of the project), the number of views produced, the amount of action, and the rendering method chosen all affect the cost of a project. Building a data base is a one-time expense but one that can be amortized when the data is used to generate many frames. The computer, after all, is a machine that works well in a repetitive mode, and graphics are no exception.

There is a joke in the animation industry that says all computer-generated movie frames take twenty minutes to compute, regardless of the speed and cost of the computer on which the computation is being performed. Faster CPUs do not necessarily produce faster throughput, only more complicated images. The twenty-minute frame seems to be bounded primarily by the limits of practicality—a thirty-second commercial computing at twenty minutes a frame requires ten days to compute.

Of course one can design an image that could take longer to compute than the universe has been in existence, no matter how fast the computer runs. The pragmatics of performing a calculation on an existing computer inside an existing time frame require planning from both a business and a production point of view. These "limits of computability calculations" are perhaps the most basic considerations in computer graphics, and they are integrally related to all creative decisions.

INTERFACE DESIGN CONSIDERATIONS

Computer graphics systems are objects of design as well as being tools for designing images, objects, and environments. Three major considerations that pertain to the design of computer graphic systems include ergonomics, man-machine interfaces, and system selection. These considerations involve the designer, who brings to the project a sense of style and direction, as well as the human factors engineer, who evaluates strategies by testing them on people.

Ergonomic Considerations

Ergonomics, the technology concerned with the application of engineering data to problems relating to man and the machine, is applied to instrumentation displays, especially in industrial applications where health and safety must be considered. In a computer graphics work station this includes not only the dimensions of the physical components of a system, but also the *visibility* of an image (visibility is to a picture what legibility is to text) and features of the work station itself, such as lighting.

The designs of these tools and environments are directly related to a worker's performance. Well-designed tools improve creativity and productivity, give people pride, and reduce health and psychological problems, including eye strain, muscular pain, and stress. The work station must be used by a large variety of people, and its components—monitor, keyboard, seat, and table—should therefore be adaptable.

Since most of a designer's contact with the system takes place through the monitor, it should not be too small, and the user should be able to tilt it to avoid light reflections and muscular discomfort. The overall quality of the image should not flicker. When color monitors are used, they should be RGB monitors, which have separate channels for red, green, and blue, and not NTSC, or composite, monitors. Image resolution should exceed seventy dots per inch so that the image is legible.

Monitors and television screens are known to emit X-ray, ultraviolet, near-infrared, radio-frequency, extremely low-frequency, and ultrasonic radiation. The long-term effects of these on an individual's health are not yet known. If health problems are suspected, the amount of radiation emitted can be measured and compared to existing occupational exposure standards. Corrective measures, like lead glass and shielding, can also be taken.

The position of the keyboard should be low enough to avoid wrist tension. Detachable keyboards allow users to reposition them. Keys should be clearly labeled and should follow one of the standard arrangements such as QWERTY. The cursor keys, numerical keys, scrolling keys, and editing keys should be separate from the alphanumeric keys. A well-designed keyboard will have a recognizable touch, so a user can feel whether a key was struck.

The design of the rest of the input and output peripherals should also conform to the best ergonomic standards available. The digitizing tablet should not be so sensitive that it registers unintended signals from mechanical vibrations. A designer should be able to adjust the tracking speed of the light pen or mouse.

The layout of the room should be considered when installing a computer work station. Light should illuminate the keyboard and work space but never fall directly on the monitor. Noisy components and those requiring air conditioning should be in a separate room from the work stations. Printers, CPUs, and disk drives usually perform better if isolated from dust, extremes in temperature and humidity, and magnetic fields.

Man-Machine Interface

Man-machine interface refers to the channels (software and hardware) and their operational characteristics that affect the communication between the system and the user. The implementation of interactive techniques and the clear display of information are two man-machine interface issues especially relevant to the design of a computer-based imaging work station. Interactive techniques are the most direct methods of controlling the computer, based on action and response operations such as picking an item from a menu or hitting a key. A quick response from the computer, even if the action is incorrect, makes the user or designer feel in control and promotes a relaxed work atmosphere.

Interaction techniques are designed to give the user control over the system, so such tasks should be made as easy as possible. Function keys allow the user to keep the number of keystrokes to a minimum. Dialogue should be structured so the user can choose options in any order. The system should also indicate where a user is in a sequence of events, possibly by displaying messages in selected parts of the screen, using split-screen techniques or multiwindow displays (see fig. 4-23). A user-friendly system allows the designer to recover gracefully from mistakes and to correct errors.

Effective information displays require consistency and legibility. *Design standards* include the careful organization of information, orderly color coding, alphanumeric and symbolic information, and positioning to ensure visual consistency and implies predetermined general guidelines or design standards. Visual information that conforms to design standards incorporates well-established graphic design principles and tests for comprehension. For example, color-coding systems operate best when the number of colors used is kept to a minimum; most people can distinguish between four to eight colors without con-

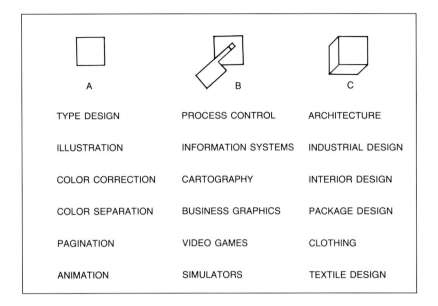

A	B	C
TYPE DESIGN	PROCESS CONTROL	ARCHITECTURE
ILLUSTRATION	INFORMATION SYSTEMS	INDUSTRIAL DESIGN
COLOR CORRECTION	CARTOGRAPHY	INTERIOR DESIGN
COLOR SEPARATION	BUSINESS GRAPHICS	PACKAGE DESIGN
PAGINATION	VIDEO GAMES	CLOTHING
ANIMATION	SIMULATORS	TEXTILE DESIGN

4-31. Two-dimensional systems for applications that require extensive manipulation of images and text in a flat, two-dimensional space. Such applications include type design, illustration, color correction, pagination, and animation (A). Interactive two-dimensional systems for applications that require the visual display of data bases and processes. Such applications include process control, information systems, cartography, business graphics, and video games (B). Three-dimensional systems for applications that are based on the representation and manipulation of three-dimensional structures. Such applications include industrial design, architecture, interior design, packaging design, and clothing and textile design. Most of these systems have tools for building and rendering three-dimensional solid objects in a schematic or realistic manner (C).

fusion. In cases where the response to color messages is critical (a process control application, for instance), users should be given color blindness tests.

Alphanumeric coding should use very common words or acronyms. Textual messages should be short, so users can remember them without difficulty, but may refer to detailed and up-to-date manuals that contain the appropriate explanations in nontechnical language. Such manuals can be printed documents or on-line documents that can be called by pressing the HELP key. In the case of symbolic or iconic coding, the symbols must be carefully and clearly designed. Tests should be conducted to ensure that symbols are self-explanatory (understandable without the aid of a code list reference). The legibility of type varies widely on computer displays and must be tailored to the resolution of the display.

System Selection

The enormous variety of tasks in the fields of design, animation, and imaging cannot be performed by a single computer system. Therefore, when selecting a computer system, the first step is to define its central application. Computer systems can be divided into several groups according to the general tasks they perform—systems usually perform a specific group of tasks

best, though they often include secondary features (fig. 4-31). It is important, therefore, to base the selection decision on the single most important application.

The second step is to consider what components it needs (both hardware and software), its size, power, and functions (fig. 4-32). Resolution, the number of colors, the syntax of dialogues, and versatility are features that must be considered, as are speed, reliability, response time, and price. These may be compared in cross-reference tables (fig. 4-33).

Computer systems can either be microcomputers (the smallest systems), minicomputers (the medium-sized systems), or mainframe or supercomputers (the largest systems). The number of designers using the system determines which of these is appropriate. A microcomputer-based system should support a single user, whereas a minicomputer system, depending on its capacity, may be shared by several users. A mainframe or a supercomputer is only cost-effective for applications that require teams of designers working on a project, or on a group of related projects.

Another consideration is whether the system should be a *turnkey* system, a finished product that is produced, integrated, delivered, installed, tested, and maintained by the vendor, or a system that can be developed and enhanced in-house. The software package in the turnkey system can only be implemented on specific equipment and leaves very little room for changes. Because it is mass-produced and marketed, it should be relatively bug-free, and may incorporate many features. On the other hand, a system assembled in-house can be tailored to specific needs. Successful in-house development requires a great deal of responsibility and expertise from the buyer as well as a programming staff. These systems usually require constant technical support that can only be provided by full-time systems and applications programmers.

Product evaluation should be made by the people who will use the system as well as by those who will be affected by its operation. Such a group includes de-

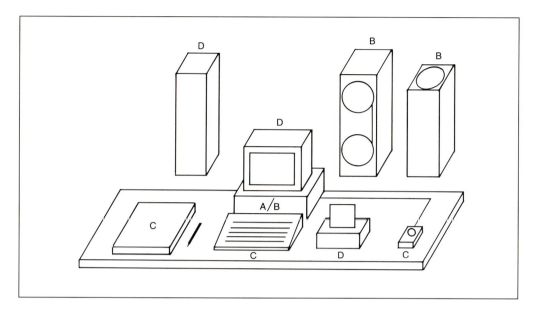

signers, data processors, engineers, managers, and administrators. If a limited number of experts are available within the company, an outside consultant could help research the optimum choice.

Installations that already have and use a system similar to the one being considered should be visited; experienced users can provide nonbiased, detailed insights about the systems that they have been using every day in their professional lives. Basing such a decision on the information printed in glossy brochures is no substitution for first-hand observations.

In order to avoid major disruptions in the production process, it is necessary to slowly move applications to a new computer system, maintaining traditional production procedures until the new system, and methods for solving design problems, are firmly in place. Diagrams of restructured design and production flow can help those involved to adjust to the new procedures.

Systems Operation and Staffs

Once the computer system is installed, special attention must be given to training personnel. Staffs in a typical system are made up of **systems programmers,** who design, repair, and maintain the operating system, languages, and application programs. Since software is complex, modifications are best made by the people

4-32. Components of a computer graphics system include the CPU or main computer (A). Memory sizes can range from a couple of kilobytes to thousands of megabytes, and memory devices include RAM, hard and floppy magnetic disks, and tapes (B). Input devices include digitizing tablets, keyboards, mice, and light pens (C), and output devices include terminals, plotters, printers, and film recorders (D). Resolution and color quality differ from one output system to the other; these may be point or pixel, refresh or static. Software is made up of systems and applications programs and is often the decisive factor in the success or failure of a computer-aided design system. Analyzing functions offered by similar programs is often a good method of choosing which program performs the operations best for a specific application.

4-33. Cross-reference table of features versus vendors.

	On-line Help	Number of Colors	Price
Vendor 1	YES	8	2,000
Vendor 2	NO	64	6,000
Vendor 3	YES	16	5,000

who define and write the systems. (In a turnkey application, the systems programmers may all work for the vendor.)

Staffs also include a **steward,** who is responsible for configuring a system. The steward does not design or use the system, but tailors its use at a particular site— enrolls users, defines their privileges, and configures the constraints or boundaries to be imposed. A system for newspaper layout, for example, should be able to accommodate many newspapers with different page sizes, numbers of columns, and column widths; a steward sets parameters and configures the system to allow some degree of flexibility. He or she therefore must know more about the overall system than a user and must be able to communicate with the systems programmers.

Users employ the capabilities of the system to typeset, create graphics, and paste-up electronically. Like the systems programmer, the user is a programmer in that he or she interacts with the system, issues commands, enters data, and checks the results. A user operates the system that a programmer constructs.

The *operator,* found in large multiuser systems, supervises the computer system and runs it or operates it on a minute-to-minute basis.

Finally, computer data is volatile, easily damaged, and can be financially devastating if lost. Backup and archival procedures are essential and require advanced planning. Backups should be done daily or weekly. Though they take time and are almost always unnecessary, they are a required precaution.

II-0. This picture is similar to figure 5-7 and like it began as a digitized black-and-white photograph that was pseudocolored and block pixed. But in this image, the pseudocoloring effect is not constant; it increases across the picture horizontally, adding one degree of freedom. Neither is the coarseness of the blocks constant; it too increases as the picture is scanned from left to right, adding a second degree of freedom (for a total of four). The result is a picture that moves from the past to the future by incorporating a visual metaphor. No additional hardware was required, only the insight, imagination, and skill that enabled the programmer to tailor the system. (Courtesy of Digital Effects Inc.)

SECTION II

VISUAL LANGUAGE

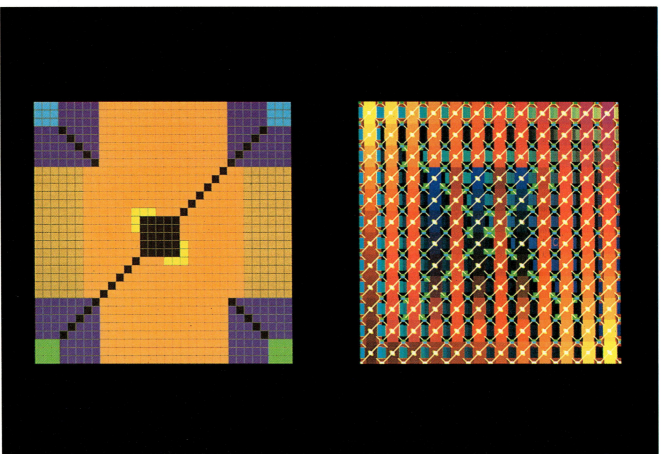

5-0. This image was cre-
ated on the Bucolic System,
which allows users to
practice color theory interactively. The simple geo-
metrical module on the left
is colored by using RGB
and HSV controls. The
module is repeated on a
12 × 12 grid at the right to
produce a pattern. The
colors in the basic module
are interpolated according
to where the module is
positioned on the 12 × 12
grid. (Courtesy of Barbara
Meier and Diana Rath-
borne, Brown University.)

COLOR
AND
BLACK-AND-
WHITE

COLOR SYSTEMS
LUMINANCE CONTROLS
COLOR CONTROLS

Some computer graphics techniques emulate traditional image making. Although certain imaging techniques are exclusive to a particular medium, programs can emulate these; they can also define techniques exclusive to the computer graphics medium. For example, a computer system cannot only make the negative of an image—an emulation of a traditional method—but it can pixelate the image as well, something a traditional system cannot do (fig. II-0).

Computers, as procedural machines, require routine methods for creating and manipulating pictures. This results in a precise *visual language*—a formal notational system used creatively by a graphic artist to communicate ideas and emotions. Indeed, most graphic artists are already

quite familiar with visual languages, whether it is a command, "enlarge picture 133 percent," or an interactive tactile process like painting. But whether the process is command driven or interactive, it is still quantified into a finite number of steps and executed in a predictable manner.

Color is an effective channel for communication and an important variable in computer graphics. Color and black-and-white processing are very similar, as both are represented numerically either in integer or real space.

COLOR SYSTEMS

Tristimulus Color Gamuts

The predominant method of implementing color on a computer employs a *tristimulus representation,* or a three-variable model in which color is described not by one, but by three channels of information represented by three numbers. The numbers may be real, ranging, for example, from zero to one, or they may be integers, ranging, for example, from 0 to 255 (fig. 5-1). Colors may be associated with a polygon or an object, for example, a cube, or with a pixel. When a pixel represents color in a tristimulus gamut, three sets of bitplanes are used—one for each channel of color (fig. 5-2).

The most common variables used to represent color are the *red-green-blue (RGB)* gamut, where the variables represent the luminance or brightness of the three additive primaries. RGB colors together become white (fig. 5-3). Although RGB is the most popular representation in computer graphics, artists and designers use other gamuts as well. Pigment-oriented systems work with the subtractive primaries, *cyan, yellow, and magenta (CYM).* The CYM gamut absorbs light, and the mixture of pigments in equal proportions produces black (fig. 5-4). CYM colors are useful in printing and painting, and like RGB, the CYM gamut can be represented as a cube.

The *hue-luminance-saturation (HLS)*

5-1. Color systems can be expressed in both integer and real notation and converted from one notation to the other. Integer notation, on the left, uses whole numbers (0 to 255 in this case). Real notation uses fractional numbers (zero to one). In this case, the formula INTEGER = 255 × REAL converts one to the other.

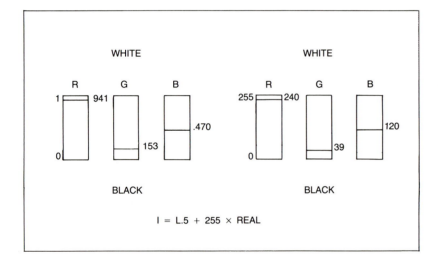

$$I = L.5 + 255 \times REAL$$

🐾 **RELATED READING**

Albers, J. *Interaction of Color.* New Haven, CT: Yale University Press, 1975.

Birren, F., ed. *The Elements of Color.* New York: Van Nostrand Reinhold, 1970.

Gerritsen, Frans. *Theory and Practice of Color.* New York: Van Nostrand Reinhold, 1975.

Hurvich, L. M. *Color Vision.* Sunderland, MA: Sinauer Assoc., 1981.

Judd, D. B., and G. Wyszecki. *Color in Business, Science and Industry.* 3d ed. New York: John Wiley & Sons, 1975.

Marx, Ellen. *Optical Color and Simultaneity.* New York: Van Nostrand Reinhold, 1983.

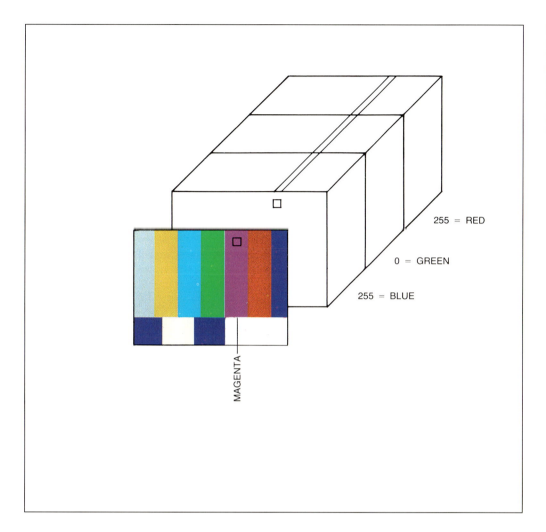

5-2. At least three bitplanes are needed to represent the color value of a single pixel in a tristimulus gamut. Each colored polygon, in this case each one of the color bars, is composed of hundreds of pixels with the same value.

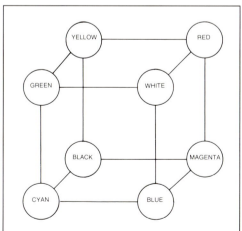

5-3. The RGB color model can be organized in a Cartesian coordinate system. The colors are distributed in a cube where each primary color is located in the corner opposite its complementary color. The values of gray are located in a diagonal between black and white.

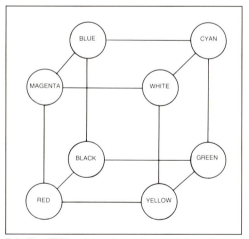

5-4. The CYM subtractive color model can be expressed in a three-dimensional cube, where primary colors are located in the corner opposite their complementary colors. The values of gray are located in a diagonal between black and white.

5-5. The hue-lightness-sat-
uration (HLS) color system
is expressed inside a six
sectioned cylinder where
luminance extends from
black to white up the vertical axis. Hue is the color
and is represented as the
angle around the vertical
axis. Saturation is the radius, or distance from the
vertical axis, and repre-
sents how much of the
color's complement makes
up the color.

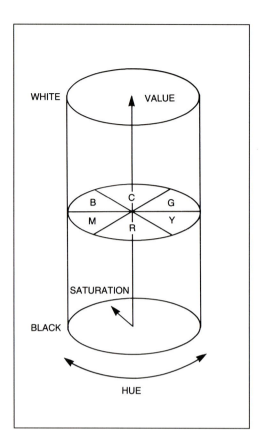

the cyan, yellow, and magenta components.

The fourth channel is also used, particularly for RGB images, to store a **matte,**
which is a bitmap that records the opacity/
transparency of an image at each pixel.
The matte pixel determines how opaque
or transparent each pixel is on a zero to
one scale, for instance; it also facilitates
the compositing of images in situations
where edges are diffuse and soft, objects
are in motion (the blurring makes them
transparent), or where transparent objects,
like glasses, are part of the scene. (Matting
is discussed in more detail in chapter 6.)

Color can also provide **multispectra
imaging,** a visual interpretation of essentially nonvisual information. Electronic
sensors can measure information at not
only many frequencies of visible light, but
at infrared, ultraviolet, ultrasound, X-ray,
and radio frequencies. By displaying these
extra channels with color, we can better
understand these instrumentational extensions of ourselves (fig. 5-7). (Multispectral
imaging is discussed in more detail in
chapter 9.)

gamut is expressed as a double cone space
that contains hue, luminance, and saturation values (fig. 5-5). The HLS model is
useful to artists and designers, because it
permits the total luminance to be held
constant while varying the other two parameters—something that cannot be done
in RGB or CYM systems.

Four-variable Color Models

Color representation in computer
graphics is not limited to three-variable
representations, but can include four or
more variables. Four-variable systems require four numbers, or four channels of
bitmap memory.

The most common four-color model is
process color, which uses magenta, yellow, cyan, and black (MYCB) inks, used
in the printing industry. Black is used in
addition to the three subtractive primaries
to improve contrast and decrease the
amount of the more expensive colored
inks that is needed (fig. 5-6). The black
represents the darker shades common to

Color Gamut Conversions

Color gamuts such as RGB, CYM, and
HLS can be converted into each other using
programs, allowing an artist to work with
alternate color gamuts (fig. 5-8).

Media that involve emitted additive light,
like television, are best commanded using
additive colors, whereas systems that are
subtractive, like print, are best commanded
using subtractive colors. HLS models are
useful when gray values are to remain
constant regardless of color.

Color Resolution Requirements

The exact number of bits needed to
represent color luminance depends on the
application. Low- and medium-resolution
full-color schemes use from eight to ten
bits per pixel total. One eight-bit approximation uses three bits for red, three bits
for green, and two bits for blue. Ten-bit
approximations, using three bits for red,
four bits for green, and three bits for blue,
provide recognizable resolutions. Green is
given more color resolution because it is

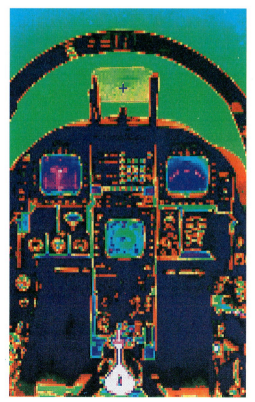

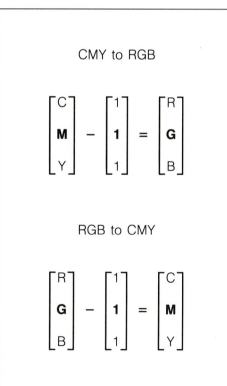

$$\begin{bmatrix} C \\ \mathbf{M} \\ Y \end{bmatrix} - \begin{bmatrix} 1 \\ \mathbf{1} \\ 1 \end{bmatrix} = \begin{bmatrix} R \\ \mathbf{G} \\ B \end{bmatrix}$$

CMY to RGB

RGB to CMY

$$\begin{bmatrix} R \\ \mathbf{G} \\ B \end{bmatrix} - \begin{bmatrix} 1 \\ \mathbf{1} \\ 1 \end{bmatrix} = \begin{bmatrix} C \\ \mathbf{M} \\ Y \end{bmatrix}$$

5-6. This image shows all the components of the MCYB system and the basic combinations. (Reprinted, by permission, from Gerritsen *Theory and Practice of Color*, 81.)

5-7. This photographic image has been pseudocolored to illustrate the concept of computer vision. Pseudocoloring can be used to make important information more visible. (Courtesy of Digital Effects Inc. for Harris Computer.)

5-8. Color gamut conversion formulas. 111 represents white in the RGB color system and black in CMY. In the example, green subtracts magenta from reflected white light.

Joblove, G. H., and D. Greenberg. "Color Spaces for Computer Graphics." *Computer Graphics* (August 1978): 20–25.

Meyer, G. W., and D. P. Greenberg. "Perceptual Color Spaces for Computer Graphics." *Computer Graphics* (July 1980): 254–61.

Montalvo, F. S. "Human Vision and Computer Graphics." *Computer Graphics* (August 1979): 121–25.

Smith, Alvy Ray. "Color Gamut Transform Pairs." *Computer Graphics* (August 1978): 12–19.

Truckenbord, J. "Effective Use of Color in Computer Graphics." *Computer Graphics* (August 1981): 83–90.

LUMINANCE CONTROLS

Histogramming

A **histogram** of an image is an inventory of the image, the number of pixels at each intensity value presented in graphic form (fig. 5-9). Color images require three (or four) histograms.

In an image that contains luminance values, one can readily determine from the histogram whether the pixel values in the image are evenly distributed in terms of light and dark, or if they are clustered, for example mostly in the middle grays in a picture lacking contrast. The information revealed in the histogram may be used to improve the visibility of an image by redistributing the pixel values and improving contrast.

Look-up Tables and Palettes

A **look-up table,** or **palette,** is a matrix of one or more columns with as many rows as there are intensity levels in an image. You will recall this number is determined by two raised to the power of the number of bitplanes—if there are three bitplanes, then there are 2^3 or eight rows in the look-up table. The number of columns corresponds to the number of color channels and would be one for black-and-white, or three for RGB color.

A look-up table is used by taking the numerical value stored in a pixel and using that value as a pointer, or index, into the look-up table memory. The value stored in the contents of that particular look-up table location is then used as the actual luminance value (fig. 5-10).

Look-up tables are often implemented as part of the frame buffer hardware, where they translate the value in each pixel at the time of image display. The hardware look-up table is loaded once at the beginning by copying a specific look-up table from a disk into the look-up table memory. There are many different palettes, and they are used by loading them into the frame buffer look-up table memory. But only one palette can be used at a time.

Look-up tables are very much a part of

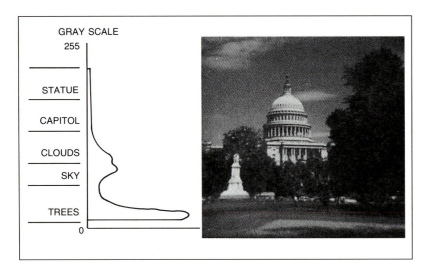

GRAY SCALE
255
STATUE
CAPITOL
CLOUDS
SKY
TREES
0

5-9. An image and its histogram. The vertical scale of the histogram represents the luminance of the image, with black at the bottom and white at the top. The horizontal scale indicates the number of pixels at each intensity level. The histogram reveals that most of the pixels are low values and make up the trees. (Courtesy of Spatial Data Systems, Inc.; a DBA Systems Company.)

the color that provides the most luminance information to the eye; blue is assumed to be less easily perceived, especially in the very subtle flesh tones.

Low-resolution HLS gamuts concentrate more bits into luminance than hue or saturation, a matter somewhat analogous to NTSC color television. One scenario might reserve six bits for luminance and two bits each for hue and saturation.

The most common color resolution is one byte-per-pixel-per-primary. This allows for 256 intensity levels in each primary, or a total color spectrum in excess of sixteen-million colors (2^{24}). The maximum is twelve bits per primary, a dynamic range in excess of most modern output media, including photography, video, and offset printing, but less than the dynamic range of the eye or daylight.

graphic arts computer systems; in an *identity look-up table* each row is loaded with its own address. The identity table contains the value of the pixel, so that when a pointer is indexed into this table, the result extracted is the same as the original number, and the picture looks as if no look-up table were involved whatsoever (fig. 5-11).

A *negative look-up table* reverses the luminance of the image by inverting the contents of the table. This is the equivalent of subtracting each pixel value from the brightest value (fig. 5-12). Pixels with low-intensity values get translated to high-intensity values and vice versa, forming a negative of the picture.

Look-up tables are useful for reducing gray levels in a picture. This is accomplished by using a look-up table that contains multiple rows with the same value (fig. 5-13). The extreme case reduces the number of gray levels to two and makes a *high-contrast* black-and-white matte ele-

ment. The luminance value that determines the break between black and white is called the *threshold* (fig. 5-14).

Remember that modifying the contents of the look-up table modifies the display but not the contents of the image. Thus, look-up tables provide a method to non-destructively preview images and are useful to correct colors, among other things. If one wants to actually change the contents of image memory, the calculation performed by the look-up table must be applied to the image itself (fig. 5-15). For example, to fix the negative of an image in frame buffer memory, one can make each pixel in the bitmap equal to the value output by the look-up table and then replace the table with an identity table. The visual results of manipulating either the look-up table or pixels are identical. The pixel method requires more computing and may not be reversible, whereas the look-up table method only requires modification of its contents.

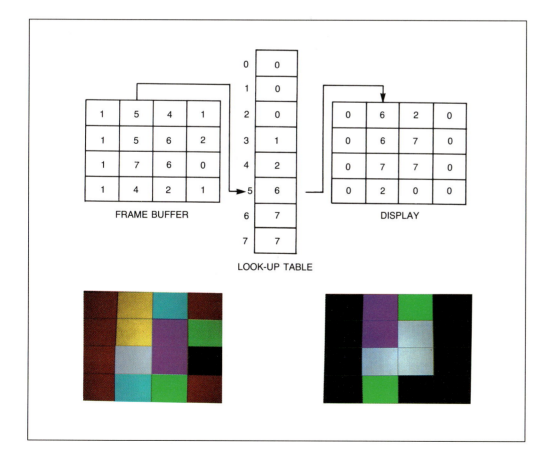

FRAME BUFFER

LOOK-UP TABLE

DISPLAY

5-10. The numerical values of the pixels that configure the image (five in this example) point the display processor to a color look-up table address. The address contains a luminance value (six) that is used to specify the brightness of the corresponding pixel in the final image.

5-11. The value in an identity look-up table is equal to its address, so the resulting picture intensity is identical to the input pixel array.

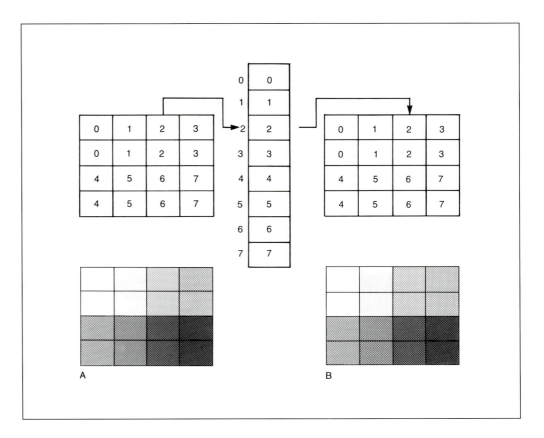

5-12. A negative look-up table reverses the luminance of the image by inverting the contents of the table. A three-bit look-up table is depicted in the illustration. At the zero address, the value seven is stored, and so on. Pixels with low values (like two) get translated to a high-intensity value (like five), and high-intensity values (like six) get translated to low-intensity values (like one).

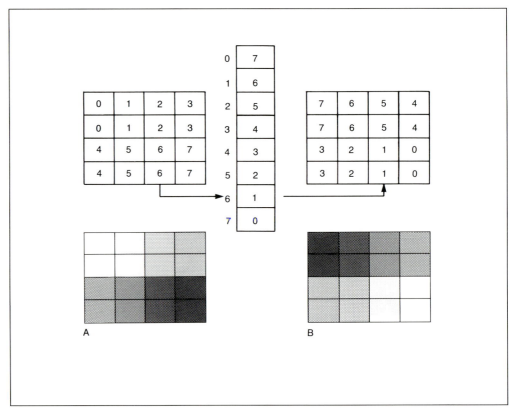

A   B   C

	32 Gray Levels (A)	16 Gray Levels (B)	8 Gray Levels (C)
0	0	0	0
1	1	0	0
2	2	2	0
3	3	2	0
4	4	4	4
5	5	4	4
6	6	6	4
7	7	6	4
8	8	8	8
9	9	8	8
10	10	10	8
11	11	10	8
12	12	12	12
13	13	12	12
14	14	14	12
15	15	14	12
16	16	16	16
17	17	16	16
18	18	18	16
19	19	18	16
20	20	20	20
21	21	20	20
22	22	22	20
23	23	22	20
24	24	24	24
25	25	24	24
26	26	26	24
27	27	26	24
28	28	28	28
29	29	28	28
30	30	30	28
31	31	30	28

5-13. Reducing gray levels. The illustration shows an image containing thirty-two gray levels and three look-up tables, each with thirty-two rows of five bits each. The first look-up table is an identity table and reproduces all the gray levels in the picture. The second look-up table uses only half the luminance values and replicates them in adjacent rows. The third look-up table is constructed in a similar manner, except it uses only eight distinct gray levels and copies each one four times. In other words, in the last look-up table, gray values of 20, 21, 22, and 23 will be reproduced as a luminance value of 20. The last look-up table maintains a dynamic range between black and white; only the number of gray levels has been reduced. (Courtesy of Spatial Data Systems, Inc.; a DBA Systems Company.)

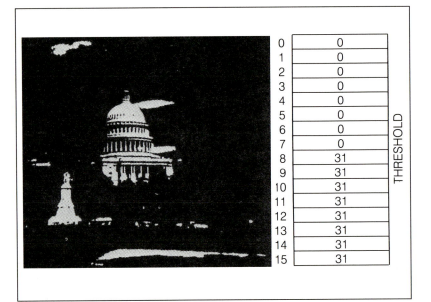

	0	0
	1	0
	2	0
	3	0
	4	0
	5	0
	6	0
	7	0
THRESHOLD	8	31
	9	31
	10	31
	11	31
	12	31
	13	31
	14	31
	15	31

5-14. In a high-contrast image, the look-up table contains only luminance values for black and white. The level or row address that determines where on the gray scale the distinction is made between black and white is called the threshold. (Courtesy of Spatial Data Systems, Inc.; a DBA Systems Company.)

Contrast and Color Correction

Look-up tables are especially useful for increasing and decreasing contrast as well as for correcting the color of images. *Contrast,* the ratio of black to white pixels in an image, is adjusted by redistributing black and white values to increase visibility. *Color correction* is a similar process that alters each color to create a balance. Histograms often provide a basis for enhancing contrast and colors. The histogram provides a diagram of the intensity levels of pixels; in an image where most of the pixels have a narrow range of intensity values, the visibility of the picture can be improved by assigning a wider dynamic range of intensity to those pixels (fig. 5-16).

Color correction on a computer system is a much more elastic process than in traditional analog electronic or photographic media, because the color look-up tables provide a wide potential for variation. In a color correction system there is one look-up table for each primary, and each is individually controlled (fig. 5-17).

COLOR CONTROLS

The techniques in this section involve methods of manipulating color. These have practical and artistic applications not only on low-resolution systems, but on full-color, high-resolution systems as well.

Color Codes and Color Mixing

In addition to representing luminance values, pixels can contain **color codes,** or numbers representing colors. Color names and codes have been widely used in the graphic arts industries, such as Pantone numbers in printing, color names in painting, and Wratten numbers for filters. The strategy in all of these cases is to identify a color by a name or number, then use a look-up table to specify the mix of ingredients.

In a computer system a color code is a number stored in a pixel that in turn points to a look-up table containing the actual RGB color. This look-up table has three columns, containing red, green, and blue color values (fig. 5-18), and it has as many rows as there are color codes.

Look-up tables expand the capability of frame buffers with only a few bitplanes of memory, because extra columns can be added to the table to provide a limited number of full colors (fig. 5-19). Because the pixel color code points to a row in the look-up table, and thus to an RGB triplet, a single color may be interactively mixed. When colors in the look-up table are manipulated, all occurrences of that color on the screen are affected, because all the values pointing to that color are being translated in the look-up table.

Tint Color

Tint color, created with a special look-up table, simulates the technique of coloring black-and-white photographs by painting over them with a color wash.

Tint coloring begins by quantifying a digitized black-and-white image with a limited number of luminance values. A special look-up table is then constructed that contains this same number of limited values, but in ranges of color as well as black-and-white (fig. 5-20). The process of tinting the picture replaces the pixel value in the image with a corresponding pointer to the look-up table value for a different color and the same intensity. Thus,

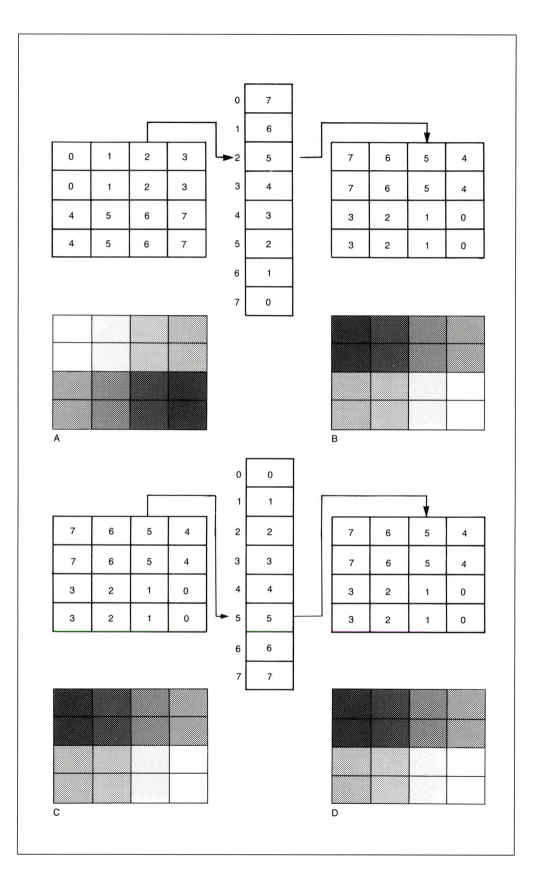

5-15. Modifying bitmap versus modifying palette. In the top illustration, a look-up table translates the original image into its negative. In the bottom, the original image has been modified to incorporate the result of the look-up table manipulation. This image must now be read into an identity look-up table if it is to be output as a negative.

5-16. In the image on the left, most details are lost in shadows; very few of the pixels are dark grays. By distributing the pixels more evenly along the histogram—adjusting contrast—we can expand the dynamic range of the look-up table. The middle-gray values are spread out in the range of the highlights and blacks, increasing the visibility of the image (right).

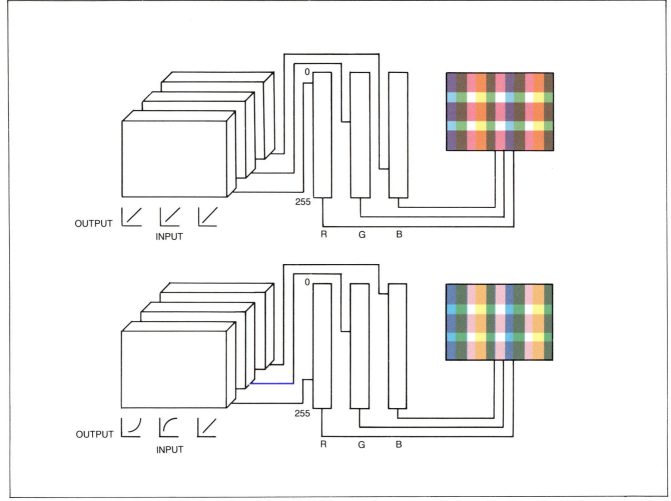

OUTPUT   INPUT   R   G   B

5-17. Shown here is the original image to be corrected. Each set of bitplanes points to one column in the look-up table. The output of the look-up table controls the RGB values on the monitor. A line graph depicts the relation between input and output. Because each look-up table is an identity table, the lines are straight. By altering the contents of the look-up tables, the linear color relationships can be changed so the intensity values of the original image are converted to new values that alter the color balance.

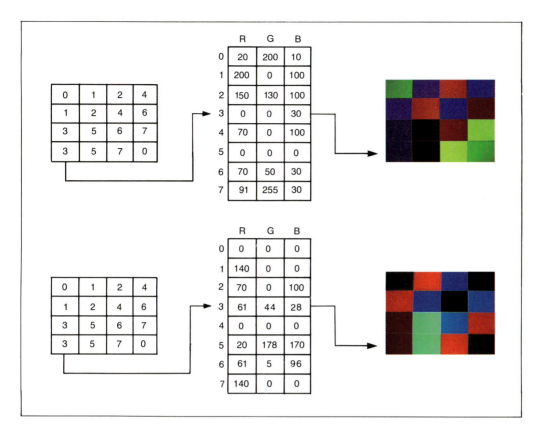

5-18. An image created with color codes and two color look-up tables. The image is colored by indexing each color code into a row in the look-up table and then reading and displaying the corresponding red, green, and blue values. The two look-up tables, or palettes, each define a unique set of color combinations. Displaying an image with alternate palettes is the software equivalent of printing a silkscreen with different color combinations.

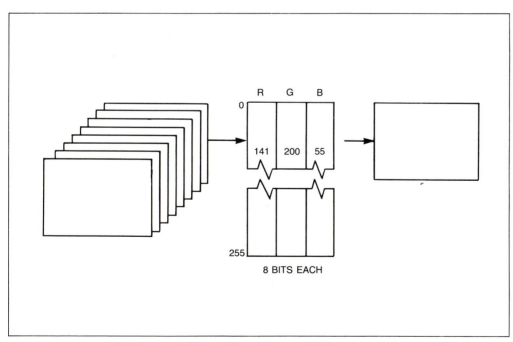

5-19. In a system with eight bitplanes of memory, there are 256 possible color codes, and any of the 256 different rows in a look-up table can be indexed. Since each of those rows can contain an eight-bit value for red, green, and blue, the system at large can display 16 million different colors, though it can display only 256 of them at once.

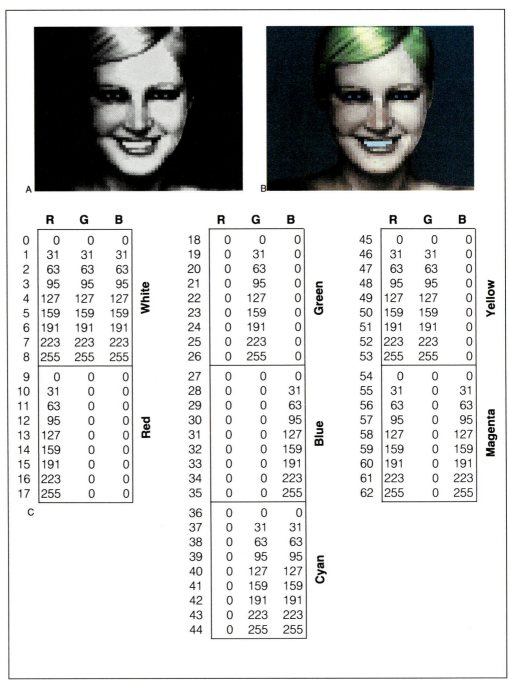

#	R	G	B		#	R	G	B		#	R	G	B	
0	0	0	0	**White**	18	0	0	0	**Green**	45	0	0	0	**Yellow**
1	31	31	31		19	0	31	0		46	31	31	0	
2	63	63	63		20	0	63	0		47	63	63	0	
3	95	95	95		21	0	95	0		48	95	95	0	
4	127	127	127		22	0	127	0		49	127	127	0	
5	159	159	159		23	0	159	0		50	159	159	0	
6	191	191	191		24	0	191	0		51	191	191	0	
7	223	223	223		25	0	223	0		52	223	223	0	
8	255	255	255		26	0	255	0		53	255	255	0	
9	0	0	0	**Red**	27	0	0	0	**Blue**	54	0	0	0	**Magenta**
10	31	0	0		28	0	0	31		55	31	0	31	
11	63	0	0		29	0	0	63		56	63	0	63	
12	95	0	0		30	0	0	95		57	95	0	95	
13	127	0	0		31	0	0	127		58	127	0	127	
14	159	0	0		32	0	0	159		59	159	0	159	
15	191	0	0		33	0	0	191		60	191	0	191	
16	223	0	0		34	0	0	223		61	223	0	223	
17	255	0	0		35	0	0	255		62	255	0	255	
C					36	0	0	0	**Cyan**					
					37	0	31	31						
					38	0	63	63						
					39	0	95	95						
					40	0	127	127						
					41	0	159	159						
					42	0	191	191						
					43	0	223	223						
					44	0	255	255						

5-20. The illustration shows an original black-and-white image (A) containing nine gray levels, ranging from black to white. The nine levels are stored in an eight-bit (256-level) frame buffer and point to rows zero through eight in a special look-up table (C). The "color values" in these rows depict a range of intensities from black to white. The look-up table continues with additional colors, each with nine intensity levels. For example, look-up table positions nine through seventeen contain a full range of reds from dark red to a fully saturated red. Other sections contain a range of blues, greens, cyans, yellows, and magentas. The colors do not have to be primaries or secondaries, each must simply have an equal range of intensity levels. Tinting the picture (B) involves substituting pointers in the image. Thus, to tint a part of the image that is 50 percent gray to the corresponding 50 percent red, the program replaces all pixels with a value of four (the look-up table pointer for medium gray) with a value of thirteen, the pointer to medium red. (Courtesy of Digital Effects Inc.)

to tint a part of the image that is 50 percent gray to the corresponding 50 percent red, the program replaces all pixel values pointing to medium gray with pixel values pointing to medium red.

Tint color can be used in many different configurations. A 256-row by 3-column look-up table can have sixteen levels of gray and sixteen different colors, or eight levels of gray and thirty-two different colors, or sixty-four levels of gray and four different colors, and so forth.

Pseudocolor

Pseudocolor is similar to posterization and is another effect that can be simulated with look-up tables. Each pixel intensity value is pointed to a red, green, and blue color triplet. Pseudocolor is really a variation on color codes, except that the bitmap image actually has luminance information, not just color numbers (fig. 5-21). The visual effect of pseudocolor is contour areas of color in what was originally a black-and-white image, either for a graphic effect or to make them more comprehensible. The use of pseudocolor is not limited to pixel matrices of luminance, however, and is also used to view matrices of zels and voxels, coloring them according to their depth or density. Pseudocolor is usually interactively controlled and is an incisive tool.

Dithered Color

Dithering is a technique used to maintain the total color information of an image while representing it with fewer colors; it is especially useful when displaying full-color pictures on displays with only eight or ten bits per pixel—for example, only three bits each for red, green, and blue, as opposed to eight bits each in an image with high color resolution.

The difference between a low- and high-resolution color space is not the dynamic range of the colors from brightest to darkest, but the number of intermediate values. Dithering compensates for the fewer number of colors first by approximating the high-resolution pixel with a low-resolution one, and by adding any surplus or deficit

5-21. Pseudocolor assigns colors to a continuous-tone image. (Courtesy of Digital Effects Inc. and Andrea D'Amico.)

5-22. Dithered color. (Courtesy of Digital Effects Inc.)

color into the adjacent pixel when it is computed. Thus, while the number of different colors in the image has been substantially reduced, the total representation of color in the picture is equal to the total color overall at high resolution (fig. 5-22).

6-0. A scroll/scale effect created with video hardware. (Courtesy of Ken Zeran Productions, Inc.)

6

TWO-DIMENSIONAL IMAGING PROCESSES

MONADIC IMAGE PROCESSES
POINT TO PIXEL TECHNIQUES
DYADIC IMAGE PROCESSES
LOCAL AND GLOBAL OPERATORS
IMAGE ENHANCEMENT
COMPUTER VISION AND IMAGE ANALYSIS

Image-processing techniques are procedures that modify images, both to enhance their visibility and to creatively alter them. Images can be photographic in origin and represent a pixel array of intensity values. They can also be synthetically generated and approximate a photographic perspective.

Bitmaps can represent natural measurements with no intensity variations; zels or a cross section of CAT scan voxels are two examples (fig. 6-1). Images may even be graphs of mathematical equations plotted in a two-dimensional space. The image is really the solution space, the contour of the equation (fig. 6-2).

Image-processing systems manipulate images rather than create them. An image to be processed is first digitized by sampling its levels of brightness, then storing them as pixels in a bitmap. (Television cameras, flying spot scanners, and laser drum scanners all can digitize images, as is discussed in chapter 3.) Image processing is often viewed interactively on soft copy displays.

MONADIC IMAGE PROCESSES

Monadic image processes, functions with one input and one output image, include the traditional photographic procedures of sizing, cropping, flipping, repositioning, and mapping. The most primitive image operation, the basic method for altering a picture, is the pixel *read* and *write*. This involves reading a pixel from the frame buffer memory, modifying its contents in the CPU, and writing the new value either back into the same frame buffer memory, or into a second one (fig. 6-3).

Some monadic image processes may be implemented as part of the frame buffer hardware. These modify the display but do not permanently alter the frame buffer memory. Look-up tables are one such feature and are discussed at length in chapter 5.

Scroll, Scale, Rotation

Scroll is the translation of the image left or right, up or down. It is computationally performed by reading a pixel and then displaying it at a different XY screen position. This is usually done with special hardware scroll registers, one for the horizontal offset and one for the vertical displacement. The part of the scrolled picture offset is usually wrapped around the image plane (fig. 6-4).

Scrolling is also used to create **pattern repeats,** repetitive areas that form a continuum (fig. 6-5). Standard repeats include half and full drops, and flips.

Scaling enlarges or reduces the number of pixels that define an image in order

6-1. A CAT scan cross section of the brain. The picture is pseudocolored so that different densities become different colors. It thus looks photographic, though it is not. (Courtesy of Digital Effects Inc.)

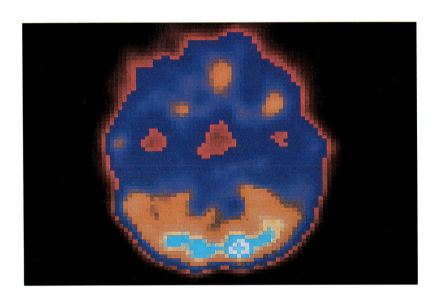

▶ **RELATED READING**

Ahuja, Narendra, and Bruce J. Schachter. *Pattern Models.* New York: John Wiley & Sons, 1983.

Cannon, T. M., and B. R. Hunt. "Image Processing by Computer." *Scientific American* (October 1981).

Gonzalez, Rafael C., and Paul Wintz. *Digital Image Processing.* Reading, MA: Addison-Wesley, 1977.

Green, William B. *Digital Image Processing.* New York: Van Nostrand Reinhold, 1983.

Pratt, William K. *Digital Image Processing.* New York: John Wiley & Sons, 1978.

Rosenfeld, Azriel, and Avinash C. Kak. *Digital Picture Processing.* 2d ed. Orlando, FL: Academic Press, 1982.

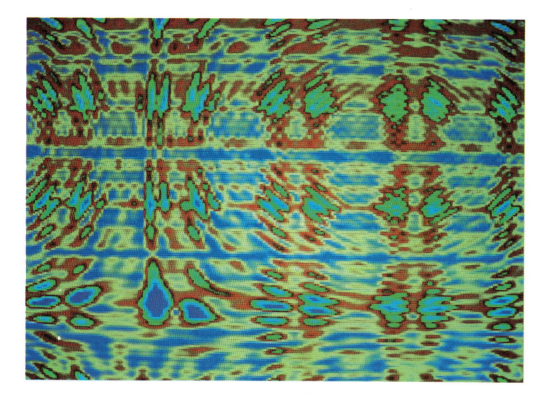

6-2. Images can represent the contour of equations in two-dimensional space. (Courtesy of Don Leich.)

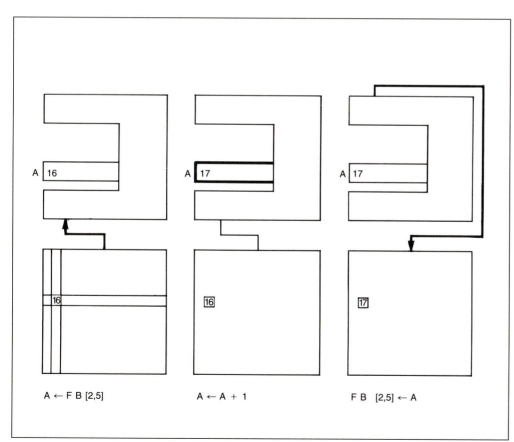

A ← F B [2,5]   A ← A + 1   F B [2,5] ← A

6-3. In this image the numerical value (16) contained in frame buffer location (2, 5) is *read* into main memory. The CPU then performs an operation and *modifies* it, in this case increasing it by one. Finally, the new value (17) is *written* back onto the frame buffer.

6-4. A hardware scroll register is set to 100, 100. The display offsets the output index counter, positions pixel 100, 100 at the origin in the lower left corner of the picture, and wraps the left and bottom portion that was cropped, so these appear at the right and top.

NORMAL

SCROLL = 100, 100

6-5. Many different patterns can be created by manipulating simple modules. Basic manipulations include constant repetition at regular intervals, repetition at offset intervals, and flipping.

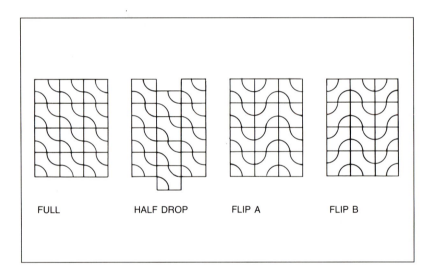

FULL　　　　HALF DROP　　　　FLIP A　　　　FLIP B

to change its size. Scalings can be either discrete, even pixel quantities, or continuous.

Scaling a picture larger by an integer amount involves simple pixel replication, since there is no new information to be added (fig. 6-6). But scaling a picture smaller by integers is not as easy. In a picture that is reduced by one-fourth its pixels, selecting every other pixel would create aliasing, because the final image would only incorporate one-fourth the information of the original picture (fig. 6-7). A proper solution is to average groups of four pixels together and store the average in the remaining pixel (fig. 6-8). This would eliminate aliasing, and although the image is only one-fourth the spatial resolution, it preserves the total luminance information.

Enlarging and reducing by noninteger amounts is also accomplished by averaging. Each pixel is treated as if it were a tiny area, a floating point domain. When the scaling process calculates averages it averages not only whole pixels but parts of pixels as well (fig. 6-9). Again, this is a technique that retains total luminance information, but changes spatial resolution.

Scaling is often accomplished using hardware scale registers that specify the number of times the pixel is to be replicated in the X and Y directions on the screen. Scale registers control how the hardware indexes the picture when it displays it on the monitor; they do not actually affect the bitmap memory. If a bitmap is scaled up by showing each pixel four times using a hardware scale register, it can be scaled back to the original. But if the image is altered, the higher-resolution data is gone and cannot be recovered (fig. 6-10).

Scaling registers are often called *zoom* registers, but strictly speaking, a zoom pertains to the focal length of a lens. Although it appears to enlarge the picture, a zoom actually narrows the field of view; it is not a two-dimensional effect. Scroll and scale registers may be used together for many purposes, including animation (fig. 6-11) and the positioning and cropping of pictures.

Rotation is the pivoting of an image about a central point, usually the origin of the coordinate system (fig. 6-12). It is usually continuous and expressed as a positive or negative angle along with the address of a pixel around which the rotation should occur. Hardware rotation also exists, although it sometimes only rotates a picture in even multiples of 90 degrees.

Flips are 90-degree and 180-degree rotations that reorient the picture and provide mirror views. Flips can transpose the left side to right, the top to bottom, and one corner to the other that is diagonally op-

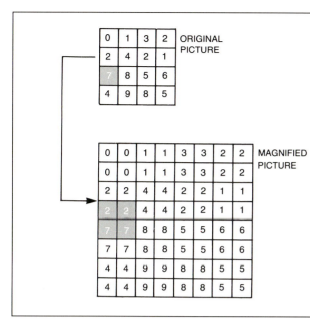

0	1	3	2
2	4	2	1
7	8	5	6
4	9	8	5

ORIGINAL PICTURE

0	0	1	1	3	3	2	2
0	0	1	1	3	3	2	2
2	2	4	4	2	2	1	1
2	2	4	4	2	2	1	1
7	7	8	8	5	5	6	6
7	7	8	8	5	5	6	6
7	7	8	8	5	5	6	6
4	4	9	9	8	8	5	5
4	4	9	9	8	8	5	5

MAGNIFIED PICTURE

6-6. Scaling, 2× integer enlargement—each pixel in the input image is repeated four times. A 3× scaling would repeat each pixel nine times. (Courtesy of Spatial Data Systems, Inc.; a DBA Systems Company.)

1	2	5	6	9	10	13	15
3	4	7	8	11	12	14	16
2	3	7	8	10	11	15	16
5	6	9	10	11	12	13	14
4	5	6	7	11	12	13	15
1	2	8	9	13	14	15	16
3	4	5	6	9	10	14	15
2	3	4	5	7	8	9	10

MAGNIFIED PICTURE

6-7. Integer reduction with point sampling. Scaling down the original picture by half will actually reduce the number of original pixels by three-fourths. In this example, the original image (sixty-four pixels) was reduced by half and only one-fourth of the original number of pixels remained (sixteen pixels).

1	5	9	13
2	7	10	15
4	6	11	13
3	5	9	14

ORIGINAL PICTURE

ORIGINAL PICTURE

AVERAGE = 3   AVERAGE = 4

6-8. Integer reduction with image averaging. The diagram shows a 2 × 2 average. The images illustrate averages at different factors of reduction. (Courtesy of Spatial Data Systems, Inc.; a DBA Systems Company.)

6-9. Scaling with continuous reduction. The input picture is a 4 × 4 matrix, the output picture is a 3 × 3 matrix. Each new resultant pixel contains parts of one or more pixels from the original image. For example, the output pixel (3, 3) is a composite of input pixels 3, 3; 3, 4; 4, 3; 4, 4.

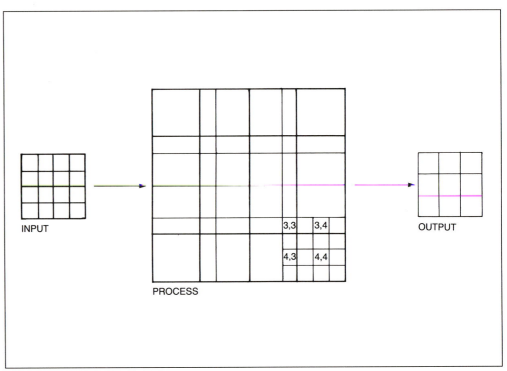

INPUT

PROCESS

OUTPUT

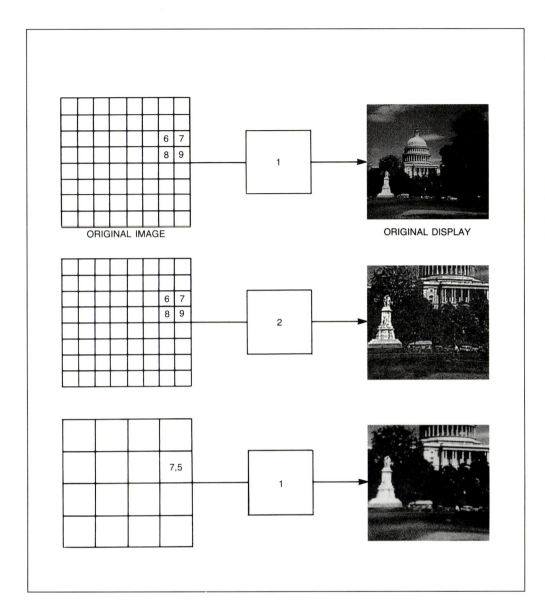

ORIGINAL IMAGE

ORIGINAL DISPLAY

6-10. Hardware and software scaling. The top row illustrates a bitmap and the corresponding picture, with the scaling registers set to identity, or one. The scale registers in the center row are equal to two, and the display of the picture is enlarged 200 percent, although the data remains untouched. On the other hand, if the bitplane itself has been enlarged then the finer resolution of the data would have been lost, and the scale registers are set to identity (bottom row). (Courtesy of Spatial Data Systems, Inc.; a DDA Systems Company.)

posite (fig. 6-13). ***Three-axis rotation*** allows an image to be pivoted anywhere in space (see chapter 7).

Image Warping and Mapping

Image warping and mapping are techniques for stretching images in nonlinear ways, much as if the image were rubber. ***Image warping*** is two-dimensional and is accomplished by either mathematically distorting the image (fig. 6-14) or by identifying key pixels in an image associated with specific features (fig. 6-15). Biologists use warping techniques to study growth and evolutionary patterns in an organism,

and plastic surgeons use the technique to study aging.

Image mapping is a similar technique that wraps two-dimensional pixel arrays around the surfaces of three-dimensional objects in perspective. Image mapping is discussed in detail in chapter 7.

POINT TO PIXEL TECHNIQUES

Line Representation

On bitmap displays lines are represented

6-11. The picture contains sixteen subframes, each 128 pixels square. Each subframe contains one frame of action in a real-time cycle sixteen frames long. The CPU can quickly change the address of the scroll and zoom register, thus cycling all the sub-pictures to a zoomed-up, full-screen animation. The resolution admittedly is rather coarse, but the animation contains all action. (Animated by Eric Ladd. Courtesy of Omnibus Computer Graphics Center.)

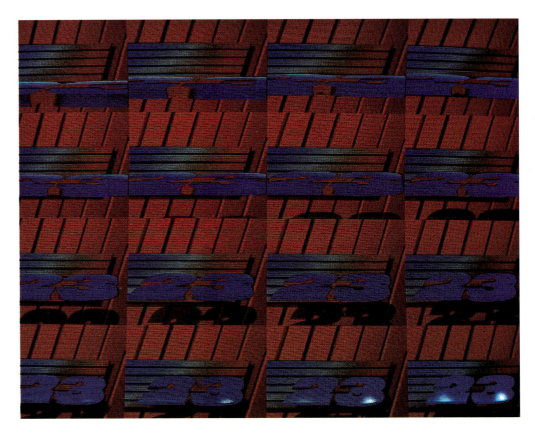

6-12. A rotation of 45 degrees about the center of the picture. (Courtesy of Spatial Data Systems, Inc.; a DBA Systems Company.)

6-13. New images can be obtained by flipping the original image (top left) three ways: from left to right, from top to bottom, and across the diagonal.

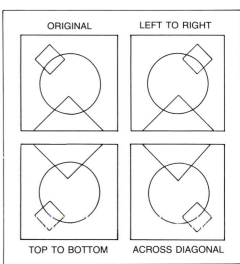

ORIGINAL   LEFT TO RIGHT

TOP TO BOTTOM   ACROSS DIAGONAL

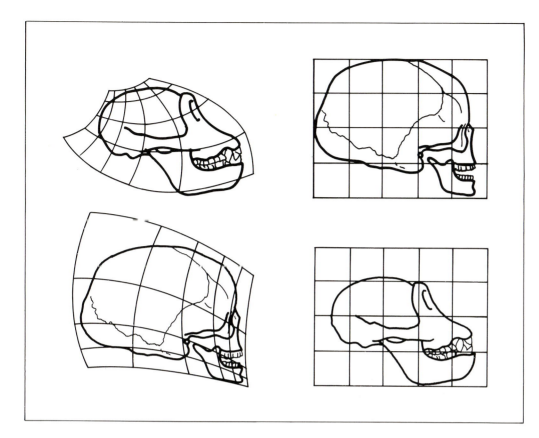

6-14. This classical illustration, from D'Arcy Thompson's *On Growth and Form*, suggests a continuity in the evolution of a chimpanzee's skull to that of a man, which may be simulated by mathematically warping the coordinate system of one to the other.

6-15. Warping aligns two or more similar images. The line drawing depicts three different faces; the grid lines, calculated by digitizing key features on each face (nose, mouth, chin, and face contour, for example), show the warping necessary to transform each face to the final composite below. The photograph is a composite image of twelve faces (six men and six women). (Photo courtesy of Nancy Burson.)

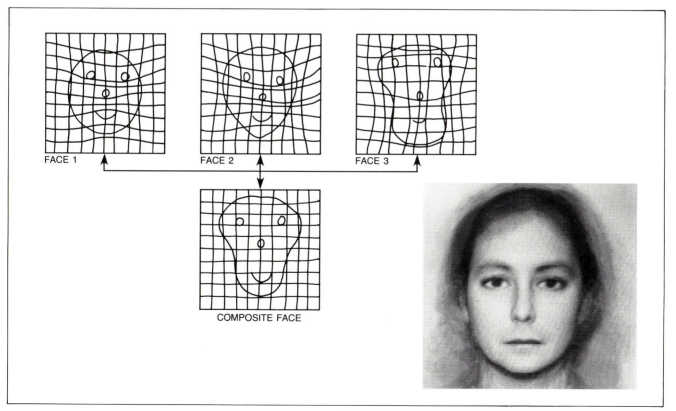

FACE 1

FACE 2

FACE 3

COMPOSITE FACE

RELATED READING

Gottschall, Edward M., ed. *Graphic Communication/Visions 80.* Englewood Cliffs, NJ: Prentice-Hall, 1981.

Kim, Scott. *Inversions.* Petersborough, NH: Byte Books, 1981.

Wong, Wucius. *Principles of Two-Dimensional Design.* New York: Van Nostrand Reinhold, 1972.

Area Fill Methods

Areas are shapes bounded either by vectors or pixels. Scan conversions and fills are two methods used in computer graphics to create areas. ***Scan conversion*** converts a polygon area, bounded by vectors, into a series of horizontal lines usually represented by pixels. Scan conversion techniques work with real, floating point numbers. However, if we scan convert a polygon into pixel memory, the process essentially involves integer numbers, since there is a one-to-one correspondence between the number of scan lines and the resolution of the bitmap (fig. 6-16). Many algorithms perform this function, some with anti-aliased edges.

A ***fill*** is similar to a scan conversion in that it converts the pixels within a boundary to a certain intensity value or number. The boundary is defined by pixels already existing in bitplane memory; furthermore, the boundary must completely surround the area to be filled (fig. 6-17).

Both methods are found in illustration and paint systems. The scan convert is used to draw solid shapes, whereas the fill is used to change the value of an already-existing patch of equal intensity pixels on a screen.

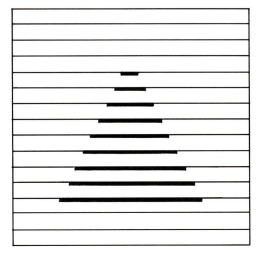

6-16. A scan conversion determines the left and right edges of a polygon and draws parallel horizontal lines between them. These can be integerized and represented on a bitmap display.

as a sequence of adjacent pixels. Horizontal or vertical lines are represented by rows or columns of pixels, but diagonal lines are represented by a staircase of pixels, and the steepness of the staircase is analogous to the steepness of the line.

The conversion from a line defined by its two end points into pixels is performed on the computer with a program called a ***digital differential algorithm (DDA).*** Several techniques for doing this implement the program in hardware. Unfortunately, if the lines are represented with only one bit per pixel, they appear aliased.

In bitmap memories that contain more than one bit per pixel, lines and edges can be anti-aliased using pixels with shades of gray adjacent to the completely dark pixels that make up the main body of the line. The pixel is really a small square of area, and it is intensified in direct proportion to what percentage of it is intersected by the line. The resulting line appears smoother and more continuous (see fig. 1-45).

Halftoning

Most two-dimensional pixel images that have a wide luminance range require several bitplanes to contain the luminance values of each pixel. An image with 256 light-intensity levels, for example, requires eight bitplanes. The process of converting a two-dimensional image with a wide range of luminance values to a matrix containing only black and white is known as ***halftoning.*** This process is very similar to the conversion of photographs to a halftone (black-and-white) screen for printing.

Halftoning represents different luminance values not as an array of pixels of constant area and varying intensity, but as an array with constant intensity (black/white) and varying area. For an image to be "halftoned," a higher spatial resolution matrix is needed, that is, more pixels in X and Y. The intensity information of each pixel is converted to and contained in several pixels. For example, a pixel with a low intensity will be equivalent to a halftone array with very few pixels turned on; a pixel with a very high intensity (white) will turn on many of the pixels in the halftone array (fig. 6-18).

DYADIC IMAGE PROCESSES

A dyadic image process involves two input images and one resultant image. The resultant image consists either of one image partly overlaying another, or of the two images combined.

Matte Compositing

Matting is a process used to lay one image over another. (In the television industry, mattes are called *keys;* in the print industry they are called *holdbacks* and *knockouts.*) Two input bitmaps include elements to be composited, such as a set of bitplanes defining a background and a set defining a foreground. A third bitplane contains the **matte,** or logical operator, which specifies which pixels from each image will be used to form the composited image.

A high-contrast matte contains only zeros and ones; the output is determined on an either/or basis (fig. 6-19). Self-mattes, or **keys,** are mattes that are shaped by the foreground object. The foreground components are placed against a flat field of black or of color, often a bright blue, which is easily referenced by the computer, that replaces the background color pixels with black pixels. Next, all the remaining pixels, depicting the objects in the foreground, are changed to white, producing a high-contrast matte (fig. 6-20). The two images are then composited in the manner just described (see fig. 6-19). Given two input images, each of which could self-matte, there are twelve ways the images could be composited (fig. 6-21).

Continuous contrast mattes represent not only black-and-white, but all shades of gray as well (fig. 6-22). This matte is often stored as a fourth image channel

6-17. A flood algorithm changes the value of all connected pixels that are of identical color or intensity.

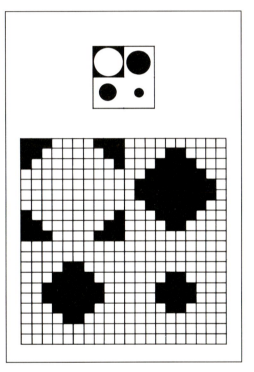

6-18. A very bright pixel is represented by many pixels in the higher spatial frequency halftone array; a dim pixel is approximated by a smaller area.

RELATED READING

Born, Robert, ed. *Designing for Television.* Tequesta, FL: Broadcast Designers' Association, 1983.

Felding, Raymond. *The Technique of Special Effects Cinematography.* New York: Hastings House, 1965.

Imes, Jack. *Special Visual Effects.* New York: Van Nostrand Reinhold, 1984.

Levitan, Eli. *Electronic Imaging Techniques.* New York: Van Nostrand Reinhold, 1977.

6-19. This figure shows foreground and background elements (A, C), the matte (B), and the final composite (D). For each zero pixel in the matte, the resultant pixel is taken from the background; for each one pixel in the matte the resultant pixel is taken from the foreground.

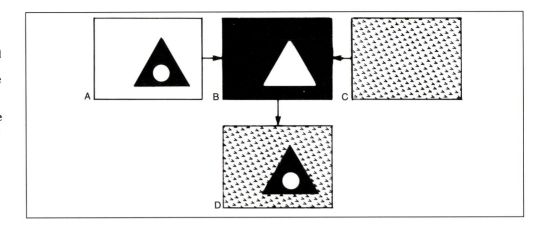

6-20. Creating a key matte. The foreground, here a headshot, is placed in front of a blue background (A). The blue background is converted to black (B) and all other colors become white, creating a matte (C). The original foreground image is then composited with a new background (D), yielding a composite (E).

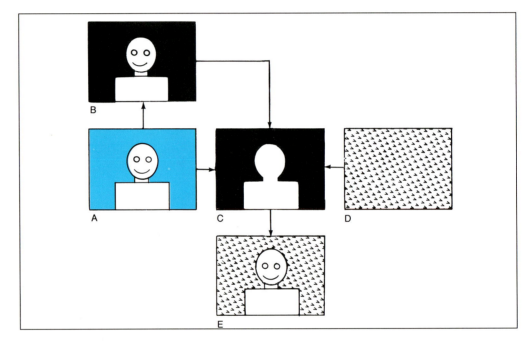

along with RGB. Continuous contrast mattes permit two images to be blended and for transparent objects, like a glass of water, to be matted over a background. When the inputs are composited, instead of each resultant pixel being from either one image or the other, the matte determines a blend of the two at each pixel. The blend, obviously, is defined as the percentage of gray in each matte pixel.

Continuous contrast mattes allow objects with soft edges or objects in motion to be combined without hard matte lines dividing the foreground and background. Hair, for example, has a soft, fuzzy edge that is difficult to matte without some de-

gree of quantization to determine what is and is not part of the hair, but when the matte has a degree of transparency to it, the soft edges of the foreground hair blend into the background.

Static mattes are often empirically determined, as in a split screen. Here the matte specifies that the left half of the picture is to come from one input image and the right half from another. Mattes can be rectangular, square, triangular, or be shaped like binoculars, keyholes, or hearts (fig. 6-23). They can also effectively crop a picture—essentially the part of the image that corresponds to the black pixels in the matte is not reproduced.

OPERATION

A	A IN B	A ATOP B
B	B IN A	B ATOP A
A OVER B	A OUT B	A XOR B
B OVER A	B OUT A	CLEAR

6-21. Compositing operators illustrate all possible combinations between images.

A

B

C

D

6-22. Continuous-tone mattes are employed in film and video as well as digital media. In this illustration, the background is a color sea scene (A); the foreground element is a transparent glass placed in front of a black background (B). A continuous-tone matte is formed next (C). The foreground and background images are then composited (D) by weighting their proportions according to the variable density matte. (Courtesy of Steve Borowski and R. Globus, Globus Brothers Studios.)

6-23. Static matte selections.

Overlays are another form of static mattes used for field guides, safety grids, registration (fig. 6-24). Overlays can also be implemented with special look-up tables and as an extra bitplane that can be turned on and off by the graphic artist.

Traveling mattes are sequences of mattes applied to a series of frames and are used in motion pictures and television. Animated traveling mattes or *wipes* are used to create a transition between two scenes (fig. 6-25). A wipe is identified by a name or number and its duration. Traveling mattes can also be prepared from a sequence of live action, where the foreground self-keys the background.

Matting and compositing processes that involve more than two input images are reduced to a sequence of individual composites, each with two inputs, a matte,

6-24. A twelve-field overlay is used to locate objects in images. A safety grid determines the limits in which to place an image or title for film projection or television broadcasting. Registration marks are used to match different images. Counting reticules are used to count sample elements in the image.

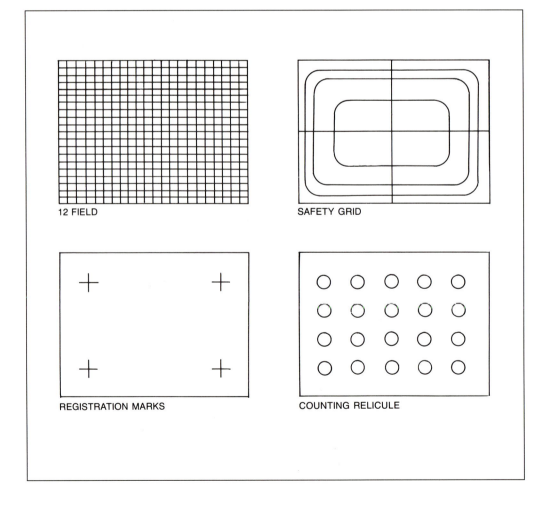

12 FIELD

SAFETY GRID

REGISTRATION MARKS

COUNTING RELICULE

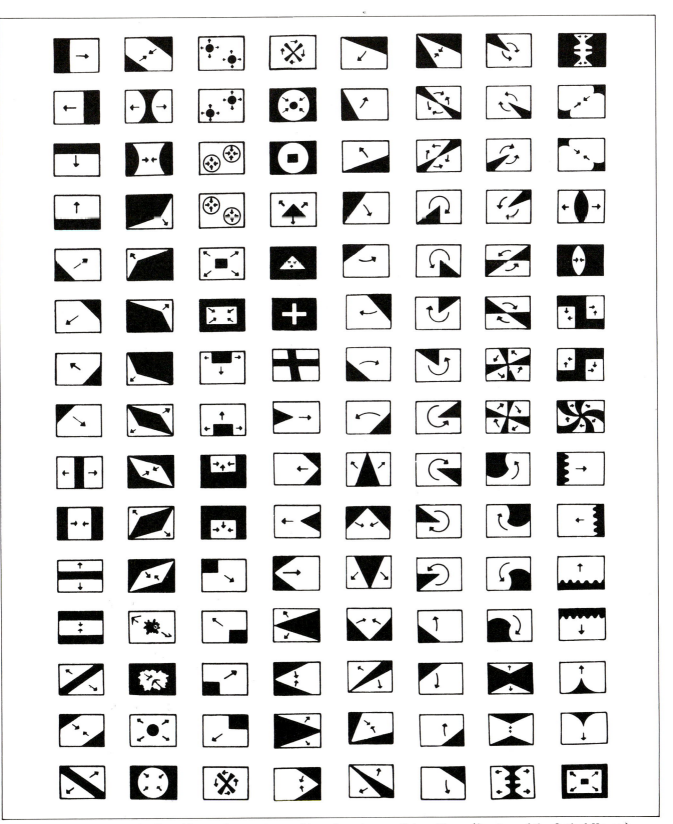

6-25. Wipe effects are used in film, video, and computer graphic systems to smooth transitions. (Courtesy of the Optical House.)

6-26. The diagram shows a virtual switching system where an input image and a black field are combined at different proportions with a fade slider that is operated at a certain speed (number of frames/length of time). The resulting image will be equal to the input image multiplied by the fade factor: RESULT ← (FADE VALUE × INPUT).

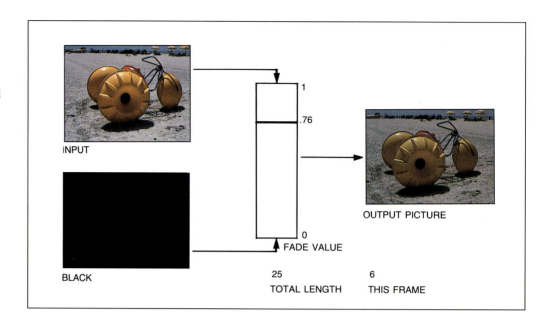

6-27. The dissolve from input image A to B is controlled with a dissolve slider. The final result is expressed as: RESULT ← (INPUT A × DISSOLVE = FACTOR) + (INPUT B × (1 − DISSOLVE FACTOR)). (Provided by Isaac V. Kerlow.)

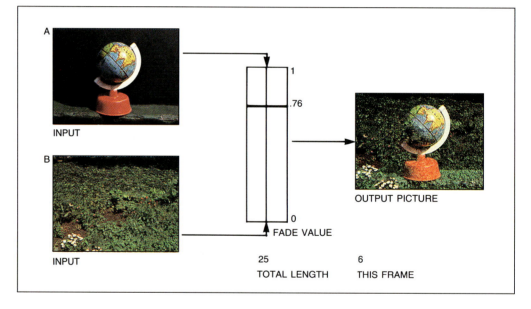

and an output. One of the main advantages of computer graphics methods is that there is no generation loss or image degradation through the succession of composites.

Fades, Dissolves, Double Exposures

Fades, dissolves, and double exposures are all operations between pairs of digital images that are arithmetically combined. (Arithmetic operations are different from logical operations in that each resultant pixel is an arithmetic combination of two input pixels, rather than a logical choice between them.) A **fade** is a traditional arithmetic operation in which a variable between zero and one is multiplied by each pixel, producing less exposure as a result (fig. 6-26). A fade usually occurs across a sequence of frames, causing them to become black.

A **dissolve** is actually two fades combined; an image fading out is added to the image fading in (fig. 6-27), creating a

6-28. Double exposure. (Provided by Isaac V. Kerlow.)

transition between the shots. Fades and dissolves are nonlinear; the manner by which the individual increments are determined is discussed in chapter 7.

Another arithmetic operation, the *double exposure (DX),* combines two images (fig. 6-28). If the dynamic range of the output image, that is, the number of luminance levels between black and white, is equal to the input image, adding the images together would produce very bright, overexposed values, as does shooting two exposures on one frame; a computer, like film, has a finite dynamic range and thus a maximum value beyond which no value may be brighter. A better strategy would be to add the two pictures and divide by two. The resultant image would not overflow the dynamic range and would appear much the same as a frame in the middle of a dissolve, where the output frame has one-half the exposure from each incoming scene. The total exposure will not exceed the total brightness permitted in the medium.

Double exposures work well to superimpose type and logos over backgrounds. The type must be completely white in order to burn out, or double expose, any background image.

Double exposures are used to make *glows,* a double exposure with a soft edge, *streaks,* traveling elements that make a motion smear, and *strobes,* which are discrete streaks (fig. 6-29).

Cells and Sprites

Cells are objects built out of polygons and recorded in a display list. *Sprites* are pixel arrays that are smaller than the total area of the picture and function as submodules. Sprites include type characters, brushes, stamps, and cursors. These small pixel arrays vary in size from less than ten squared and one bit deep, to full-color areas hundreds or thousands of pixels square. Sprites may be rectangular as well as square in shape and incorporate transparency as well as luminance information.

In *dot matrix type,* the raw sprite letter is stored in a character generator chip as a table of zeros and ones. Bitmapped characters are often defined in ROM; they can be plugged in and out of a computer to provide different fonts, characters, sets, and patterns. The letters are indexed by the American Standard Code for Information Interchange (ASCII) code.

In the sprite, the bits of value one are part of the letter; zero bits are transparent. When the sprite is matted over a corresponding set of pixels in an image, the bits in the image that correspond to the ones are made a color, while the zero

6-29. Glows are created by double exposing the recording medium—first with the artwork in focus and then with the artwork diffused. (Courtesy of Animotion.)

6-30. A sprite two bits deep can be three colors and transparent. Like acetate cartoon cells, sprites self-matte the background. The colored bits are overlaid, the zero bits are transparent, and the corresponding pixels on the image are unchanged. Here we see the original sprite and background separately and the overlaid result.

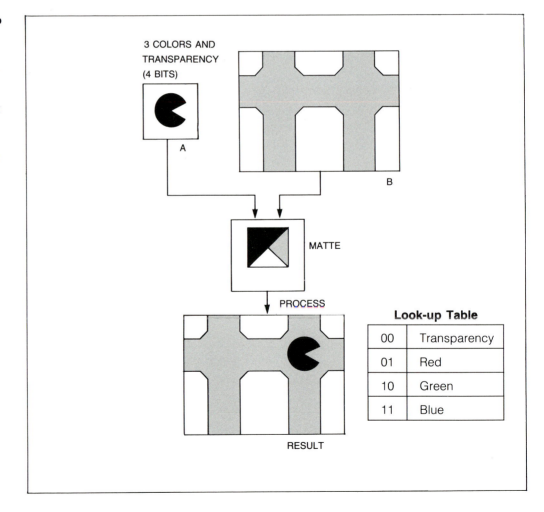

3 COLORS AND
TRANSPARENCY
(4 BITS)

A

B

MATTE

PROCESS

RESULT

Look-up Table

00	Transparency
01	Red
10	Green
11	Blue

transparent bits do not alter the image (fig. 6-30).

Cells, because they are stored on a display list, may be repositioned and rescaled interactively and then scan converted and displayed. Sprites too often reside in special memories structured much like frame buffers. Sprites are positioned and sized using registers that specify the XY location on the screen and the size. Sprites can be more flexibly positioned in a graphics system than in a dot matrix character display, which simply shows a fixed number of dot matrix letters per line and a fixed number of lines. Often the sprite location is interactively determined using a graphics peripheral, like a joystick in a video game. This hardware permits the sprite to be positioned anywhere over the image without being written or fixed into the bitmap.

Cursors essentially are cells or sprites that can be moved around on an image and that are controlled by a pen, mouse, or joystick. Because the system knows the location of the cursor, it can identify the object to which it is pointing. Blinking cursors are simply cursors that are alternately displayed and blanked.

Sprites are easily animated and are ideal for creating limited real-time computer animation. First, a cycle of action, such as the cells that animate a PAC-MAN running or the position of talking lips, is defined as sprites. Second, the cells are defined in sequence (fig. 6-31). The animation is either interactively composed or composed using a scripting system much like an animation sheet, which specifies a sequence of cells and positions. Once the preview is complete, a second process composites the animation, fixes each sprite into the background, then stores the composite image for future playback.

A *brush* is a sprite that can be fixed into the image immediately and is used for painting digital pictures as well as for retouching. Brushes often function in a preview or movable mode, so they may be positioned correctly, and then entered, or fixed into the image (fig. 6-32). Brushes, like sprites in general, can be solid as well as transparent and can paint over images

as a wash. A *stamp* is a sprite, or brush, formed by excising a rectangular matrix of pixels from an image. This is then positioned and drawn somewhere else in the picture.

LOCAL AND GLOBAL OPERATORS

An image-processing function is designated either as local or global. This distinction is subtle, and depends on how the resultant image is calculated. *Global operators* are functions applied to each pixel independently of the other pixels in the image. For example, the process of making a negative reads each pixel in the image, uses each in a calculation, and replaces each with a result. Almost all of the processes that we have discussed so far involve global operators.

Local operators are also procedures applied to each pixel, but the result of the calculation incorporates information about the pixels that surround and touch it (fig. 6-33). In a local operation, changes to a pixel are affected by the values of adjacent pixels.

A local operator can be visualized by thinking of a theater audience with people sitting in rows of seats. The occupied seats equal one, and the empty seats zero. The audience is told: "Look to your right and if the seat to your right is empty, move into it." Each member of the audience does this simultaneously, as if it were one iteration of a machine. The people with empty seats to their right move over, while everyone else remains stationary.

Computer language would state that each pixel with a value of one in the bitplane should examine the value of the pixel immediately to its right, and if the

▶ **RELATED READING**

Gardner, Martin. "Mathematical Games." *Scientific American* (October 1970, February 1971).

Knowlton, Ken. *EXPLOR.* Murray Hill, NJ: Bell Laboratories, 1974.

6-31. Sprites (or cells) can be animated by displaying them in sequence over the background image. The position of the sprite can be controlled either by the program or with a joystick. In this case, eight sprites represent the shapes of the lips effected by pronouncing different combinations of letters. The sequence of sprites is controlled by a sequence of numbers fed into the computer. (Courtesy of Jan Svochaak and Susan Bickford.)

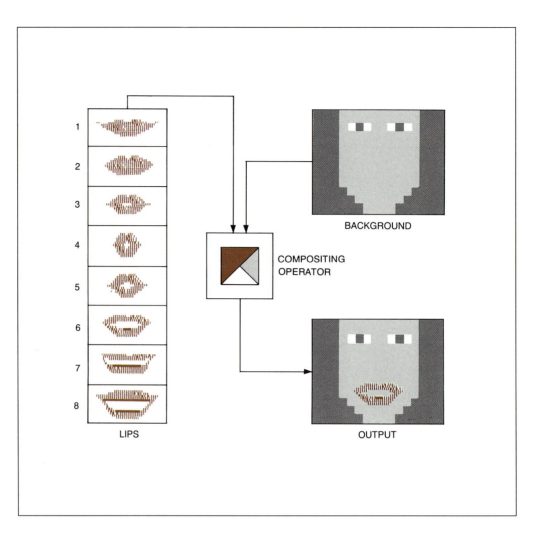

6-32. A *line-drawing brush* can create strokes of varying thicknesses (as used to create the sailor holding the telescope). A *blending brush* mixes the colors of the pixels it overlays (as in the violet waves). An *airbrush* deposits a solid central spot of color, which fans out to transparency. A *stencil* is an area of the screen that cannot be affected by a brush—like a frisket, it allows colors to surround an object without damaging it (as on the boat), protecting it from the blending brush that creates waves. (Courtesy of New York Institute of Technology.)

value of that pixel is one, do nothing, but if the value of that pixel is zero, set it to one and set the original pixel to zero (fig. 6-34).

A program called *Life* (fig. 6-35) is one example of a local operator in computer graphics and was invented by John Conley. Another illustration of local operators is the language *Explor*, written by Ken Knowlton of Bell Labs (fig. 6-36). Explor is a collection of FORTRAN subroutines and has been widely circulated as a teaching tool. It also allows artists to define local operators.

Another kind of local operation is *image averaging* (also called *pixelation, block pix, mosaic*), the averaging of small areas of an image to reduce picture resolution (see fig. 6-6). This can be a creative

method, one that aggregates areas of pixels into patterns or shapes (fig. 6-37) and at different resolutions in either black-and-white or color. The procedure involves reading a group of pixels, calculating an average, then writing the average back out to each pixel in the pattern.

Brushes that blend colors in an image and simulated air brushes also involve local operators.

IMAGE ENHANCEMENT

Numerous digital techniques are unavailable using optical, photographic, or analog electronic methods. Many of these techniques originated in the field of image processing. *Image enhancement* tech-

6-33. A pixel and its eight neighbors.

6-34. Local operator animation. Each member of the theater audience changes position depending on surrounding seat availability. Repeating the procedure described in the text eventually stacks everyone to the right of the theater—the result of successive iterations depends on previous ones.

6-35. The game of *Life* is played on a one-bitplane matrix and has three rules for turning bits on and off. The rules are based on neighborhood conditions and simulate the conditions and patterns necessary to create colonies of pixels that are stable, divide, reproduce, and die. The three rules are: (1) every pixel with two or three neighboring pixels survives for the next move; (2) each pixel with four or more neighbors dies from overpopulation, and each with one or no neighbor dies from isolation; (3) each empty cell adjacent to exactly three neighbors will generate a new pixel on it at the next move.

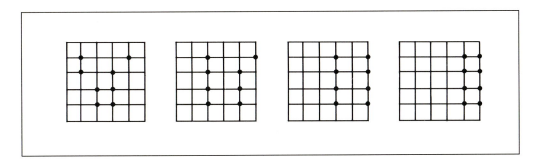

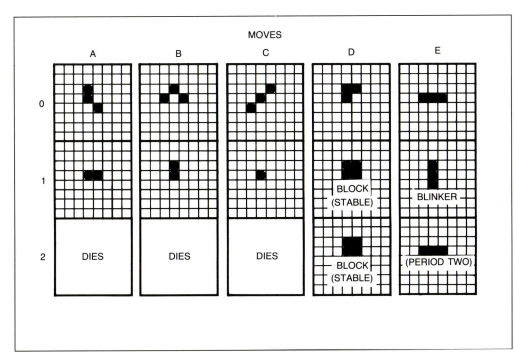

6-36. Ken Knowlton may have been inspired to write *Explor* by his research on growing silicon chip wafers. In Knowlton's model—an example of how pixel graphics can represent things other than images—the bitplane represents a molecular array of silicon and each pixel represents one atom. The pixel value describes how many atoms deep the layer of silicon was (essentially a zel). Growing the crystal begins with a layer that is one atom thick; each atom has a random chance that an atom will stick on top of it. The growth simulation hypothesis states, however, that (for each discrete moment in time of the process) this chance is increased if the value of the neighboring pixels is greater, because the pocket or shoulder attracts the atom from the side. (Courtesy of Ken Knowlton.)

6-37. Image averaging is performed by reading the values inside each diamond, adding them, and dividing them by the number of pixels in the diamond. The result is the average intensity value, which is written back out to each pixel. (Courtesy of Digital Effects Inc.)

niques are used to improve the visibility of images, bringing out details that would otherwise remain latent. These include diffusion and sharpening filters, noise reduction methods, and spatial frequency techniques, which are becoming part of the graphic artist's vocabulary. (Many of the techniques described in the section on color in chapter 7 also involve enhancement.)

Diffusion Filters

A *low-pass,* or *diffusion, filter* softens an image. The procedure works locally by averaging each pixel and its eight neighbors, then writing that average value back in the pixel (fig. 6-38). This is somewhat similar to image averaging, except that the average is only written back into the central pixel of the resultant image. This moving average essentially blends areas of the picture and is often used in interactive paint systems to meld colors and retouch.

The amount of blurring in a diffusion filter depends on the size of the sampled neighborhood and can vary in width as well as height. The minimum (and identity case) is a one-pixel region that simply averages the pixel and replaces it with its own contents. A wider filter might sample a 3 × 3 matrix of pixels (see fig. 6-38), 5 × 5 pixels, 7 × 7 pixels, or larger areas, producing increasingly blurred pictures. The average can also be *weighted;* this means that the value of the central pixel affects the resultant value more than the value of the surrounding pixels (fig. 6-39).

Sharpening Filters

The opposite of a low-pass filter is a *high-pass* or *sharpening* filter, which reveals details only. High-pass filtering subtracts the low-pass filter from the original image, leaving only details (fig. 6-40).

Noise Reduction

Noise reduction in digital pictures uses a collection of ad hoc procedures and subjective evaluations to increase visibility. *Noise* in a picture refers to spurious, abnormal pixel values, whatever their source (fig. 6-41). Noise reduction is seldom

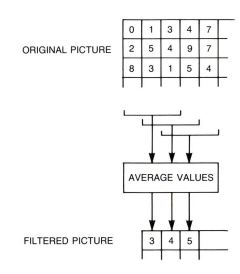

6-38. A low-pass filter calculates a moving average that blurs and smooths the image. (Courtesy of Spatial Data Systems, Inc.; a DBA Systems Company.)

6-39. Weighted average. In the 3 × 3 pixel array illustrated, the central pixel accounts for 50 percent of the value of the result, whereas the eight surrounding pixels each account for one-eighth of the remaining 50 percent of the averaged value, or 6.25 percent each.

9 × .5	=	4.5
6 × .0625	=	.375
7 × .0625	=	.4375
6 × .0625	=	.375
7 × .0625	=	.4375
6 × .0625	=	.375
8 × .0625	=	.5
5 × .0625	=	.3125
6 × .0625	=	.375
		7.688

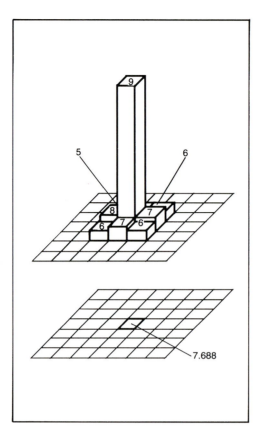

6-40. A high-pass filter sharpens an image. (Courtesy of Spatial Data Systems, Inc.; a DBA Systems Company.)

completely effective—for example, a low-pass filter can smooth out noise, but it smooths out details, as well.

Distortions resulting from camera lenses, time smears, or movements of the camera during an exposure can sometimes be corrected with *restoration techniques,* which use facts about the defect to improve picture quality (fig. 6-42).

Spatial Frequency Processing

Pixels describe an image in terms of its luminance, but images can also be represented and perceived in other ways. We suggested that horizontal resolution is one kind of *spatial frequency,* or the number of samples across the space of the picture.

The contents of an image also exhibit spatial frequencies, which appear as changes in luminance across a scan line. For example, a photograph of a picket fence contains a spatial frequency roughly equal to the number of pixels from the center of one picket to the center of the next (fig. 6-43). Spatial frequency in an image is associated with the perception of the degree of detail. The more detailed an image, the higher its spatial frequency (fig. 6-44).

The spatial frequencies of an image may be analyzed to discover latent properties and to provide quantitive measures of its contents. Spatial frequency analysis begins by taking inventory of all the spatial frequencies in the image. For example, a picture of a picket fence will have a spatial frequency that is quite different from the spatial frequency of a picture of rain. A picture of a picket fence in the rain will contain both; the sharp spatial frequencies associated with a picket fence can be isolated from the lower spatial frequencies of the rain, and the frequency of the rain removed. The result is a picture where the picket fence is more visible and the rain is gone (fig. 6-45).

This approach can also be used to search images and identify objects associated with specific spatial frequencies. For example, satellite images of the ocean can be searched for ships by establishing

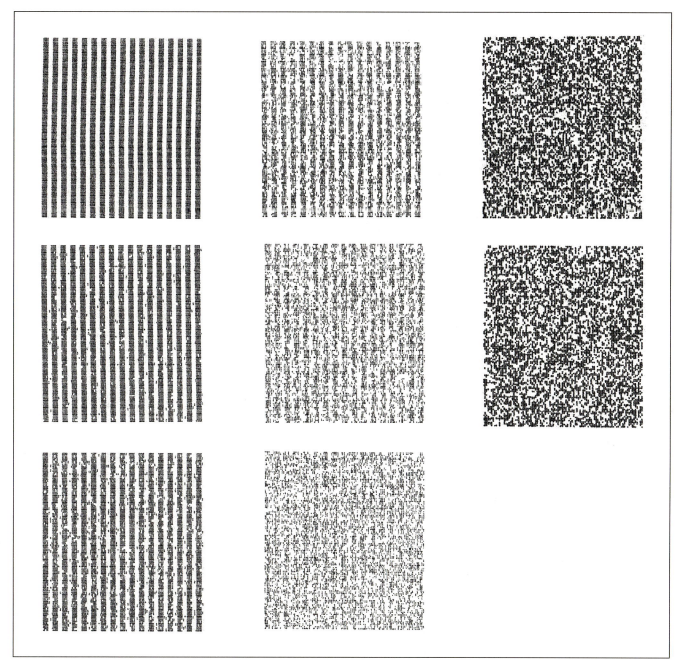

the background frequencies for waves, then flagging images with dramatically different frequencies.

COMPUTER VISION AND IMAGE ANALYSIS

Computer vision systems are concerned with the perception of images and with identifying objects and physical features such as shapes and volumes. Computer vision not only converts pixels into lines and shapes, but determines the relation of shapes and what they signify. Computer vision is the opposite of computer graphics and is closely related to *perception,* the science and art of forming mental constructs of the world and then navigating in that volumetric space.

6-41. Noise mixed with a set of vertical bars in various percentages. (Provided by Isaac V. Kerlow.)

6-42. Image-processing techniques can restore the blurred image by eliminating the original movement.

 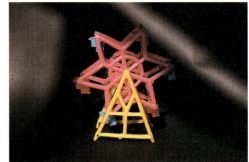

6-43. Spatial-frequency analysis can be used to detect and remove regular interference patterns, such as the out-of-focus bars in the illustration on the left.

6-44. A gothic image is very detailed and has a high spatial frequency (right). A Renaissance image (left) has less detail, smoother edges, and a lower spatial frequency.

6-45. Spatial frequency enhancement can reduce irregular picture noise, such as rain, provided the noise has characteristic spatial frequencies. The image is converted into the spatial domain, the unwanted frequencies are subtracted, and the picture is converted back.

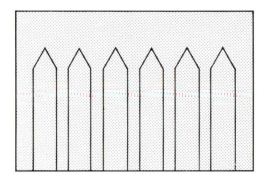 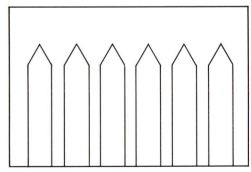

Computer vision is a prerequisite for machines that navigate, and its widespread applications complement the graphic arts. These include the development of measures that relate to visibility. Computer vision is used to read typographic characters and bar codes, recognize faces, signatures, or thumbprints, and inspect parts on an assembly line. Image analysis is used in medicine, where CAT scan data is reconstructed into volumetric organs and X rays are analyzed for tumors.

Inputs to computer vision systems include a variety of light and imaging devices, which are often complemented with pressure, molecular, and temperature sensors, as well as with a range of electronic extensions, such as radar, ultrasound, and sonar.

Edge and Boundary Determination

Edge detection and boundary determination are used to assist in converting pixel images back into point and polygon representations; they are the opposite of scan conversion and DDAs. An *edge* is a sharp distinction in color or intensity values between adjacent pixels. Edges are keys to finding surfaces that intersect should the image depict a three-dimensional environment. Long straight edges often mark intersections of ceilings and walls, corners of rooms, or outlines of furniture.

In its most primitive form, an edge is simply the difference in value between two adjacent pixels; an edge detection algorithm subtracts the value of each pixel from the value of its neighbor and stores the results in a bitmap (fig. 6-46). The result looks much like a bas-relief image.

Edges imply a structural bias in an image and are a first step in finding polygons; an edge is essentially one side of a polygon, a vector between two points. Different algorithms produce different kinds of edges and are worth creatively exploring (fig. 6-47). An edge matrix added back into an original image sharpens it by enhancing the shapes of things, making the image more distinct (fig. 6-48).

More sophisticated software can convert a gradient of pixels, adjacent pixels that

 RELATED READING

Ballard, Dana H., and Christopher M. Brown. *Computer Vision.* Englewood Cliffs, NJ: Prentice-Hall, 1982.

Gordon, Richard, Gabor T. Herman, and Stephen A. Johnson. "Image Reconstructions from Projections." *Scientific American* (October 1975).

Gregory, Richard L. *Eye and Brain, the Psychology of Seeing.* 3d ed. New York: McGraw-Hill, 1978.

Harmon, Leon. "The Recognition of Faces." *Scientific American* (November 1973).

Poggio, Tomaso. "Vision by Man and Machine." *Scientific American* (April 1984).

Rock, Irvin. *Perception.* New York: W. H. Freeman & Company, 1984.

have similar intensity and slope, into lines in the point/vector domain. A *boundary* is similar to an edge, but is a contour, formed by pixels that can be converted into a curving line or a polygon. Boundary determination works by identifying a contour of pixels and then converting it into a series of floating point numbers that define a polygon outline (fig. 6-49).

Matching

Template matching compares preexisting shape definitions, usually a small pixel array, to an input image, in order to identify specific details or features (fig. 6-50). It is used for quality control on assembly lines, in surveillance (computerized searches for missile silos in satellite images and for tumors in X rays) and for robotic vision. Computerized matching systems do not necessarily work if the object being matched is viewed at a different size, from a different angle, or with different lighting. This problem is now being actively researched for artificial intelligence purposes.

Reconstruction

Bitmap images that depict three-dimensional spatial environments, such as a digitized photograph of a house, are analyzed and possibly reconstructed into three-dimensional environments using a variety of procedures (fig. 6-51).

Three-dimensional reconstruction often uses edge and boundary detectors to discern shapes, and *normal determination,*

6-46. Edges are depicted with a matrix that shows the difference between the value of a pixel and its horizontal or vertical neighbor. This resultant bitmap is a matrix of changes and is called the *first derivative* of the image. (Courtesy of Spatial Data Systems, Inc.; a DBA Systems Company.)

6-47. Gradient edge detection. (Courtesy of Spatial Data Systems, Inc.; a DBA Systems Company.)

6-48. Laplacian edge detection plus original image. (Courtesy of Spatial Data Systems, Inc.; a DBA Systems Company.)

which evaluates information about the location of light, the comparative color of the surfaces, reflected brightness, foreshortening, and texture patterns, in order to ascertain surface orientation (fig. 6-52). One normal is calculated for each pixel, and stored in a bitplane memory. When associated with contours, normals assist in locating surfaces in a three-dimensional spatial environment, because they indicate their orientation.

Another tool for three-dimensional reconstruction is *photogrammetry,* a method that correlates two perspective views of a scene and derives three-dimensional spatial locations (see fig. 7-10). The two-view technique requires some knowledge of points in the three-dimensional environment in order to yield a proper result, because apparent two-dimensional size depends on both object size and its distance from the observer.

Computerized three-dimensional reconstruction, like an individual's perception, is not always perfect. Accurate interpretations require some preexisting data structure and memory on the part of the observer (fig. 6-53). The Necker cubes and the Rubin vase (fig. 6-54) are examples of failed psychological "algorithms," because they yield two solutions, or multistable images.

6-49. The same image before and after boundaries have been determined. The top illustration shows the original continuous-tone image. The bottom shows the result of a process that determines the boundaries between sharp distinctions of gray levels. (Courtesy of Allen R. Hanson, Edward M. Riseman, and members of the VISIONS research group at the University of Massachusetts.)

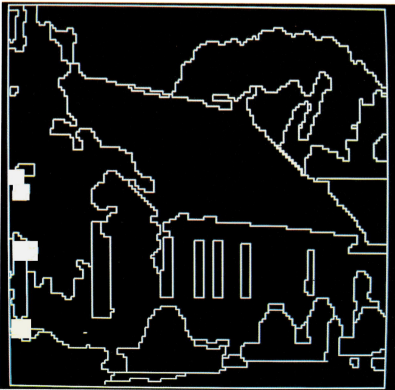

6-50. Pattern matching uses a template for hexagonal nut against which it will be matched. Photograph by Dana H. Ballard and Chris M. Brown, *Computer Vision.* © 1982, p. 67. Reprinted by permission of Prentice-Hall, Inc.

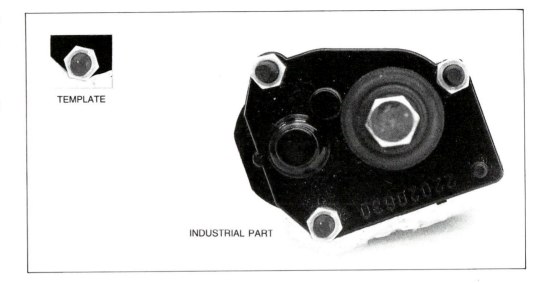

TEMPLATE

INDUSTRIAL PART

6-51. In three-dimensional reconstruction, the general features of landscape and object are extracted from a photograph (see fig. 6-49) and reconstructed in three dimensions. The spatial relationships between them are established in the form of a relational data base. (Courtesy of Allen R. Hanson, Edward M. Riseman, and members of the VISIONS research group at the University of Massachusetts.)

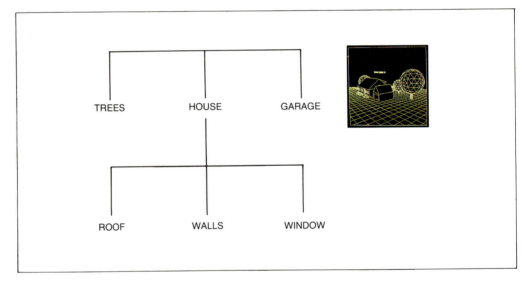

TREES   HOUSE   GARAGE

ROOF   WALLS   WINDOW

6-52. Characteristics of a surface depicted in an image may be used to determine the orientation of the surface in space (normal determination). These techniques include perspective (A) and fore-shortening texture patterns (B).

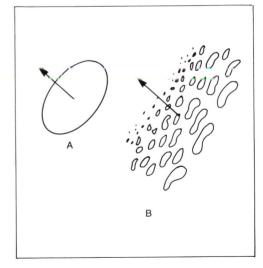

A

B

6-53. Three-dimensional reconstruction based on two-view photogrammetry.

6-54. A Rubin vase—a multistable image—can be seen as the silhouette of a vase or as two faces.

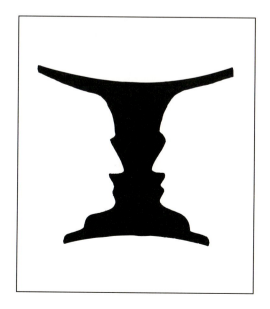

7-0. This Robot with Good Taste in Wallpaper, an example of realistic figurative animation, illustrates the advanced computer graphics techniques that are explored in this chapter. (Courtesy of New York Institute of Technology, Computer Graphics Lab. Image by Ned Greene.)

7

THREE-DIMENSIONAL MODELING

MODEL CONSTRUCTION
COMBINATORIAL GEOMETRY
PRIMITIVE TRANSFORMATIONS
PERSPECTIVE, WINDOWS, AND PORTS
ACTORS AND ACTIONS
SURFACE ATTRIBUTES
LIGHTS AND LIGHTING
RENDERING

Visual language as it applies to three-dimensional graphics, particularly points, lines, planes, and volumes, is considerably different from the pixel representational form and includes objects as opposed to images. *Objects* are virtual entities in a continuous environment, whereas images are discrete picture areas. Objects include points, lines, and shapes in two-dimensional space as well as three-dimensional volumes. The principles are basically the same. The focus of this chapter is to define, position, manipulate, light, and render objects in three-dimensional graphics.

In many respects three-dimensional solid modeling is a lot like constructing theater props. Positioning models in the imaginary computer space is analogous to classical set design. Action, characterization, and lighting are all comparable, but rendering and visualization apply only to graphics.

MODEL CONSTRUCTION

Shape and Volume Representation and Digitization

Objects that are stored in a computer can either be concrete—a tape recorder or a building—or abstractions—a model of an atom, a subatomic particle, or a psychological variable. Objects, static or mobile, can be geometrically built or composed freehand. Very basic objects, like stars, are represented as points. A list of points can be connected with lines and can define a surface or the edge of a volume (fig. 7-1). All objects are represented as numbers, but they are often composed and manipulated using commands or procedures, which address them using a variable name.

The definition of objects in a computer, whether they are simple lines bounded by two points, or complicated shapes, requires that the objects be stored in the machine. Digitization and procedural descriptions are two ways of inputting that information. Both techniques can be controlled either explicitly or interactively.

Objects are digitized using a keyboard, tablet, camera, or special measuring device. Extrusion is a technique that turns two-dimensional inputs into three-dimensional objects; three-dimensional objects are also digitized from serial sections and coplanar blueprints. Photogrammetry is used to reconstruct three-dimensional objects from photographic images; and spatial measuring tools specify either points, zels, or voxels that are already three dimensional.

Objects are also described using predefined computer programs. Procedural descriptions include geometric figures such as boxes, cylinders, doughnuts, surfaces, such as those in an automobile fender, and irregular forms, such as trees. The graphic artist controls the position, size,

7-1. A scene composed of lines, surfaces, and volumes.

  RELATED READING

Barnhill, Robert E., and Richard F. Reisenfeld. *Computer Aided Geometric Design.* New York: Academic Press, 1984.

Chasen, Sylvan H. *Geometric Principles and Procedures for Computer Graphic Applications.* Englewood Cliffs, NJ: Prentice-Hall, 1978.

Faux, I. D., and M. J. Pratt. *Computational Geometry for Design and Manufacture.* New York: John Wiley & Sons, 1979.

Gasson, Peter C. *Geometry of Spatial Forms.* New York: John Wiley & Sons, 1983.

Mortenson, Michael E. *Geometric Modelling.* New York: John Wiley & Sons, 1985.

Pavlidis, Theo. *Algorithms for Graphics and Image Processing.* New York: Springer-Verlag, 1982.

and shape of these objects with simple commands and arguments.

Closely allied to the object definition methods in this section are combinational methods such as clipping and unions, and animation techniques such as in-betweening and interpolation.

Point Digitizing

The most basic way to enter points into a computer is on a keyboard. This is essential in situations where the data exists at higher resolutions than the digitizer. Regular shapes, such as rectangles, can easily be entered on a keyboard, because only a few points need to be defined (fig. 7-2).

Objects that are more irregular—the outline of a letter or logo—are usually digitized by placing the artwork on a digitizing tablet and picking points or tracing around the perimeter with a stylus. Another strategy is to redraw the object onto graph paper, identify key coordinates and curves such as arcs, then enter them via a keyboard. This is often best, because the lines produced are smoother (fig. 7-3), and because many objects, for example, type, often have a geometric basis.

Extrusion

Extrusion is used to convert a two-dimensional outline into a three-dimensional space and defines the sides of the object (fig. 7-4). The term comes from machinery containing dies through which metal or plastic is pulled. Computationally, it is a procedure that translates a copy of the front surface back into Z space and then connects sides between the front and back edges, creating a three-dimensional shape.

Objects of Revolution

Another model-constructing technique is used to make symmetrical surfaces of revolution, such as a bell (fig. 7-5). *Objects of revolution* begin by digitizing only a cross section of the object. The cross section only consists of X and Y data and is centered around the Y axis. A computer program then spins, or rotates, this line

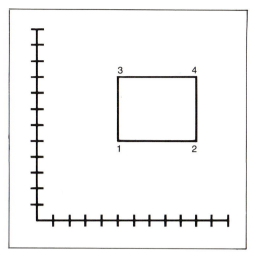

7-2. Only two points, opposite corners, must be entered to point digitize a rectangle. The computer recombines the X and Y values for the other two points—the lower left corner and the lower right corner have the same Y value, and the lower right corner and the upper right corner have the same X value.

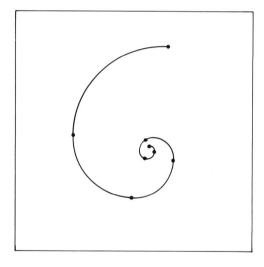

7-3. When digitizing objects the number of points needed depends on the rate of change. It is useful to enter more points for a rapidly curving line, and fewer points for a slowly curving line. This makes the sharp curves smoother without wasting points.

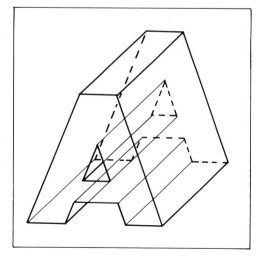

7-4. Extrusion of an alphanumeric letter into a three-dimensional volumetric representation.

7-5. Surfaces of revolution
are created by spinning a
curved line about an axis.

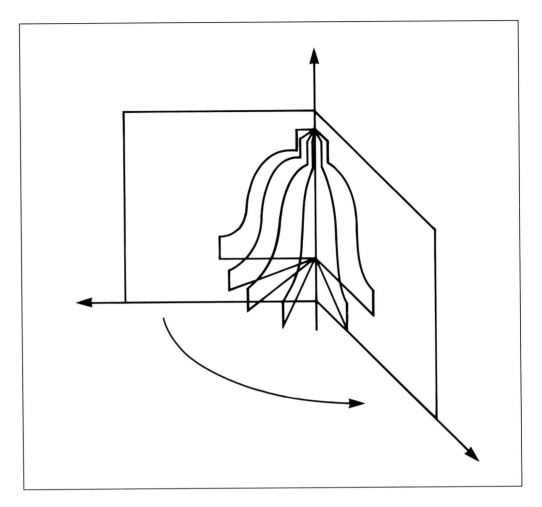

around the central axis to make a solid object, either a mesh of polygons or a continuous surface. Objects of revolution need very little data to construct complicated objects and work much like a vase that is thrown on a potter's wheel or turned on a lathe.

Sections

Another way to build three-dimensional objects with a computer is to construct a series of sections that are lifted into position (fig. 7-6). A **section** is a cross section of an object, a contour line of a quantized elevation, and allows organic, nongeometric shapes such as a biological organ or topographic terrain contours to be digitized.

Contour perimeters are digitized one at a time by picking points on a tablet, or by typing numerical coordinates on the keyboard. Each contour is assigned a layer number. After all layers have been digitized, a computer program constructs a surface mesh by automatically constructing polygons that connect each contour to the contour above and below it, creating a solid object (fig. 7-7).

Using a polar coordinate scheme and digitizing a data point at a constant angular interval is the easiest way of building objects with contours. Thus sections are easily connected, because each section point can be connected to the section point directly above (and below) it, forming planar triangular facets. The disadvantage of this method is that it does not compensate for quickly curving places in the contour (which require additional points in order to appear smooth), places where a section may curve back on itself and form an overhang, or holes (fig. 7-8). In these sit-

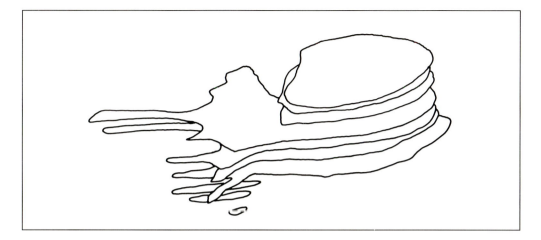

7-6. A human vertebra defined by three-dimensional contours.

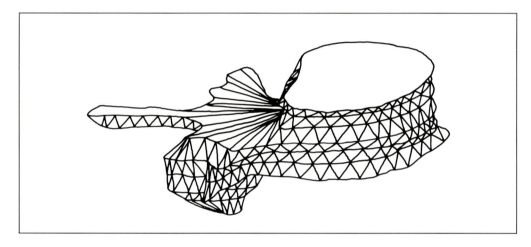

7-7. A mesh can be formed by connecting adjacent contours of the human vertebra into polygons.

uations, a more sophisticated surface-meshing algorithm is required, one that is able to build a mesh surface when the points are not evenly distributed along each contour.

Coplanar Technique

The coplanar technique of building models is used to create three-dimensional objects from blueprints. *Coplanar* signifies two planar views, a plan and an elevation, both two dimensional (fig. 7-9). The elevation, or front view, contains X and Y data. The plan, or top view, contains X and Z data. Each data point—for example, each corner—appears in both views and is assigned a point number—its address in a point list.

The two drawings are digitized by being taped to a digitizing tablet, and a graphic artist first digitizes a point from the plan

and then the corresponding point from the elevation. A computer program merges the X and Y value digitized from the first view with the Z value digitized from the second view into a single three-dimensional point stored in computer memory. (The second Y value is discarded.)

A *point list table* results from this process and has as many rows as there are points, and three columns, one for X, Y, and Z. The table contains no connectivity information between the points; that is, there is no indication of what points together form polygons or polyhedra. This information is contained in *connect lists,* which define the sequences of point numbers that form a boundary of an object. In defining a cube, for example, the point list will consist of eight points, each point representing one vertex of the cube. There will then be six connect lists, each con-

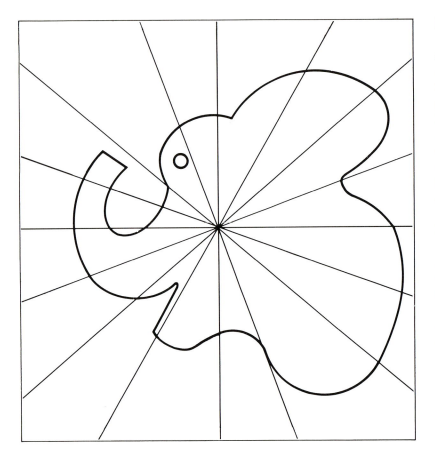

7-8. When a curve is changing gradually, as on the right, a sample point is taken at even angular intervals. Here 5 degrees approximate the contour. Contours that change quickly or curve back on themselves, as on the left, cannot be meaningfully sampled using the even-angular technique. Holes and overhangs are particularly problematic.

taining the four points needed to describe one of the polygons that make up the surface of the cube. Each point in the cube will appear in three different connect lists—the three surfaces that connect at that corner.

The coplanar method is efficient in computer memory because points are only stored once, yet may be used in multiple connect lists. If a point needs to be repositioned, then all the polygons that use it automatically incorporate the change. Usually the process begins by digitizing *rectification points,* or registration marks, in the two views. These points permit the program to relate the position of the drawings on the tablet with the internal data base and provide a way to correctly reposition artwork, for example, so new points can be added in the future.

Point and connect lists do not necessarily require blueprints beforehand. They can also be captured with XYZ stylus digitizers and can be explicitly declared.

Photogrammetry

Surfaces can also be defined with *photogrammetry* techniques that project a grid onto an actor or scene and then digitize the grid points as they appear in perspective photography, which uses two cameras (fig. 7-10). Single points appearing in both views are merged into three-dimensional points using a reconstruction technique; the point mesh is then replicated in the machine. Photogrammetry is useful for objects that cannot be sectioned or are in motion.

Zels

Another digitizing technique represents an object or a surface as a matrix of depth values called *zels.* The depth matrix may be orthogonal, or cylindrical (fig. 7-11). The matrices of zels can be converted from polar to Cartesian forms; they can also be converted to mesh surface representations as well as to contours.

Voxels

Voxels are digitized by hardware such as a CAT scanner and provide a discrete approximation of densities of space. Voxels can be organized in many ways and, like zels, may be converted to and from polygon surface meshes (fig. 7-12).

Procedural Methods

Another way of defining objects is to use the computer to calculate the sequence of points rather than directly digitizing the objects. This is done with a command that activates the procedure. A circle, for example, is best defined using a procedure, or formula, that determines the X and Y positions for each angular distance about the circle. This method can calculate extremely accurate circles with an arbitrary number of points or sides. This is quicker than digitizing the circle using a tablet and stylus, and the result is more uniformly round. By using a procedural method to construct a circle, we can calculate a circle with ten points, one hundred points, a thousand points, or a million points. The circle is not a predefined object, but is created whenever it is needed, and at whatever resolution is needed.

In a vector graphics system a circle is represented as a series of straight sides. In order to make a circle look round, the number of sides needed depends on the size of the circle in the field of view; as little as two dozen or as many as a few hundred sides may be required. Because the circle is calculated using a procedure, one can calculate the number of points needed (fig. 7-13).

Circles are not the only objects that can be procedurally built and parametrically controlled. Most computer graphics systems come with a fairly rich set of *primitive functions,* including a circle, rectangle, box (defined by its length, width, height, and center position), sphere (defined by its center position and radius), cylinder, doughnut (or torus), prism, and other basic geometric figures (fig. 7-14).

Statistical Distributions and Fractals

Procedurally defined parametrically controlled objects do not have to be regular; they can include irregular, bloblike vol-

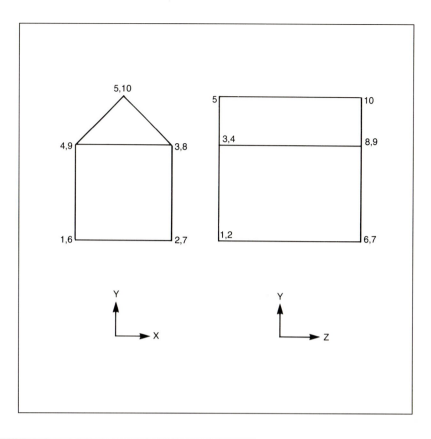

POINT LIST				CONNECT LIST
	X	Y	Z	1, 2, 3, 5, 4, 1
1	0	0	15	6, 7, 8, 10, 9, 6
2	10	0	15	5, 10, 9, 4, 5
3	10	10	15	5, 10, 8, 3, 5
4	0	10	15	2, 7, 8, 3, 2
5	5	15	15	6, 1, 4, 9, 6
6	0	0	0	
7	10	0	0	
8	10	10	0	
9	0	10	0	
10	5	15	0	

7-9. This drawing depicts the side and front views of a house. Each point is assigned a number common to both views; this number is not a spatial coordinate but an identifying number. Many points in each elevation actually represent two points (one in front and one behind) and therefore have two identification numbers associated with them. The three-dimensional coordinates of each point are determined by merging an X, Y coordinate from the left drawing and a Y, Z coordinate from the right drawing. The list of points and the spatial coordinates are shown in the point list, and a separate connect list defines the boundaries of each polygon in the structure.

7-10. Three-dimensional reconstruction using two-view photogrammetry. A grid is drawn or projected onto a three-dimensional object, which is in turn photographed using two cameras (see fig. 6-33). The camera positions and focal lengths are known. Each point in both photographed grids is assigned a number and then separately digitized. The two sets of points are mathematically merged creating a three-dimensional data base.

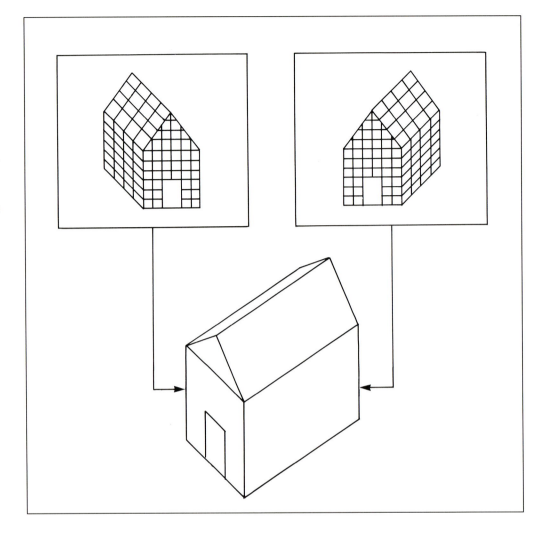

7-11. Orthogonal and polar zels are matrices of depth values. In the orthogonal case (A), they are the distances from a plane in space to the surface of an object behind it. In the polar case (B), they are a matrix of radial distances, for example, from the center of a cylinder to a point on it.

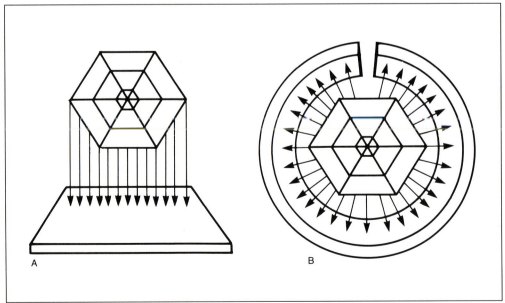

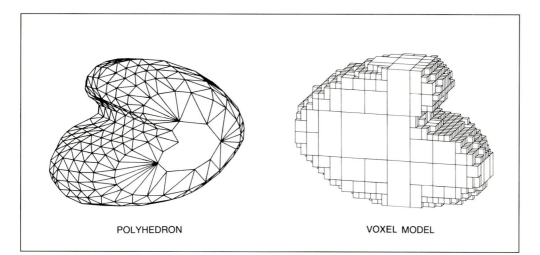

POLYHEDRON

VOXEL MODEL

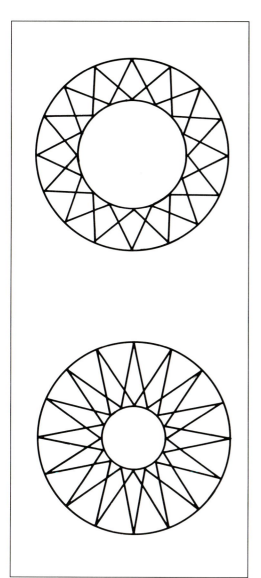

```
10    REM    KR.CIRCLE
20    REM    DRAWS CIRCLE USING
             ANGULAR INCREMENTS
30    CX = 140:CY = 96
40    TH = 0
50    DTH = 6.2832 / 40
60    DIM SX(40),SY(40)
70    RADIUS = 90
80    FOR I = 1 TO 40
90    X = RADIUS * COS (TH)
100   Y = RADIUS * SIN (TH)
110   SX(I) = X + CX
120   SY(I) = Y + CY
130   TH = DTH * I
140   NEXT I
150   HGR2 : HCOLOR= 3:PEN = 0
160   FOR I = 1 TO 40
170   IF PEN = 1 THEN GOTO 190
180   HPLOT SX(I),SY(I):PEN = 1
190   HPLOT  TO SX(I),SY(I)
200   NEXT I
210   END
```

7-14. Procedurally defined objects also include complicated models such as the eye and the iris. A single parameter controls the opening and closing of the iris, and the procedure might be called by typing "EYE .5," where the argument is the percentage of the opening of the iris.

7-13. In a computer graphics system, procedures are invoked by calling them by name. Arguments for a circle include the number of sides, the X and Y coordinates for the center, and the radius. The command might be: "90 Circle 140 96 40."

7-15. Statistical distribution. Random points on a plane.

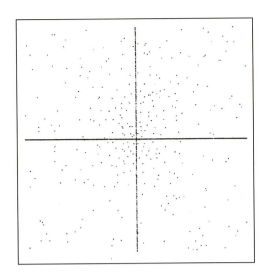

7-16. Particle systems were used to make this fire in "Star Trek II: The Wrath of Khan." (© 1982 by Paramount Pictures Corporation. All rights reserved. Courtesy of Lucas Film Ltd. and Paramount Pictures Corp.)

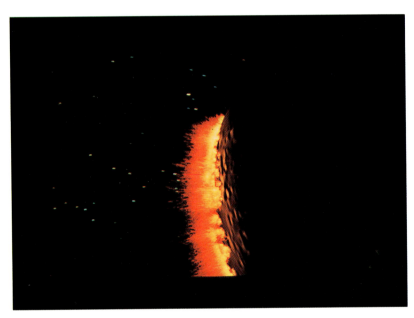

 RELATED READING

Cundy, H. Martyn, and A. P. Rollett. *Mathematical Models.* 2d ed. London: Oxford University Press, 1961.

Hildebrandt, Stefan, and Anthony Tromba. *Mathematics and Optimal Form.* New York: W. H. Freeman, 1984.

Lalvani, Haresh. *Transpolyhedra.* New York: Red Ink Productions, 1977.

Pearce, Peter. *Structure in Nature as a Strategy for Design.* Cambridge, MA: MIT Press, 1978.

Thompson, D'Arcy. *On Growth and Form.* London: Cambridge University Press, 1971.

Wenninger, Magnus J. *Polyhedron Models.* London: Cambridge University Press, 1971.

umes, flowing surfaces, statistical distributions of points (fig. 7-15), and even ***particle systems*** that are used to represent fireworks, explosions, or dust (fig. 7-16). ***Fractal*** procedures involve not only geometric parameters like position, length, width, height, and radius, but random parameters, like the density of points, their standard deviation, or the minimum and maximum boundary by which the points are constrained.

Fractals provide an alternative to constructing objects from geometric shapes and are primarily used in modeling natural and organic objects such as clouds, mountains, rivers, and coastlines (fig. 7-17). Fractals that simulate nature recursively divide the initial structure into increasingly smaller detail.

Surface Patches

Parametric surface patches also describe three-dimensional objects. These objects are created with a limited number of control points that define the shape and curve of the surface (fig. 7-18) and determine the remaining points computationally. The advantage of patches is that large, continuously curving surfaces can be defined and controlled with very few points. Patches are widely used in applications such as automobile and aircraft design as well as in sculpture that involves complex surfaces.

SET CONSTRUCTION: COMBINATORIAL GEOMETRY

Union Operators

Chapter 6 inventoried a collection of matting operations between pictures— logical operators like AND or OR that specify how images are combined (see fig. 6-21). This same concept can be used three dimensionally on solid models. In three-dimensional space, these logical combinations are called ***union operators*** and combine two volumetric shapes to form a new shape (fig. 7-19).

This is easiest to conceptualize if the three-dimensional objects are made up of

voxels and are compared voxel by voxel, using logical operators. Unions not only provide a way to aggregate primitive objects into more complicated ones, but also subtract parts from the whole.

Clipping and Capping

Clipping is a process that slices an object into two parts as if cut with a knife. A fundamental tool for objects in three-dimensional space, clipping is used to eliminate objects that are outside the field of view as well as to chop objects into pieces (fig. 7-20).

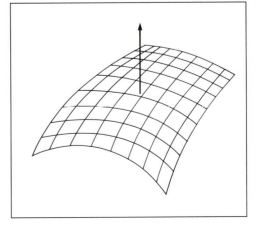

7-17. Fractal mountains. (Courtesy of Boeing Aerospace.)

7-18. Parametric surfaces are formed first by defining control points and then by calculating the intermediate points using these parameters. The result is often a mesh of polygons.

7-19. The union of a cube and a sphere, where the sphere has a diameter equal to the width of the cube and bisects its circumference. The OR union results in a volume that contains both the cube and the sphere. The logical AND union produces a resultant volume that is common to both volumes. The NOTAND operator produces the volume of the cube and the sphere that are not common, or shared. The NOTOR union eliminates everything. The sphere MINUS the cube produces a hemisphere, and the cube MINUS the sphere results in a box with a depression.

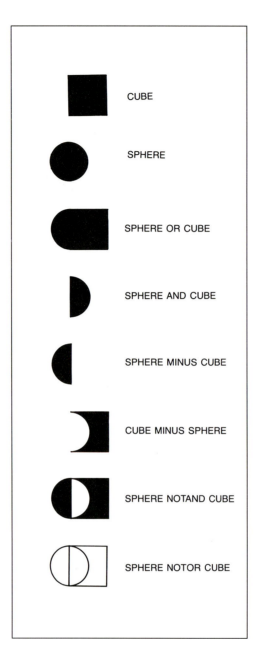

CUBE

SPHERE

SPHERE OR CUBE

SPHERE AND CUBE

SPHERE MINUS CUBE

CUBE MINUS SPHERE

SPHERE NOTAND CUBE

SPHERE NOTOR CUBE

Clipping defines a plane in space (essentially a giant rectangle) and then sorts the objects between the two sides of the plane. Where a line or edge crosses the clipped plane, the procedure calculates a new point at that location (fig. 7-21).

Capping is a process that defines new surfaces formed where a clipping plane truncates an object (fig. 7-22). This prevents an object from appearing hollow; capping constructs a new side so the polyhedron looks opaque or solid. Clipping is much like unions; clipping, however, involves an intersection between a plane and a volume, while unions involve the intersection of two volumes.

PRIMITIVE TRANSFORMATIONS

Geometric transformations are operations that move and position objects in either two- or three-dimensional spaces. Translate, size, rotate, and shear are four primitive computer graphics transformations.

These transformations describe the ways in which a rigid object can be manipulated in space. Primitive transformations can always be undone or combined to describe a single position that includes more than one primitive transformation, such as rotation and size.

Transformational functions use arguments to specify the magnitude of the transformation and store the result as data, much as an object is stored—positions and motions are entities just as objects are entities. Transformational data is independent of the data of the object being positioned. For example, a transformation specifies the *position* of an aircraft, but not any information as to what kind of aircraft is at that location.

Translation

Translation, or offsetting, is a transformation that moves an object left or right, up or down, or in or out in three-dimensional space. A translation of some combination of X, Y, and Z repositions an object anywhere in space by adding the amount of the displacement to each point in the object to be transformed (fig. 7-23).

An *identity translation,* a translation of 0, describes a situation in which an object is not to be moved. Positive number translations displace objects along the corresponding positive axis; in other words, right, up, or toward the viewer. Negative values move that object to the left, down, or away from the viewer.

Sizing

Sizing transformation either reduces or enlarges objects. By definition, sizing always occurs around the origin, which is one reason why objects tend to be defined with the origin at their center. Sizing transformations change the size of an object, multiplying their coordinates by the scaling factor(s) (fig. 7-24).

As in translation, there are three sizing transformations, one for X, Y, and Z, and it is not necessary to size an object equally in all three dimensions. Sizing a sphere in X and Y, but not Z, will create an ellipsoidal shape, for example. Sizing a letter in X, but not Y, will condense or expand it.

An *identity sizing* (leaving the size of an object unchanged) is a sizing of 1. Scaling factors greater than 1 enlarge the object; scaling factors between 0 and 1 reduce it. A sizing of 0 reduces the entire object to a point, and negative numbers flip the object into mirror image positions.

Sizing should not be confused with *zooming,* which changes the focal length of a lens and does not make an object larger or smaller. Nor should sizing be confused with *dollying,* which translates a camera closer to an object. Sizing, zooming, and dollying all affect the apparent size of an object on a screen, but only sizing affects its actual dimensions.

Rotation

A *rotation* specifies a pivoting, or angular, displacement about an axis. In two-dimensional computer graphics rotations only occur around the origin (fig. 7-25). An example of two-dimensional rotation

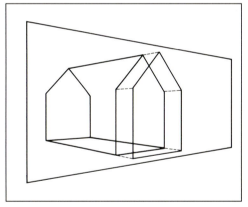

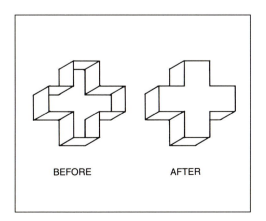

BEFORE   AFTER

7-20. The "3" has been clipped in X, Y, and Z to create smaller cubes, which are then translated away from the center. (Provided by Judson Rosebush.)

7-21. This clipping diagram shows how a single clipping plane intersects a three-dimensional house. The part of the house outside the field of vision is eliminated.

7-22. An extruded cross before and after capping.

7-23. Adding three horizontal units to a point located at 6, 5, 1 will translate that point to location 9, 5, 1. The displacement must be added to each and every point that describes a shape in order to translate a shape or a group of shapes.

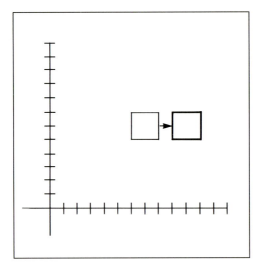

7-24. A letter T sized by a factor of two would become twice as large. But the same letter sized by two in the X dimension, and three in the Y dimension, will result in a larger letter with different proportions. In either case, each of the eight coordinates that describe the letter are multiplied by the scaling factor and result in a new set of coordinates.

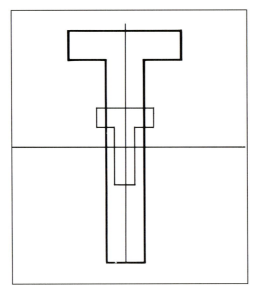

7-25. Two-dimensional rotation of 310 degrees about the origin.

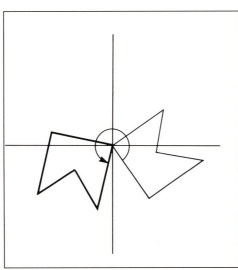

is the movement of the hands of a clock. In three-dimensional graphics there are three rotations, one each around the X, Y, and Z axes (fig. 7-26).

Objects are rotated by specifying an angle of rotation and using trigonometric functions to determine the new position. Rotation angles are usually expressed in degrees; but they can also be in other rotary measures, such as radians. These angles can be positive or negative; the identity rotation is 0 degrees (or any multiple of 360 degrees).

Rotations are said to be either *left-handed* or *right-handed,* specifying whether a positive angle rotates clockwise or counterclockwise. The handedness rule is based on the curl of fingers, on either hand, around into a fist with the thumb pointing out. The fingers curl in the direction of a positive angle rotation (fig. 7-27).

Remember that rotations, like sizings, always occur around an axis, and this is different from rotating a figure around its own center (fig. 7-28).

Shear

The ***shear transformation*** displaces points relative to the origin. Shear is similar to italicization and can work forward or backward (fig. 7-29). A shear involves the displacement of two axes against a third, and although there is only one way to shear in two-dimensional graphics, there are six different ways to shear in three-dimensional space.

Inverse Transformation

All primitive transformations can be ***inverted,*** for example, the inverse of a 10-degree positive rotation is a 10-degree negative transformation, and inversion is a common command in three-dimensional systems (fig. 7-30). Inverting a transformation is simple, as it is not necessary to know how the transformation was made, but only to have the transformation as data, in order to invert it.

Concatenation of Transformations

The four primitive, singular transformations, position, size, rotate, and shear, are not only methods for representing single positions, but can be combined, or **concatenated,** to specify a position that incorporates a sequence of two or more individual, primitive transformations (fig. 7-31). The sequence of transformations affects the result. Rotations and sizings are especially sensitive to sequence, because they occur around an axis (fig. 7-32). The proper sequence of transformations can only be achieved after the location of the origin is identified, without confusing it with the center of the object.

Transformations can be concatenated ad infinitum and result in a single transformation. Often functions exist or can be written that describe complex transformations yet only require simple arguments. For example, a command ZCENTEROTAT with arguments XPOS, YPOS, and ANGLE might describe a rotation about an arbitrary

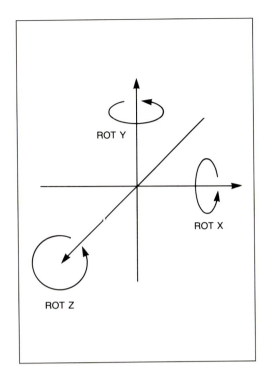

7-26. Right-handed rotations in three-dimensional graphics.

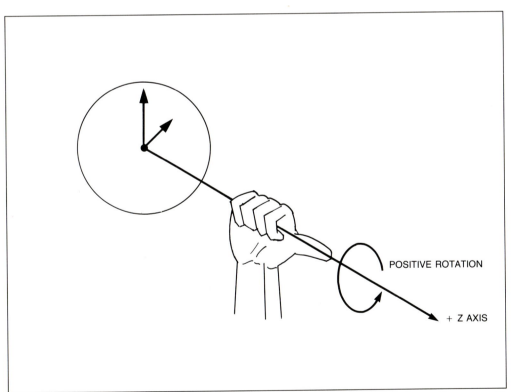

7-27. Left-handed rotations specify a positive angle rotation that goes clockwise when viewed from the positive axes. On the clock illustrated, the X axis is right, Y up, and Z toward you. If you curled the fingers of your left hand around the Z axis, your thumb will point toward you, in the positive Z direction, and your fingers would curl clockwise. Positive Z angle rotations would make the clock go forward in time. With a right-handed system, positive angles would go counterclockwise, and negative rotation angles would have to be used to make time go forward.

7-28. Rotation and size occur around an origin. A Z rotation of a rectangle (A) pivots the rectangle around the origin, not its own center. A rotation around its own center is accomplished first by translating the center of the rectangle to the origin (B). The rectangle is then rotated (C) and translated back to its original position (D).

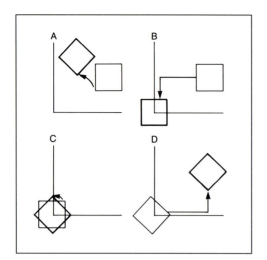

7-29. Identity shears have a value of 0. Positive number shears make objects lean forward, in the positive direction. Negative number shears make objects lean backward, like backward-slanting letters. Shears are sometimes used in animation to "race" type into a scene horizontally, and as the type comes to a rest, it relaxes, shears backward, and then returns to normal.

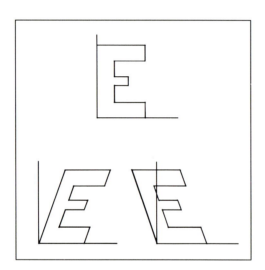

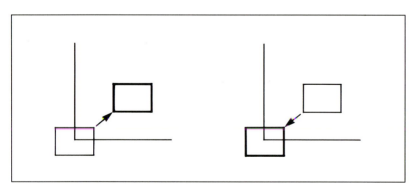

7-30. The drawing on the left shows the translation of a rectangle from its initial position at the origin to a new location. The second drawing shows an inverse transformation, the translation of a new rectangle located at 4, 3, 0 back to the origin.

point. In this case, three transformations are combined—a translation from XPOS, YPOS to the origin, the rotation of ANGLE degrees, and the translation back.

Many applications require that a single object be repeated in many positions. This is accomplished with a technique called *instancing,* which uses a model object only, but defines a series of transformations that represent all the positions. Examples of instancing include multiple columns on a building, the location of houses in a subdivision, the position of trees in a forest, and textile pattern repeats (fig. 7-33).

Transformations may also represent serial events or *animation,* a pathway of motion or a sequence of positions across time, like the position of hands on a clock, a turning water wheel, or a falling rock. Transformations merely specify the position and do not specify what is at the position.

PERSPECTIVE, WINDOWS, AND PORTS

Perspective is a technique for representing three-dimensional environments on two-dimensional surfaces, such as the surface of a monitor or a sheet of paper. Perspective is related to point of view and to a window, or frame. Together these function like an eye or camera. Computer graphics can model many kinds of perspective, but this discussion will center on the single-vanishing-point perspective evolved during the Renaissance.

The Point of View and the Window

The *point of view (POV)* is the position in space from which a three-dimensional environment is viewed. It is defined by an XYZ point analogous to the location of a camera or an eye. The viewing point is the location at which all perspective lines converge.

Along with the **POV** is the *aim point,* which is the point that the camera or eye is looking toward. The **aim point** lies on the *window,* a rectangular image plane perpendicular to the viewing point and located between it and the viewing envi-

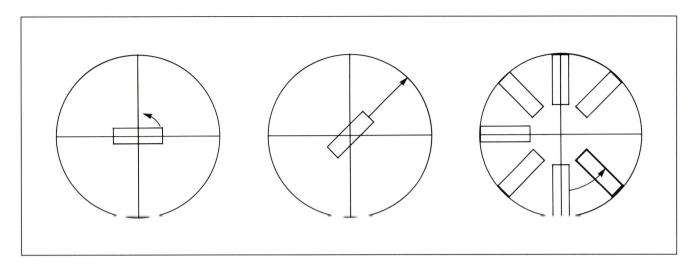

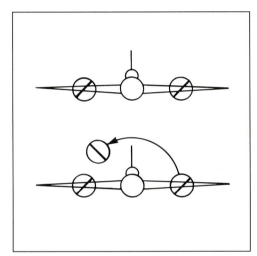

7-32. This figure shows a propeller, centered at the origin and translated to an engine shaft on a wing. If the propeller is rotated and then translated, the result is a spinning propeller sitting on the engine. But should the translation precede the rotation, then the propeller would orbit around a central axis of the aircraft.

7-31. Concatenated transformations involve a sequence of transformations: a paddle on a water wheel is positioned using two successive transformations, one that rotates the paddle, and a second that translates the paddle onto the circumference of the wheel.

—

7-33. Instancing a single object, in this case a column, repeatedly translates it to create a pattern.

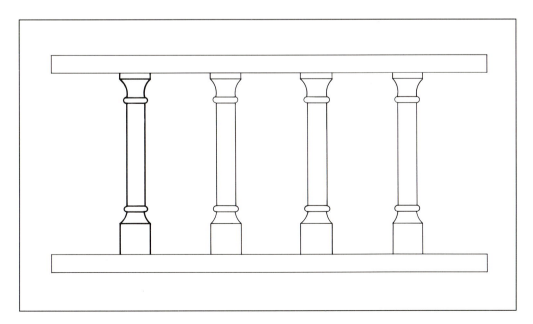

Descargues, Pierre. *Perspective.* New York: Van Nostrand Reinhold, 1982.

Dubery, Fred, and John W. Illatz. *Perspective and Other Drawing Systems.* London: Herbert Press, 1983.

Lipton, Lenny. *Foundations of the Stereoscopic Cinema.* New York: Van Nostrand Reinhold, 1982.

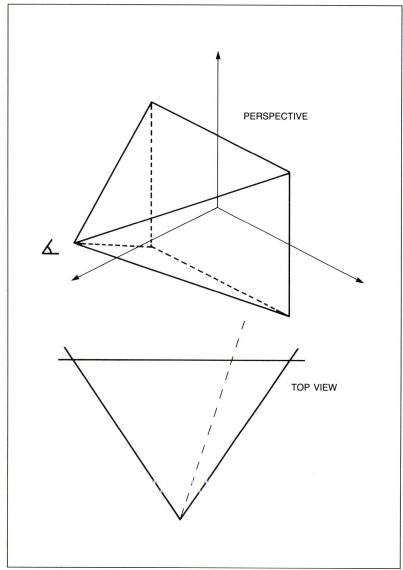

PERSPECTIVE

TOP VIEW

7-34. A three-dimensional environment can be viewed from a point of view, located anywhere in space, through a window connected to the point of view by a viewing pyramid (the pyramid of vision), which defines an expanding field of view. Rays drawn between a point in the environment and the point of view intersect the window, or image plane, and form a perspective projection of the environment.

ronment (fig. 7-34). The window is analogous to the film in a camera or the retina of an eye, except it is located in front of the POV instead of behind it.

A perspective view is created by projecting each point of an object onto the window by drawing a ray between the point and the POV, and determining where that ray intersects the window. Thus the points in the object coordinate system are transformed to the window coordinate system. A *lens* is the aggregation of a window and POV, and the *focal length* of the lens is the distance between the window and the POV. For a normal lens, the distance between the POV and the window is equal to the diagonal of the window. A POV that is close to the window functions like a wide-angle lens, and a POV that is far away functions like a telephoto lens.

As the POV pulls away from the window, the perspective gets flatter. When the POV is at infinity, points orthogonally project, that is, the XY location of a point in the window is the same as the XY location in the environment—the depth (or Z value) is not represented (fig. 7-35).

Distortions that accompany increasingly wide-angle glass lenses, such as curved lines, or barrelhousing, and fish eye, do not occur in computerized perspective, although these effects can be created. Many other kinds of perspective, including isometrics, sphericals, anamorphics, and even the unreal imaginings of M. C. Escher, or the formal but pre-Renaissance perspective of Pompeii, can be generated with computer graphics.

A *zoom* is a change in the focal length of the lens during a shot. Pivoting the POV is akin to a *pan;* and translating the POV during a shot is called a *dolly.* The window, like the eye, may be moved; it may also be scaled bigger or smaller so that the imaginary computer camera can look at things on an atomic or interplanetary scale. One can even tip a window to reduce keystoning, the apparent distortion of parallel lines.

The point of view is connected to the four sides of the window to form a perspective pyramid. All the objects that are

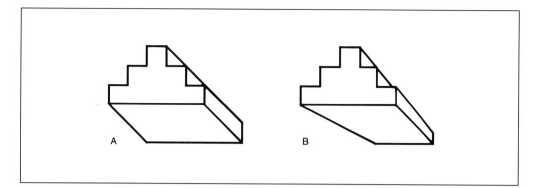

7-35. Orthogonal and vanishing-point perspectives create different images and have different purposes. Orthogonal perspectives are used in blueprints (A); vanishing-point perspectives are used to create the illusion of depth (B).

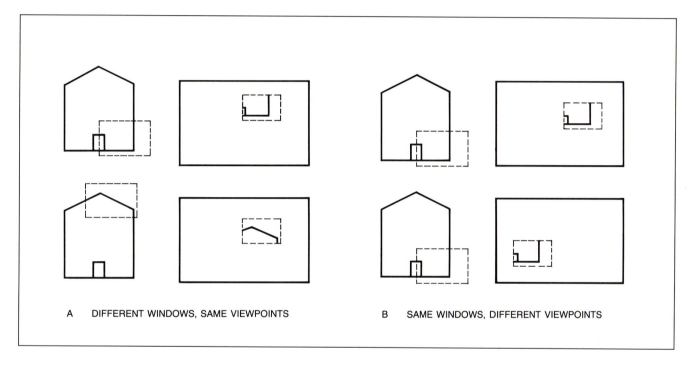

A   DIFFERENT WINDOWS, SAME VIEWPOINTS   B   SAME WINDOWS, DIFFERENT VIEWPOINTS

outside this pyramid are clipped and excluded from the final image.

Windows and Ports

A window corresponds to what we see on a screen; but a window and screen usually have different coordinate systems. The coordinate system of the window is related to the size of the data; the coordinate system of a screen is described by hardware. It is thus necessary to scale the image window into the address space of the device itself (fig. 7-36).

A *port,* usually rectangular, is that part of the display screen where the window is presented. A port may be the full resolution of the display; thus, a port on a

frame buffer might be 0, 640 in X and 0, 480 in Y. Or, a port may be smaller than the total area of the display. In a newspaper, for example, the full port is the total area of the newspaper with smaller ports used to display pictures. A traditional window-to-port conversion is done by cropping a photograph and scaling it. The activity is no different in computers—the crop is the window and the scaling is the ratio between the width of the window and the width of the port.

The three window-to-port conversion methods are illustrated in figure 7-37. Remember that the computer is an elastic machine, and that a window and its port need not have the same aspect ratio. Ports

7-36. A window exists in the coordinate system of the environment and its units of measurement are changeable. A port exists in the coordinate system of the display and its units of measurement are defined by the hardware. Windows and ports together provide a way to represent environments of arbitrary scale on displays of arbitrary resolution by freeing the mechanics of the virtual environment from the mechanics of the display.

are a fundamental element in the graphic arts, and figure 7-38 lists some of their variables.

Stereopsis

Stereopsis, the dimensional perception provided by two different views of the same scene—such as the two eyes of a human being—can be simulated in computer graphics by calculating two slightly different views of the same scene. The two are then independently viewed by each eye using a simple viewer or with crosseyes (fig. 7-39).

7-37. There are three ways to map windows into ports when the aspect ratios are different. The first solution is simply to stretch the window to fit the port (on both axes) and is used in situations where pixels on the port are not square—in Cinemascope with its squeezed aspect ratio, for instance. The second solution fits the window into the port, and the third fits the port into the window.

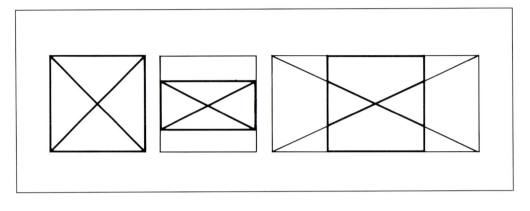

7-38. Variables associated with a port.

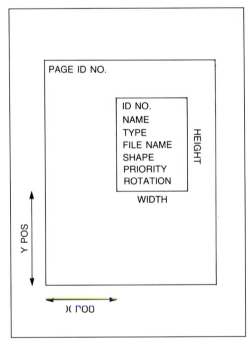

Variable	Description
IDno.	This is a number identifying a particular port.
PageIDno.	This is the number of the page the port is on.
Name	Any name used to identify the port; it need not be unique.
Type	Kind of port: text or pictures.
Xposition	X position of the center of the port.
Yposition	Y position of the center of the port.
Width	X size of the port.
Height	Y size of the port.
Filename	File name referring to the data that goes into the port. In other words, the contents of the data.
Shape	Rectangle, circle, other (most ports are rectangular).
Priority	Closeness of port to viewer. Ports closer to viewer obscure ports further away.
Rotation	Angle of port to frame. Default is zero.

ACTORS AND ACTIONS

Computer animation is the representation and display of objects and movement across time, using a rapid sequence of individual frames. Animation is a fundamental part of computer graphics, because it captures motion and thus enhances our perception and understanding of images. Animation is a sequence of pictures in which at least one parameter is changed each frame. The variable of time is controlled in animation and can be used to represent not only time but other variables as well, such as pressure, tension, or affection. Animation extends the range of visual artists and enables them to evoke emotions, communicate ideas, and tell stories.

Traditional visual language includes scripting notations to manipulate animation and lay out optical effects. Computer graphics animation languages use a special vocabulary to specify when actions begin and end, their duration, and rates of change.

Action refers to all kinds of motion—of objects in space, changes in their shape, changes in camera position, changes in lighting, and special effects.

Many aspects of computer graphics involve action. Objects can move, size, rotate, deform, and shear over time. Patterns on surfaces may themselves be in motion. The camera may change position (dolly), rotate (pan), or change its focal length (zoom). Lights, too, may pan across a scene, fade up and down, and change color.

An action is usually thought of as a singular change over a sequence of frames and conceptualized with one or a few degrees of freedom. Creativity in computer animation, however, often involves a search for new actions, that is, new parameters that can be controlled. If it varies, move it; if it does not vary, find out how to vary it.

Rates of Change: Eases

Action seldom occurs in equal increments. Usually it begins in small increments that become larger as the object approaches a cruising speed, then become smaller again as the object slows down to a stop (fig. 7-40). An example of this is an ordinary automobile accelerating to a speed, cruising, then braking to a stop.

In computer graphics accelerations and deaccelerations are modeled using ***eases,*** or ***farings,*** which calculate rates of change. Eases are used in all animation—hand-drawn, motion graphics, and computer-generated.

Eases are used to control the movement of objects, cameras, zooms, colors and lights, and special effects. Fades and dissolves require eases, as do curves that change their slope. Eases are designed using different mathematical formulas, including linear acceleration and deacceleration (the simplest), sine waves, and logarithmic progressions. The parameters

7-39. Two views calculated from two different positions and viewed with two eyes (normal binocular vision) create a sense of depth for the viewer. (Provided by Judson Rosebush.)

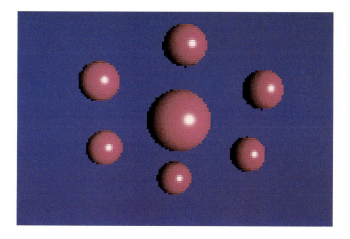
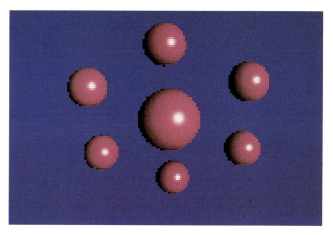

7-40. This ease illustrates linear acceleration or deceleration. A command such as "17 EASE .3 .2" produced the ease in this drawing. It is 17 frames long, accelerates for 30 percent of the time, and decelerates for 20 percent of the time. The drawing shows an object moving from bottom to top, with time plotted on the horizontal axis. The initial increments of distance are small, but increase from frame to frame until the motion consists of a constant velocity; the increments are equal here. Finally, as the object slows to a stop, each increment of distance gets progressively smaller.

7-41. A compound ease is defined first by selecting points at specific space/time intervals (X, Y coordinates in the graph) and then fitting a curve through the points.

7-42. The number two illustrates the motion pathway of an object. The pathway is defined so the length, or number of frames, can vary.

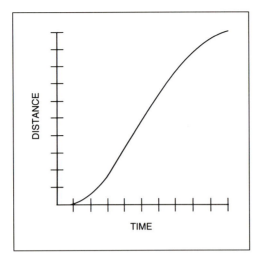

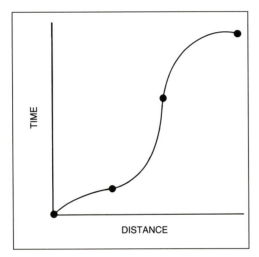

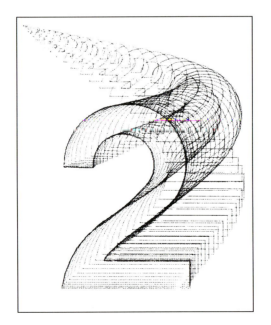

of an ease include the length of time the ease should accelerate and deaccelerate. Compound eases specify motions consisting of a series of changes in speed, which often have constraints, say, that require an object to be at certain places at certain times (fig. 7-41).

Action Using Transformations

Action is produced by defining a *motion pathway,* a series of transformations that define the successive positions of an object. Motion pathways are usually defined by functions and this data is independent of the data that describes the traveling object (fig. 7-42).

A single motion pathway is an example of a *global action,* an action that is applied to an entire object or group of objects. A *local action* applies only to a component of the object (fig. 7-43).

Global and local actions are accomplished by organizing the individual actions in a hierarchical tree, which is similar to the way objects are stored. Global and local actions are assembled by concatenating a series of individual transformations. Complex figures, for example, a robot character, or actor, might use a *hierarchical tree* of articulated local transformations propagating throughout its joints (fig. 7-44). A complex character often requires many simultaneous arguments, or parameters, to specify actions. There is at least one parameter for every joint in the actor. A *parameter table,* a matrix that contains one column for each parameter and one row for each position of the joints in the body, defines these parameters.

In animation, a sequence of static positions is defined, either by filling in the parameter table or interactively manipulating the figure. More sophisticated systems permit an animator to simply refer to the static position by name, just as a choreographer would score a ballet. Then, the length of each *gesture,* or move from one static position to another, is specified. After this is completed, the computer animates each gesture by positioning all the joints to the parameters specified in the first static position; it then eases those parameters to the final static position in a specified number of frames.

Cycles are often designed to incorporate the entire tree of transformations and are controlled using a single parameter. Consider animating an automobile engine, a complicated but predictable collection of pistons and rods connected to a crankshaft (fig. 7-45). The action is controlled by specifying an angle for the crankshaft and letting the computer determine the positions of all the parts of the engine. The engine is not defined for a finite number of positions; it is procedurally defined for any position, or angle, specified by the argument.

Animating the engine is therefore a process, invoking a function with a series of arguments that specify the **phase,** or rotary angle, of the engine. In animation terms, the action is being absolutely drawn, as if it were responding to the turn of a crank. By changing the sequence of arguments the animation can make the engine run faster, slower, or even backward. Accelerations and deaccelerations are accomplished with easing applied to the rotary angle.

Simulation

Simulation is a way of producing animation by copying the physical laws that actually affect objects, as opposed to positioning objects where they are supposed to be. For example, the cycling automobile engine described above is not a simulation. The procedure does model the motion of the engine, but it does so by declaring

7-43. A global action makes an airplane loop, spin, and bank. A local action applies only to parts of the airplane, for example, spinning propeller blades or a rotating rudder. The global transformation of the airplane flying loops effects local transformations—so the propellers continue to spin on their shafts as the airplane twists and turns.

7-44. The two-dimensional robot has an origin in its chest and an arm with an articulated shoulder, elbow, and wrist. Each of these joints is rotated to move the arm. Whereas a global transformation might apply to the entire body, increasing local actions applied to the shoulder would affect the movement of the elbow, which in turn would concatenate to the wrist. (After all, a shoulder pivots everything below it.) Also shown is the parameter table used to describe the robot, which shows frame numbers and the corresponding angles for key positions of each of the three joints. A computer program will evaluate the table, construct the appropiate transformations, and calculate intermediate frames.

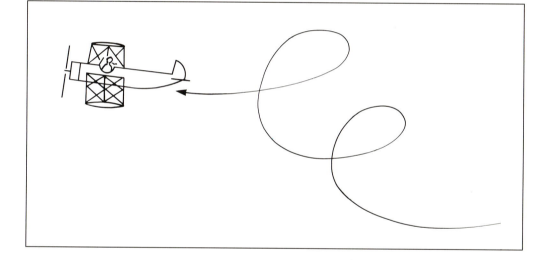

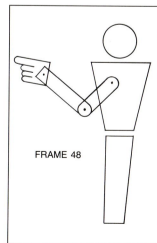

FRAME 48

Frame Number	Shoulder Angle	Elbow Angle	Wrist Angle
1	0	0	0
48	45	40	−10
72	90	0	0
100	90	30	10
120	0	0	0

where it is to be positioned.

An engine simulation would consider the physics of engine operation: it would calculate the rate of exploding gas in the top of the cylinder, the resistance of the piston and the connecting rod, and determine how far down the piston gets pushed, then draw it. The position of the piston is calculated this way for each successive discrete frame in time, creating animation.

Parameter-controlled actions, like cranking the automobile engine, require no history. The sequence of frames can be calculated in any order, as successive frames are not dependent on previous frames but on the argument alone. A simulation, however, is a scientific experiment, and is incrementally solved. A simulation of an automobile engine must solve the position for frame one before it can begin to solve the position for frame two. Indeed, to get to an advanced state like frame one

hundred, it is necessary to calculate all ninety-nine prior frames. Each successive frame is dependent on the calculation of the previous frame (fig. 7-46).

Simulation is used when it is necessary to evaluate the circumstances in order to determine the result, rather than simply drawing the result. (Simulation is discussed in more detail in chapters 9 and 10.)

Deformations

Another way of creating action is to deform the basic objects, whether they are two- or three-dimensional. Deformations are not changes that result from sizing or rotating an object, where shapes maintain their rigid body character. Deformations are changes in the geometry of the object.

The simplest method of deforming an object is to **in-between,** or create a series of transitional stages between two static positions (fig. 7-47). The in-betweens, or the sequence of intermediate shapes, are

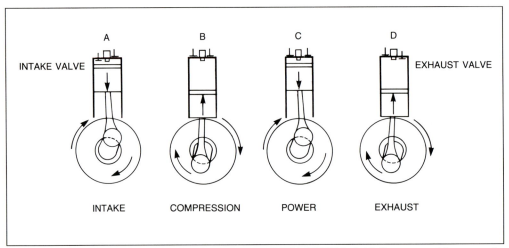

7-45. A single parameter often controls the action of many connected parts—here, a simple engine is controlled by the rotary angle of its crankshaft. The rate of change of this parameter controls the speed at which the engine turns. For example, if the engine were running at 10 rpm (3,600 degrees per minute) and the animation consisted of 24 frames per second (1,440 frames per minute), then the engine would advance 2.5 degrees per frame (3,600 ÷ 1,440). The animation would be performed by calling the function once for each frame, with a sequence of arguments: 0, 2.5, 5, 7.5, 10, 12.5 . . . degrees. The program might look like this, with function ENGINE taking a single argument

ANGLE. ANGLE is initially zero, and increases in increments of 2.5 per frame:

```
ANGLE ← 0

BEGIN 1440

    DRAW ENGINE ANGLE

    ANGLE ← ANGLE + 2.5

    FRAMEADVANCE

END
```

all generated from the given beginning and final static positions; these are also called **key positions** or **extremes.**

At its most basic, in-betweening migrates each point in the initial object, the first extreme, to its corresponding point in the final object, the second extreme. The two extremes are designed to contain the same number of points. **Interpolation** is the method of calculating any number of new values between two existing values (fig. 7-48). The new, interpolated points are used to define intermediary objects.

Whether computerized in-betweening can substitute for hand-drawn in-betweening in cell animation is subject to debate. Cartoon characters may involve a level of creativity that cannot be equaled by a simple interpolation between the two extreme positions.

In-betweening can be performed on three-dimensional objects too; the effect is one volumetric shape metamorphosing into another (fig. 7-49).

Deformations can be performed on geometric shapes or objects that are procedurally defined, such as fractals and surface patches. Curves or surfaces are also controlled with tension points, much as a suspension cable on a bridge is supported at only two points. By manipulating the control point alone, the graphic artist can modify the entire curve, surface, or a large three-dimensional structure (fig. 7-50).

Another type of deformation especially related to animation involves **stretch** and **squash,** the elongation of objects that are gaining velocity and the foreshortening of objects that are losing velocity (fig. 7-51). These are much like **motion blur,** which tends to elongate an object on a frame in the direction of its action. Stretch and squash also give an object the appearance of weight: the object stretches against gravity and squashes to a stop when moving with gravity. These movements do not necessarily follow physical laws; they are often done for artistic graphic effects, which should above all look good and seem correct.

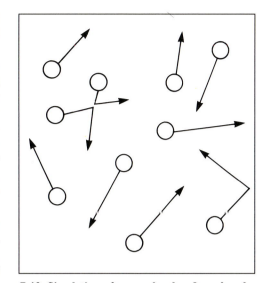

7-46. Simulation of gas molecules. In a closed room, each molecule in a simulation has a location, a direction in which it is moving, and a speed. For each frame of the simulation, the computer advances the molecule the distance in space along the direction of its motion. It then tests to see if any molecule has collided with any other molecule or if any molecule has collided with the exterior. When two molecules collide, they ricochet away from each other like two Ping-Pong balls hitting in space, and the simulation program calculates a new direction vector and speed for each. Should a molecule hit the wall, it will bounce off in a new direction. The gas pressure in the room is the number of molecules that hit the wall each second, and this simulation determines how the pressure changes when the temperature is increased and the molecules move faster.

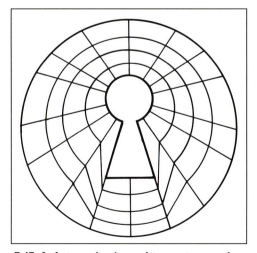

7-47. In-betweening is used to create smooth transitions between two extreme or key positions. Here, a key-hole shape becomes a circle.

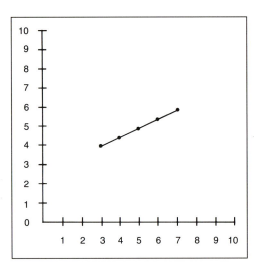

7-48. Positions, scalings, rotations, color values, and even normals can be interpolated. One merely supplies initial and terminal values and a frame count. The intermediary values, which the computer calculates, are equally spaced

between the initial and terminal positions; the number of values plus the beginning and end points equals the number of iterations. The illustration shows a five-step interpolation between an initial position of (3, 4) and a final position of (7, 6). The interpolated positions can be described with a table:

3, 4

4, 4.5

5, 5

6, 5.5

7, 6

The interpolation is calculated by subtracting the initial position from the final position, thus creating a value that is equal to the total displacement. In this case, it would be 7, 6 − 3, 4 = 4, 2. Each increment of the displacement is equal to the displacement divided by one less than the count, here 4 (5 − 1). Thus the incremental displacement per frame is equal to 4, 2 ÷ (5 − 1) = 1, .5. This incremental value is then successively added into the original position value to create the sequence of interpolated positions in the table above.

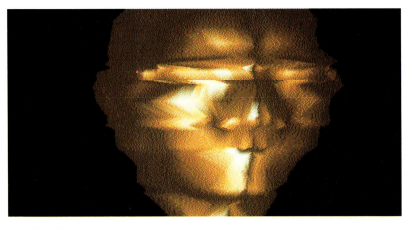

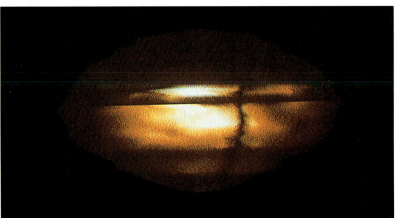

7-49. Three-dimensional objects as well as two-dimensional shapes can be interpolated to produce extremely innovative computer graphics. This face moves as a result of three-dimensional interpolation. (Courtesy of Nathalie Lambert.)

SURFACE ATTRIBUTES

Three-dimensional computer graphics deals not only with the geometry of objects, their position and size, but also with the properties of their surface. Indeed, the description and treatment of the surface of an object is at least as complicated as the geometric description of the object itself.

Surface attributes include color, transparency, pattern, and a host of properties that determine how the surface reflects light. All of these properties are simulated in advanced three-dimensional computer graphics.

Color

The color of a surface is usually represented as a red, green, and blue triplet (RGB), but can also be described with subtractive primaries, cyan, yellow, and magenta. Colors are often represented as real numbers between zero and one, rather than as integers, allowing for greater resolution and a constant system. Low-resolution systems are more limited in three-dimensional graphics where a full range of continuously varying colors is essential for *chiaroscuro,* pictorial representations of light and shade (see chapter 5 for an extensive treatment of color).

Luminescence

Luminescence is the amount of light a surface emits, without reflecting light from an outside source. In other words, if you were to look at a surface in a totally dark room, the luminescence would be the color that glows. The luminescence property of a surface is usually not considered a light source; it is used with lighting to ensure that certain surfaces of objects will not get too dark. In situations where lighting is not used luminescence is the same as color, and, like color, it is an RGB triplet with a range from zero to one.

Transparency and Filters

Transparency describes the amount of light that passes through a surface. A transparent surface transmits light without appreciable scattering, so that surfaces behind it are partially visible (fig. 7-52). Transparency is expressed as a real value between zero and one. A transparency value of zero describes an opaque surface. A surface with a transparency value of one is fully transparent and therefore invisible.

Transparency is usually represented as an RGB triplet so that different colors can have different degrees of transparency, permitting the implementation of colored filters. Thus, while a value of 0, 0, 0 indicates that the surface is completely opaque, a value of 0.7, 0.7, 0.5 indicates that red and green are 70 percent transparent, but blue is 50 percent transparent.

Transparent surfaces also have color, and the two attributes should not be confused. For example, a blue filter might have a *color* of 0, 0, 0 and a *transparency* of 0, 0, 0.5. A blue filter that was colored yellow might have a color of 1, 1, 0 and a transparency of 0, 0, 0.5. Again, there is a world of strange creative nooks here for anyone wishing to explore them.

Pattern and Image Mapping

Mapping takes an image, a two-dimensional bitplane memory, and treats it as if it were a surface in three-dimensional

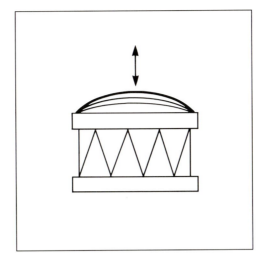

7-50. By raising or lowering the control point, the entire surface, here depicted as a line, moves up and down. Large three-dimensional structures can thus be deformed using only a few control parameters.

7-51. Motion seems real when moving objects acquire elasticity relative to the direction in which they are headed. This phenomenon, called *stretch* and *squash*, can be used to minimize temporal aliasing by simulating the shape and position of distortions that real objects undergo while accelerating and decelerating, as illustrated in this pencil test.

 RELATED READING

Blinn, J. F. "Simulation of Wrinkled Surfaces." *Computer Graphics* (August 1978): 286–92.

Carpenter, L., A. Fournier, and D. Fussell, "Fractal Surfaces." *Communications of the ACM*, 1981.

Crow, F. "Shadow Algorithms for Computer Graphics." *Computer Graphics* (Summer 1977): 242–47.

Gouraud, H. "Continuous Shading of Curved Surfaces." *IEEE Transactions on Computers* (June 1971): 623–28.

Phong, Bui-Tuong. "Illumination for Computer-Generated Pictures." *Communications of the ACM* (June 1975): 311–17.

Sutherland, I. E., R. F. Sproull, and R. A. Schumacker. "A Characterization of Ten Hidden-Surface Algorithms." *Computer Surveys* (March 1974): 1–55.

Whitted, T. "An Improved Illumination Model for Shaded Display." *Communications of the ACM* (June 1980): 343–49.

7-52. The extent to which an object is transparent depends on how much light can pass through it. Fully transparent objects transmit light, so bodies lying beyond them are visible. (Courtesy of Intelligent Light.)

7-53. Planar mapping pivots a bitmap image in three-dimensional space. (Courtesy of Digital Effects Inc.)

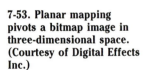

7-54. Curved mapping takes a two-dimensional bitmap image and wraps it onto a three-dimensional curved surface. (Image by Brian A. Barsky, Tony D. DeRose and Mark D. Dippé. Courtesy of University of California at Berkeley, Computer Graphics Lab.)

space. Images and patterns can be mapped onto surfaces with color, or onto transparent or reflective surfaces.

At its simplest, mapping places a flat image in perspective (fig. 7-53). More sophisticated methods wrap an image onto curved surfaces, much as a label is wrapped around a can (fig. 7-54). In the case of the can or cylinder, the image is not distorted, but an image mapped onto a sphere or parametric surface needs to be distorted or stretched to fit—much like a map of the earth, which needs to be distorted at the poles.

Mapping provides a way to define massive amounts of photographlike detail, such as a brick wall or water, without resorting to geometric objects. Rather than creating a data base for a brick wall, the graphic artist need only create a data base for an image of a brick wall and then map it onto a polygon.

Pixel images are not the only kinds of bitplane memory that can be mapped. Normals are mapped using a technique called bump mapping described in the texture section. A reflection map, which is a spherical projection of an environment around a point, is used to make objects seem reflective.

Luster

Luster is the property of a surface that determines how shiny it is. Shiny objects, like chrome, reflect sharp highlights and have high luster. Objects with low luster, like newsprint, are dull and scatter light (fig. 7-55).

Luster can be defined as a RGB triplet with a range from zero to one, allowing different lusters to be set for each primary. Lusters of zero have no specular reflection whatsoever; lusters of one are completely shiny like mirrors.

Texture

A *texture* is a flat representation of an uneven surface that is created by manipulating the reflection of light (fig. 7-56).

Texture mapping, like image mapping, does not alter the actual geometry of the surface. The texture, like an image, is defined by a two-dimensional bitmap matrix of values; but whereas the image-mapping matrix contains pixels with luminance values, the texture matrix contains elements with normals. The normals have subtle deviations that are either patterned or random and that microscopically recreate the way light is reflected, causing an object to look smooth or rough (fig. 7-57).

Texture is similar to shine or luster, but luster applies to the entire surface, whereas texture supplies a "grain" to the surface.

LIGHTS AND LIGHTING

Lighting is a subtle art and requires perception, technical skill, and sensitivity. Lighting in computer graphics is in many ways analogous to lighting for theater or film, and, like model building or action, is responsive to the touch of a creative artist.

A *light* is a source of illumination. Lights interact with a surface and determine the chiaroscuro, the amount of light that a surface reflects, as well as cast *shadows,* volumes of space where light has been removed. In computer graphics, lighting can be controlled using English language-like commands that specify the position of lights and their properties.

Properties of Lights

Lights have a number of properties. First,

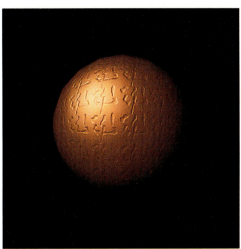

7-55. Luster refers to the reflecting qualities of a surface. ("Artist's Table" by Glenn Entis for Pacific Data Image, Inc.)

7-56. Bump mapping is a technique that creates surface texture, not by altering the geometric integrity of the object, but by wrapping a two-dimensional matrix of normals onto a surface. Texture can also be simulated by perturbing the normals of the objects in a random or constant fashion. (Courtesy of Digital Effects Inc.)

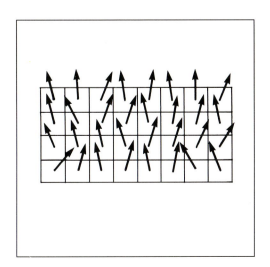

7-57. A bump map is a matrix of normals that can be randomly directed or follow a pattern. Surface normals represent the orientation of a surface, the direction the surface is pointing, and determine reflected light. When a bump map is wrapped onto a surface, the original surface normals are modified, which affects the lighting calculation, as the surface no longer uniformly reflects light. Bump maps will reflect light in many different directions and can therefore approximate the way light is microscopically reflected by materials such as cotton, silk, rayon, or linen.

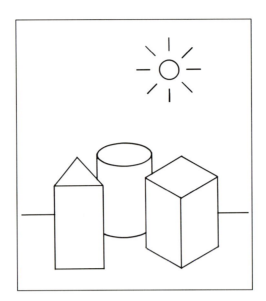

like objects they have **position,** an XYZ location in space. Lights may be located at infinity (like the sun) and behave like point sources, or they may be located outside or within the field of view. Second, the **brightness,** or quantity of light emitted, is expressed as an RBG triplet, usually on a scale of zero to one or infinity, which determines the color of light.

An **omnidirectional** light radiates equally in all directions (fig. 7-58). A **spotlight** radiates in a single direction, which is expressed as a normal (fig. 7-59). Spotlights can have a **fall-off** parameter, which controls the brightness of light relative to the axis of directionality. **Barn doors** may be used to control where light falls, and **cookies** cause the light to fall in patterns.

Reflection: Interaction of Lights and Surfaces

Reflection is the bouncing of light waves from a surface back to the environment and the POV. Light is not always modeled in computer graphics; when it is not, the color of a surface is the color recorded on the image. When lighting is employed, the reflective properties of the surface as well as the color of the lights determine the imaged surface color; this is the color of the light reflected to the camera lens.

Reflection calculations involve surface normals, because the normal specifies the directionality of a surface, and the amount of reflected light varies according to the relationship between the **angle of incidence**—the angle between the light source and the normal—and the **angle of view**—the angle between the normal and a camera or eye (fig. 7-60).

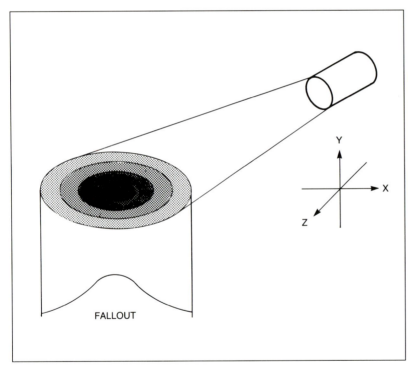

FALLOUT

**7-59. Spotlights are like
omnidirectional lights—
they have a position and
brightness—but they emit
light in one direction, specified by a normal. Spotlights can usually be
focused on an area or
flooded out, and their
brightness relative to their
normal can be defined.**

**7-60. The angle of incidence (LPN) is the angle
between a light source (L)
and the surface normal
(PN). The angle of reflection (NPR) is the angle
between the normal and a
perfectly reflected ray (R)
and is equal to the angle
of incidence.**

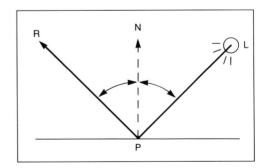

A **diffuse,** or matte, surface is one that reflects light randomly and evenly in all directions; the surface appears as a dull, flat color, like the felt on a pool table (fig. 7-61a). Diffuse reflection scatters light equally in all directions and depends solely on the angle of incidence; the smaller this angle, that is the more directly above the surface the light source is, the more light is reflected. Different surfaces reflect different percentages of light, but the diffuse reflection remains unaffected by the viewing angle.

Specular reflections are not uniformly distributed; they are concentrated around the **angle of reflection**—the angle between the surface normal and a perfectly reflected light ray. In the shiniest case the surface functions like a mirror. Specular reflections create highlights on an object;

the concentration of the highlight depends on the luster of the object. Objects with high luster reflect pinpoint highlights; objects with lower luster create more softened highlights (fig. 7-61b). Specular reflections tend to be the color of the lights; diffuse reflections are the color of the surface. Different surfaces have different amounts of specular reflection.

A lighting calculation involving both diffuse and specular reflection requires information about the color, luster, position of the surface, the proportions of diffuse and specular reflection, a point of view, and the position, color, and brightness of the light(s). These are then manipulated to simulate surfaces ranging from metals like gold and aluminum, to plastics, glass, paper, and paint (fig. 7-61c).

Surfaces with texture, or bumpmaps,

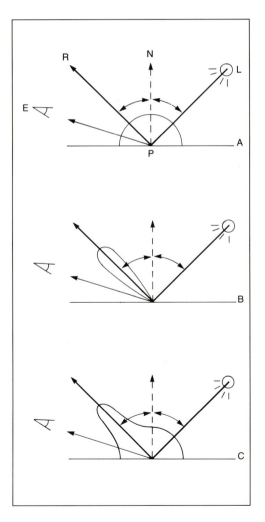

7-61. A matte or diffuse surface reflects light in all directions, signified by the hemisphere in the diagram (A). The amount of light reflected to an eye or camera is a function of the angle of incidence and has nothing to do with the location of the eye, since light is reflected in all directions. The amount of diffuse reflection is also called the coefficient of diffuse reflection and is essentially the radius of the hemisphere. Specular reflection (B) is the tendency of some surfaces to reflect light only in the direction of the angle of reflection. The specular light reflected to the eye is a function of both the angle of incidence as well as the location of the eye. In a perfectly reflecting surface, one with very high luster, the reflected light is concentrated only on the angle of reflection and the surface becomes a mirror. But surfaces with lower luster cause some spreading of light, as in this diagram with its teardroplike reflection. Luster adjusts the width of the teardrop, and the magnitude of the teardrop along the angle of reflection is controlled by the quantity of specular reflection, also called the coefficient of specular reflection. When diffuse and specular reflection are combined (C), the result is a composite curve. Changing the two coefficients alters the ratios between the hemisphere and teardrop shape and provides a way to mix varying amounts of diffuse and specular components. The relation between diffuse and specular reflection, the luster, and the amount of light reflected in red, green, and blue for each, provide important visual clues about the composition of objects.

are calculated in a similar way to surfaces with properties of diffuse and specular reflection. The reflection properties do not change, but the calculation uses the mapped normals instead of a single normal when calculating lighting, which gives the surface more life.

Shadows

Shadows, areas of an environment that are blocked from light by other objects, provide important depth cues and heighten realism. Multiple lights, of course, produce multiple shadows, which are automatically calculated by programs in most computer systems. Shadows in computer graphics may be hard edged, or they may have an umber or penumbra to them (fig. 7-62). Transparent surfaces cast shadows that are not completely black, and when

7-62. Shadows are cast by light sources onto other objects in the scene; multiple lights cast multiple shadows. (Courtesy of Raster Technologies, Inc.)

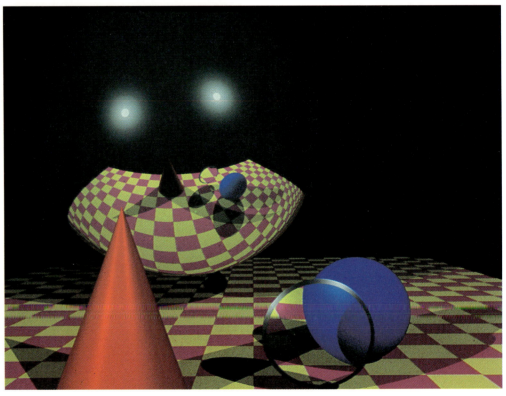

7-63. The refraction in this image was computed using a technique called *ray tracing.* (Courtesy of Intelligent Light and Todd Rodgers.)

superimposed create deeper, blacker shadows.

Images can be drawn with or without shadows. Specific lights in a scene may be designated to cast shadows just as some objects can be designated to cast shadows, depending on whether or not the goal in a particular application is realistic simulation. The designer creatively and imaginatively tells stories and communicates ideas either by simulating reality or by mixing the components of reality and surreality to create visually striking effects.

Refraction

Light not only interacts with surfaces but with volumes as well. One volumetric light property is **refraction,** which causes light to bend or change direction whenever it travels from one medium to another, for example, from air into glass into water. Refraction can be modeled in computer graphics as a single constant, the refractivity of the material (fig. 7-63), and is used to model curved surfaces such as lenses, crystal balls, and gem cuts.

Atmospherics and Translucency

Light is affected when it passes through volumes that contain air, glass, fog, and water; the changes it undergoes are sometimes called *atmospherics,* similar to what Leonardo da Vinci called aerial perspective.

The atmospheric effects that can be created in a computer include haze, fog, rain, clouds, and translucent substances that are not appropriately represented as opaque surfaces, such as quartz (fig. 7-64). Atmospherics often involve an un-

7-64. Atmospheric effects simulate the absorption of light as it passes through air, smoke, water. (Courtesy of the Mathematical Applications Group, Inc.)

RELATED READING

Born, Robert. *Designing for Television.* Tequesta, FL: Broadcast Designers' Association, 1983.

Ching, Francis D. K. *Space, Form and Order.* New York: Van Nostrand Reinhold, 1977.

Jankel, Annabel, and Rocky Morton. *Creative Computer Graphics.* Cambridge, England: Cambridge University Press, 1984.

Levitan, Eli. *Electronic Imaging Techniques.* New York: Van Nostrand Reinhold, 1977.

Wong, Wucius. *Principles of Three-Dimensional Design.* New York: Van Nostrand Reinhold, 1977.

even absorption of light, and a softening of edges, and produce effects such as depth in a landscape by graying areas that are farther away.

RENDERING

Rendering refers to the way objects are actually represented or drawn on a screen: is a cube drawn as a wire frame skeleton or as a solid object; do lights cast shadows; by what rules do lights and surfaces interact?

The rendering or viewing algorithm is fundamentally concerned not with what objects are but with how they are drawn. Rendering is a tool of the graphic artist, and, though renderings sometimes model our physical world, they often involve ad hoc procedures to improve visibility—how effectively pictures communicate.

Points

The most basic rendering involves drawing points, which can describe things inherently pointlike, such as atoms or stars (fig. 7-65), as well as surfaces, such as a rippling flag.

In addition to having alterable spatial positions, points can also have a variety of intensities, colors, and sizes.

Often, because of their small size and tendency to get lost in transmission, points are drawn with a surrounding glow that makes them seem larger.

Wire Frame or Line Rendering

The simplest way to represent an object is with lines (fig. 7-66). These ***wire frame,*** or vector graphic, displays are the most economical ways to display data and are the stock and trade of plotters and storage tubes.

Wire frame renderings may be monochromatic (black-and-white), colored, or even shaded. In addition to intensity and color, lines may have variable width and a dot or dashing pattern (fig. 7-67).

Because they show the backs as well as the fronts of objects, wire frame renderings are often difficult to comprehend

7-65. The stars in this universe have been created with point-rendering techniques and diffusion filters. (Courtesy of Digital Effects Inc.)

and make it hard to distinguish between objects that are closer and those that are farther away. One technique to improve visibility is **depth cueing,** which, with a simple calculation, draws lines that are farther away with a dot pattern, a darker value, or a narrower width (fig. 7-68). Depth cueing is also used to color elevations, like those found in contour maps (fig. 7-69).

Line does not necessarily bound and define surface; it can exist in very free forms and imply surface without actually enclosing an area (fig. 7-70).

Occultation

Often, especially when lines are being used to represent the outlines of volumes, it is desirable to draw only the lines that would be visible to a viewer, and to omit the lines that would be obscured by solid objects. **Occultation** is the determination of the edges and surfaces that would be visible from the observer's point of view. Only visible surfaces are drawn, and all occulted, or hidden, ones are removed (fig. 7-71). This is also called *hidden line* or *hidden surface removal.*

Renderings with occultation are much more complex computationally than simple

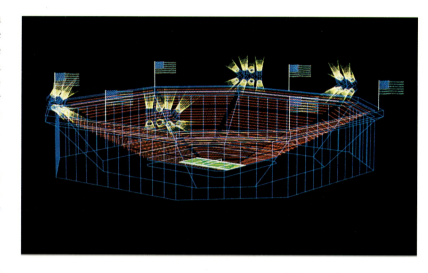

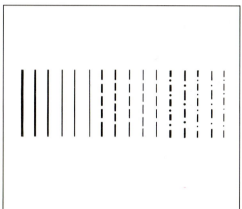

7-66. Wireframe rendering of the National Tennis Center in Flushing. (Courtesy of Digital Effects, Inc.)

7-67. Line widths and dashing patterns provide graphic variety and improve clarity in computer-generated images.

7-68. Depth cueing draws lines that are farther away with either different line widths (A) or darker values (B). (Courtesy of Digital Effects Inc.)

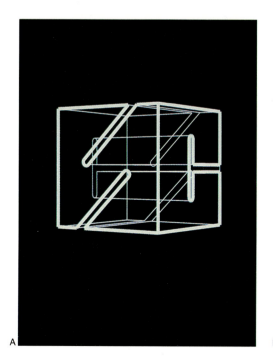

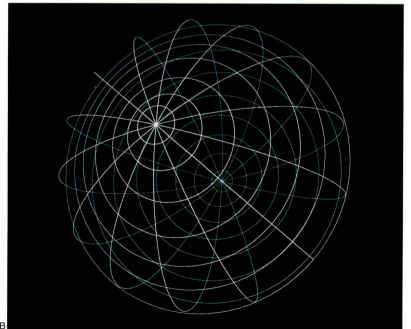

A

B

7-69. Different elevations have different colors; the higher the elevation, the lighter the color. (Courtesy of Digital Effects Inc.)

7-70. Lines can suggest surface without actually defining a closed, bounded, area. Compare this to figure 7-66, where the lines define edges that bound a surface. (Courtesy of Digital Effects Inc.)

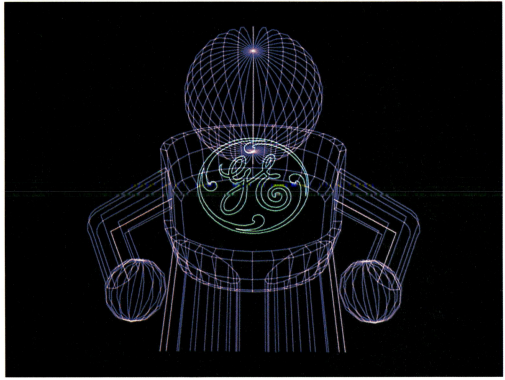

7-71. Occultation systematically sorts the data base and displays only the edges and surfaces of an object that are visible. (Courtesy of Pixel, Inc. Software written and designed by Manuel de Landa.)

wire frames, and, depending on the application, may or may not be worth the added expense.

Opaque Surface Rendering

Surfaces can be represented not only by their outlines or edges, but as **opaque,** solid areas of color (fig. 7-72). Renderings with occulted, opaque surfaces are often called *solid renderings.* **Scan conversion,** one method of creating an opaque area of color, draws many touching parallel lines inside the surface or superimposes the surface over a bitmap and changes the value of all the pixels that lie within the surface (fig. 7-73).

Another method involves **crosshatching,** diagonal lines or a pattern drawn on the surface. Like scan conversion, crosshatching is done at screen, not data, resolution. **Close-packed vectors** (CPV) draw a series of parallel lines from one side of a polygon to the other (fig. 7-74). CPVs are different from the scan conversion method, because scan conversion works at screen resolution, whereas the CPVs are part of the data and get bigger or smaller as the data gets bigger or smaller. These provide a dynamic graphic feel and are often used to simulate streak photography.

Chiaroscuro (Shading)

Chiaroscuro, or shading, is the representation of opaque surfaces with a range of dark to light values, as if they are illuminated by lights. Chiaroscuro is computed after visible surface determination; it is the result of the surface orientation, color, and luster and the light color, position, and brightness.

The simplest chiaroscuro technique is called constant value face shading, or polygonal shading. **Polygonal shading** performs a single calculation for each polygonal surface and renders the entire surface of each polygon with a single intensity of light (fig. 7-75). Polygonal shading makes each polygon easily distinguishable from

7-72. In solid surface rendering, the hidden surfaces are occulted and the objects are rendered with opaque surfaces using scan conversion. (Courtesy of Digital Effects Inc.)

7-73. Scan conversion (left) opaques a surface at the screen resolution. Thus, if the object gets bigger or smaller, it will still be evenly colored. Close packed vectors (right) are parallel lines drawn on the face of a surface and are part of the object. When an object gets bigger, smaller, or rotates, the closed packed vectors change accordingly.

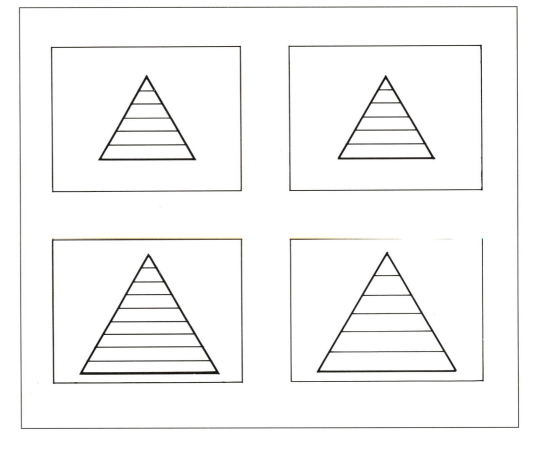

the others, causing objects like spheres to look faceted. If a smoother figure is required, one solution is to add more facets. This is not the best approach, however, because too many facets must be added to make the object smooth.

A better solution is to employ intensity interpolation, or ***continuous shading*** (fig. 7-76), which produces a smoothly varying surface. Continuously shaded surfaces may also have luster and highlights as well as texture or image maps. Continuous shading produces the most realistic results, but takes longer to compute than polygonal shading.

Color-graduated surfaces are closely related to continuously shaded surfaces but do not involve chiaroscuro; rather each corner of the polygon is assigned a color and the software then interpolates a color for each pixel of the resultant image in a manner similar to interpolating a shading value. This is a common technique for graphically creating a sky or background, where color must vary from one hue to another (fig. 7-77).

Drafting

Engineering drawing, or ***drafting,*** is a specialized rendering technique that consists of lines, dimensions, and standard symbols designed to represent the way parts and machinery are manufactured and assembled. Drafts represent not only the geometry of an object, using a variety of perspectives, but its dimensions, surface-finishing properties, such as how it is polished, and cross-sectional assembly details.

Drafting perspectives are often or-

7-74. Close-packed vectors have many artistic uses and produce lightweight, semi-transparent surfaces. (Courtesy of Walt Disney Productions and Robert Abel Associates. © 1982 Walt Disney Productions.)

7-75. Polygons are *shaded* by calculating one normal per polygon and then using that normal to calculate a single reflected light value to opaque the polygon. The lighting calculation can employ diffuse as well as spectral reflection, although it is normally only done with diffuse reflection, because highlights simply do not show up unless there are a large number of polygons. (Courtesy of Digital Effects Inc.)

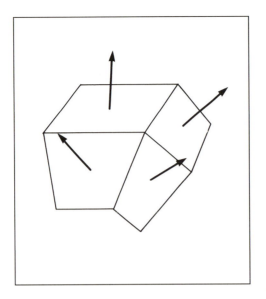

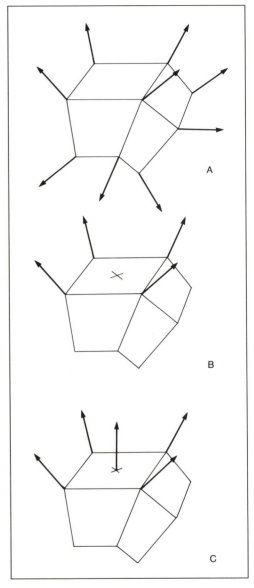

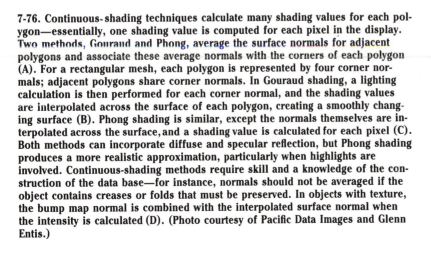

7-76. Continuous-shading techniques calculate many shading values for each polygon—essentially, one shading value is computed for each pixel in the display. Two methods, Gouraud and Phong, average the surface normals for adjacent polygons and associate these average normals with the corners of each polygon (A). For a rectangular mesh, each polygon is represented by four corner normals; adjacent polygons share corner normals. In Gouraud shading, a lighting calculation is then performed for each corner normal, and the shading values are interpolated across the surface of each polygon, creating a smoothly changing surface (B). Phong shading is similar, except the normals themselves are interpolated across the surface, and a shading value is calculated for each pixel (C). Both methods can incorporate diffuse and specular reflection, but Phong shading produces a more realistic approximation, particularly when highlights are involved. Continuous-shading methods require skill and a knowledge of the construction of the data base—for instance, normals should not be averaged if the object contains creases or folds that must be preserved. In objects with texture, the bump map normal is combined with the interpolated surface normal when the intensity is calculated (D). (Photo courtesy of Pacific Data Images and Glenn Entis.)

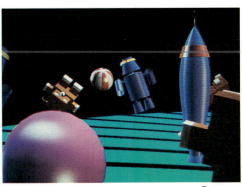

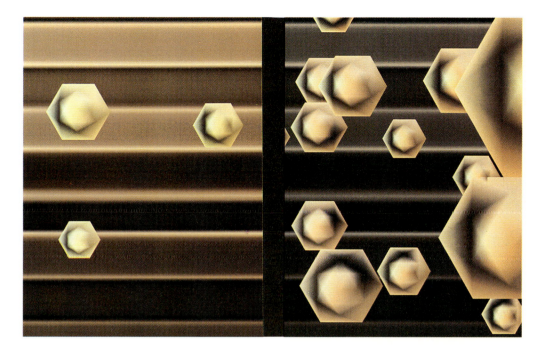

7-77. Color-interpolated surface, or color per vertex. The colors are interpolated by attaching them to different vertices in the polygons. (Courtesy of Gleckler and Spiegel Advertising.)

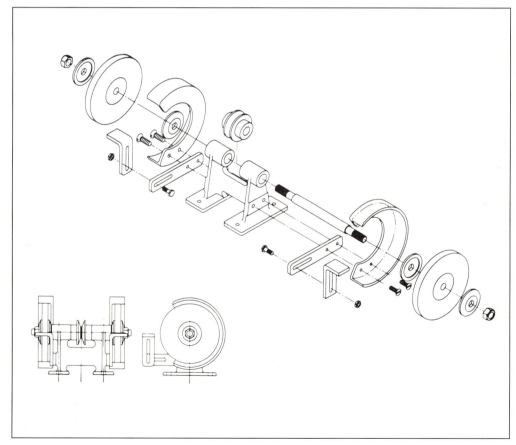

7-78. Multiview and exploded renderings relate parts to the whole. (Courtesy of International Business Machines Corp.)

7-79. Isometric and oblique projections.

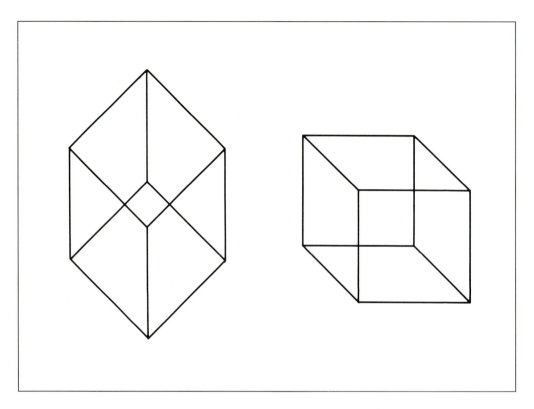

7-80. Dimension drawings are used to incorporate measurements and tolerance information. (Courtesy of the Mathematical Applications Group, Inc.)

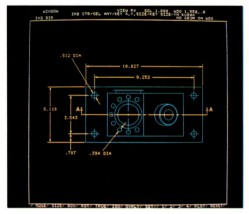

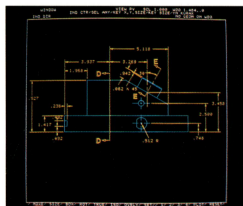

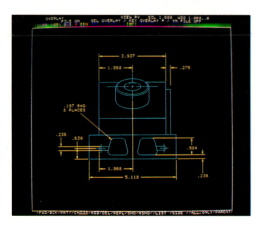

thogonal and include exploded and multiviews (fig. 7-78). Axonometric and oblique projections are also used instead of the more familiar perspective projection, since they employ true distances along some axes (fig. 7-79). ***Dimension drawings*** include measurements, dimension lines, and arrows, and often center lines and tolerances (fig.·7-80). ***Assembly drawings*** (fig. 7-81) show how the components of an assembled mechanism fit together, and ***auxiliary views*** (fig. 7-82) show parts and dimensions in perspective.

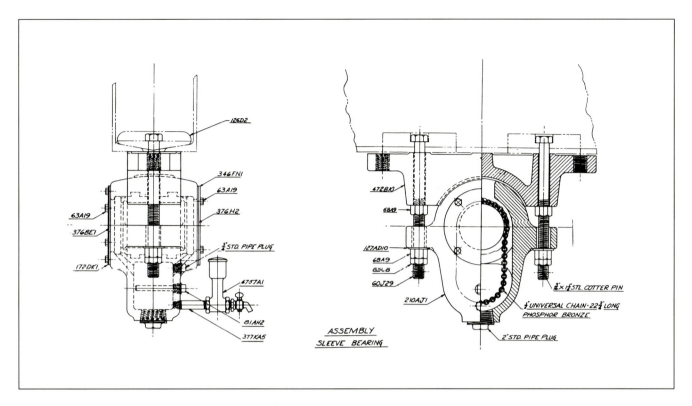

126D2

346FNI

63A19

376H2

63A19

376BEI

172DKI

¼"STD. PIPE PLUG

6757AI

172DKI

81AN2

377KA5

ASSEMBLY
SLEEVE BEARING

472BKI

68A9

127ADIO

68A9

85L8

60J29

210AJI

⅛"x I½"STL. COTTER PIN

¼"UNIVERSAL CHAIN-22½"LONG
PHOSPHOR BRONZE

2"STD. PIPE PLUG

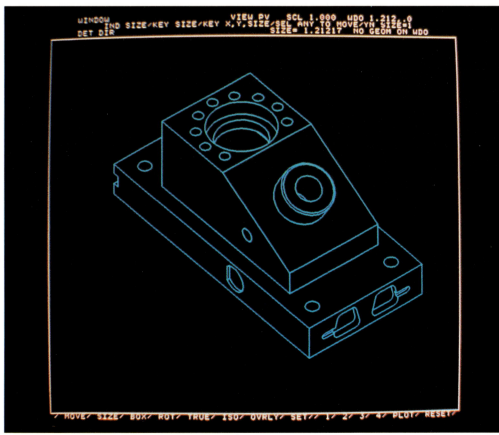

WINDOW
IND SIZE/KEY SIZE/KEY X,Y,SIZE/SEL ANY TO MOVE/YN SIZE=1
DET DIR
VIEW PV   SCL 1.000   WDO 1.212 , 0
SIZE= 1.21217 NO GEOM ON WDO

/ MOVE/ SIZE/ BOX/ ROT/ TRUE/ ISO/ OVRLY/ SET// 1/ 2/ 3/ 4/ PLOT/ RESET/

7-81. Assembly drawings.
(Reprinted, by permission
of Harper & Row Publish-
ers, Inc., from Lombardo
Engineering Drawing, Fig.
257.)

7-82. Auxiliary views are
planar projections of slant-
ing or oblique surfaces.
(Courtesy of the Mathematical Applications Group,
Inc.)

III-0. Courtesy of the Mathematical Applications Group, Inc.

SECTION III

APPLICATIONS IN DESIGN

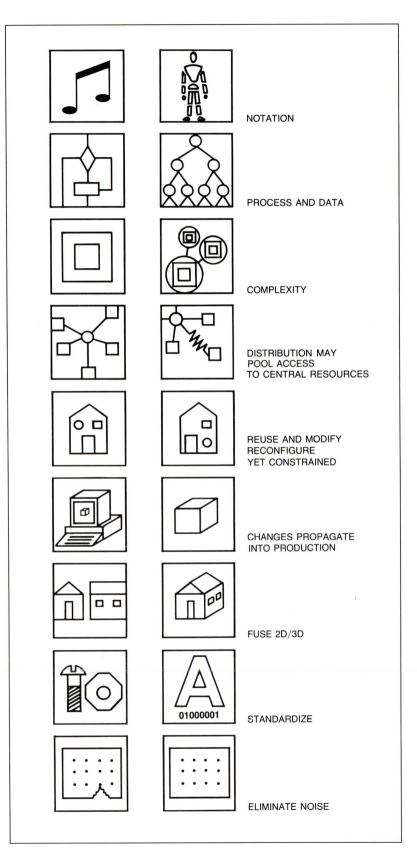

NOTATION

PROCESS AND DATA

COMPLEXITY

DISTRIBUTION MAY
POOL ACCESS
TO CENTRAL RESOURCES

REUSE AND MODIFY
RECONFIGURE
YET CONSTRAINED

CHANGES PROPAGATE
INTO PRODUCTION

FUSE 2D/3D

01000001 STANDARDIZE

ELIMINATE NOISE

The introduction of computer technology into the design studio is changing the way images are being created and manipulated. Computers are also shaping the management and engineering of creative projects, analyzing structures before they are built, and controlling and monitoring production. The computerization of the design office implies a continued integration of tools in the tradition of the typewriter, the copying machine, and the press (or television set). Computerization should be gradually introduced into an existing system, since it requires designers to learn new ways of thinking and to learn to operate new tools. A support structure for computerization is required too; as in other graphic arts, partnerships with other professionals are inevitable.

In a design environment computers merge design and production/distribution into a single process. These integrated systems are finding increased use in both two-dimensional and three-dimensional applications, from newspaper publishing to textiles and package design.

Integrated systems incorporate all computing basics—the ability to execute many kinds of notation, to store and maintain processes as well as data, particularly processes that reliably define increasingly complex tasks. Integrated systems incorporate advantages indigenous to computer graphics, too, including data bases, the ability to fuse two-dimensional and three-dimensional representations, and the ability to eliminate noise. They are the media as

III-1. The benefits of computerized design systems increase when the tasks involve groups of people rather than individuals, as common data bases provide ways for individuals to share information. Standardization can occur at many levels—field guides, test charts, conversion factors, as well as dimensions of standard parts. Digital data and processes can be communicated to remote, geographically diverse sites. Finally, computer graphic systems have no noise and provide a method whereby a blueprint or a piece of graphic art can be sorted, transmitted, and reproduced with no loss of fidelity or quality. Many mechanical problems that have frustrated the artist, the designer, the producer, and even the engineer are gone forever.

well as the message (fig. III-1).

In an integrated system scattered users can share access to centralized problems and solutions, providing a way to reuse good ideas and to adapt them anew. Integrated systems can be reconfigured or constrained, interactive or batch, and broadcast or network oriented.

In general, integrated systems reduce the time between the design and manufacturing stages. Designs are previewed on soft copy displays, and then automatically produced as material goods. The designer is more involved with the final product and less concerned with the mechanics of production.

In a computerized system, last-minute design or spelling changes propagate forward—that is, they are automatically incorporated into the production run—allowing design changes close to, if not during, press or air time.

Integrated systems fuse the design and production of the individual item with the operation of the plant (or the medium) as a whole (fig. III-2). All facets of a production cycle, including modeling, previsualization, manufacturing, quality control and research, management, and sales, become part of a single business system.

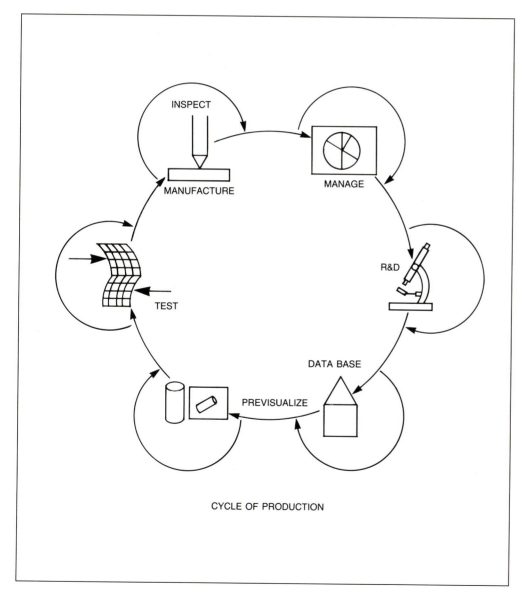

CYCLE OF PRODUCTION

III-2. Integrated systems involve a cycle of production: modeling depicts structures such as buildings, vehicles, and products, as well as systems such as networks, data bases, and production flows; previsualization includes rendering and drafting; testing includes aerodynamics, structural analysis, and audience research; manufacturing includes lists of parts, the costs of materials, and the actual creation, assembly, and inspection of parts; managing the system involves inventory as well as sales and expense journals.

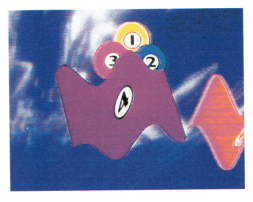

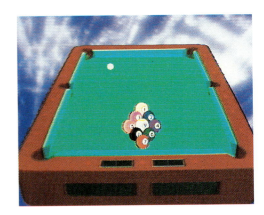

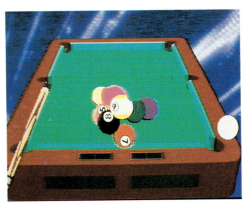

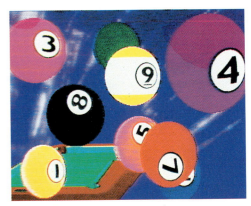

8-0. Key frames from an animated sequence produced with a video special-effects generator. (Courtesy of Broadway Video, Inc., and ESPN. Produced by Ralph Molé, edited by Roger Tyrrell, and programmed by Lorene Lavora. © 1984 by ESPN.)

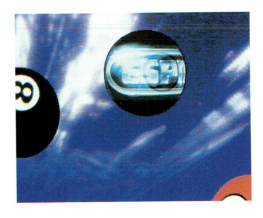

8

TWO-DIMENSIONAL MEDIA APPLICATIONS

DIGITAL TYPOGRAPHY
ILLUSTRATION SYSTEMS
COLOR CORRECTION AND SEPARATION
PAGINATION
ANIMATION
FINE ARTS

The processes involved in the production of two-dimensional graphics include typesetting, painting, illustration, chart makeup, photography, *lensing*—recording through a lens—color correction, pagination, and animation (two-dimensional media across time).

Integrated publishing is the consolidation of all of the steps of production into a single system (fig. 8-1). A two-di-

mensional integrated design system includes conceptualization, typography, illustration, photography, pattern design, compositing, pagination, analysis, run control, distribution, sales, media surveys, and accounting.

Integrated publishing is best designed and composed on interactive soft copy terminals. It therefore has the capacity to migrate the printing and distribution of

8-1. In an integrated publishing system, text, illustrations, and photographic color corrections terminate in a pagination system and go to press.

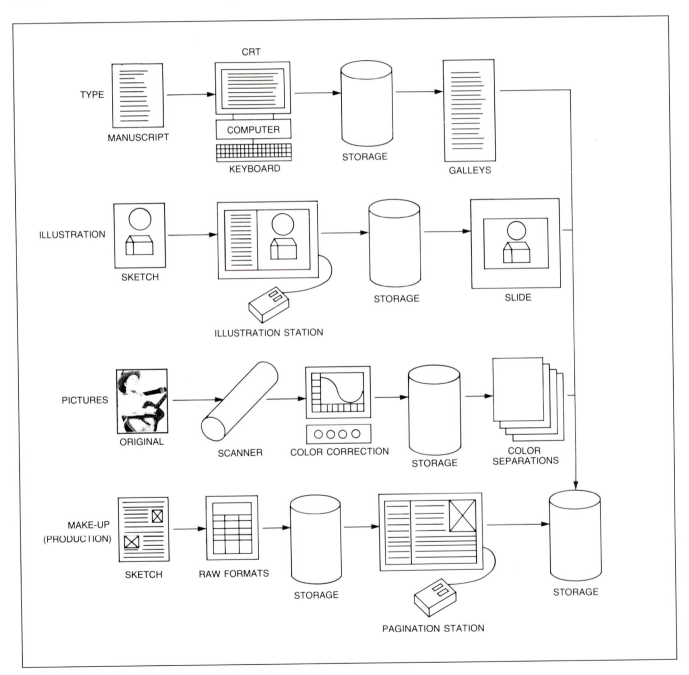

published materials to locations that are remote from the production center. Newspapers, for instance, may be composed in a central location, then facsimiles are transmitted to multiple printing plants via satellite (fig. 8-2). This decreases shipping costs, while expediting product distribution.

Electronic publishing provides alternatives to plate making and printing. Hard copy, should it be desired, can be created by consumers at their homes or offices.

The basic components of integrated publishing systems are terminals for text input and editing and stations for graphic illustration, photographic digitization, color correction and separation, and page makeup. The output devices include laser scanners, plate-making equipment, impact printers, and televisions.

DIGITAL TYPOGRAPHY

Type is one of the fundamental tools of the graphic artist, a tool that the graphic artist has in common with the writer. ***Digital typography*** involves not only typesetting, but the design and creation of type as well. Whether type is ideographical, as in Chinese, or phonetic, as in Western languages, word processing and typesetting specify how letters and ligatures are positioned, and how lines are organized and graphically formatted.

RELATED READING

Barnett, M. P. *Computer Typesetting.* Cambridge, MA: MIT Press, 1965.

Becker, Joseph D. "Multilingual Word Processing." *Scientific American* (July 1984).

Bigelow, Charles, and Donald Day. "Digital Typography." *Scientific American* (August 1983).

Gerstner, Karl. *Compendium for Literates: A System of Writing.* Cambridge, MA: MIT Press, 1974.

Zapf, Herman. "Changes in Letterforms Due to Technical Developments." *Journal of Typographic Research* (October 1968): 351–68.

Type Creation and Design

The design and creation of type is a specialized field that employs computer-assisted techniques. The shape of digital type, like the shape of type through history, is influenced not only by the designer but by design and reproduction technologies as well. Effective type requires accurate transcriptions of traditional typefaces and type designs that are tailored to the new medium.

Digital type design must consider leading, justification, letter spacing, and kerning, as well as features that are unique to the new media, such as data storage, portability, and anti-aliasing.

As we suggested before, ***type*** is a one-dimensional sequence of symbols each of which is visually represented as a two-dimensional graphic element. Each symbol can be encoded either as a polygon outline

8-2. A centralized factory transmits to remote printing and distribution centers (left). A centralized facility transmits directly to the consumer (right). Computerizing the production process and transmitting to remote sites for printing and distribution is becoming a common method for newspaper and magazine circulation.

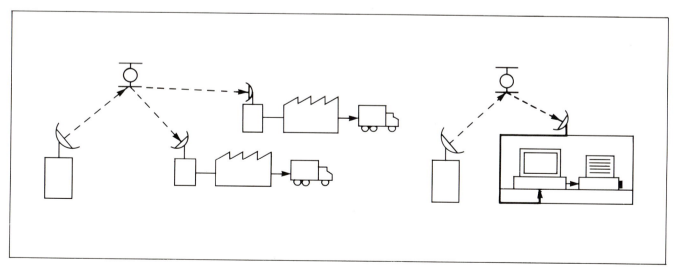

8-3. Letterforms can be represented with codes, contours, and bitmaps.

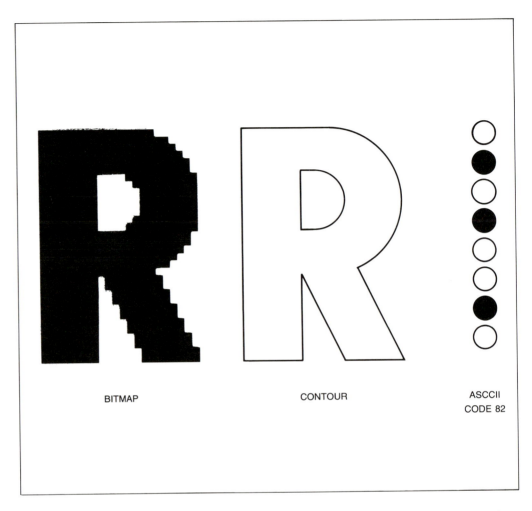

BITMAP

CONTOUR

ASCCII CODE 82

8-4. Building a character with points and arcs.

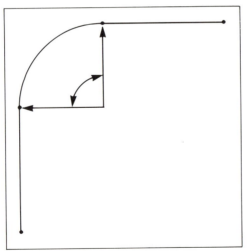

or as a bitmap. All three representations are used in computer graphics hardware (fig. 8-3).

Typewriter displays use a code number to cause a striker to impact the paper. Vector displays, and applications that need to scale type, represent letters as polygon outlines. Video displays and many pixel displays use bitmaps.

The vertices that describe the contour of a character can be digitized on an electronic tablet or geometrically constructed by digitizing only critical points and then connecting them with straight lines, arcs (fig. 8-4), or curve-fitting equations (fig. 8-5).

Procedural methods, whether plane geometry or brush-stroke simulation, are harder to use at first but often produce smoother, faster results, especially when the letter shapes are complex or must have dynamic range in scale.

Computer technology can foster innovations in type design. Interpolation techniques make it possible to derive hybrid typefaces from two existing styles. Although thousands of variations can be generated using this method, it is up to the designer to select those that can be worked and refined into a consistent alphabet (fig. 8-6).

An alphabet can also be drawn with different computer-simulated pen tips, which is especially useful for alphabets where stroke direction and sequence are important. The characters in figure 8-7 were created by specifying key points, describing the paths of the strokes, and choosing the shape of the pen. Describing letterforms with a program allows the designer to explore systematic variations by just altering one or two variables.

Mathematical distortions of type designs can also be easily achieved with computer-based design systems (fig. 8-8). These possibilities include the simulation of effects and distortions traditionally realized with lenses and mechanical apparatuses.

The conversion of polygon type into bitmaps is accomplished by positioning and sizing the polygon outline and then scan converting it to pixels (fig. 8-9). The results, however, often leave much to be desired, as problems include not only aliasing, but uneven weight that results from subtle changes in alignment and resolution. Anti-aliasing, higher pixel resolutions, and adequate planning in the design stage lead to satisfactory results.

Overstriking, variable intensity pixels, and careful alignment are techniques for enhancing the visibility of bitmap typography, especially in low-resolution output devices (fig. 8-10). Bitmaps may also be manually created, which is a preferred method for low-resolution bitmaps used in dot matrix printers and video display terminals (fig. 8-11). The designer's role is not to design at high resolution regardless of what becomes of the design in the transmission process, but to understand that communication involves many resolutions, and to design at the resolution

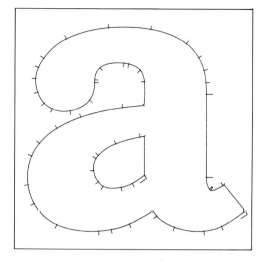

8-5. Building a character with curve-fitting equations. (Courtesy of URW Unternehmensberatung.)

8 6. Interpolation between serif and sans serif typefaces. (Courtesy of URW Unternehmensberatung.)

that suits the message space.

Although a polygon letterform contour can be sized to a small or large point size, the two must be different shapes. Smaller type, for example, is proportionally thicker than larger type and is designed to be easily read at some real world size. Traditional lead and phototypography therefore design different type for each point size. Computerized type defines a series of contours for each letter in a font. For example, three different contours might be made for each letter, one for normal book size type (9–14 points), one for smaller sizes (4–18 points), and one for headlines and display type (16–64 points).

Typesetting

Typesetting, or the placement of letters and words on a page to compose legible text, is a command-oriented process with a rich historical tradition. **Body type,** used to set text that will be read as a linear continuum, tends to be used in fixed integer sizes. **Display** or headline type is used

8-7. Stroke simulation. Variables describe the finished character; an experimental Chinese font by Go Guoan and John Hobby (left); AMS Euler Fraktur by Hermann Zapf and The Stanford Digital Typography Group (right). Both characters were created using the Metafont program. (Courtesy of Scott Kim.)

8-8. The calligraphic module has been digitized and arranged in a spiral with a special program. (Courtesy of Scott Kim.)

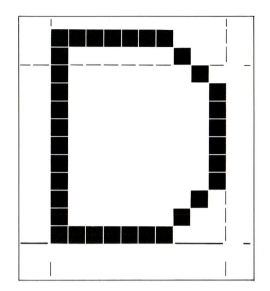

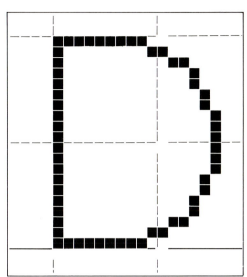

8-9. Type in a polygon format can be converted to bitmaps at different resolutions. (Courtesy of URW Unternehmensberatung.)

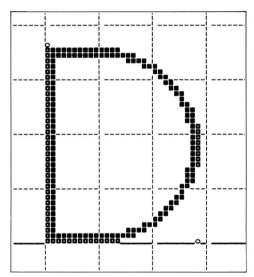

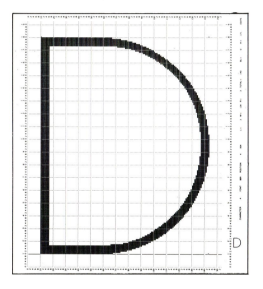

8-10. The legibility of low-resolution bitmaps is enhanced with anti-aliasing techniques—even four levels of gray provide a significant improvement. (Provided by Isaac V. Kerlow.)

The Real Hawkeye Pierce
  "What city?" inquired
the operator for Maine
Information.
  "Crabapple Cove," re-
plied the magazine writer.
  "Oh, that's where Hawk-
eye lives," came her quick
response. "You know, the
guy in 'MASH'."

A

The Real Hawkeye Pierce
  "What city?" inquired
the operator for Maine
Information.
  "Crabapple Cove," replied
the magazine writer.
  "Oh, that's where Hawkeye
lives," came her quick response. You know, the guy
in 'MASH'."

B

The Real Hawkeye Pierce
  "What city?" inquired the operator
for Maine Information.
  "Crabapple Cove," replied the
magazine writer.
  "Oh, that's where Hawkeye lives,"
came her quick response. "You
know, the guy in 'MASH'."
  We know, and it's also the name
of the inlet where the real Hawkeye

C

8-12. Text and display
typefaces.

Body Type

DISPLAY TYPE

for larger copy and is often sized to fit; it is continuously scalable (fig. 8-12).

Typesetting production involves the *input text,* a string of letters, numbers, and punctuation, and *formatting* commands, which specify how the text is to be justified, tabulated, and letter spaced (fig. 8-13). Text is entered into a computer either with a keyboard or an optical character reader (OCR). The text and commands are edited using a *word processor,* a program that allows the text to be modified, augmented, and cut; it also allows the integration of the formatting commands. After the text is edited, it is saved on a digital disk or output as a formatted file that contains the input text interspersed with *control characters* (special characters that are recognized by the typesetting system and control indents, tabs, carriage returns, letter spacing, and justification). This formatted file is input to a typesetter, which outputs either film galleys or soft copy type that is displayed on a screen or forwarded to a pagination system (fig. 8-14).

Typesetting systems are related to other computerized procedures that can index, correct spelling errors, hyphenate, and analyze readability. The ability to input ASCII text files to a typesetting system makes typesetting more accessible to authors with personal computers, by eliminating a whole series of intermediate production steps (fig. 8-15).

Typesetting variables can be controlled and adjusted, often on a letter by letter basis, with contemporary digital typesetters. The visual language variables that are involved in typesetting include font name, case, boldness or weight, italicization, color, drop shadows, point size, letter spacing, leading, line width, column depth, and justification.

The face, or *font,* is a collection of characters and special symbols in a particular size and style (fig. 8-16). Thousands of fonts exist in script, serif, and sans serif styles. Fonts may be condensed, regular, or extended; bold or italic; solid or outline.

Case, as in upper- and lowercase, distinguishes capital and "small" letters. Many fonts also have a control case, which contains punctuation, numerals, and special characters. Case is usually controlled by a button on a keyboard, just as it is on a typewriter (fig. 8-17). **Drop shadows** give the illusion of depth, but are actually two dimensional, whereas **extruded sides** do extend into space and are three dimensional (fig. 8-18).

The **type size** of a font is determined by measuring the font from the lowest to the highest extension of a letter, from the bottom of a lowercase **g** to the top of a capital **M**, for instance. Type size is specified in *points*—seventy-two points equal one inch. Type sizes created with digital media generally range from six to seventy two points in increments of one-half point.

Leading is the vertical distance in points between lines of text; this book is set in ten-point type with two points of lead. Line **length** refers to the width of a line measured in **picas.** Approximately six picas equal one inch and this copy is fifteen picas wide. **Depth** is the length of a column from top to bottom and is measured in inches (fig. 8-19).

Systems tailored to hard copy display often use windows that contain real world coordinates. But points, picas, and inches are all measures that have less meaning in soft copy displays where the screen can vary in size. In these situations type size is either measured relative to an arbitrary

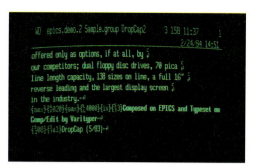

8-13. Inputs to typesetting include text and commands.

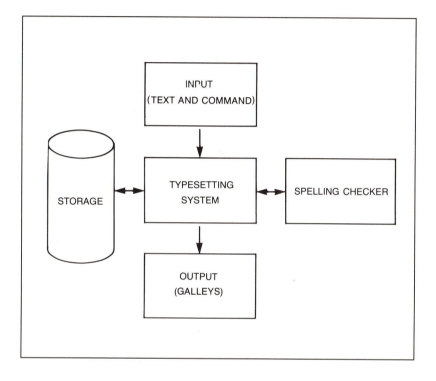

INPUT
(TEXT AND COMMAND)

STORAGE

TYPESETTING SYSTEM

SPELLING CHECKER

OUTPUT
(GALLEYS)

8-14. Computer graphics systems often support many different cases and switch back and forth between them using ASCII control codes activated by the buttons on the keyboard.

8-15. The word-processing files created with this Radio Shack portable computer can incorporate commands that will drive a typesetting system. (Provided by Isaac V. Kerlow.)

SERIF

SANS SERIF

𝔖𝔠𝔯𝔦𝔭𝔱

CONDENSED

NORMAL

EXPANDED

BOLD

ITALIC

OUTLINE

8-16. A variety of fonts.

8-17. Uppercase, lowercase, and pi case.

UPPERCASE
lowercase
!#$&*"¢@[]()

8-18. Drop shadow and extrusion.

DROP SHADOW

EXTRUSION

8-19. Leading, width, and depth. Twelve points equal one pica and six picas equal one inch.

window or by predefined, fixed sizes referred to by number or name.

Letter spacing is the space between individual characters, or how closely they butt up against each other, and is regulated to enhance the aesthetic qualities or to improve the readability of text (fig. 8-20). Letter spacing should not be confused with condensation or extension, which makes the actual letters wider or narrower. Nor should it be confused with **kerning,** which adjusts the space between individual letters for differences in their width and relationship (fig. 8-21).

Justification, or the fitting of type into lines of equal length, proportionally spaces letters, giving different characters more or less space according to their width to flush out the surplus width in the line.

In addition to being justified (left and right), type can be left justified (ragged right), right justified (ragged left), or centered (fig. 8-22). Paragraph indents and tab settings are additional parameters usually specified as a number of spaces.

ILLUSTRATION SYSTEMS

Computerized paint and makeup systems complement and, to some degree,

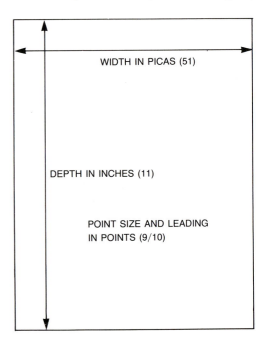

WIDTH IN PICAS (51)

DEPTH IN INCHES (11)

POINT SIZE AND LEADING
IN POINTS (9/10)

approximate traditional methods, though computer systems have unique benefits and liabilities (fig. 8-23).

Interactive illustration systems allow color mixing, freehand drawing, and the sizing and positioning of shapes. Many include type display and image digitizing capabilities. Most systems are operated by selecting options, in any order, from a soft copy menu (fig. 8-24); these often call other menus that offer further options.

Much of the "brainstorming" involved in the design process can be easily implemented on a computer design station. For example, the technique of interpolation can be very effective for generating variations of a seed idea by changing one shape into another (fig. 8-25). Color variations, label and copy positions, and bottle shapes can also be explored.

In addition to designs, news graphics for television, audiovisual slides, industrial illustrations, limited animation, and charts and graphs are produced at a computer design station.

Computer-generated business graphics are very accurate and significantly reduce the time involved in creating presentation art. The graphic work stations can format raw data that is downloaded from mainframes as well as data directly keyed in.

TOUCHING
TIGHT
NORMAL
LOOSE

8-20. Letter spacing: tight, touching, normal, loose.

WOLVES

WOLVES

8-21. Kerning tailors the space between individual letters, so it varies from combination to combination. In a word set without kerning all letters are evenly spaced. Kerning tightens up spaces and makes combinations such as "wo" tighter than combinations such as "ol."

Computer graphics are expanding the role of graphic designers beyond the traditional imaging media. The future is open for designers who know how to combine the structuring of information with effective visual design.

Computer graphics are expanding the role of graphic designers beyond the traditional imaging media. The future is open for designers who know how to combine the structuring of information with effective visual design.

Computer graphics are expanding the role of graphic designers beyond the traditional imaging media. The future is open for designers who know how to combine the structuring of information with effective visual design.

Computer graphics are expanding the role of graphic designers beyond the traditional imaging media. The future is open for designers who know how to combine the structuring of information with effective visual design.

8-22. Justification: both sides justified, flush left, flush right, and centered copy.

8-23. An illustration system comprises a computer with memory, a color monitor, one or more input peripherals (a mouse or a graphics tablet), and sometimes a hard copy device. (Courtesy of Artronics, Inc.)

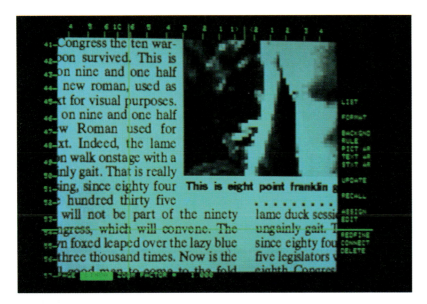

This data can then be displayed on low-resolution video monitors, recorded on videotape, and drawn with pen and ink plotters to make 8-inch by 10-inch overhead transparencies, or transmitted to a remote 35 mm slide film recorder, often at a service bureau, where they are drawn at high resolution in full color (fig. 8-26). The selection of resolution and medium depends on the audience and will be discussed in more detail in chapter 9.

The resolution and the features of a computer system are connected to the underlying technology of the work station. Two major technologies exist in real time interactive graphics work stations for graphic artists: polygon display list machines and bitplane machines. The dif-

8-24. Integrated text and image in a what-you-see-is-what-you-get newspaper pagination system. Compare this system with the one illustrated in figure 8-30. (Courtesy of *Time* Magazine.)

8-25. This 5 × 5 matrix interpolates a different design variable in each axis to create a cross-reference table of symbol variations. (Courtesy of Scott Kim.)

ference is comparable to the distinction between line copy and continuous tone; the features and functionality of the two technologies vary substantially, and although both technologies can coexist in a machine, this is often not the case.

Color Features

Color is associated with polygons as well as pixels, often in conjunction with look-up tables, for both display list and bitplane architectures. As explained in chapter 5, the maximum number of colors is related to the width of the look-up table, and the total number of colors that can be simultaneously displayed is related to the number of bits/pixel.

Other features most illustration stations support include the ***mixing*** of primary or secondary colors and ***ramping,*** the ability to create all the shades of color that exist between two extreme colors using interpolation (fig. 8-27). Colors can be picked up and moved, and some illustration systems also have limited animation capabilities based on color table animation, described later in this chapter.

Display List Features

Display list machines are well suited for the makeup of business charts and graphics, because the graphic elements can be manipulated and positioned individually or in groups. Polygons do not,

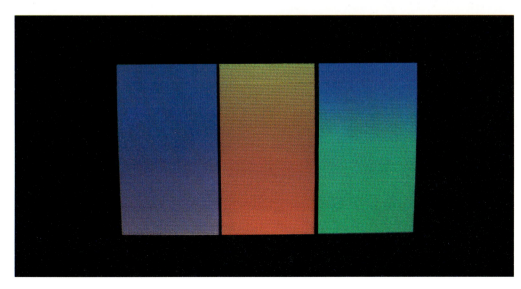

8-26. A medium-low-resolution image preview and a finished color graphic. Color and spatial resolution are inferior in the preview image, though the preview image may be suitable for certain applications. (Courtesy of Judson Rosebush and Atlantic Motion Pictures.)

8-27. The user selects and mixes two end colors in color ramping, and the system calculates a series of colors between the two by interpolating each primary. (Provided by Isaac V. Kerlow.)

however, describe continuous tone images like photos and paintings; this needs to be done with bitplane machines.

Display list machines store graphic objects like blocks of type, logos, and iconic elements as polygon shapes stored on a display list (fig. 8-28). Individual elements or groups of elements can be repositioned, continuously sized, rotated, and assigned priorities (which objects are to appear in front of other ones). Basic capabilities also include parallel lines, T squares, tangents, base lines, grids, and alignment guides.

Because the polygons on the display list are stored as real numbers, they are not affected by the resolution of the display. This allows the work to be interactively previewed at 640 × 480 pixel resolution video, and then output to film at higher resolutions, ranging from 4,000-pixel 35 mm slides to 8,000-pixel 8½ by 11-inch color transparencies. Obviously, the output can also be directed to a page makeup system, color separation system, or satellite transmitter.

Bitplane Features

Paint systems are machines that use bitplanes to represent an image. Bitplane systems produce images that resemble painted forms, by creating soft edges as in airbrushing and area blending. Photographs can be scanned into a paint system, color corrected, and retouched. Paint functions include the ability to draw lines and shapes, fill areas with different colors or patterns, and create and use electronic brushes. A paint system can excise a block

8-28. Although this image— display list output— appears to be three dimensional, it comprises only two-dimensional elements. The rivets, the door, and handle are all created with circles. The inside of the safe door is made of three concentric circles, one overlaying the other, and colored with different shades of gray to approximate shading. The tubular components of the safe door, as well as the locking pins, are similarly composed of two-dimensional rectangles carefully spaced and color ramped. Color ramping was also used in the pathway leading into the safe, in the clouds, and in the background. The software permits individual objects, such as a cloud, or assemblages of objects to be repositioned. (Provided by Judson Rosebush.)

of pixels from an image, reposition it, and use it as a stamp, but it cannot isolate one object from the rest of the scene, because everything (the bitplane) is represented as a collection of pixels (fig. 8-29). Paint systems are therefore good for illustration, but do not easily manipulate the individual components of a frame.

Resolution of bitplane systems is limited to the size of the bitplane itself and varies from home computer systems at 150×200 pixels to video resolution systems at 640×480 pixels—resolutions above 1,000 square are state of the art. A variety of hard copy and digital outputs are discussed in chapter 3.

COLOR CORRECTION AND SEPARATION

Color correction is the process of adjusting the color balance of an image. Transparent or reflective art is first scanned into the machine and stored as the three additive primaries, red, green, and blue. The color values are interactively manipulated and balanced on the screen, with corresponding graphic readouts showing the correction curves (see fig. 5-17).

In color printing, the RGB components are converted into subtractive pigment colors, cyan, magenta, yellow, and black. The black channel is biased to accentuate the deep tones and shadows and was originally produced with a special amber filter that extracted luminance common to the CMY. Color and image processing are discussed in more detail in chapters 5 and 6.

Color separations are separate high-contrast, or halftone, images composed of variable area dots, with one separation for each of the four colors. The outputs vary in the number of dots per inch, the shape of the dots, and rotary screen offsets. The four separations can be represented as one-bit-deep bitplanes, but at a spatial resolution substantially higher than the original pixel resolution or the number of dots per inch. In fact the resolution is high enough so that each dot of the halftone

🐾 **RELATED READING**

Born, Robert, ed. *Designing for Television: The New Tools.* Tequesta, FL: Broadcast Designers' Association, 1983.

Gottschall, Edward. *Graphic Communication/Visions 80.* Englewood Cliffs, NJ: Prentice-Hall, 1981.

8-29. Image created on a paint system. (Courtesy of Mark Lindquist at Digital Effects Inc.)

is actually made up of many pixels (see fig. 6-18). This is then output to a laser plotter for hard copy black-and-white high-contrast film negatives; these are used to create the printing plates, one for each of the four colors (CMYB).

PAGINATION

Pagination is the integration of text, illustrations, and pictures into a whole page. A pagination system is essentially a digital pasteup and stripping machine (fig. 8-30). In addition to coordinating the placement of the integral elements of the page, such as headlines, subheads, type, photographs, illustrations, captions, and rules, pagination assists in managing *jumps,* the flow of copy and graphics from page to page. Many systems can display *folios,* a whole sequence of pages where

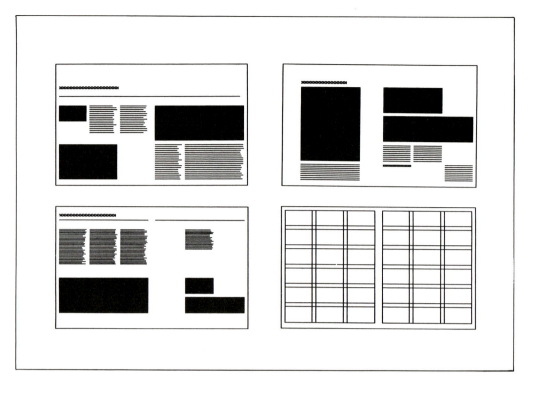

8-30. Layout grid used in a low-resolution pagination system, and three double spreads indicating positions of images and headlines. (Courtesy of James ver Hague, Rochester Institute of Technology.)

8-31. Eight pages of a classified ad section are displayed on the screen at once. (Courtesy of Atex, Inc.)

each page is viewed at a smaller than actual size (fig. 8-31), especially useful in newspaper or magazine makeup.

Interactive work stations paginate by previewing the assembled page, so that type can be directed to a specific page and column, justified, and hyphenated to fit. Pictures, drawings, and graphs are assigned cropping information and ports.

Shorter lead times, faster assembly, soft copy preview, digital data management, and archiving are the benefits of computerized pagination, which renders the production aspects of publishing more accessible to the writer, editor, illustrator, and graphic designer. Changes such as a spelling correction propagate forward into the final assembly electronically, not mechanically. All parties, therefore, can better coordinate their efforts, as each is aware of last-minute changes that affect the final product.

Inputs to pagination systems include formatted type files, illustrations, graphics, and digitized photographs. The graphic artist assembles the page interactively, directing the various inputs to specific ports on the page. Many pagination systems allow

PortID#	1	2	3	4	5
PageID#	0	0	0	0	0
Name	Title	Subtitle	Graph	Legend	Reference
Type	Text	Title.text	Picture	Text	Text
FileName	Title.text	Title	Dec.sales	Dec.sales	Title.text
Shape	Rect	Rect	Rect	Rect	Rect
Priority	1	1	1	1	1
Rotation	0	0	0	0	0

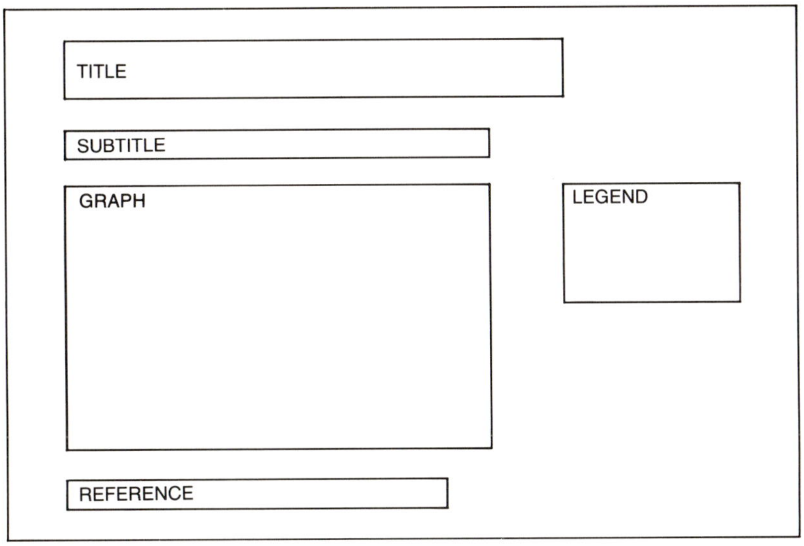

8-32. Design standards for a business graphic define several ports where the various components of a business graphic slide are displayed. Type, sizes, lengths, leading, and color constraints can be stored along with the text in the source file. The design standards may also specify graphic parameters like the maximum number of slices in a pie chart. The table lists the variables associated with each port in the format described in figure 7-38.

the artist to composite with mattes, lay down flat areas of color, and perform a number of the imaging techniques discussed in chapter 6. The paginator coordinates the output from many different graphics systems. The typical output from a pagination system is a digital file, usually an extremely high-resolution, possibly color, bitmap that is either digitally transmitted or converted to hard copy, often with a laser scanner or plate maker. A detailed pagination strategy is presented in figure 8-1.

Design parameters in computer systems can be implemented as permanent specifications in the pagination system, indicating general format guidelines for preferred composition and layout schemes. Specific variables include column widths, typefaces and point sizes, headline grids, margins, and safety areas (areas that will always be visible regardless of the format). In a computerized pagination system, these design standards may conform to rigid formats, or they may be flexible, allowing greater visual variety (fig. 8-32).

Pagination systems offer a wide range of capabilities: some display true typefaces,

TITLE

SUBTITLE

GRAPH

LEGEND

REFERENCE

RELATED READING

Badler, Norm, ed. "Special Issue on Character Animation." *IEEE Computer Graphics and Applications* (November 1982).

Halas, John, ed. *Computer Animation.* New York: Hastings House, 1974.

Halas, John. *Graphics in Motion.* New York: Van Nostrand Reinhold, 1984.

Halas, John, and Roger Manvell. *The Technique of Film Animation.* 3d ed. New York: Hastings House, 1971.

Levitan, Eli. *Electronic Imaging Techniques.* New York: Van Nostrand Reinhold, 1977.

Thomas, Frank, and Ollie Johnson. *Disney Animation: The Illusion of Life.* New York: Abbeville, 1981.

(the ability to move data), and sophisticated input-output capabilities.

Most integrated publishing systems allow a variety of hard copy output resolutions. Proofing printers are available that can output text and images at 240 lines per inch. More expensive phototypesetting systems can output to plate-making equipment at 1,000 lines per inch.

ANIMATION

Computer animation is the bridge between the static picture and interactive graphics. **Animation** is the representation and display of objects and motions across time, using a rapid sequence of individual frames. The representation of time, the fourth dimension, involves the study of changes and variance and the telling of stories.

Animation production is different from print production, as animation perception responds to a sequence of images, as in film and video delivery media. The animation process begins with a clearly defined **concept,** the basic idea or design, of the project. A **script** is the text, including dialogue; it is often included with the **storyboard,** which illustrates the general characteristics of the objects, actors, and sets. The storyboard shows the composition of each shot (fig. 8-34). Camera movements and transition effects are also plotted on storyboards, and these are often filmed or taped with a rough soundtrack called an **animatic** and used to create a sense of action.

Action and lighting are previewed on interactive displays and often test frames are made on film or videotape. Interactive systems move a finite number of objects with sophisticated display processors that execute graphic processes (fig. 8-35). In productions too complex to preview interactively, wire frame or low-resolution motion tests are produced before computing the final, fully detailed version. This motion test is recorded on film or video.

Once rendering and motion tests have been approved, the animation is computed

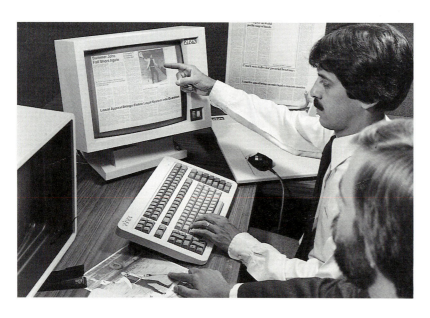

8-33. Text and image integrated. (Courtesy of Atex, Inc.)

others simulate type; some allow for the integrated display of image and text, and others use boxes to indicate position (fig. 8-33). These systems are evolving and have only recently approached their full capacity.

Microcomputer-based pagination systems that can illustrate, create business graphics, and do page makeup are becoming common for smaller publishing environments. Many of these systems offer integrated software packages to handle accounting, telecommunications, word processing, data-base management, and image scanning. Color graphics work stations with more powerful computers and high resolution require a large memory capacity, wide communication bandwidths

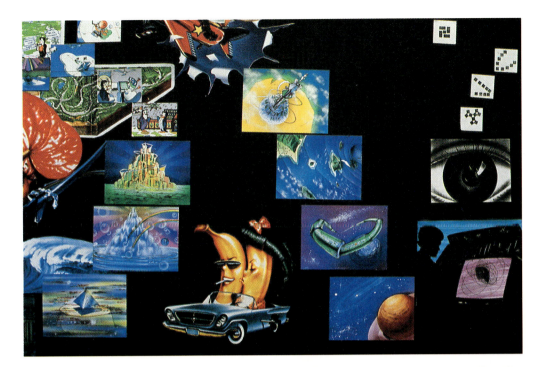

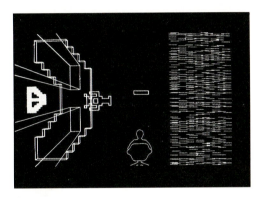

8-35. Motion tests often use diagrammatic representations of actions over time. In this example they are used to show size and position of live action as well as computer graphics. (Courtesy of Robert Abel Associates.)

frame by frame and either stored on digital magnetic tape, viewed on color CRTs, or transferred to film or video. Formats and resolution vary widely, from 640 × 480 pixel video to 1,800 × 2,400 pixel 35 mm film.

Animation must usually be combined with sound and the individual scenes edited together (see fig. 9-7). This post-production process often requires optical or video effects involving combinations with live action (fig. 8-36).

Animation is produced using interactive and batch tools, but remains a compositional medium, distinct from interactive video synthesis, which is an improvisational medium. Animation systems incorporate interactive design stations and real time displays to preview results, but the visually richest and more complex imagery is often batch computed in nonreal time, since the extra computation can add production value, an economic assumption that increased capital investment in a product increases its market value.

The difference between interactive systems and notated animation is similar to the difference between an improvising jazz musician and a composer. Animation, with its concern for story, music, and of course, visuals, is seldom a wholly interactive process, and often requires time for people to develop ideas. Some computer processes enhance traditional animation, whereas

8-36. Post-production involves many techniques to combine computer graphics and live action. These figures show a computer-generated background that is front projected onto a pair of actual bicycle riders. The top image illustrates the shooting rig and the bottom illustrates the final composite. (Courtesy of Robert Abel Associates.)

others are techniques that never before existed. ***Computer-aided animation*** uses computers to control hardware, but uses traditional photographic techniques. In ***computer-generated animation*** all objects and actions are produced numerically, often in a three-dimensional space with perspective.

Motion Graphics

Motion control systems are computer-controlled hardware, such as an animation stand or live action camera. These systems can generate and repeat very precise camera moves as well as reposition artwork. In addition to a camera, a typical motion control system includes a ***platen,*** a place where artwork is mounted. Both the camera and platen are equipped with one or more computer-controlled motors that serve to focus and move the camera rig and position the platen (see figs. 3-15 and 3-16).

Applications include multiple pass cinematography, shaft encoder tracking, and camera rigs that can record and then repeat the motions of a human cameraman. The computer control of cameras makes it possible to synchronize live action with computer-generated imagery (fig. 8-37).

Types of graphic sequences optimized

8-37. Computer graphics and live action combined. In this image, the computer graphics are composited in front of live action, and a live action car is composited on the computer graphics. Photogrammetry techniques assist in synchronizing the graphics and live action. (Courtesy of Digital Effects Inc.)

8-38. Streaks are made by opening a camera shutter and then either moving the camera or the artwork to create a smear of light. (Courtesy of Shadow Light Productions, Inc., Director/Designer Marc Chelnik.)

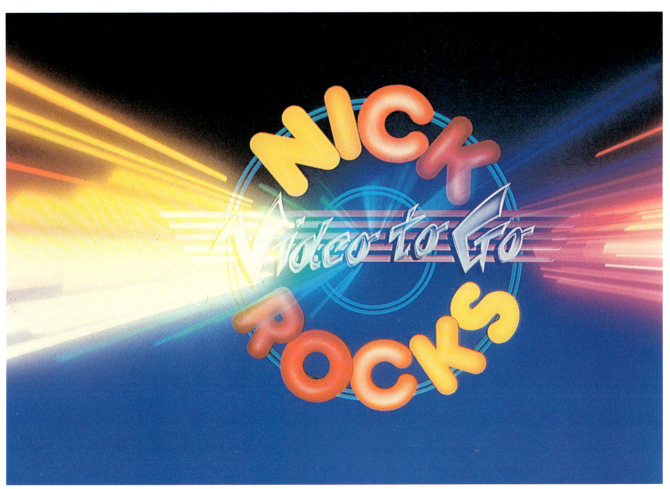

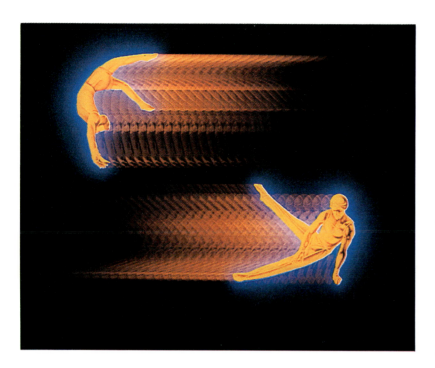

8-39. A strobe is a multiple exposure made by moving the camera or platen from position to position while the camera shutter is closed.

acetate, nor is there cell flair or dirt. Mistakes are corrected and reshot without other mistakes occurring. And the final output can be directed to videotape or film.

Many animation systems are interactive and screen oriented, directed with keystrokes or menus. Flexible systems can create, edit, and replay action sequences in real time, often with color, sound, and several cells moving over a background (fig. 8-41).

Color Table Animation

Color table animation, also called a *marquee,* is a way of producing limited animation on static display. The action is created by sequentially illuminating areas that are positionally predefined (fig. 8-42). It is related to the process of painting by number. An object in the scene to be animated is assigned a color number that corresponds to a color in a color table. The positions of the object at each successive frame are assigned successive numbers that correspond to specific colors (fig. 8-43). The look-up table is then rotated, creating action as the colors move through different positions.

Color table animation can also animate the effects of daylight, seasons, and changing weather (fig. 8-44). When the weather is sunny we use the "sunny color table," which assigns blue to the sky, and shades of white to the color numbers of the clouds. When the weather is stormy we use the "stormy color palette," where the sky is yellow-gray and the clouds are dark purple-grays. To animate a storm approaching we dissolve one color table into the other.

Three-dimensional Animation

Model animation uses computer procedures to define, move, and display three-dimensional objects in an imaginary environment. Using a combination of solid modeling, transformations, and perspective, the artist describes objects once, with the computer calculating the intermediary positions and perspectives.

Once the three-dimensional models have been designed, they are converted

by motion control systems include slit-scans and multipass strobes. *Slit-scans* and *streaks* (fig. 8-38) are created by leaving the shutter open while simultaneously zooming the camera and panning the artwork. *Strobes* (fig. 8-39) are made by reshooting artwork with multiple passes in exact alignment and registration.

Computer-assisted Cartoon (Cell) Animation

Hand-drawn animation can be facilitated with the computer by systematically routinizing simple operations. Today's cell animation systems range from implementations that computerize virtually all facets of production, to systems that assist at only certain stages. These include scripting (word processing), storyboarding (illustration systems), composing cells and backgrounds (spread sheets for layout), drawing (illustration systems), in-betweening (interpolation), inking and painting the cells and backgrounds (scan conversion), and shooting the artwork (image compositing) (fig. 8-40).

Computerized cell animation also eliminates the problems that come with numerous cell levels, because there is no graying due to the physical density of the

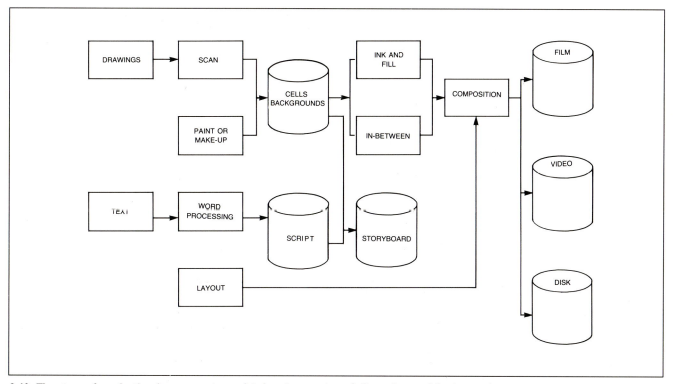

8-40. The steps of production in a computer-assisted cartoon system. Cell overlays and backgrounds are either hand drawn and scanned into the system, or made on a digital paint or display list system. Text is keyed in via a word processor. Illustrations and text are merged to form electronic storyboards. The cells are stored as polygon outlines, scan converted to make them opaque, and interpolated to calculate intermediary positions or in-betweens. Compositing or layout commands specify what cells and backgrounds are to be combined in what order, and the results are output to film, video, or digital disk.

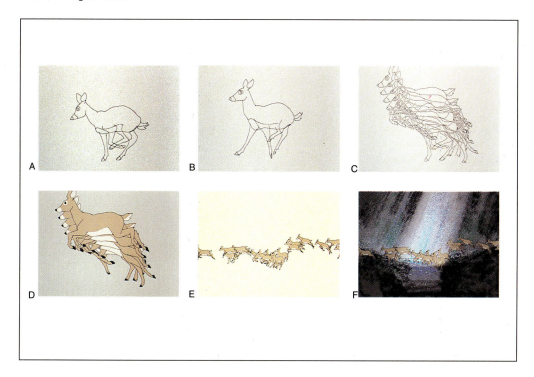

8-41. Beginning and end line drawings (A, B) specify two extreme, or key, positions that are used to determine the in-between drawings shown here both in line (C) and color (D). Apparent movement is achieved by repositioning successive in-betweens in a scene (E). The final animation is overlaid on a color background (F). (Courtesy of New York Institute of Technology.)

8-42. A marquee, like the light bulbs on a theater marquee, creates action simply by illuminating pre-defined areas in sequence, so limited animation is achieved without actually moving any shapes.

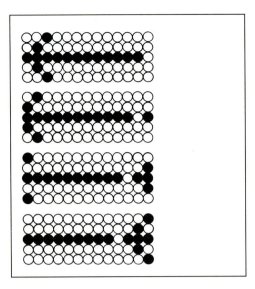

into numerical data bases. These digitizing techniques, described in chapter 7, include point digitizing, sectioning, coplanar blueprints, photogrammetry, and procedural methods.

Set construction is the positioning of objects in three-dimensional space and begins once the objects are defined. They are positioned in the virtual three-dimensional space by declaring the spatial coordinates for each object. Next, the animator determines the position of the camera for the ***extremes,*** or beginning and end frames, of each shot. These *key frames* determine the composition of the frame as well as objects in space (fig. 8-45).

Lighting and effects such as reflection, refraction, and shadows depend on the location, intensity, and diffusion of the light sources as well as on the surface properties of objects. Decisions about how to render the objects are closely related to lighting decisions.

FINE ARTS

Computer graphics introduces a wide range of techniques that lead our imaginations down artistic paths never before explored. Computers are used not only to create pictures, but are used in conjunction with traditional painting, sculpture, and conceptual art techniques. Computer-generated images can be created by modeling concepts and events and embodying them in a program and visualizing the result. This creative process, called ***procedur-***

	R	G	B
0	0	0	0
1	0	0	0
2	0	0	0
3	0	0	0
4	0	0	0
5	0	0	0
6	0	0	0
7	255	0	0

	R	G	B
0	255	0	0
1	0	0	0
2	0	0	0
3	0	0	0
4	0	0	0
5	0	0	0
6	0	0	0
7	0	0	0

	R	G	B
0	0	0	0
1	255	0	0
2	0	0	0
3	0	0	0
4	0	0	0
5	0	0	0
6	0	0	0
7	0	0	0

8-43. Screen action (left) and an eight-row color look-up table (right) depict three successive animation frames. Between each frame, each row in the look-up table is translated one row down, and the last row is written in the first one. The design and format of the objects, in this case chevrons, and in particular their color-by-number assignments, set up the animation. Because the computation only involves the table and not the objects, it can be completed quickly. The effect on the screen is to blank certain pixels and to color others, so a single chevron appears to be descending.

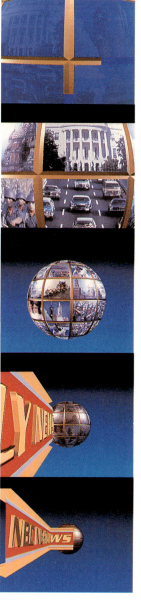

8-44. Look-up table animation showing sunny and stormy color palettes. The first twelve values in the look-up table dissolve from "sunny" to "stormy"; the values 13 and 14 are toggled on and off to simulate lightning. (Provided by Isaac V. Kerlow.)

8-45. A set of key frames from a thirty-second commercial animation illustrate critical compositions, coloring, and lighting. (Courtesy of Digital Effects Inc.)

RELATED READING

Deken, Joseph. *Computer Images.* New York: Stewart, Tabori & Chang, 1983.

Greenberg, Donald, Aaron Marcus, Allan H. Schmidt, and Vernon Gorter. *The Computer Image.* Reading, MA: Addison-Wesley, 1982.

Jankel, Annabel, and Rocky Morton. *Creative Computer Graphics.* Cambridge, England: Cambridge University Press, 1984.

Kawaguchi, Yoichiro. *Digital Image.* Tokyo: Ascii Publishing, 1981.

Reichardt, Jasia. *Cybernetic Serendipity.* New York: Praeger, 1969.

Scott, Joan. *Computergraphia.* Houston: Gulf Publishing, 1984.

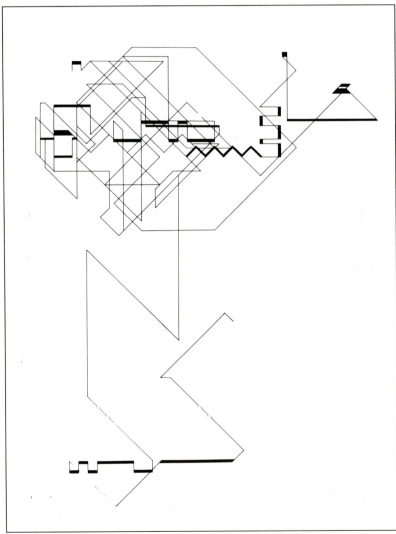

8-46. Two-dimensional vector drawing was one of the first computer outputs used in the fine arts. (Courtesy of Manfred Mohr.)

alism, allows an artist to produce a concrete image based on a concept.

Artists have been using computers as creative tools since the 1960s. Early computer-generated art was predominantly two-dimensional with a focus on geometric patterns, drawings using interpolation, and randomness (fig. 8-46). Many early computer artists used programming language as their creative and expressive tool and have become proficient programmers after continued practice. Some artists sought ways to use computer technology without learning how to program, by collaborating with professional programmers or using predefined systems.

The development of interactive paint and illustration systems has provided opportunities for skillful artists to discover new ways to paint and draw (fig. 8-47). The development of three-dimensional techniques during the 1970s, and their refinement during the 1980s, focused attention on both the simulation of reality and the creation of a new breed of abstract and surrealistic imagery (fig. 8-48).

Original hard copy in two dimensions is produced with printers and plotters with colored ribbons and pens, customized photocopying machines, and even painting machines, unique to computers (fig. 8-49). Image-processing devices, like pseudocolor and edge detection, provide new ways to manipulate pictures and search for new truths. And animation, spurred by computerized motion control and three-dimensional modeling, has enjoyed a popular resurgence. Computers can also be used to create sculptures and installations that interactively respond to participants (fig. 8-50). Other artists have used the computer as an art design tool, rather than as the central means of production, for anything from designing templates and patterns to creating paint-mixing formulas.

Whereas early computer artists had to gain access through research or educational institutions, today's desktop computers provide artists with a variety of software, from languages to paint boxes, for their personal expression.

The technical possibilities for computer-

8-47. Image created with a paint system. (Courtesy of New England Technology Systems. Image by Tom Christopher.)

8-48. Three-dimensional computer graphics shaped by a fertile imagination produce abstract yet seemingly tangible imagery. (Courtesy of Yoichiro Kawaguchi.)

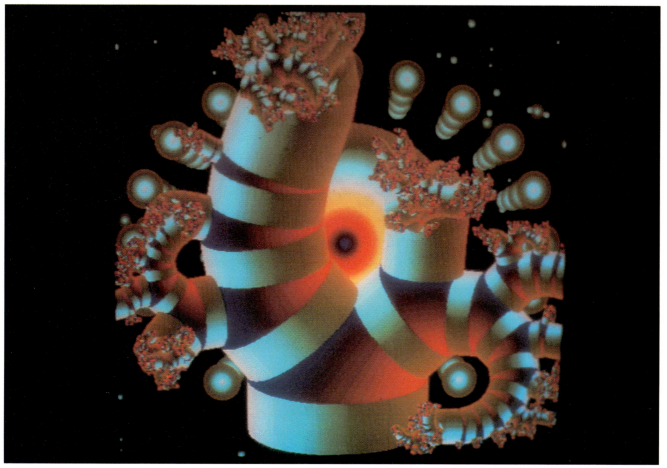

8-49. Artists have never limited themselves in hard copy technologies. This computer-driven painting machine allows the fabrication of very large-scale images. (Courtesy of Ron McNeil, MIT Visible Language Workshop.)

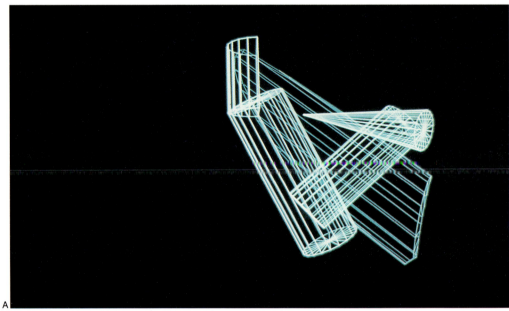

A

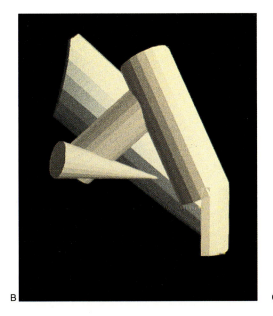

B

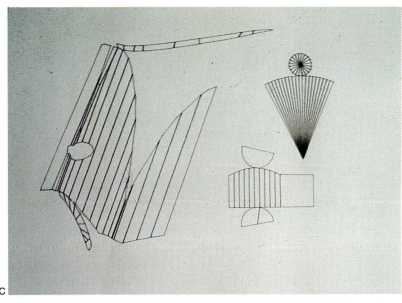

C

D

8-50. Computer-aided sculpture. A wire frame representation of a sculpture allows the artist to examine all of its components (A). Viewing the finished solid model from different angles allows him or her to understand its multiple configurations (B). A blueprint of the piece is created by transferring the three-dimensional model onto a flat surface (C). Finally, a three-dimensional paper model is created from the computer-generated blueprint (D). (Courtesy of New York Institute of Technology and Michael O'Rourke.)

generated art continue to evolve, thus attracting artists who see its great potential for aesthetic expression and who are, in turn, finding new ways to extend this capacity.

9-0. Flight simulators and real aircrafts include many aspects of monitor and control systems, including cartography, process control, and simulation. This image depicts a synthetic environment representing views outside an airplane window. (Courtesy of Evans & Sutherland Corp.)

TWO-DIMENSIONAL INTERACTIVE SYSTEMS

MONITOR AND CONTROL SYSTEMS
INFORMATION SYSTEMS
CARTOGRAPHY
BUSINESS GRAPHICS/MANAGEMENT SYSTEMS
INTERACTIVE VIDEO INSTRUMENTS AND GAMES
EDUCATION AND TRAINING

Computer graphics is not only affecting the design and production of traditional graphic arts, but it is sponsoring the creation of new media as well. Graphic interfaces are being used in an increasingly wide range of applications that involve human and system communications, including process control, data basing, cartography, management, interactive entertainment, and education. These operations are expanding the role of the graphic designer beyond the traditional broadcast media—print, film, and television (fig. 9-1). A rich future awaits those designers who know how to couple the structuring and presentation of information with effective visual design. The designs must not only be legible, but operable as well.

An interactive system, whether it is a Sears and Roebuck videodisc catalog or a command and control center for a power plant, provides a network of options to a user, who can be either an operator, a player, or an artist. The user or operator in an interactive system manipulates the contents of the screen by selecting options.

This chapter concentrates on interactive computer graphics systems and the way that these shape the information that is presented to, and selected by, a user. Some of these applications, for example cartography, combine traditional diagrammatic representations with new techniques for analysis. Other applications, for example

flight simulators, involve interactive control using graphics that approximate the real world.

MONITOR AND CONTROL SYSTEMS

A *monitor and control system* operates complicated pieces of machinery, networks, and processes. Examples include railroad switching towers, factories, and power plants. Monitor and control systems are often called *process control systems* in industry and *command-and-control systems* in the military.

The computer and data base, input sensors, a control console with interactive screens, the machine or process itself, and one or more operators constitute the monitor and control system (fig. 9-2). Instead of an operator running the machine directly, he or she runs the computer that controls the machine via interactive graphic tools on a screen (fig. 9-3). The operator views the system status depicted by the instruments on the screen and configures the system accordingly—how fast to run it and what to do when it breaks. In a sense the operator "drives" the machine.

The *sensors* are instruments that measure conditions in the process environment and can include thermometers, depth gauges, microphones, cameras, and radars.

9-1. The graphic designer now assists in the visual interface between the user and the system, a more complicated role than interfacing between the reader and the message.

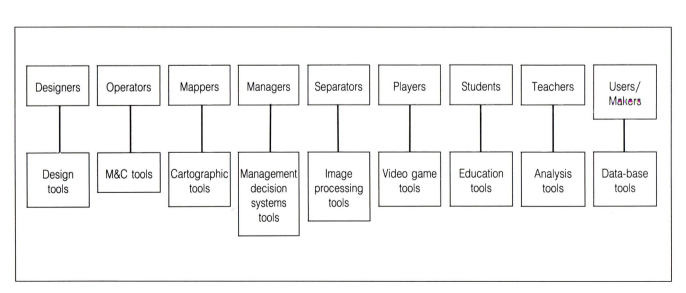

Designers	Operators	Mappers	Managers	Separators	Players	Students	Teachers	Users/ Makers
Design tools	M&C tools	Cartographic tools	Management decision systems tools	Image processing tools	Video game tools	Education tools	Analysis tools	Data-base tools

The sensors feed this data into a computer, where it is evaluated, often by comparing it to data bases, and formatted onto screens.

The **control console** consists of interactive display screens that combine text, two-dimensional diagrammatic graphics, and devices that when manipulated operate the machines or processes. These devices may include menus as well as diagrammatic icons that allow the operator to select options using a touch-sensitive screen, a mouse, or a keyboard. The screens are often low to medium resolution and are continuously altered to show the operator the current status of the process.

The **machine** or process run by the computer is essentially a peripheral containing knobs, levers, and switches that are controlled with stepping motors and relays. The computer manipulates these in response to the operator and to programmed directives. The machine can be physical or virtual.

Personnel are particularly important when executing procedures, such as navigational directions given to a pilot by an air traffic controller. Navigational systems aboard the aircraft theoretically may interact with ground radars, cross-checking results with the pilot and with data transmitted from the ground CPU.

Benefits and Ergonomics

Introducing the computer into process control allows geographically dispersed events to be correlated, ensures quality controls, optimizes time and materials, and performs interlocking and fail-safe procedures, which inhibit certain actions and neutralize the system if it goes haywire. Complex applications may be designed to allow several users to control different aspects of a process. Because the controls are software, they are easily modified and tested as an application evolves.

The designer's function is to formulate the instrumentation display and visual interface between operator and machine. Displays need to be very clear, legible, and visually consistent, particularly in cases where the operator's response time is crit-

RELATED READING

Oliver, Bernard M. "The Role of Microelectronics in Instrumentation and Control." *Scientific American* (September 1977).

Spector, Alfred Z. "Computer Software for Process Control." *Scientific American* (September 1984).

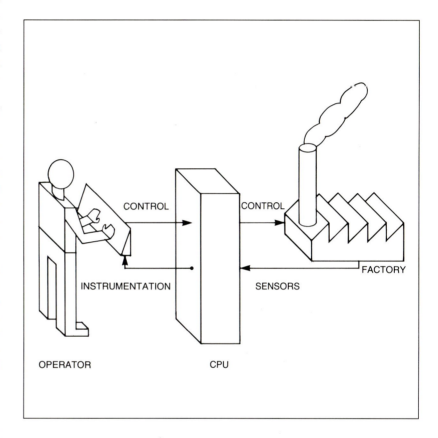

9-2. Components of a monitor and control system include a computer, a data base, input sensors, a control console, an operator and the process itself.

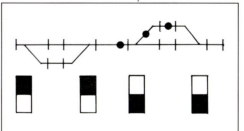

9-3. A process control board for a section of the main line of a railroad diagrams track, the position of switches, and the location of trains. Operations performed by the system determine the best route through switches, test the tracks to make sure they are empty, set and lock switches in position, and set signals. The design is engineered to be fail-safe, that is, mechanical and human failures should bring all trains safely to a stop.

ical. Numbers and text should be used when appropriate, but should not substitute for graphics. In short, a display must be readable at a glance.

The monitoring and control of complex dynamic processes are often simplified once the process can be diagrammed; the abstract diagram with icons clearly rendered can be more efficiently manipulated than the actual machine or process (fig. 9-4). Visual codes cannot contradict the conventional signs of industrial environments, such as the meaning of red (stop), yellow (pause), and green (go).

The process operation should make use of an extensive array of graphics techniques, including subwindows reached by touching menus containing icons (fig. 9-5). Typefaces and color, indeed, the entire layout, must be tested for legibility, per-

ception, and ease of operation; and practical experience should periodically be incorporated into the system.

In a broad sense, *information systems* are also interactive monitor and control systems; but instead of controlling machinery, they search, organize, and manipulate data (fig. 9-6). Information systems can store, analyze, and retrieve text, numbers, and graphics, and most use soft copy screens, often a color television set, as a primary interface to a user's personal data base as well as to public memories accessed worldwide via a communication network.

Information systems include data bases, automated office tools like electronic mail and desk organizers, and electronic publishing systems like teletext and videotex. Each differs somewhat, but all are aimed at making a decision or producing new information.

Data Bases and Information Banks

Graphic data bases are stored in a variety of ways and with varying degrees of interactivity. Storage hardware includes digital tapes and disks, ROM, and videodiscs. Data can be stored as text, numbers, pictures, movies, three-dimensional objects, drawings, and maps. Access times may range from less than a second to days and depend on just where the data is stored.

Graphic data bases can occupy an enormous amount of space in memory and are thus not always easily accessed via a *modem*, a modulator-demodulator device that permits communication between two processing systems over large distances by using existing telephone lines; they take too long to transmit at these rates. Data can also be electronically communicated through larger bandwidth carriers. It is sometimes fastest to transport data volumes physically.

Data-base technology also incorporates *videodiscs,* a mass produced high-density storage medium. Any data in digital form

9-4. This virtual recording console simulates a traditional audio mixing board, displaying data generated from the microphone in real time. (Courtesy of Visual Intelligence Corporation.)

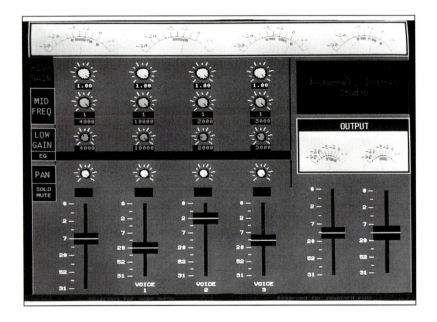

9-5. A tower operator on a main railroad line touches the train indicator and the computer system presents a submenu displaying information about the train in question.

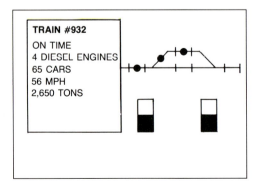

TRAIN #932

ON TIME
4 DIESEL ENGINES
65 CARS
56 MPH
2,650 TONS

can be stored in this fashion, including moving and still images, software, text, and sound. The storage capacity is large, and any frame can be quickly accessed in any order. A videodisc driven by a microcomputer provides a way for a user to select alternate sequences of video resolution images (see fig. 2-5).

High-density picture storage, such as a videodisc, makes it possible not only to select between preprogrammed pathways, but to *edit* these as well, that is, to organize and arrange a sequence of pictures or shots. Computerized editing allows the editor to make and preview cuts, change where the edits occur, extend or shorten a scene, insert or delete shots, and create transitions with dissolves and wipes (fig. 9-7).

Data-base interfaces include ***spatial data-base managers,*** which use nontextual menus and spatially organize information (fig. 9-8). A spatial data-base manager combines the selection process with graphics and indicates "where the user is." Other data bases, for example ***Xanadu,*** allow individual users to overlay the original data base with their own organization of data. This permits users to collect and organize information from their points of view with their needs in mind.

The Automated Office

Office work in our society is becoming increasingly conceptual: what was once a paper-pushing operation now requires screen entry, electronic mail, algorithmized management, and passwords. It is the role of the graphic designer to facilitate and shape office communications.

Information systems often use graphic displays to assist in formatting textual data. A ***desk organizer,*** for example, is an interactive command-and-control system that contains an appointment calendar, clock, pocket calculator, address file, and correspondence (fig. 9-9). Many systems use ***ticklers,*** preprogrammed messages that are displayed at a specific date and time, alerting a user to work due or an upcoming event. ***Electronic mail*** routes words, pictures, and voice messages

 RELATED READING

Bolt, Richard. *Spatial Data-Management.* Cambridge, MA: MIT Press, 1979.

Greenberger, Martin. "The Uses of Computers in Organizations." *Scientific American* (September 1966).

Lesk, Michael. "Computer Software for Information Management." *Scientific American* (September 1984).

Lipetz, Ben-Ami. "Information Storage and Retrieval." *Scientific American* (September 1966).

Minsky, Marvin L. "Artificial Intelligence." *Scientific American* (September 1966).

Siegel, Efrem. *Videotex: The Coming Revolution in Home/Office Information Retrieval.* White Plains, NY: Knowledge Industry Publications, 1980.

NAME
ADDRESS
PHONE
WEIGHT
HEIGHT
COLOR EYES
COLOR HAIR
SEX
AGE
CREDITS
EDUCATION

through one or more computer systems so that individuals can communicate privately or as user groups.

Electronic Publishing

Electronic publishing combines interactive data-base techniques with real time interactive graphics. ***Videotex*** and ***teletext*** are two emerging technologies that permit textual data, icons, and formatting information to be transmitted via

9-6. Information system screen for a personnel data base. File contains names, pictures, statistics, and actors' and models' credits.

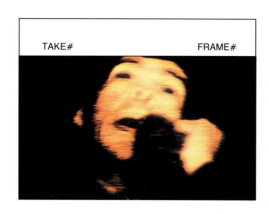

TAKE#   FRAME#

EDIT LIST

TAKE#	FR#B	FR#E
1	60	96
3	15	181
2	126	177

BIN 1

TAKE

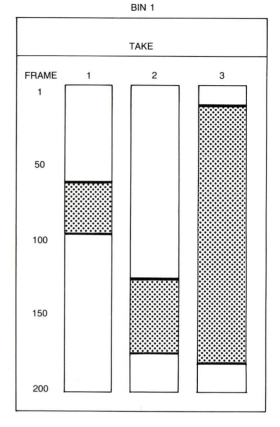

FRAME   1   2   3
1
50
100
150
200

9-7. This virtual editing system shows the current frame plus the complete list of takes that make up a sequence in both graphic and alphanumeric fashions.

9-8. The spatial data-base manager organizes information in a logical manner. The first illustration depicts a collection of ships in a task force, including the name of the ship, its commanding officer and profile. Selecting any one ship zooms it up to full screen and expands the amount of information displayed. (This drawing is based on material created by Computer Corporation of America, 1969.)

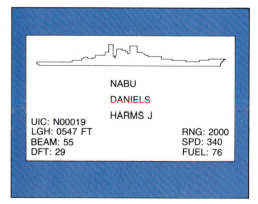

a low bandwidth channel, such as a telephone, and then stored in the local memory of a user's "smart" terminal. Depending on the system, the data is updated every few seconds or accessed interactively by the user. It is often organized into pages through which a user can flip (fig. 9-10).

Applications often involve situations with a modest amount of constantly changing data, such as flight schedules, news, bank account balances, and food prices. They can even include *exchanges,* which list buy-and-sell offers, and a *ticker,* a data stream transmitted once that contains all recent transactions (fig. 9-11).

Most microcomputers can be connected to a videotex or teletext service, with special chips used to decode and graphically display information without taxing the CPU. North American Presentation Level Protocol Standard (NAPLPS) is the most popular standard for encoding and transmitting videotex in North America. NAPLPS uses ASCII notation for character representation, and Picture Description Instructions (PDI) for image description (fig. 9-12). PDI works with very few instructions and can be economically transmitted. Because the graphic icons are represented as polygons, they are transmitted in a compact form and then drawn by the user's machine, making NAPLPS device independent and adaptable to displays of different resolution.

From the design point of view, teletext and videotex offer an interactive graphic environment with limited resolution and typefaces. Clear design guidelines are extremely important, as is typography, readability, and layout. The designer today must be able to design at many resolutions so that the information is effectively understood in the medium through which it is communicated (fig. 9-13).

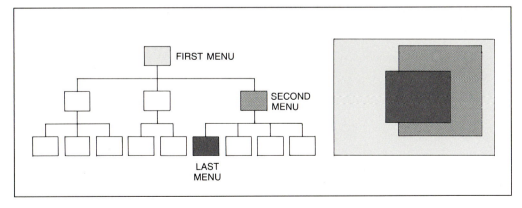

9-9. Desk organizer includes a virtual pocket calculator, calendar, word processor, and data base.

9-10. A complex data base is transmitted over the phone lines to a "smart" terminal where it is stored locally in hierarchical form. The user accesses the data base by making menu selections and calling up new pages of information that are overlaid on the screen.

9-11. Exchange tickers are used in electronic publishing, because a computer can be programmed to pick off pertinent information, for example, the transactions in certain currencies or commodities. The role of the graphic designer is to assist in displaying this information in a meaningful way. The figure illustrates a system that displays information on spot currency prices. (Courtesy of Reuters Limited.)

```
1114                SPOT CURRENCIES - 24 HR WORLD INPUT          WRLD
TIME CY    PAGE    SOURCE      LATEST         PREV      HIGH    LOW
                                                              N.AMERICA HI/LO
1114 DMK   RBCM    ROYAL BK    3.0540/50      40/55     3.0585  3.0480
1113 STG   MHTN    MAN HAN     1.2700/10      00/10     1.2720  1.2680
1114 SFR   UBZA    U B S       2.5660/80      60/80     2.5700  2.5625
1111 YEN   MHTN    MAN HAN     247.95/05      95/05     248.50  247.30
1111 FFR   BMMA    BK MTL      9.3125/75      30/80     9.3250  9.3000
1058 GLD   UBZB    U B S       315.00/315.50  00/50

1058 SIL   UBZB    6.14/6.16         0723   3 MTH EUR EDLR   7.50-.62
0828 FED   PREB    7 11/16 3/4       1113   T BND CGO JUN        79%16



            S1-K1-1         REUTER MONITOR       0355
```

Escape	32	15	45	31	52	27
Graphics mode		Start line	X coordinates		Y coordinates	

9-12. Table shows numerical codes that represent commands.

9-13. Bold graphic design and clear typography, as in this videotex page, are essential for successful medium-resolution graphics. (Courtesy of Stanley Bernesche, Office of External Affairs, Canada.)

CARTOGRAPHY

Computerized systems have revolutionized *cartography*—the gathering, analysis, and display of maps. Maps today are no longer flat sheets, but are complex socio-geographic information systems that would have been impossible to implement, or even conceive of, several years ago.

Maps now provide information about an environment by analyzing landscape, cultural features, and bedrock. Maps for navigation involve movement through space and include real time training simulators for teaching the operation of ships, aircraft, and automobiles (fig. 9-14).

Up-to-the-minute information is vital for creating useful maps; digital cartography permits a data base to be quickly updated, enabling changes to propagate into map displays at the speed of light.

One distinctive feature of this evolution is the multispectral image. **Multispectral images** are not limited to tristimulus color, but incorporate photographic, topographical, and sociological features that can be overlaid and compared (fig. 9-15).

Photographic data includes aerial as well as satellite data imaging and is usually

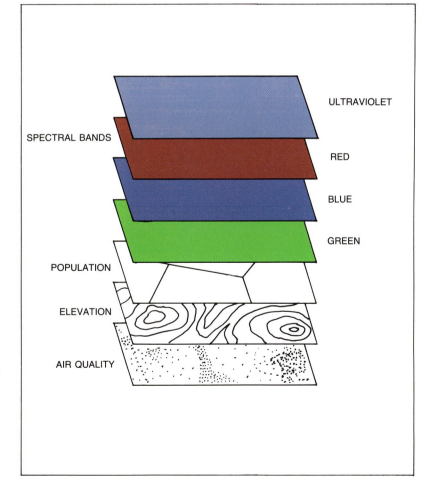

SPECTRAL BANDS

ULTRAVIOLET

RED

BLUE

GREEN

POPULATION

ELEVATION

AIR QUALITY

9-16. LANDSAT photograph of New York state coastline. (Courtesy of Celco.)

9-17. Topographical data plotted in perspective. Each square plots one zel, or Z elevation. In the rendering, the lines have been smoothed between pixels of different elevation. (Reprinted, by permission, from Mitchell *Computer Aided Architectural Design*, 140.)

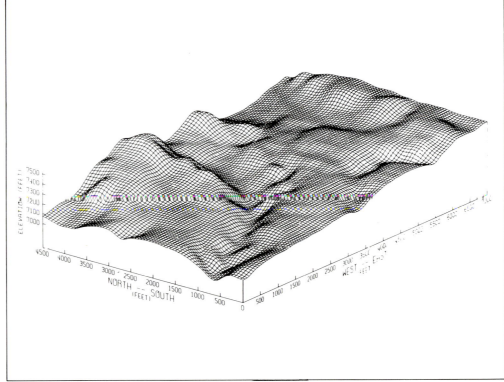

represented as pixels (fig. 9-16). *Topographical* data, usually zel data, contains elevations of land and water and is determined from field survey techniques and stereometric methods (fig. 9-17). Population census data, air quality measurements, and political boundaries that constitute *sociological* data are stored as a matrix of numbers, and may be graphically represented (fig. 9-18).

By aligning all of these spectral representations as bitmaps, the computer can calculate areas, densities, and selectively compare topographical and sociological features. This simple pixel-by-pixel analysis can compare different spectral planes to discover whether population densities tend to be higher in low elevations or in mountains (fig. 9-19).

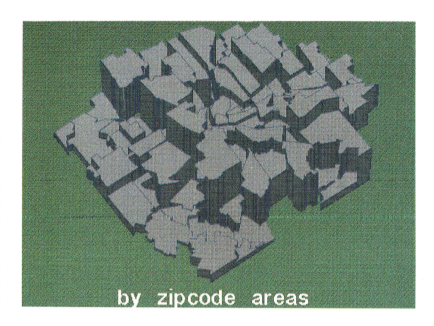

by zipcode areas

A

9-18. Sociological data—population density—is expressed with columns whose heights are proportional to the number of residents, who are separated by zip code. (Courtesy of Morgan Fairfield, Inc.)

B

9-19. These images were created with a computer program that analyzes altitude information (A) before creating snow on the mountain peaks (B).

9-20. Flat diagrammatic projection of contours. This is the same data as in figures 9-17 and 9-21. (Reprinted, by permission, from Mitchell *Computer Aided Architectural Design*, 262).

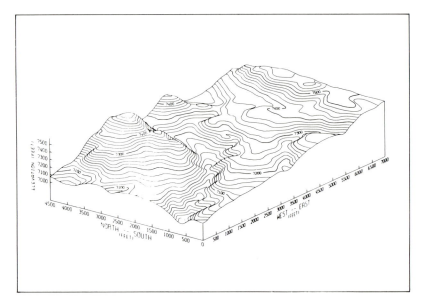

(a)

9-21. Perspective projections of contours. This is the same data as in figures 9-17 and 9-20. Note how scale and heavier line contours aid representation. (Reprinted, by permission, from Mitchell *Computer Aided Architectural Design*, 263.)

 RELATED READING

Monmonier, M. S. Computer Assisted *Cartography*. Englewood Cliffs, NJ: Prentice-Hall, 1982.

These pixel representations can be converted into lines and contours using the standard techniques discussed for image processing (fig. 9-20), and plotted in perspective (fig. 9-21). Icons, measurements, networks for transportation and power, and text may be overlaid in different colors, either on a screen or on paper (fig. 9-22). Color may also be used with three-dimensional perspective renderings of terrain, both to show elevation (fig. 9-23) as well as a realistic, photographlike rendering (fig. 9-24).

Since it is impossible to map a sphere to a plane without distortions, a variety of projection methods have been developed with various strengths, weaknesses, and purposes; some are equal area and others are not, for instance (fig. 9-25). These are readily produced using computers.

BUSINESS GRAPHICS AND MANAGEMENT SYSTEMS

Management decision systems control the administration of money and resources; the manager of the future may

246 APPLICATIONS IN DESIGN

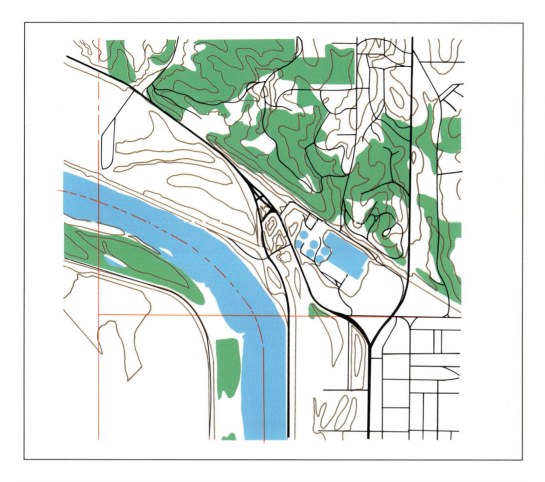

9-22. Maps often relate overlays and colors. In a real time system the overlays can be switched on and off in different combinations. In this example, topographical elevations are represented in brown, rivers and water deposits in blue, floral areas in green, roads and cultural features in black, and political boundaries in red.

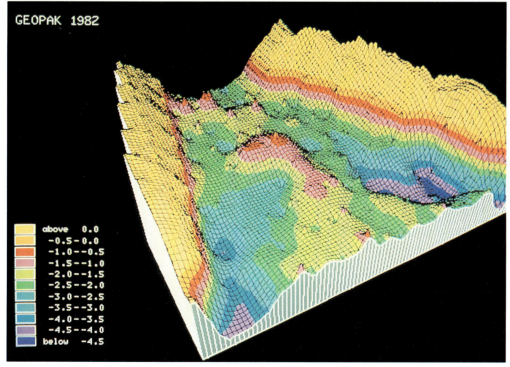

GEOPAK 1982

above	0.0
-0.5 - 0.0	
-1.0 - -0.5	
-1.5 - -1.0	
-2.0 - -1.5	
-2.5 - -2.0	
-3.0 - -2.5	
-3.5 - -3.0	
-4.0 - -3.5	
-4.5 - -4.0	
below	-4.5

9-23. Altitude information is color coded and rendered in perspective. The display is of medium resolution but is clear. Do not confuse the spatial resolution of the display with the topographical resolution. (Courtesy of European Software Contractors A/S. Image created on the UNIRAS system.)

9-24. Realistic renderings of cartographic data (Mt. St. Helens) can include natural features like snow (light blue), rock (rust), and water (deep blue). Seasons, too, can be modeled. This image is from an aircraft system that works in a real airplane cockpit and updates the display in real time as the pilot flies, which is useful for flying in the dark, especially over and around things at low altitude. The data is digitally stored aboard, or down loaded from an earth satellite, and then cross-correlated by radars on the plane that validate position and view. The images generated are similar to a flight simulator, but in this case the pilot is using simulated displays for real flight. (Courtesy of Hughes Aircraft Company, Radar Systems Group.)

9-25. Illustrated here are Albers equal area projection (A), Lambert conformal projection (B); Mercator projection (C); sinusoidal projection (D).

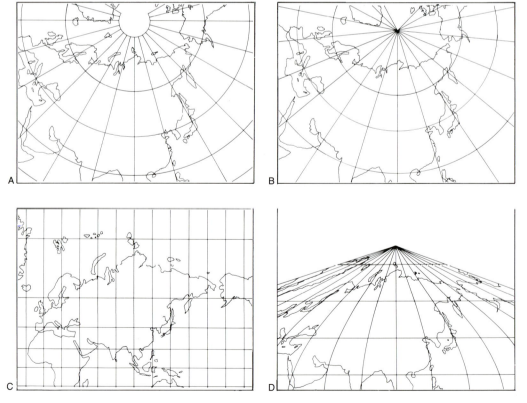

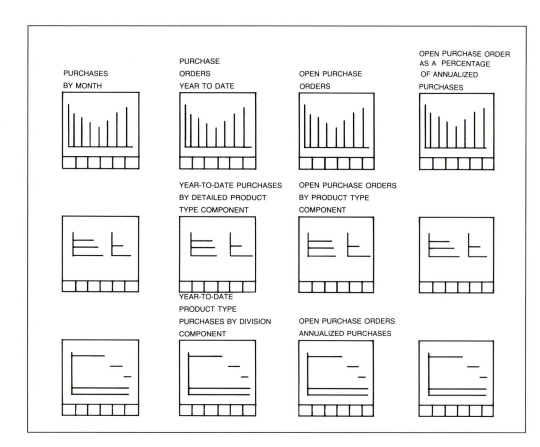

9-26. Management-decision-system console incorporates graphics showing critical financial information about various aspects of the company.

	A	B	C	D	E
1	Concept/Month	January	February	March	Total Quarter
2	Cost	10,987.00	08,700.25	09,254.32	28,941.57 (SUM B2 . . . D2)
3	Sales	16,842.82	15,495.57	15,392.13	47,730.52 (SUM B3 . . . D3)
4	Profit	05,855.82 (+B3–B2)	06,795.32 (+C3–C2)	06,137.81 (+D3–D2)	18,788.95 (+E3–E2)

well be a player sitting at a command-and-control console. Today's business systems format financial reports, analyze market research, and forecast (fig. 9-26).

Spread Sheets

A manager's graphic tools include *spread sheets,* interactive displays containing a matrix of numbers and labels (fig. 9-27). The number in each cell of a spread sheet can be either a *value,* original data entered into the system or captured

by it, or a *value rule,* the result of an equation that incorporates the values from other cells. For example, a certain row can contain the column totals of all the rows above it. A change in one cell produces a change in any other cell that uses it in a value rule calculation—change propagates forward. The cells can also contain text, labels, formatting instructions (for example, how many decimal places to show), and pointers to other spread sheets.

9-27. Spread sheet.

RELATED READING

Cardamone, T. *Chart and Graph Preparation Skills.* New York: Van Nostrand Reinhold, 1981.

Chambers, John, William S. Cleveland, Bert Kleiner, and Paul A. Tukey. *Graphical Methods for Data Analysis.* Belmont, CA: Wadsworth, 1983.

Jarett, Irwin. *Computer Graphics and Reporting Financial Data.* New York: John Wiley & Sons, 1983.

Kay, Alan. "Computer Software." *Scientific American* (September 1984).

Paller, Alan, K. Szoka, and N. Nelson. *Choosing the Right Chart, A Comprehensive Guide.* San Diego: ISSCO, 1981.

Spear, Mary Eleanor. *Practical Charting Techniques.* New York: McGraw-Hill, 1969.

Tufte, Edward R. *The Visual Display of Quantitative Information.* Cheshire, CT: Graphics Press, 1983.

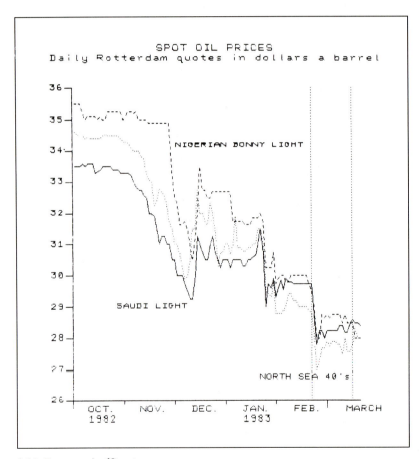

9-28. Peer graph. (Courtesy of Ron Couture and the *New York Times*.)

Spread sheets are similar to local operators except the cells represent quantities such as dollars. The value rules, input, and output are all in the same matrix. The value rules can be used not only to account for the past, but to simulate the future by describing hypothetical situations. Spread sheets can also be used for hierarchical data retrieval and may interface to database managers, as well as to graphs.

Graphs

A *graph* represents numerical information in a defined pictorial format, often an XY display. The most common graphs, line and bar graphs, pie charts, and scattergrams, are used in all facets of science and industry to monitor and communicate events and cash flows.

Many integrated computer systems allow data to be automatically fed into a preformatted chart and graph template. Graphic presentation simplifies complex numerical information and describes problems and trends. Graphs, coupled with numerical information, provide a valuable correlation between the left brain and right brain, which helps an analyst or audience understand the representation.

Graph design is often divided into either a *peer graph* (fig. 9-28), used for internal analysis and decision making, or a *presentation graph* (fig. 9-29), a slicker, simpler, often color, visual designed to persuade a particular group of people or to focus attention on specific data. Peer graphs tend to be rougher and more complex.

The designer determines graph formats and ensures that layouts are easy to understand and use an appropriate style. Each of the common forms for creating graphs works well for specific applications. Business graphs evolve from an ongoing dialogue between designers (experts in the composition of messages) and analysts (those who compile and analyze the data).

Line and bar graphs are often used for plotting data with one variable and one constant—a graph across time, for example (fig. 9-30). A *line graph* suggests continuous change whereas a *bar graph* depicts discrete measures. Both allow multiple variables to be superimposed and compared.

Pie charts are best used to express data as parts or percentages of a whole (fig. 9-31). Well-designed pie charts picture a small amount of data.

Polar graphs are used to chart measurements made at different angular positions. The radius at each angle can represent a distance or an elevation (fig. 9-32).

The **scattergram** shows the relationship between two variables (fig. 9-33). Scattergrams are XY point pairs such as the height and weight of an individual, and are used

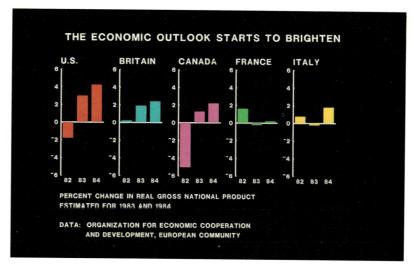

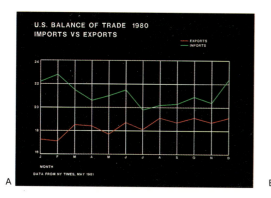

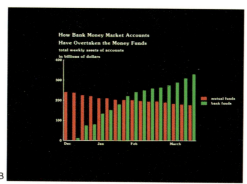

9-29. Presentation graph. (Courtesy of Christine Shostack.)

9-30. Line (A) and bar graphs (B). (Courtesy of Christine Shostack.)

9-31. Pie chart. (Courtesy of Image Resource Corporation, Westlake Village, CA.)

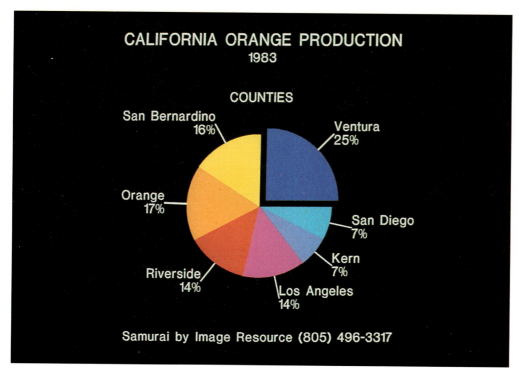

9-32. Polar graphs. The first of these (A) depicts the field strength of a radio transmitter. The transmitter is located in the center of the graph and the concentric circles represent radial distances in miles. The wavy line represents a constant signal strength where a listener can get good reception. Perhaps the physical contours of the terrain explain why the line indicating field strength is uneven. The second of these graphs (B) depicts the angular clearances for a ship-mounted projectile weapon. In this drawing the concentric circles represent elevations. Straight up is at the center, with larger circles representing progressively lower angles. The plot shows how the deck house and bow obscure part of the field of vision.

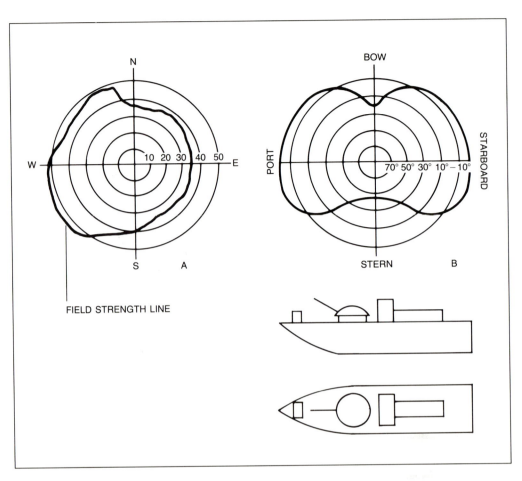

9-33. Scattergram.

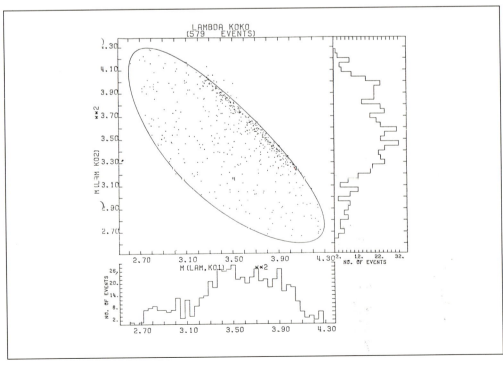

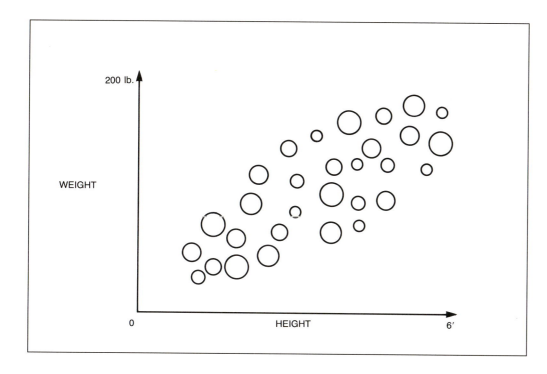

9-34. In this bubble graph the radius of the bubble relates to intelligence. Heavier people tend to be taller, but are they more intelligent?

9-35. Surface chart. (Courtesy of Genigraphics.)

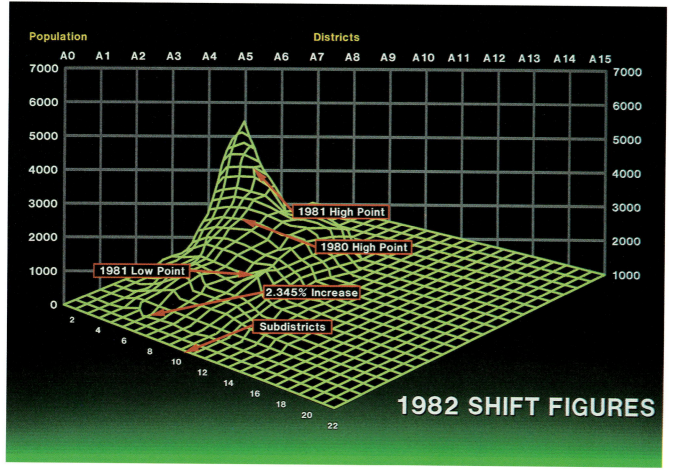

RELATED READING

Crawford, Chris. *The Art of Computer Game Design.* Berkeley, CA: Osborne/McGraw-Hill, 1984.

Gayeski, Diane, and David Williams. *Interactive Media.* Englewood Cliffs, NJ: Prentice-Hall, 1985.

Krueger, Myron W. *Artificial Reality.* Reading, MA: Addison-Wesley, 1983.

Schachter, Bruce J., ed. *Computer Image Generation.* New York: John Wiley & Sons, 1983.

to identify correlations: taller people generally weigh more.

Graphs can also plot three or more variables. **Bubble graphs** represent three variables on a two-dimensional planar surface (fig. 9-34) and differ from scattergrams in that they plot a radius at each point. A **surface net,** like the bubble graph, depicts three degrees of variance and displays a three-dimensional perspective (fig. 9-35) that looks like a topographical map.

On the bubble graph the magnitude of the point is plotted as a circle radius; on a surface net the magnitude of each point is projected as an elevation (a zel); and on a **balloon graph,** a point is projected as a volumetric icon in three dimensions, perhaps with color, transparency, and luster, which can represent even more variables (fig. 9-36). **Isobars,** used on weather maps, show wind direction and speed as well as cloud cover at a geographic (XY) location (fig. 9-37). **Chernoff** graphs (fig. 9-38) can display twenty or more variables, often econometric, by connecting them to the various parts of a graphic icon. Often these icons are cartoon faces with the variables controlling the length of a smile, size of an eye, and position of an eyebrow. This anthropomorphization of abstract data makes it more readily perceived—the face is "happy" or "sad"—and a single feature astray is immediately obvious. We find the researcher, then, like the animator, bringing a figure to life, so its moods and expressions communicate a state of affairs.

Features of graphing systems vary widely and range from the best display list machines to punch card input. Graph software controls formatting techniques, such as *automatic scaling,* which ensures that a graph fits into its window and its axes have logical tic marks (fig. 9-39). Other formatting variables determine if bars are **stacked** (on top of each other) or **grouped** (side by side), if pies are to be pulled from pie charts, or if grids, high/low/close marks, and average lines are to be overlaid.

INTERACTIVE VIDEO INSTRUMENTS AND GAMES

The marriage between video and interactive computer graphics is a profound and serendipitous one. Video, after all, is a real time picture-processing system with medium resolution and is a dominant distribution medium in our culture. With computer graphics, video becomes an interactive medium.

The **Video synthesizer,** an instrument that allows a "visual musician" to form and modify images in real time—often in conjunction with music (fig. 9-40)—is one such interactive system that is controlled with knobs, piano-styled keyboards, and typewriter keyboards.

The **interactive video game,** which has brought computers closer to more people than any other technology to date, is a closed system with interactive computer graphics displayed on a color screen. These games require cognitive skills, strategy, and fast reflexes.

Video games both educate and entertain. A highly participatory medium that relies on a variety of graphic techniques, the game is based on either a conflict between the player and the machine—a skill and action game—or a problem posed by the machine for the player to solve—a strategy game.

The skill and action video game is reflex oriented and pits the player against an antagonist—often in an unfriendly environment. Played by the computer, the antagonist becomes increasingly fiendish as the player's skills improve (fig. 9-41). Examples include Pong (the first computer game), PAC-MAN, and sports contests.

The strategy game involves thinking and

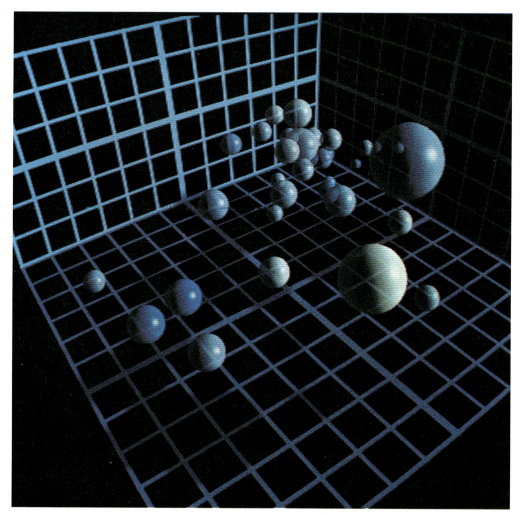

9-36. The balloon graph, a three-dimensional perspective plot, depicts the universe within 50 million light years of earth. Each bubble represents a cluster of galaxies; the radius of the bubble is proportional to the number of galaxies in that region in space. (Courtesy of Floyd Gillis, Omnibus Computer Graphics.)

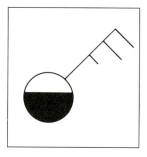

9-37. Wind direction and speed are represented by the position of the flag and the number of bars on this isobar; the cloud cover is represented as shading.

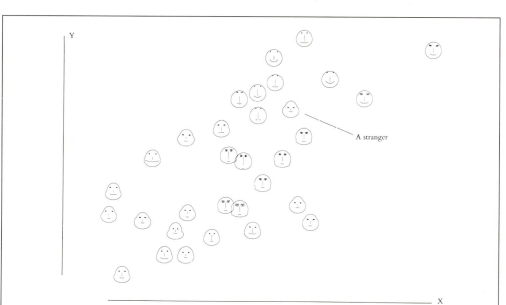

A stranger

9-38. In this Chernoff graph, the faces have not only X,Y positions, but their expressions are determined by a multitude of variables. The aggregate effect is not only to condense a complex set of situations into a "look," but also to recognize deviations from the norm. (Courtesy of Edward Tufte. Image by Herman Chernoff.)

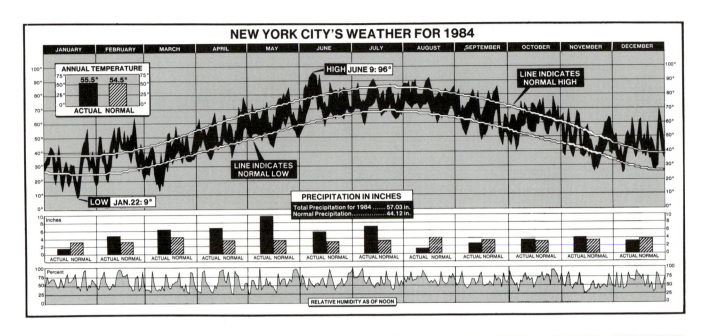

9-39. This weather chart combines a multitude of data into a single diagram. It includes daily highs, lows, and averages, bar graphs of monthly precipitation, and a line graph of relative humidity. (Courtesy of the *New York Times*.)

9-40. Visual music. (Courtesy of Tom DeFanti.)

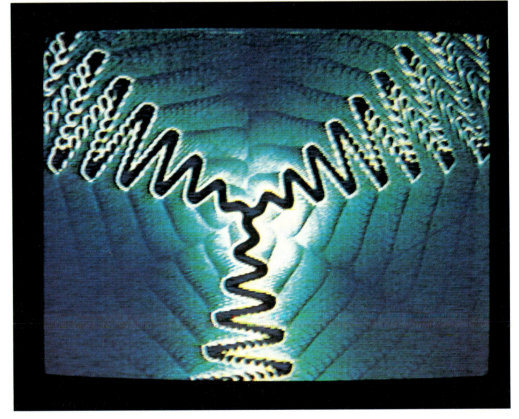

CITY'S PK ENERGY: 2873 $3000

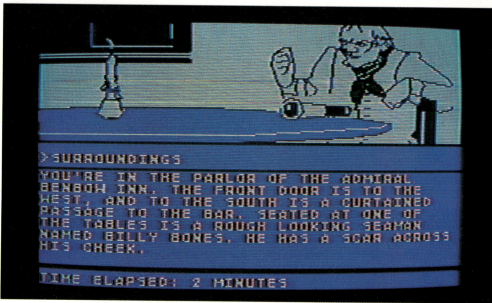

>SURROUNDINGS
YOU'RE IN THE PARLOR OF THE ADMIRAL
BENBOW INN. THE FRONT DOOR IS TO THE
WEST, AND TO THE SOUTH IS A CURTAINED
PASSAGE TO THE BAR. SEATED AT ONE OF
THE TABLES IS A ROUGH LOOKING SEAMAN
NAMED BILLY BONES. HE HAS A SCAR ACROSS
HIS CHEEK.

TIME ELAPSED: 2 MINUTES

9-41. Action video game.
(Courtesy of Activision.
Graphics by Hillary Mills.)

9-42. Strategy game. (Courtesy of Byron Preiss Video
Productions.)

9-43. Star Rider, a laser disk video game created by Computer Creations for Williams Electronics, presents a computer-generated race through a futuristic city. The images are retrieved from a videodisc and displayed on a video monitor while the view through a rearview mirror is calculated by the computer. (Courtesy of Computer Creations. Game design by Python Anghelo; animation by Eric Brown; software by Tom Klimek and Herman Towles.)

9-44. A system for teaching layout to design students. (Courtesy of the College of Fine and Applied Arts, Rochester Institute of Technology.)

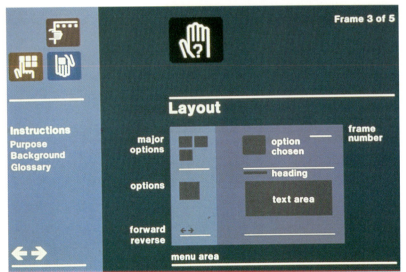

cognitive skills; it is less action and reflex oriented. Examples include Adventure, which involves a search or a quest through a complex spatial world (fig. 9-42), and Star Trek, a war game that creates environments, shows the status of deployments, and offers options displayed on a command-and-control panel.

Video game design incorporates graphic technologies that range from sprites to the integration of on-line videodiscs that store still frames and animated sequences (fig. 9-43). Graphic design requires an understanding of characterization, action, and environment, and progresses from storyboards to flowcharts that contain alternate pathways and show visual style.

EDUCATION AND TRAINING

Teaching and training systems can incorporate process control, data-base retrieval, cartography, and interactive game playing, but focus on education. Applications include console training and practice, drill skills like typing, and organized curriculums for learning, which can in-

◤ RELATED READING

Kaye, Allen C. "Microelectronics in the Personal Computer." *Scientific American* (September 1977).

Oettinger, Anthony G. "The Use of Computers." *Scientific American* (September 1966).

Suppes, Patrick. "The Uses of Computers in Education." *Scientific American* (September 1966).

9-45. An instrumentation display of a small aircraft is combined here with a moderately realistic view on the screen. Instrumentation includes an altimeter, artificial horizon, throttle, and rates of climb and descent. (Portrayed here is *Flight Simulator* by Microsoft, Inc.)

9-46. The virtual environment of an airplane cockpit includes full-scale seats and working controls. The views out the window are synthetically generated while the plane is "in flight." (Courtesy of Evans & Sutherland Corp.)

9-47. A rocker platform is used to support virtual environments, such as the one in figure 9-46, and adds an element of realism to the learning experience. The platform is mounted on hydraulic arms that can make it pitch or roll. (Courtesy of The Singer Co., Link Flight Simulation Division.)

corporate a mixture of cognitive and reflex skills. Programmed learning systems involve interactive interface between trainers and trainees, plus a program of instruction.

From the point of view of the trainee, the system presents an interactive network that the student can explore at his or her own pace. This system must anticipate how a student learns the correct information and must recognize when a student is confused or using incorrect methods. The system presents the information again with more precise examples and retests the student.

The system permits instructors to monitor the individual student as well as the teaching algorithm. They can thus tailor the curriculum to stress a student's problem areas or analyze the entire educational process. Both teacher and student are "plugged into" the support structure of computerized classroom rosters, scheduling, testing, grading, and financial exchange.

Imaginative graphics can be implemented on eight- and sixteen-bit home computers using sprites, look-up tables, and pull-down windows (fig. 9-44). The graphics can reinforce basic concepts even in nonvisual and abstract disciplines, such as typing, spelling, composition, science, history, or music.

Education and training systems often use **instrumentation displays,** which are similar to those in process control and many video games (fig. 9-45) and teach topics as diverse as golf, weight reduction methods, astrology, poker, chemistry, and instrument flight—a real time task. **Virtual environments** instruct by displaying synthetic physical environments, for example, a full-scale cockpit mock-up with working controls and a view out the window of land, clouds, airports, and other aircraft (fig. 9-46). Obviously, if you bank the plane, the point of view out the window changes. In fact, the cockpit can even be mounted on a hydraulically controlled platform, so the plane can pitch, bank, and bounce from turbulence (fig. 9-47).

Image generation in virtual environments incorporates three-dimensional shaded computer graphics, using hardware and software to animate the screens in response to controls. Videodiscs can also be used by selecting from prerecorded images made from different points of view. One novel application by researchers at MIT's Architecture Machine Group recorded views down the streets of Aspen, Colorado, as well as all the corner turns. These fragments were stored on a disk, allowing a user to drive around the city without leaving the room.

A virtual environment can take many forms (fig. 9-48) and includes synthetic environments as well as synthetic instrumentation displays. The former includes visualizations of reality, the latter does not. As virtual environments become more tactile they can be used as substitutions for real world experience: training machines can already be connected, so two fighter pilots can practice dogfights. This is high-tech video, requiring motor skills to perform a precision task, and a closed environment is thus large enough to seem real.

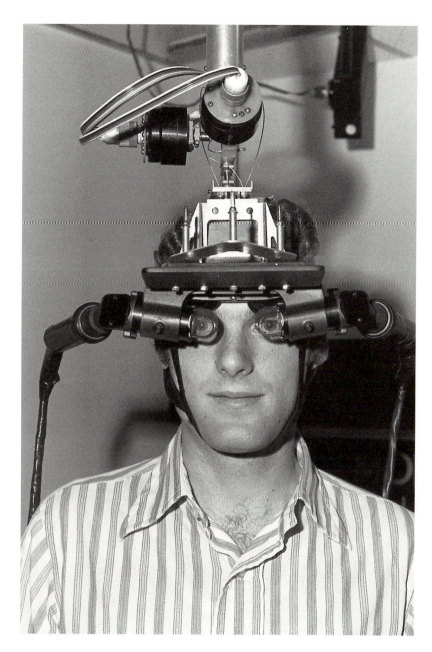

9-48. A head-mounted display tracks the user's eye movements and simulates a three-dimensional environment that changes accordingly. (Courtesy of the University of Utah.)

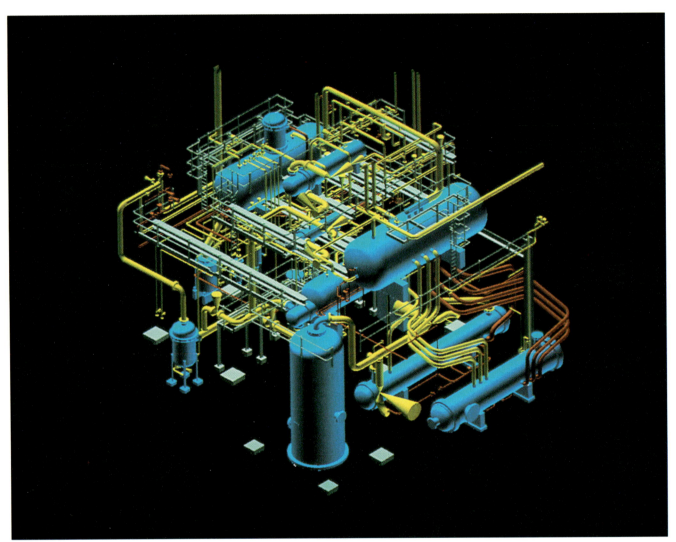

10-0. Production processes can be computer controlled. Different colors are used to illustrate different sections of this piping installation. (Courtesy of Computervision Corp.)

THREE-DIMENSIONAL MEDIA: THE PRODUCTION OF MATERIAL GOODS

INDUSTRIAL DESIGN
ARCHITECTURE AND INTERIOR DESIGN
PACKAGE DESIGN
CLOTHING AND TEXTILE DESIGN

Computer-aided design and manufacturing (CADAM) consolidates the design and production of three-dimensional material goods—packages, products, clothing, vehicles, and architecture.

The computer-aided design (CAD) component conceptualizes, models, previsualizes, tests, and documents the progress of a project. The computer-aided manufacturing (CAM) component automatically produces drafts, process plans, assembles—using numerically controlled robots and assembly tools—performs quality control, and accounts.

CADAM allows designs to be easily refined, increases design variety and accuracy, and shortens the cycle from design to production. Designers using CADAM

10-1. An overall view of an electronic circuit design (A), and a close-up of the area inside the rectangle (B). (Courtesy of NEC Information Systems.)

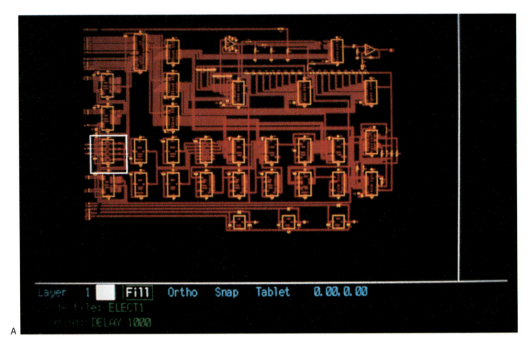

A

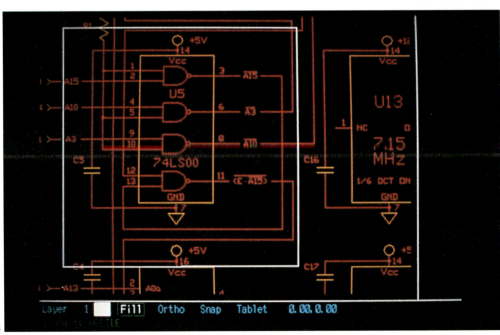

B

systems work in the positive, designing actual objects, rather than in the negative, where a mold is required. Since the data is digital, it can be archived when it becomes obsolete, yet restored and easily adapted should there be a need to redesign.

CADAM systems provide an alternative to the mass production of goods and can efficiently produce *prototypes* and *one-offs,* products manufactured in unit quantities, using mass production techniques.

INDUSTRIAL DESIGN

Applications in Industrial Design

Industrial design includes three-dimensional products used both by consumers and in manufacturing, such as hand tools, appliances, power and machine tools, furniture, electronic circuit components and products, farm equipment, automobiles, airplanes, musical instruments, drugs, and factories (fig. 10-1).

The products of industrial design can be solid objects made from a single material, such as a fork or baseball bat; static objects made from a combination of materials, such as a pencil; nonpowered objects built of moving parts, such as a stapler; or powered objects with many moving parts, such as a gasoline engine. The products may be manufactured by machine, cast from molds, stamped from dies, extruded, laminated, and grown, to name a few methods.

In all of these applications, whether objects are as small as atoms or as large as planets, computer graphics provides a way to model and preview the virtual product before it is actually manufactured, to test it in its domain, at a scale comfortable to the designer, and to convert the virtual model into a real product.

The CADAM Cycle of Production

The cycle of production of material goods begins with a design and concludes with a three-dimensional solid object. The steps of this production include needs analysis, three-dimensional solid modeling, visualization, simulation, drafting, process

▶ RELATED READING

Coons, Stephen A. "The Uses of Computers in Technology." *Scientific American* (September 1966).

Encarnacao, J., and E. G. Schlechtendahl. *Computer Aided Design.* Berlin: Springer-Verlag, 1983.

Groover, Mikell P., and Emory W. Zimmers, Jr. *CAD/CAM Computer Aided Design and Manufacturing.* Englewood Cliffs, NJ: Prentice-Hall, 1984.

Gunn, Thomas G. "The Mechanization of Design and Manufacturing." *Scientific American* (September 1982).

Lange, Jerome C., and Dennis P. Shanahan. *Interactive Computer Graphics Applied to Mechanical Drafting and Design.* New York: John Wiley & Sons, 1984.

Oliver, Bernard M. "The Role of Microelectronics in Instrumentation and Control." *Scientific American* (September 1977).

Teicholz, Eric. *CAD/CAM Handbook.* New York: McGraw-Hill, 1984.

planning, production, quality control, and accounting (fig. 10-2).

The *design concept,* a marketing-related term that refers to the design of the physical container or appliance as well as to the design of the idea, is the first concern when employing a CADAM system. The product design of frosted flakes, for example, refers not only to the design of the box and the graphics, but to the concept of frosting cornflakes and selling them as a breakfast cereal.

The development of a product in this context is shaped as much by the market research analyzed with a computer as by its interactive creation and the display of the product. Products today are often designed to fill sociological, psychological, and physical voids; a design that attracts buyers, therefore, is often not a physically innovative design, but one that has been shaped by a marketing plan based on demographics, research, and economics.

Once conceived, a product is modeled three dimensionally on an interactive vector graphic, or raster, work station that can rotate, size, and position the model. Modeling for a CADAM system is not functionally different from the methods of three-dimensional modeling described in chapter 7. Models are constructed by digitizing and procedural techniques and are stored in graphics data bases. Standardized parts

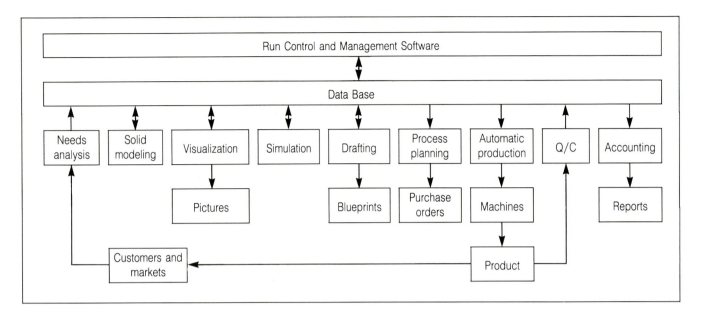

10-2. The CADAM cycle of production.

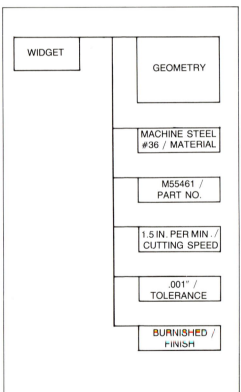

10-3. CADAM data bases combine geometric and nongeometric information.

such as screws, nuts, brackets, and washers are modeled once and stored in on-line libraries.

A reliable and flexible data base is required at each stage, storing all relevant information about the product and how it is manufactured. *Geometric* data, about the shape of the object, as well as *associated data,* nongraphic information such as the materials used to make an object, manufacturing tolerances, and a part number are data-base components (fig. 10-3). Most CADAM data bases are relational and show how subassemblies together form a whole, and how parts are connected and move, their order of assembly, and functional relationships.

Previsualization provides a way to see the computer models before they are manufactured. The virtual models can be displayed either as wire frames, solid objects, or even cutaway views (fig. 10-4). Solid, shaded renderings are useful for thoroughly evaluating the look of a design, and realistic visualization routines include all of the aspects of surface and light interactions already discussed. Even animated movies and holograms can be made.

Simulation is the analysis· of product design—testing the product while it is still a numerical model. The exact simulations performed depend on the product that is being designed; for example, a refrigerator design might be simulated to determine its heat loss under a variety of room temperatures. In all cases the results of the experiment are used to validate and modify designs.

Designs can be physically tested as well as market tested. Physical simulations include analyzing structures, calculating areas, testing electrical requirements and fracturing conditions, aerodynamics, and confirming tolerances between moving parts. Air-conditioning, cooling, and power requirements can be simulated, as can human factors (fig. 10-5).

Market testing uses computerized previsualizations in research to test human responses to designs, determining which styles have appeal and which do not. The ability to generate variations in color, shape, and detail permits a researcher to quantify variations and hone in on successful design concepts within tight deadlines.

Drafting produces engineering drawings—geometric visualizations that represent data so that machinists, die makers, or assembly workers can follow it. Engineering drawings augment the basic geometry of a part with center lines, tolerances, surface finish, and measurements. Drafting is a characteristic of CADAM systems that distinguishes them from three-dimensional solid-modeling software.

When machines are computer controlled, engineering drawings are obsolete as communicative devices between designer and machinist. Applications that involve large constructions, such as ship building, architecture, or factory design, require drafting as a fundamental communication tool. In all cases drafting provides basic documentation, often in multiple colors, that depicts relationships between different systems (fig. 10-6).

Process planning techniques include assembly plans (fig. 10-7), schedules, pert and gant charts, which graphically depict critical paths of production, time allotments, raw materials and components lists used to generate purchase and work orders, and interfaces to sales, manage-

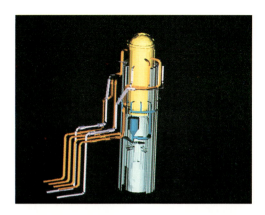

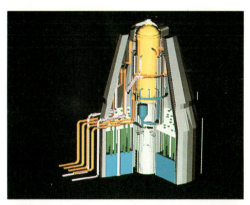

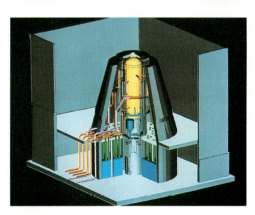

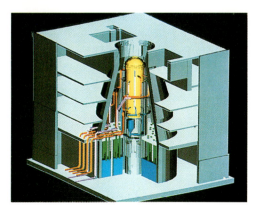

10-4. Previsualized cutaway views of nuclear reactor containment facility in varying degrees of complexity. (Courtesy of Everett I. Brown Company.)

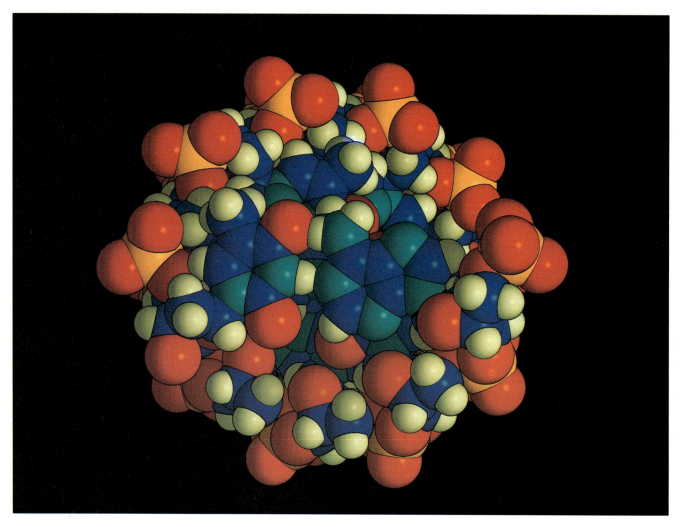

10-5. Simulation allows a product to be tested before it is created. For example, a new drug might be tested for side effects by simulating how it reacts chemically with other molecules in the body. The simulation uses calculations based on the rules of chemistry and molecular reactions. (Top view of DNA molecule courtesy of Nelson Max and Lawrence Livermore, National Laboratory.)

ment, accounting, and production departments.

CADAM systems were developed to connect the three-dimensional digital data base directly with the manufacturing process for automated parts production and assembly. ***Run control procedures*** manage the entire design and manufacturing processes. Run control software interrelates the various components of a CADAM system and is akin in many respects to monitor and control processes, tracking production from order entry through delivery. The exact strategies involved vary according to the production methods, but include numerically controlled machine tools and assembly robots. ***Numerically controlled tools*** are computer driven lathes, milling machines, and specialized machine tools

of all types used to either make molds or to cut the material directly (fig. 3-46). ***Assembly robots*** (fig. 10-8) include machines that weld, integrate, and assemble products. Some are programmed to perform exact moves; others have computer vision and tactile sensors that allow them to pick up pieces in a random bin, or to orient themselves in situations that are not completely predictable.

After a product has been manufactured, each part can be tested to ensure *quality control*. These controls are computerized and are therefore clearly defined; solutions to past mistakes can be integrated into the present system. The monitoring hardware can include digital scales that check weight, cameras and pattern recognition software that verify the shape of the part

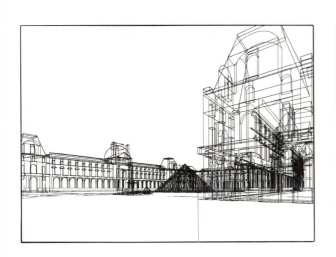

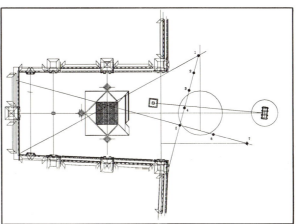

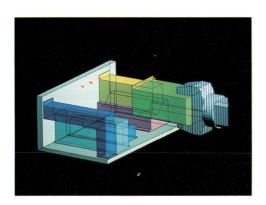

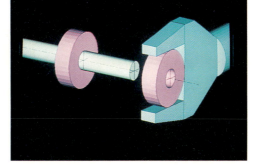

10-6. Drafting is a specialized visualization method used to show the relationships between different components of a project. Drafting includes plan and elevation drawings; structures can be also drawn in perspective. Depicted here is a remodeling of the Louvre Museum by I. M. Pei. (Courtesy of Computervision Corp.)

(fig. 10-9), and testing jigs, which operate the product (fig. 10-10).

Finally, **accounting software** produces reports either in a tabular or graphic format that detail profits, costs associated with specific jobs, and statistics about the production unit, such as what percent of its capacity is being used.

ARCHITECTURE AND INTERIOR DESIGN

Computers used in architecture and in interior design locate elements in three-dimensional space and simulate their appearance and performance. Computers assist in space design and planning, landscape studies, and the detailing and spec-

10-7. A Tokyo University research group led by Professor Kunii solves a product assembly problem. The product here is a copying machine that has been designed on a CAD system. The assembly solution begins by disassembling the product with a virtual disassembler, which tests pieces to see which can be removed, then removes them one by one—by sliding a bearing off a shaft, for example. After the disassembly sequence is stored, it is easily reversed, so either a virtual assembler or a real machine performs the assembly. Kunii envisions a future with a standardization that enables real disassemblers to take apart real objects, service them, and put them together again. (Courtesy of Tosiyasu L. Kunii. © Tsukasu Noma, Tosiyasu L. Kunii, and Ricoh Co., Ltd.)

10-8. The robot (A) is first programmed using an interactive computer graphics display that simulates the robot's movements and checks for interferences (B). A variety of grippers can be affixed to the end of the robot arm. (Courtesy of Calma Company.)

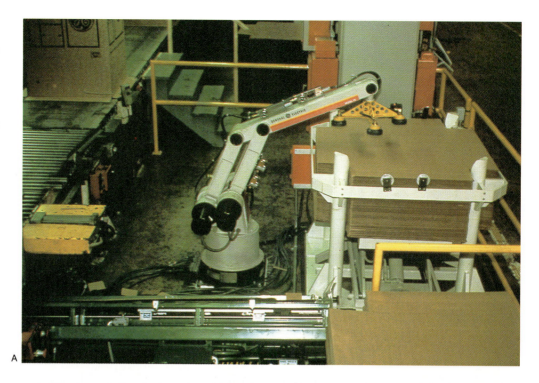

A

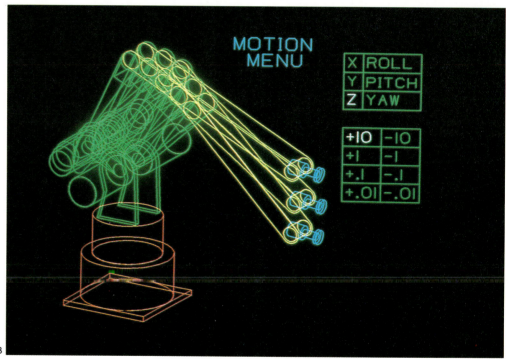

B

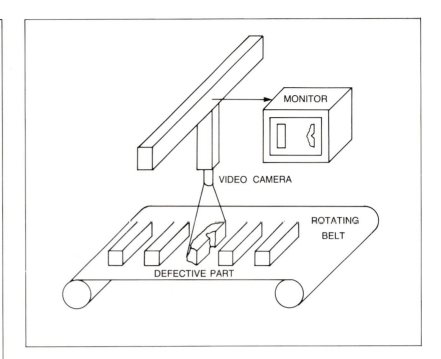

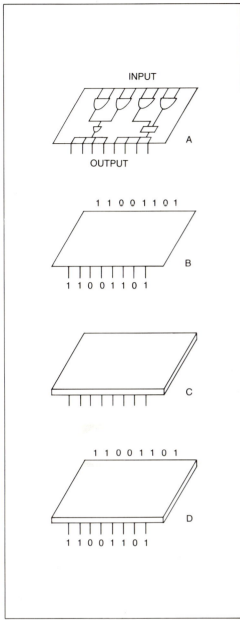

10-10. Testing may be closely allied to simulation. For example, a designer might make a computer model of a product such as a microprocessor chip (A). Next, a simulated electrical signal, essentially a machine language program, is applied to the virtual computer model to see if the results are predictable (B). If errors result, the original design is changed and retested. Once the virtual chip is perceived to be working, a real one is fabricated, using an automated production facility (C). The finished chip is mounted on pins and plugged into a testing machine, which applies the same software simulator, only this time to the real device (D). Once in production, the chips can be similarly tested on an individual basis.

ifications of individual parts (fig. 10-11).

The design process for architecture generally follows the CADAM pattern and has much in common with the design of large structural objects like ships and airplanes. Models are input from coplanar blueprints, cross sections, and procedural techniques, and relational data bases and sophisticated software correlate designs for the various subsystems of a structure, such as the flow of water, electricity, communications, air conditioning, heat, and sewage.

Visualizations of an architectural project may be enhanced by color and realistic rendering techniques (fig. 10-12). Ground and air views of the structure in its proposed environment can incorporate the structure into existing urban data bases (fig. 10-13). The designer can animate the design and thus move through it, evaluating physical and social aesthetics.

Tests for structural properties, wind loading, and earthquakes, are performed on the digital architectural model (fig. 10-14). Energy studies analyze lighting, heating, and air-conditioning requirements. Color, light, and shadow studies (fig. 10-15) preview the structure as it might appear in the summer or winter. Zoning

10-9. A vision system checks gear tooth deviations using a video camera.

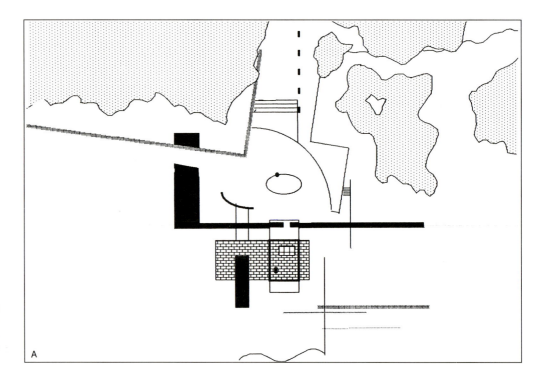

10-11. A site plan (A) as well as north (B) and east (C) elevations of a proposed residence created on a Macintosh personal computer. (Courtesy of UKZ: S. Ungers, L. Kist, T. Zwigard, and M. Whitmore.)

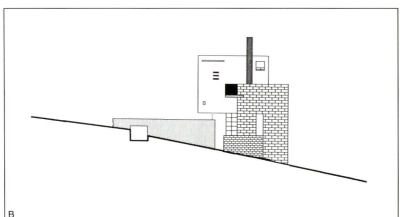

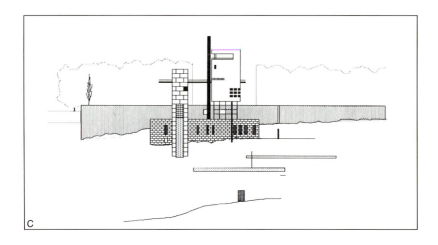

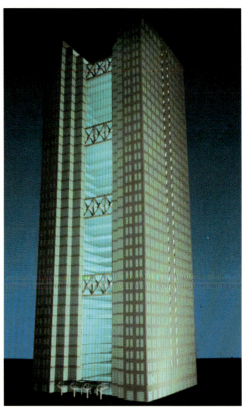

10-12. Realistic renderings can be produced with specialized software and assist in evaluating design decisions. (Courtesy of Cranston-Csuri Productions. Animation by Michael Collery.)

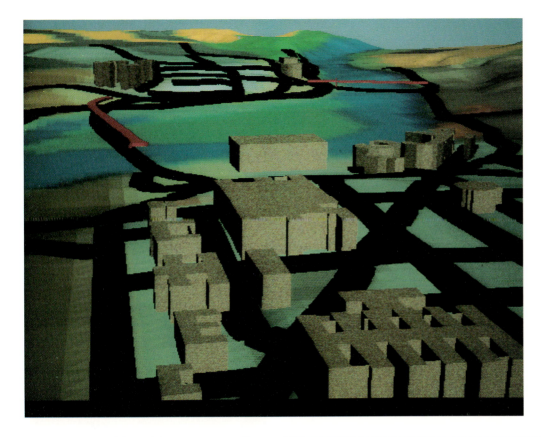

10-13. Medium-resolution color displays incorporate structures of the future into today's environments. (Courtesy of David M. McKeown Jr., Carnegie-Mellon University. Computer-generated scenes of Washington, D.C., using MAPS System, a three-dimensional map generation system.)

analysis plots allowable structures (fig. 10-16).

Finally, the graphic and nongraphic data in the relational data base are used to produce blueprints and engineering drawings that show any combination of subsystems, testing them against each other to ensure they are properly structured and do not collide (fig. 10-17). The data bases can also feed numerically controlled machining of made-to-order parts, schedules of work orders, and material goods purchases.

The type of CAD system needed for an architectural application varies according to the size of the project. Initial sketching and massing studies, simple blueprints, line drawings, and even some structural analysis can be executed with a small computer (fig. 10-18). Only a larger system, however, can handle a complex project with extensive data bases that call for exhaustive analysis and realistic rendering with solid volumes, transparencies, light reflections, shadows, and textures.

 RELATED READING

Ching, Francis D. K. *Space, Form and Order.* New York: Van Nostrand Reinhold Co., 1979.

Greenberg, Donald P. "Computer Graphics in Architecture." *Scientific American* (May 1974).

Leighton, Natalie Langue. *Computers in the Architectural Office.* New York: Van Nostrand Reinhold, 1984.

Milne, M. *Computer Graphics in Architecture and Design.* New Haven, CT: Yale School of Art and Architecture, 1969.

Mitchell, William J. *Computer Aided Architectural Design.* New York: Van Nostrand Reinhold, 1977.

Negroponte, Nicholas. *The Architecture Machine.* Cambridge, MA: MIT Press, 1970.

Negroponte, Nicholas, ed., *Computer Aids to Design and Architecture.* New York: Van Nostrand Reinhold, 1975.

10-14. Structural testing allows a structure to be stressed while still in the design stage. (Courtesy of Skidmore, Owings & Merrill.)

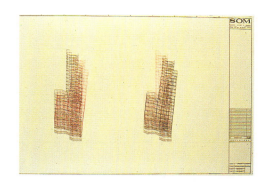

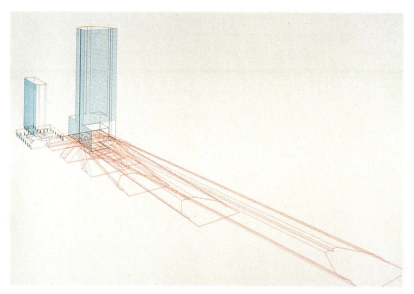

10-15. Shadow studies incorporate not only the location of shadows falling from a new structure, but how shadows from existing structures will affect heating and air-conditioning requirements. Shadow studies can be diagrammatic, as shown here, or incorporated into realistic renderings. (Courtesy of Skidmore, Owings & Merrill.)

10-16. This illustration depicts a variety of allowable zoning setbacks (relationship between height and setbacks) in a New York City site study. (Courtesy of Skidmore, Owings & Merrill.)

PACKAGE DESIGN

Package design considers the volume and shape of a container as well as its surface information (fig. 10-19). In other words, computer graphics in package design combines three-dimensional solid modeling with two-dimensional illustration, typography, and pagination. Graphic systems must therefore be highly flexible with two-dimensional makeup capabilities as well as the ability to map these designs on three-dimensional objects and view them in full color in perspective. An attractive alternative to building mock-up packages, computer systems can test a variety of positions, proportions, and colors before creating the final package design (fig. 10-20).

Once the artwork is mapped onto a three-dimensional container, the finished model can be previewed as a full-color solid object, which permits many difficult container shapes to be explored and tested. The package, simulated in perspective on a supermarket shelf next to competing products, can be exposed to extensive market research in the early stages of de-

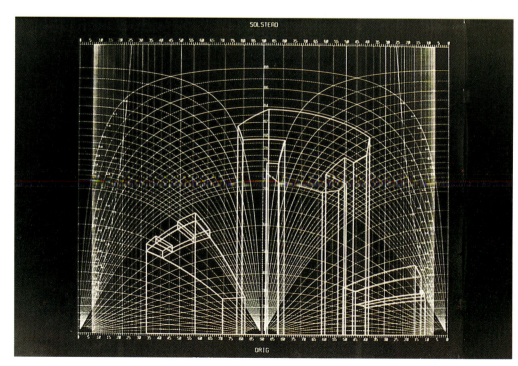

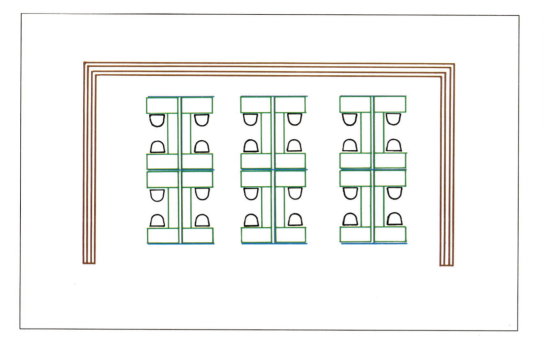

10-17. Overlays depict physical, electrical, and mechanical subsystems of the floor plan of a building. The furniture is drawn in black, the inner walls in green, the outer walls in red, and the lighting grid in blue.

10-19. Computer graphics can realistically simulate products and their packages. This Comet can is built by wrapping type and label information around a cylinder. The observant reader will notice that the effects of lighting do not appear in the label area, improving readability and creating a more effective graphic. (Courtesy of Digital Effects Inc.)

10-18. This small architectural system is built around a personal computer and can display color-shaded images of parts of structures. (Courtesy of Cubicomp Corp.)

10-20. Computer graphic systems allow a variety of designs to be created for a single product. These two pictures show how a brand name, a bowl, and ears of corn form different design combinations. (Courtesy of Artronics.)

10-21. Computer-simulated products can be drawn in pattern repeats and in perspective as if they were actually on display. (Courtesy of Cranston-Csuri Productions, Inc. and Kornick Lindsay, Chicago.)

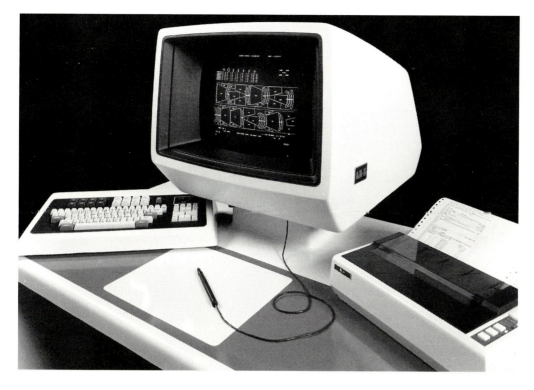

10-22. Pattern design systems are used to find the most effective way of cutting raw materials and arranging them in a limited shipping volume. (Courtesy of Gerber Camsco, Inc.)

sign (fig. 10-21). Advertisements that incorporate the computer-generated packages can also be tested.

A package design system must also be able to calculate the volume of the package and its gross weight; alternate materials can be compared for strength, weight, and cost. The distribution of a product, boxing and palletizing finished packages in a truck, also affect the final design (fig. 10-22).

Finally, prototypes can be produced quickly and cheaply using numerically controlled machine tools, thus allowing one to test physical objects. These same machines can then be used to fabricate production tools and dies. Computerized package design includes methods for identifying market appeal, optimizing resources, and reducing costs.

CLOTHING AND TEXTILE DESIGN

Computer graphics has a long tradition in the textile industry. Pixels are used in weaving and needlepoint, two-dimensional polygonal graphics are used for pattern design and textile printing, and two- and three-dimensional systems relate patterns for cutting cloth with the three-dimensional structure of a finished garment. The Jacquard loom, created in the beginning of the nineteenth century, is an early example of a programmed machine. It used punch cards to weave complex patterns.

Weaving, like most textile applications, combines two-dimensional and three-dimensional technologies. In terms of pattern, weaving, like needlepoint and knitting, is a rectangular grid—an imaging technology that employs pixels. Cloth, however, is not just pattern, it is a material good, a matrix of yarn organized three dimensionally so it knots together.

Cloth is woven by stretching many parallel threads of yarn, called a **warp,** and then threading a horizontal thread, called a **weft,** back and forth through the warp (fig. 10-23) on a loom (fig. 10-24). Patterns are formed by varying which warp strings each weft string goes above and below. The control of this, along with the resulting pattern, can be represented in **draft notation**—a Boolean bitmap of the process and the result (fig. 10-25).

RELATED READING

Creager, Clara. *Weaving*. Garden City, NY: Doubleday, 1974.

Davison, Marguerite. *A Handweaver's Pattern Book*. Swarthmore, PA: Davison Publishing, 1974.

Frey, Berta. *Designing and Drafting for Handweavers*. New York: Collier Books, 1958.

Lourie, Janice R. *Textile Graphics/Computer Aided*. New York: Fairchild Publications, 1973.

Draft notation can be executed on a computer, just as it can be executed on a real loom, allowing a designer to preview patterns. Furthermore, a computer, unlike a loom, can invert the operation—analyze a pattern and compose the draft notation.

Computer graphics are also employed in pattern design, textile printing, and are used to calculate pattern repeats (fig. 10-26), preview color combinations, alter designs, and calculate **traps,** which separate areas of different colors, so the textile inks have room to run without bleeding.

Computer systems to design and manufacture clothing combine two- and three-dimensional graphics and are similar to some metalworking processes, including the stamping of a steel sheet to form an automobile. Computers are used to preview patterns as they would appear three dimensionally (fig. 10-27) and also to determine the position of the pattern on the raw material, minimizing the amount of material wasted.

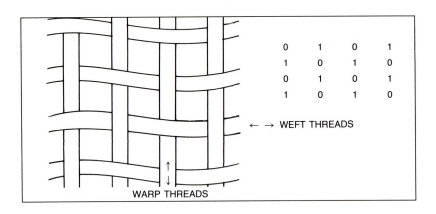

10-23. Cloth is composed of weft threads, which alternatively stretch over and under warp threads. The over-and-under pattern of threads, a plain weave, can be represented as a Boolean bitmap.

10-24. On a loom the alternate warp threads pass through a heddle so they can be lifted up or depressed, allowing weft threads to be inserted between alternate warp threads. Two stages of the process are illustrated: lifting the heddle lifts the warp strings. The strings that are not connected to the heddle that is being lifted or depressed remain stationary.

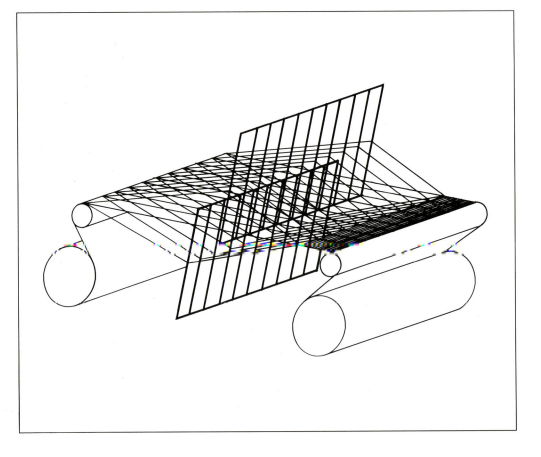

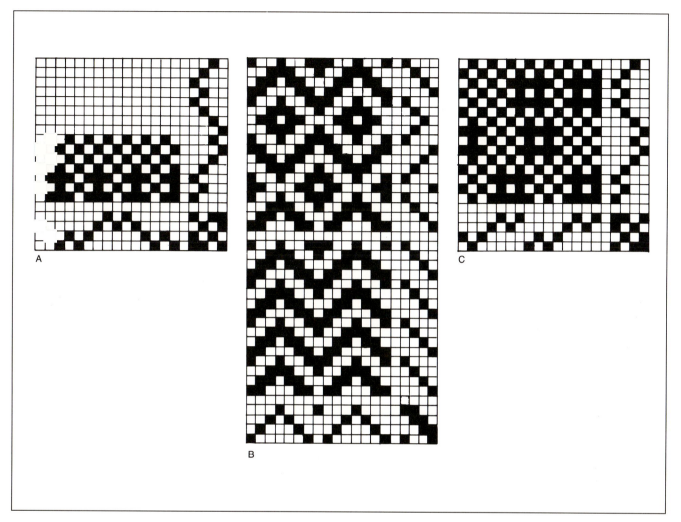

10-25. Draft notation consists of the threading draft, the tie-up, the treadling, and the web, or final pattern created by operating the loom. The threading draft, written across the bottom of each of these three diagrams, depicts four heddles. Black squares indicate that the heddle is connected to a string. The tie-up, in the lower right corner, indicates what foot pedals, or treadles, are connected to what heddles. For example, in diagram A treadle 1 is connected to heddles 1, 3, and 4; treadle 2 is connected to heddles 2 and 4, treadle 3 is connected to heddles 1 and 3, and treadle 4 is connected to heddles 1, 2, and 4. The treadles are the vertical column to the right of the drawing, and the black squares here indicate what treadle is pushed in what order. Finally, the web is the large area in the upper left of each drawing. The loom process works by depressing the treadles in the order indicated in the draft notation which in turn raises one or more heddles according to the tie-up; the heddles then lift up the corresponding warp threads so a new weft thread can pass underneath these strings horizonally. Thus the web grows away and up, with black web squares indicating where the warp threads will be visible in the final pattern, and white web squares indicating where the weft threads will be visible in the final pattern.

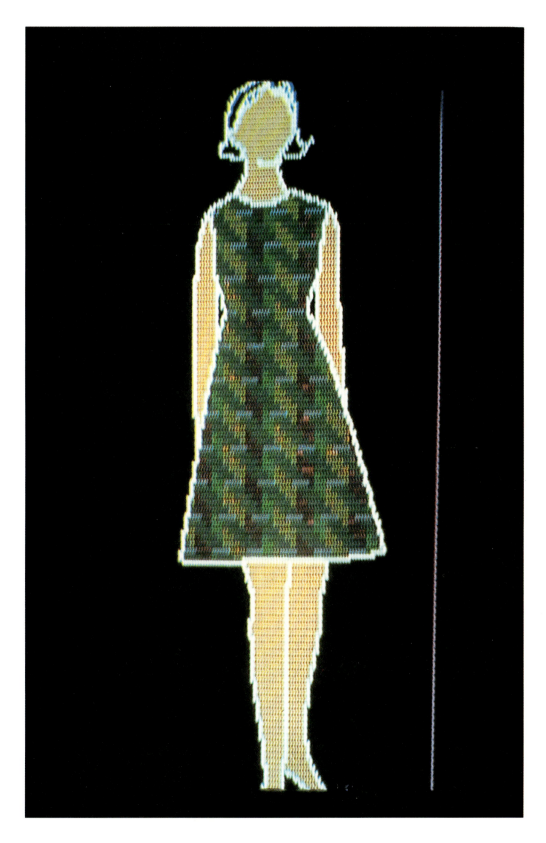

10-27. This pattern preview system provides the designer with views of a piece of clothing, both on a model and laid flat. The designer can interactively alter the style, view the results, and generate patterns in different sizes. (Courtesy of Tosiyasu L. Kunii, Tokyo University.)

CONCLUSION

Computer-aided design systems are not yet capable of delivering a finished product at the touch of a button, but their effects on the theory and practice of design have been profound. Computers, like technologies that have emerged in the past, are changing and expanding the language of visual creation, as design is directly related to the technical resources that support it.

In the next few years, much progress will result from integrating the latest advances in computer technology into widely available computer graphics systems. The touch-sensitive display screen will become our next drawing table, reprogrammable so that it can be a workbench for a national news magazine, a CADAM design station in the aerospace industry, or a control panel for a business or physical plant. Iconographic and/or three dimensional, it will be manipulated by hand and will respond to subtler aspects of touch—not only to pressure and direction, but to moisture and oils, temperature, heartbeat, and galvanic skin responses.

Media extensions in the future—input as well as output—will approximate all of our senses, while making those that can already be simulated respond more effectively to manipulation. Holographically projected, three-dimensionally colored spatial displays will incorporate information about the location of light in the environment and use this information to create images that are seemingly more realistic.

Computer graphics can already be used to animate the transformation between two different states of an object—a blueprint of an appliance fading to the real thing, a sphere of the earth interpolating into a head, or ice crystalizing. The post-realistic phase of the medium will include a more expansive analysis of growth, the fabrication of structure, and thought processes.

Computer graphics, along with its inverse, robotic vision, provides a formal structure for defining what and how we see. As an extension of our senses, computer graphics is not bound either by its history or by the reality it models and simulates. Thus, by accident and exploration, images can be defined or perceived that do not conform to our preconceived notions. Our vision of reality will therefore continually expand.

Today's powerful microcomputers are bringing computer systems to most design studios. With this widespread computerization comes new design challenges and opportunities—finding appropriate methods for particular design situations and exploring novel solutions. Only a realistic and comprehensive examination of the current state of computer-aided design technology will allow us to evaluate the benefits that can be expected from future systems. Designers who can foresee change will, in turn, have realistic expectations and original proposals for new and more efficient methods of using and executing computerized design.

BIBLIOGRAPHY

BOOKS AND PERIODICALS

Adler, Mortimer J., and Warren Preece, eds. *Encyclopaedia Britannica.* 15th ed. Chicago: Encyclopaedia Britannica, Inc., 1979.

Ahuja, Narendra, and Bruce J. Schachter. *Pattern Models.* New York: John Wiley & Sons Inc., 1983.

Albers, J. *Interaction of Color.* New Haven, CT: Yale University Press, 1975.

Amano, Akira. *Computer Graphics '83.* Tokyo: Sendenkaigi, 1982.

Anderson, Allan Ross, ed. *Minds and Machines.* Englewood Cliffs, NJ: Prentice-Hall, 1964.

Artwick, Bruce. *Applied Concepts in Microcomputer Graphics.* Englewood Cliffs, NJ: Prentice-Hall, 1983.

Atherton, P., K. Weiler, and D. Greenberg. "Polygon Shadow Generation," *Computer Graphics* (August 1978): 275–81.

Auble, J. Woodward. *Arithmetic for Printers.* 2d ed. Peoria, IL: Bonnett, 1954.

Backer, David, and Andrew Lippman. "Future Interactive Graphics: Personal Video." Massachusetts Institute of Technology, Architecture Machine Group, 1980.

Badler, Norman, ed. *Motion Representation and Perception.* New York: Association for Computing Machinery, 1983.

Badler, Norman, ed. "Special Issue on Character Animation." *IEEE Computer Graphics and Applications* (November 1982).

Ballard, Dana H., and Christopher M. Brown. *Computer Vision.* Englewood Cliffs, NJ: Prentice-Hall, 1982.

Barnett, M. P. *Computer Typesetting.* Cambridge, MA: The MIT Press, 1965.

Barnhill, Robert E., and Richard F. Reisenfeld. *Computer Aided Geometric Design.* New York: Academic Press, 1984.

Beatty, John C., and Booth Kellog. *Tutorial: Computer Graphics.* 2d ed. Long Beach, CA: IEEE Computer Society, 1982.

Becker, Joseph D. "Multilingual Word Processing." *Scientific American* (July 1984).

Bertin, Jacques. *Semiology of Graphics.* Madison, WI: University of Wisconsin Press, 1983.

Bigelow, Charles, and Donald Day. "Digital Typography." *Scientific American* (August 1983).

Birren, F., ed. *The Elements of Color.* New York: Van Nostrand Reinhold, 1970.

Blinn, J. F. "Simulation of Wrinkled Surfaces." *Computer Graphics* (August 1978): 286–92.

Blinn, J. F., and M. E. Newell. "Texture and Reflection in Computer Generated Images." *Communications of the ACM* (October 1976): 542–47.

Bolt, Richard. *Spatial Data-Management.* Cambridge, MA: The MIT Press, 1979.

Bonifer, Michael. *The Art of Tron.* New York: Simon & Schuster Inc., 1982.

Booth, Kellogg S. *Tutorial: Computer Graphics.* Long Beach, CA: IEEE Computer Society, 1979.

Boraiko, Allen A. "The Chip." *National Geographic* (October 1982): 421–57.

Born, Robert, ed. *Designing for Television: The New Tools.* Tequesta, FL: Broadcast Designers' Association, 1983.

Bourgoin, J. *Arabic Geometric Patterns and Design.* New York: Dover Press, 1973.

Bradbeer, Robin, Peter DeBono, and Peter

Laurie. *The Beginner's Guide to Computers.* Reading, MA: Addison-Wesley Publishing Co. Inc., 1982.

Burtnyk, Nestor, and Marcelli Wein. "Computer Animation." In *Encyclopaedia of Computer Science and Technology.* New York: Marcel Dekker Inc., 1976.

Cage, John. *Notations.* New York: Something Else Press, 1969.

Cakir, A. D., D. J. Hart, and T. F. M. Stewart. *Visual Display Terminal.* New York: John Wiley & Sons Inc., 1980.

Campbell, Russell. *Photographic Theory for the Motion Picture Cameraman.* San Diego: A. S. Barnes & Co., 1970.

Cannon, T. M., and B. R. Hunt. "Image Processing by Computer." *Scientific American* (October 1981).

Cardamone, T. *Chart and Graph Preparation Skills.* New York: Van Nostrand Reinhold, 1981.

Carey, Tom. "User Differences in Interface Design." *Computer* (November 1982): 14–20.

Carpenter, L., A. Fournier, and D. Fussell. "Fractal Surfaces." *Communications of the ACM,* 1981.

Chambers, John M., William S. Cleveland, Bert Kleiner, and Paul A. Tukey. *Graphical Methods for Data Analysis.* Belmont, CA: Wadsworth Publishing Co., 1983.

Chasen, Sylvan H. *Geometric Principles and Procedures for Computer Graphic Applications.* Englewood Cliffs, NJ: Prentice-Hall, 1978.

Ching, Francis D. K. *Space, Form and Order.* New York: Van Nostrand Reinhold, 1979.

Clark, David R., ed. *Computers for Imagemaking.* Oxford: Pergamon Press, 1981.

Conrac. *Raster Graphics Handbook.* Covina, CA: Conrac, 1980.

Cook, R. L., and K. Torrance. "A Reflectance Model for Computer Graphics." *Computer Graphics* (August 1981): 307–16.

Coons, Stephen A. "The Uses of Computers in Technology." *Scientific American* (September 1966).

Cornog, D. Y., and F. C. Rose. *Legibility of Alphanumeric Characters and Other Symbols: A Reference Handbook.* Washington, DC: U.S. Government Printing Office, 1967.

Crawford, Chris. *The Art of Computer Game Design.* Berkeley, CA: Osborne/McGraw-Hill, 1984.

Creager, Clara. *Weaving.* Garden City, NY: Doubleday Publishing Co., 1974.

Crow, F. "Shadow Algorithms for Computer Graphics." *Computer Graphics* (Summer 1977): 242–47.

Cundy, H. Martyn, and A. P. Rollett. *Mathematical Models.* 2d ed. London: Oxford University Press, 1961.

Cunningham, Steve. "Computer Graphics Education Directory." *Computer Graphics* (October 1984).

David, Douglas. *Art in the Future, History/Prophecy of the Collaboration Between Science, Technology and Art.* New York: Praeger Publishers, 1973.

Davison, Marguerite. *A Handweaver's Pattern Book.* Swarthmore, PA: Davison Publishing, 1974.

Deken, Joseph. *Computer Images.* New York: Stewart, Tabori & Chang, Publishers, 1983.

Deken, Joseph. *The Electronic Cottage.* New York: William Morrow & Company, 1982.

Denning, Peter J., and Robert L. Brown. "Operating Systems." *Scientific American* (September 1984).

Dennis, Ervin A., and John D. Jenkins. *Comprehensive Graphic Arts.* 2d ed. Indianapolis: The Bobbs-Merril Company, 1983.

Descargues, Pierre. *Perspective.* New York: Van Nostrand Reinhold, 1982.

Diffrient, Niels, Alvin R. Tilley, Joan C. Bardagjy, and David Harman. *Humanscale.* Cambridge, MA: The MIT Press, 1981.

Dreyfuss, H. *Symbol Sourcebook.* New York: Van Nostrand Reinhold, 1984.

Dubery, Fred, and John W. Illatz. *Perspective and Other Drawing Systems.* London: Herbert Press, 1983.

Eastman Kodak Company. *Ergonomic Design for People at Work.* Rochester, NY: Eastman Kodak Company, Human Factors Section, 1983.

Encarnacao, J., and E. G. Schlechtendahl. *Computer Aided Design.* New York: Springer-Verlag, 1983.

Evans, David C. "Computer Logic and Memory." *Scientific American* (September 1966).

Faux, I. D., and M. J. Pratt. *Computational Geometry for Design and Manufacture.* New York: John Wiley & Sons Inc., 1979.

Feigenbaum, Edward A., and Pamela McCorduck. *The Fifth Generation.* Reading, MA: Addison-Wesley Publishing Co. Inc., 1983.

Felding, Raymond. *The Technique of Special Effects Cinematography.* New York: Hastings House, 1965.

Finch, Christopher. *Special Effects.* New York: Van Nostrand Reinhold, 1984.

Foley, James D., and Andries Van Dam. *Fundamentals of Interactive Computer Graphics.* Reading, MA: Addison-Wesley Publishing Co. Inc., 1982.

Fox, David, and Mitchell Waite. *Computer Animation Primer.* New York: McGraw-Hill, 1983.

Frank, Mark. *Discovering Computers.* Washington, DC: Stonehenge Press, 1981.

Franke, Herbert. *Computer Graphics— Computer Art.* 2d ed. Berlin: Springer-Verlag, 1985.

Frates, Jeffrey, and William Moldrup. *Computers and Life.* Englewood Cliffs, NJ: Prentice-Hall, 1982.

Freeman, H., ed. *Tutorial and Selected Readings in Interactive Computer Graphics.* Long Beach, CA: IEEE Computer Society, 1980.

Frey, Berta. *Designing and Drafting for Handweavers.* New York: Collier Books, 1958.

Frutiger, Adrian. *Type Sign Symbol.* Zurich: ABC Editions, 1980.

Fu, K. S., and T. L. Kunu, eds. *Picture Engineering.* New York: Springer-Verlag, 1982.

Gardner, Martin. "Mathematical Games." *Scientific American* (October 1970, February 1971).

Gasson, Peter C. *Geometry of Spatial Forms.* New York: John Wiley & Sons, 1983.

Gayeski, Diane, and David Williams. *Interactive Media.* Englewood Cliffs, NJ: Prentice-Hall, 1985.

Gerritsen, Frans. *Theory and Practice of Color.* New York: Van Nostrand Reinhold, 1975.

Gerstner, Karl. *Compendium for Literates: A System of Writing.* Cambridge, MA: The MIT Press, 1974.

Glassner, Andrew S. *Computer Graphics User's Guide.* Indianapolis, IN: H. W. Sams & Co. Inc., 1984.

Gonzalez, Rafael C., and Paul Wintz. *Digital Image Processing.* Reading, MA: Addison-Wesley Publishing Co., 1977.

Gordon, Richard, Gabor T. Herman, and Stephen A. Johnson. "Image Reconstructions from Projections." *Scientific American* (October 1975).

Gottschall, Edward M., ed. *Graphic Communication/Visions 80.* Englewood Cliffs, NJ: Prentice-Hall, 1981.

Gouraud, H. "Continuous Shading of Curved Surfaces." *IEEE Transactions on Computers* (June 1971): 623–28.

Graham, Frank. *Mathematics and Calculations for Mechanics.* New York: Audel & Co., 1948.

"Graphics Standards." *ACM Computing Surveys*, Special Issue, 1978.

Green, William B. *Digital Image Processing.* New York: Van Nostrand Reinhold, 1983.

Greenberg, Donald. "Computer Graphics in Architecture." *Scientific American* (May 1974).

Greenberg, Donald, Aaron Marcus, Allan H. Schmidt, and Vernon Gorter. *The Computer Image: Applications of Computer Graphics.* Reading, MA: Addison-Wesley Publishing Co. Inc., 1982.

Greenberger, Martin. "The Uses of Computers in Organizations." *Scientific American* (September 1966).

Gregory, Richard L. *Eye and Brain, the Psychology of Seeing.* 3d ed. New York: McGraw-Hill, 1978.

Grimson, Eric Leifur. *From Images to Surfaces: A Computational Study of the Human Early Visual System.* Cambridge, MA: The MIT Press, 1981.

Groover, Mikell P., and Emory W. Zimmers, Jr. *CAD/CAM Computer Aided Design and Manufacturing.* Englewood Cliffs, NJ: Prentice-Hall, 1984.

Gunn, Thomas G. "The Mechanization of Design and Manufacturing." *Scientific*

American (September 1982).

Hahn, G. J., C. B. Morgan, and W. E. Larsen. "Color Face Plots for Displaying Product Performance." *Computer Graphics and Applications* (January-February 1983): 23–29.

Halas, John, ed. *Computer Animation.* New York: Hastings House, 1974.

Halas, John. *Graphics in Motion.* New York: Van Nostrand Reinhold, 1984.

Halas, John, and Roger Manvell. *The Technique of Film Animation.* 3d ed. New York: Hastings House, 1971.

Hanson, Dirk. *The New Alchemists.* Boston: Little, Brown & Co. Inc., 1982.

Harmon, Leon. "The Recognition of Faces." *Scientific American* (November 1973).

Harmon, Leon, and Kenneth Knowlton. "Picture Processing by Computer." *Science* (April 4, 1969).

Harrington, Steven. *Computer Graphics: A Programming Approach.* New York: McGraw-Hill, 1983.

Heckel, Paul. *The Elements of Friendly Software Design.* New York: Warner Books, 1984.

Herr, Laurin, and Yuriko Kuchiki, eds. *Siggraph '83 Exhibition of Computer Graphics.* Tokyo: Hakuhodo, Inc., 1983.

Hershey, Allen. "Calligraphy for Computers." Naval Weapons Laboratory Report #2101, Dahlgren Laboratory, VA, 1967.

Hildebrandt, Stefan, and Anthony Tromba. *Mathematics and Optimal Form.* New York: W. H. Freeman and Co., 1984.

Hofstadter, Douglas R. *Godel, Escher, Bach.* New York: Basic Books, 1979.

Hofstadter, Douglas R., and Daniel C. Dennett. *The Mind's I.* New York: Basic Books, 1981.

Holden, Alan. *Shapes, Space, and Symmetry.* New York: Columbia University Press, 1971.

Holton, William C. "The Large Scale Integration of Microelectronic Circuits." *Scientific American* (September 1977).

Hoskins, Janet A., and M. W. King. "An Interactive Database for Woven Textile Design." Proceedings of the Textile Institute Annual Conference. Hong Kong, September 1984.

Hurvich, L. M. *Color Vision.* Sunderland, MA: Sinauer Assoc., 1981.

IBM, *Informatique #13.* Paris: IBM, 1975.

Imes, Jack. *Special Visual Effects.* New York: Van Nostrand Reinhold, 1984.

Jankel, Annabel, and Rocky Morton. *Creative Computer Graphics.* Cambridge, England: Cambridge University Press, 1984.

Jarett, Irwin M. *Computer Graphics and Reporting Financial Data.* New York: John Wiley & Sons, 1983.

Joblove, G. H., and D. Greenberg. "Color Spaces for Computer Graphics." *Computer Graphics* (August 1978): 20–25.

Judd, D. B., and G. Wyszecki. *Color in Business, Science and Industry.* 3d ed. New York: John Wiley & Sons Inc., 1975.

Kawaguchi, Yoichiro. *Digital Image.* Tokyo: Ascii Publishing, 1981.

Kawaguchi, Yoichiro. *The Computer Graphics.* Tokyo: Graphic-sha Publishing, 1982.

Kay, Alan C. "Computer Software." *Scientific American* (September 1984).

Kay, Alan C. "Microelectronics in the Personal Computer." *Scientific American* (September 1977).

Kay, D., and D. Greenberg. "Transparency for Computer Synthesized Images." *Computer Graphics* (August 1979): 158–64.

Kerlow, Isaac. "Illusion and Technology." Master's Thesis, Pratt Institute. New York, 1983.

Kim, Scott. *Inversions.* Peterborough, NH: Byte Books, 1981.

Klein, Stanley. *The S. Klein Directory of Computer Graphics Supplies.* Sudbury, MA: Technology and Business Communication, Inc., 1984.

Knowlton, Ken. *EXPLOR.* Murray Hill, NJ: Bell Laboratories, 1974.

Knuth, Donald E. *TEX and Metafont: New Directions in Typesetting.* Bedford, MA: American Mathematical Society, Digital Press, 1979.

Knuth, Donald E. "Algorithms." *Scientific American* (April 1977): 63–80.

Korites, B. J. *Graphic Software for Microcomputers.* Duxbury, MA: Kern Publications, 1981.

Kranz, Stewart. *Science and Technology in the Arts.* New York: Van Nostrand Reinhold, 1974.

Krueger, Myron W. *Artificial Reality.* Reading, MA: Addison-Wesley Publishing Co. Inc., 1983.

Kunii, Tosiyasu, ed. "Computer Graphics: Theory and Applications." Proceedings of Intergraphics. Berlin: Springer-Verlag, 1983.

Lalvani, Haresh. *Transpolyhedra.* New York: Red Ink Productions, 1977.

Lange, Jerome C., and Dennis P. Shanahan. *Interactive Computer Graphics Applied to Mechanical Drafting and Design.* New York: John Wiley & Sons Inc., 1984.

Laurie, Peter. *The Joy of Computers.* Boston: Little, Brown & Company, 1983.

Leavitt, Ruth, ed. *Artist and Computer.* New York: Harmony Books, 1976.

Leighton, Natalie Langue. *Computers in the Architectural Office.* New York: Van Nostrand Reinhold, 1984.

Lesk, Michael. "Computer Software for Information Management." *Scientific American* (September 1984).

Levitan, Eli. *Electronic Imaging Techniques.* New York: Van Nostrand Reinhold, 1977.

Lewell, J. *Computer Graphics.* New York: Van Nostrand Reinhold, 1985.

Lipetz, Ben-Ami. "Information Storage and Retrieval." *Scientific American* (September 1966).

Lipton, Lenny. *Foundations of the Stereoscopic Cinema.* New York: Van Nostrand Reinhold, 1982.

Lombardo, Josef V., Lewis S. Johnson, W. Irwin Short, and Albert J. Lombardo. *Engineering Drawing.* New York: Harper & Row, 1956.

Lourie, Janice R. *Textile Graphics/Computer Aided.* New York: Fairchild Publications, 1973.

Machover, Carl. "A Guide to Sources of Information About Computer Graphics." *IEEE Computer Graphics and Applications* (January 1981): 73–85.

Machover, Carl. "An Updated Guide to Sources of Information About Computer Graphics." *IEEE Computer Graphics and Applications* (January-February 1983): 49–59.

Machover, Carl. "Background and Source Information About Computer Graphics." *IEEE Computer Graphics and Applications* (January 1985): 68–81.

Machover, Carl. *Display Systems: Computer Graphics.* Pittsfield, MA: Optical Publishing Co., 1979.

Machover, Carl. *Understanding Computer Graphics.* New York: Van Nostrand Reinhold, 1980.

Madsen, Roy. *Animated Film.* New York: Interland Press, 1970.

Malina, Frank J., ed. *Kinetic Art Theory and Practice.* New York: Dover, 1974.

Marks, Robert W. *The New Mathematics Dictionary and Handbook.* New York: Bantam, 1981.

Marquis Who's Who Inc. *Marquis Who's Who Dictionary of Computer Graphics.* Chicago: Marquis Who's Who Inc., Professional Publications Division, 1984.

Martin, J. *Design of Man-Computer Dialogues.* Englewood Cliffs, NJ: Prentice-Hall, 1973.

Marx, Ellen. *Optical Color and Simultaneity.* New York: Van Nostrand Reinhold, 1983.

Mayo, John S. "The Role of Microelectronics in Communications." *Scientific American* (September 1977).

McCarthy, John. "Information." *Scientific American* (September 1966).

McCorduck, Pamela. *Machines Who Think.* San Francisco: W. H. Freeman and Co., 1979.

Meadows, A. J., ed. *Dictionary of New Information Technology.* New York: Random House, 1983.

Meyer, G. W., and D. P. Greenberg. "Perceptual Color Spaces for Computer Graphics." *Computer Graphics* (July 1980): 254–61.

Milne, M. *Computer Graphics in Architecture and Design.* New Haven, CT: Yale School of Art and Architecture, 1969.

Minsky, Marvin. "Artificial Intelligence." *Scientific American* (September 1966).

Mitchell, William J. *Computer Aided Architectural Design.* New York: Van Nostrand Reinhold, 1977.

Monmonier, M. S. *Computer Assisted Cartography.* Englewood Cliffs, NJ: Prentice-Hall, 1982.

Montalvo, F. S. "Human Vision and Computer Graphics." *Computer Graphics* (August 1979): 121–25.

Moore, Patricia, ed. "Harvard Library of Computer Graphics." Cambridge, MA: Harvard University Laboratory for Computer Graphics, 1980.

Morris, Joseph. "Using Color in Industrial Control Graphics." *Control Engineering* (July 1979).

Mortenson, Michael E. *Geometric Modelling.* New York: John Wiley & Sons, 1985.

Muller, W., ed. *Dictionary of the Graphic Arts Industry.* Amsterdam: Elsevier Scientific Publishing, 1984.

Negroponte, Nicholas. *The Architecture Machine.* Cambridge, MA: The MIT Press, 1970.

Negroponte, Nicholas, ed. *Computer Aids to Design and Architecture.* New York: Van Nostrand Reinhold, 1975.

Nelson, Theodore H. *Dream Machines/Computer Lib.* Chicago: Hugo's Book Service, 1977.

Nelson, Theodore H. *Literary Machines.* Strathmore, PA: Nelson Publishing, 1983.

Nevatia, R. *Machine Perception.* Englewood Cliffs, NJ: Prentice-Hall, 1982.

Newell, M. E., R. G. Newell, and T. L. Sancha. "A New Approach to the Shaded Picture Problem." *Proceedings ACM 1972 National Conference,* p. 443.

Newman, William M., and Robert F. Sproull. *Principles of Computer Graphics.* 2d ed. New York: McGraw-Hill, 1979.

Nouri, Guy, and Eric Podietz. *Moviemaker.* Reston, VA: Reston Publishing Co., 1982.

Oettinger, Anthony G. "The Use of Computers." *Scientific American* (September 1966).

Oliver, Bernard M. "The Role of Microelectronics in Instrumentation and Control." *Scientific American* (September 1977).

Paller, Alan, K. Szoka, and N. Nelson. *Choosing the Right Chart, A Comprehensive Guide.* San Diego: ISSCO, 1981.

Pavlidis, T. *Algorithms for Graphics and Image Processing.* New York: Springer-Verlag, 1982.

Pearce, Peter. *Structure in Nature as a Strategy for Design.* Cambridge, MA: The MIT Press, 1978.

Phong, Bui-Tuong. "Illumination for Computer-Generated Pictures." *Communications of the ACM* (June 1975): 311–17.

Poggio, Tomaso. "Vision by Man and Machine." *Scientific American* (April 1984).

Pooch, Udo. "Computer Graphics, Interactive Techniques and Image Processing 1970–75: A Bibliography." *IEEE Computer* (August 1976).

Porter, Tom, Bob Greenstreet, and Sue Goodman. *Manual of Graphic Techniques.* 4 vols. New York: Charles Scribner's Sons, 1980, 1985.

Potts, Jackie. *Computer Graphics Bibliography.* Report 4062, Naval Ship Research and Development Center, Bethesda, MD, January 1975.

Pratt, William K. *Digital Image Processing.* New York: John Wiley & Sons, 1978.

Prueitt, Melvin. *Art and the Computer.* New York: McGraw-Hill, 1984.

Prueitt, Melvin. *Computer Graphics.* New York: Dover, 1975.

Pulgram, William L., and Richard E. Stonis. *Designing the Automated Office.* New York: Whitney Library of Design, 1984.

Reeves, William T. "Particle Systems—A Technique for Modeling a Class of Fuzzy Objects." *Computer Graphics* (July 1983): 359–76.

Reichardt, Jasia. *Cybernetic Serendipity.* New York: Praeger, 1969.

Reichardt, Jasia. *The Computer and Art.* New York: Van Nostrand Reinhold, 1971.

Roberts, L. G. "Machine Perception of Three Dimensional Solids." MIT Lincoln Lab, May 1963. Photocopy.

Rock, Irvin. *Perception.* New York: W. H. Freeman & Company, 1984.

Rogers, David F., and J. Alan Adams. *Mathematical Elements for Computer Graphics.* New York: McGraw-Hill, 1976.

Rogers, David F. *Procedural Elements for Computer Graphics.* New York: McGraw-Hill, 1985.

Rosenfeld, Azriel, and Avinash C. Kak. *Digital Picture Processing.* 2d ed. Orlando, FL: Academic Press, 1982.

Russett, Robert, and Cecile Starr. *Experimental Animation: An Illustrated Anthology.* New York: Van Nostrand Reinhold, 1976.

Sachter, Judy. "3-D Computer Graphics for Artists." Proceedings of the 3rd Symposium on Small Computers in the Arts. Philadelphia (1983): 68–73.

Schachter, Bruce J., ed. *Computer Image Generation.* New York: John Wiley & Sons, 1983.

Schillinger, Joseph. *The Mathematical Basis of the Arts.* New York: Philosophical Library, 1966.

Schneider, Jerry B. "A Bibliography of Applications of Computer Graphics to Transportation Planning and Engineering Problems." Seattle, WA: Dept. of Urban Planning and Civil Engineering, University of Washington, 1980.

Schrack, G. F. "Literature in Computer Graphics for the Year 1983: A Bibliography." *Computer Graphics* (May 1984): 69–95.

Schrack, G. F. "Literature in Computer Graphics for the Year 1982: A Bibliography." *Computer Graphics* (October 1983): 173–209.

Schroeder, Manfred R. "Images from Computers and Microfilm Plotters." *Communications of the ACM* (February 1969).

Scott, J. E. *Introduction to Interactive Computer Graphics.* New York: John Wiley & Sons, 1982.

Scott, Joan. *Computergraphia.* Houston: Gulf Publishing, 1984.

Siegel, Efrem. *Videotex: The Coming Revolution in Home/Office Information Retrieval.* White Plains, NY: Knowledge Industry Publications, 1980.

Skidmore, Owings and Merrill. *Computer Capacity.* Chicago: Skidmore, Owings and Merrill Co., 1980.

Smith, Alvy Ray. "Color Gamut Transform Pairs." *Computer Graphics* (August 1978): 12–19.

Smith, David. *Computer Literacy: Coping with Terminal Anxiety.* New York: McGraw-Hill, 1983.

Soppli, Charles. *Microcomputer Dictionary.* Ft. Worth, TX: Radio Shack, 1981.

Spear, Mary Eleanor. *Practical Charting Techniques.* New York: McGraw-Hill, 1969.

Spector, Alfred Z. "Computer Software for Process Control." *Scientific American* (September 1984).

Speer, Richard, and Bill Kovacs. *An International Guide to Computer Animated Films.* Roseda, CA, 1979. Photocopy.

Strachey, Christopher. "Systems Analysis and Programming." *Scientific American* (September 1966).

Suppes, Patrick. "The Uses of Computers in Education." *Scientific American* (September 1966).

Sutherland, Ivan. "Computer Displays." *Scientific American* (June 1970).

Sutherland, Ivan. "Computer Inputs and Outputs." *Scientific American* (September 1966).

Sutherland, Ivan, R. F. Sproull, and R. A. Schumacker. "A Characterization of Ten Hidden-Surface Algorithms." *Computer Surveys* (March 1974): 1–55.

Teicholz, Eric. *CAD/CAM Handbook.* New York: McGraw-Hill, 1984.

Thalmann, Nadia and Daniel. *Computer Animation.* New York: Springer-Verlag, 1985.

Thomas, Frank, and Ollie Johnson. *Disney Animation: The Illusion of Life.* New York: Abbeville Press, 1981.

Thompson, D'Arcy. *On Growth and Form.* London: Cambridge University Press, 1971.

Toong, Hoo-Min D. "Microprocessors." *Scientific American* (September 1977).

Torrance, K. E., and E. M. Sparrow. "Polarization, Direction Distribution, and Off-Specular Peak Phenomena in Light Reflected from Roughened Surfaces." *Journal of the Optical Society of America* (July 1966): 916–25.

Torrance, K. E., and E. M. Sparrow. "Theory for Off-Specular Reflection from Roughened Surfaces." *Journal of the Optical Society of America* (September 1967): 1105–14.

Truckenbord, J. "Effective Use of Color in Computer Graphics." *Computer Graphics* (August 1981): 83–90.

Tufte, Edward R. *The Visual Display of Quantitative Information.* Cheshire, CT: Graphics Press, 1983.

Tukey, John W. *Exploratory Data Analysis.* Reading, MA: Addison-Wesley Publishing Co. Inc., 1977.

Van Dam, Andries. "Computer Software for Graphics." *Scientific American* (September 1984).

Van Deusen, Edmund, ed. *The Graphics Standards Book.* Laguna Beach, CA: CC Exchange, 1985.

Von Arx, Peter. *Film Design.* New York: Van Nostrand Reinhold, 1984.

Waltz, David L. "Artificial Intelligence." *Scientific American* (October 1982).

Warn, David R. "Lighting Controls for Synthetic Images." *Computer Graphics* (June 1983): 13–21.

Warnock, J. A. "A Hidden-Surface Algorithm for Computer Generated Half-Tone Pictures." University of Utah, Computer Science Department, 1969. Mimeograph.

Watkins, G. S. "A Real-Time Visible Surface Algorithm." University of Utah, Computer Science Department, June 1970.

Wenninger, Magnus J. *Polyhedron Models.* Cambridge, England: Cambridge University Press, 1971.

Wenninger, Magnus J. *Principles of 3-Dimensional Design.* New York: Van Nostrand Reinhold, 1977.

Wexelblat, Richard L. *History of Programming Languages.* New York: Academic Press, 1981.

Whitney, John. *Digital Harmony: On the Complimentarity of Music and Visual Art.* Petersborough, NH: McGraw-Hill, 1980.

Whitted, T. "An Improved Illumination Model for Shaded Display." *Communications of the ACM* (June 1980): 343–49.

Wilson, Mark. *Drawing with Computers.* New York: The Putnam Publishing Group, 1985.

Wirth, Niklaus. "Data Structures and Algorithms." *Scientific American* (September 1984).

Wong, Wucius. *Principles of Three-Dimensional Design.* New York: Van Nostrand Reinhold, 1977.

Wong, Wucius. *Principles of Two-Dimensional Design.* New York: Van Nostrand Reinhold, 1972.

Woodson, W. E. *Human Factors Design Handbook.* New York: McGraw-Hill, 1981.

Yoshinari, Mayumi. *Computer Graphics/ SIG.* Tokyo: Genkosha, 1982.

Youngblood, Gene. *Expanded Cinema.* New York: E. P. Dutton Inc., 1968.

Zapf, Herman. "Changes in Letterforms Due to Technical Developments." *Journal of Typographic Research* (October 1968): 351–68.

SPECIALIZED COMPUTER GRAPHICS PERIODICALS

ACM Transactions on Graphics. Association for Computing Machinery. 11 West 42 Street, New York, NY 10036.

Anderson Report. 4265 Avenida Simi, Simi Valley, CA 93063.

Byte. 70 Main Street, Peterborough, NH 03458.

CAD/CAM Digest. P.O. Box 8100, Dallas, TX 75205.

Cinefex. Box 20027, Riverside, CA 92516.

Computer Aided Design. IPC Science and Technology Press, Ltd. 32 High Street, Guildford, Surrey, England GU1 3EW.

Computer Aided Publishing Report. 52 Dragon Court, Woburn, MA.

Computer Graphics, ACM/Siggraph. 11 West 42 Street, New York, NY 10036.

Computer Graphics and Applications. IEEE. 10662 Los Vaqueros Circle, Los Alamitos, CA.

Computer Graphics and Image Processing. Academic Press, Inc. 111 Fifth Avenue, New York, NY 10003.

Computer Graphics Today. 8401 Arlington Blvd., Fairfax, VA 22031.

Computer Graphics World. 1714 Stockton St., San Francisco, CA 94133.

Computer Pictures. Backstage Publications, Inc. 165 West 46 Street, New York, NY 10036.

Computers and Graphics. Pergamon Press, Inc. Maxwell House, Fairview Park, Elmsford, NY 10523.

Klein Newsletter. Box 89, Sudbury, MA 01776.

Millimeter. 12 East 46 Street, New York, NY 10017.

Pixel: The Computer Animation Newsletter. 217 George Street, Toronto, Ontario, M5A 2M9, Canada.

PROFESSIONAL SOCIETIES

National Computer Graphics Association. 8401 Arlington Blvd., Fairfax, VA 22031.

Siggraph (Association for Computing Machinery). 11 West 42 Street, New York, NY 10036.

SMPTE, 862 Scarsdale Avenue, Scarsdale, New York 10583, annual.

SOURCES OF VISUAL MATERIAL

DeFanti, Tom, ed. *Siggraph Video Review.* UIC/EECS, MS 154, Box 4348, Chicago, IL 60680.

George, James, and Steven Levine, eds. "Frontiers in Computer Graphics." Microfiche supplements to *Computer Graphics.* Association for Computing Machinery, 11 West 42 Street, New York, NY 10036.

Siggraph Slide Sets. Association for Computing Machinery. 11 West 42 Street, New York, NY 10036.

INDEX

Accounting software, 269
ACM Core System, 46
Action, 177. *See also* Animation
  deformations to create, 180–81
  global and local, 178
  rates of change of, 177–78
  simulation of, 179–80
  using transformations, 178–79
Active area, on-screen, 91
Ada (language), 45
Address of ports, 33
Address of words in memory, 7
Aerial perspective, 189
ALGOL (language), 43
Algorithm, 35, 36
Aliasing, 23–24, 128
  anti-, 134
Alphanumeric printers, 71
ALU. *See* Arithmetic and logic unit
American Standard Code for Information Interchange. *See* ASCII code
Analog media, 20–23
Angles, 12–13
  of incidence and reflection, 186
Animatic, 222
Animation, 172. *See also* Action
  computer, 143, 177, 222–28
APL (language), 45
Application programs, 38
Architecture, 269–73
Area fill methods, 134
Arguments of a program, 34
Arithmetic and logic unit (ALU), 29
ASCII code, 141, 212, 241
Aspect ratio, 15
Assembler, 41, 42
Assembly drawings, 195
Assembly language, 41
Assembly robots, 268
Atmospherics, 189
Automated offices, 239
Automatic scaling, 254
Auxiliary views, 198

Backup and archival procedures, 104
Backup facility, 95

Balloon graph, 251
Bar graph, 250
Barndoors and light control, 186
BASIC (language), 45
Batch processes, 39–40, 41, 49
Binary numbers, 5
Bitmaps and bitplanes, 14, 15, 126
  memory storage. *See* Frame buffer memory
Bits, 4
Blanking, film, 23
Blueprints, 161
Body type, 210
Boundary determination, 151
Break key, 86
Brightness, 186
Broadcasting, 50
Brush spite, 143
Bubble graph, 251
Budgeting systems, 97
Bus, 28–29
Business graphics, 246–55
Buttons, 90
Bytes, 4

C (language), 45
CADAM. *See* Computer-Aided Design and Manufacturing
CAD/CAM. *See* Computer-Aided Design and Manufacturing
Called programs, 35
Capping, 168
Cartesian coordinates, 11–12
Cartography, 243–46
Case, type, 212
CAT scans, *See* Computer-Aided Tomography scans
Cell animation, 13, 226
Central processing unit (CPU), 29–30
  time ratio, 100
Chernoff graphs, 254
Chiaroscuro, 193–95
Clipping, 167
Clock, 29
Close-packed vectors (CPV), 193
Clothing and textile design, 277–78

COBOL (language), 41, 43, 45
Codes, computer, 5
Color,
  codes, 118
  correction, 118, 219
  dithered, 123
  gamut conversions, 112
  and illustration systems, 217–18
  mixing and ramping, 217
  process, 112
  pseudo, 123
  resolution requirements, 112, 114
  separations, 219
  of surfaces, 182
  tint, 118, 123
Coloring techniques, 118–23
Color systems, 101, 110–14
Color table animation, 226
Combinational geometry, 166–68
Command and control systems, 236
Command language interpreters, 94–96
Communications between user and computer, 94–96, 101–2
Compilers, 41
Compositing,
  mattes, 112, 135, 140
  pagination, 219–22
Computer-Aided Design and Manufacturing, (CADAM), 264–65, 283–84
  cycle of production, 265–69
Computer-Aided Tomography (CAT) scans, 17, 74, 80, 126
Computer animation. *See* Animation
Computer-assisted cartoon. *See* Cell animation
Computer graphics systems. *See also* Integrated systems; Three-dimensional media; Two-dimensional interactive systems; Two-dimensional media
  basic concepts of, 3–24
  in the future, 283
  producing and directing, 96–100
  production rules of thumb, 98, 100
  system operations and staff, 104
  system selection, 102–3

user interface design, 100–4
Computer systems,
    basic principles, 4–24
    hardware, 28–33
    interfacing users with, 83–104
    software, 28, 33–40
Computer vision, 149–52
Computing environment, 96
COM units, 67, 71
Concatenated transformations, 170–72
Contact switches, 58
Continuous contrast mattes, 136
Continuous data, 13–18
    and cartesian space. *See* Point(s)
    conversions, hybrid forms, zels, 20
Continuous shading, 195
Contour, 191
    areas of color. *See* Pseudocolor
    digitizing with sections, 160–61
Contracting for computer graphics pro-
    duction, 97–98
Contrast, 118
Control characters, 212
Control console, 237
Cookies, and light patterning, 186
Coordinate systems, and dimensional-
    ity, 9, 11–13
Coplanar techniques, 161–62
CPU. *See* Central processing unit
Crosshatching, 193
CRT displays,
    direct view storage tube, 66–67
    photographing, 67, 72–73
    refresh vector, 32–33, 65, 218
    video raster display, 31–32, 71–72
Cube, defining, 161–62
Cursor, 85–86, 143
Cyan-yellow-magenta (CYM) gamut,
    110, 182
    conversions, 112
Cycles, and animation, 179
CYM. *See* Cyan-yellow-magenta gamut

Data, 6–7
    associated, 266
    continuous and discrete, 13–18
    geometric, 266
    photographic, 243
    sociological, 245
    topographical, 245–46
Data bases, 8–9, 96–97, 100, 238–39
Data structures, 7–9
Datatypes, 5. *See also* Codes; Numbers
Decimal numbers. *See* Real numbers
Defaults, 95
Deformations, and action, 180–81

Density scanners, 17
Depth, 76, 226. *See also* Zels
Depth cueing, 190–91
Desk organizer, 239
Device-independent subroutines, 46
Dialogue, user-machine, 86, 90, 101
    properties of, 94–96
Dials, 63
Diffuse surface, 186–87
Diffusion filters, 147
Digital differential algorithm, 134
Digital media, 20–23
Digital typography, 207–14
Digitizing, 21–22
    and model construction, 158–59
    point, 159
Digitizing tablet, 64
Dimensionality,
    and coordinate systems, 9, 11–13
    and graphics peripherals, 54, 58–80
Dimension drawings, 195
Direct view storage tube, 66–67
Discrete data, 13–18
    and cartesian space. *See* Pixel
    conversions, hybrid forms, zels, 20
Display list,
    features, and illustration, 218
    memory, 32–33
    systems, 218
Displays. *See* CRT displays; Refresh
    vector displays; Monitors; Video
    raster display
Display type, 210–11
Dissolve, 141
Distributed processing, 48–50
Dollying, 169, 174
Dot matrix printers, 56, 59, 61, 71
Dot matrix type, 141
Double exposure, 141
Drafting, 195–98, 267
Drafting perspective, 195
Draft notation, 277
Drop shadows, 213
Drum plotters, 64
Drum scanners, 71
Dyadic image processes, 135–43
Dynamic range of pixels, 15–16

Eases, 177
Edge determination, 151
Edges of a polygon, 17
Education and training, 258–61
Electronic mail, 239
Electronic publishing, 207, 239–41
Electrostatic plotters, 71
Enter key, 86

Ergonomics, and user-computer inter-
    face, 100–101
Error message, 86
Escape, 86, 90
Exchanges, 241
Explor (language), 145
Extremes, and action, 181
Extruded sides, type, 213
Extrusion, 159

Fades, 140–41
Fall-off parameter of spotlights, 186
Farings, 177
Filters, 147, 183
Fine arts, and computer graphics, 228
Firmware, 31
Flat scanners, 67
Flips of images, 128, 131
Flood imaging, 134
FLOWMATIC (language), 45
Flying spot scanners, 67
Focal length, 174
Folios, 220
Font, type, 212
Formatting commands, 93, 212
Forms entry, 93–94
FORTRAN (language), 41, 43, 145

Four-variable color models, 112
Fractals, 166
Frame buffer memory, 31–32
Function keys, 59, 101
Functions (program), 35

Geometric transformations, 168–72
Gesture, 178
Global action, 178
Global operators, 143
Glows, 141
Graph, 250
Graphic languages, 45–48
Graphics Kernel System (GKS), 46
Graphics peripherals. *See* Peripheral
    devices for graphics
Graphics proprocessor, 46
Graphics tablet, 64

Halftoning, 134–35
Hardware, 28–33
Hidden line removal, 191
Hierarchically articulated tree, 178
High-pass filters, 147
Histogram, 114, 118
HLS. *See* Hue-luminance-saturation
    gamut
Holdbacks, 135

Holograms, 74, 75, 283
Hue-luminance-saturation (HLS)
    gamut, 112, 114

Identity look-up table, 115
Identity transformations, 169
Illustration systems, 215–19
Image analysis. *See* Computer vision
Image averaging, 145
Image enhancement, 147–49
Image mapping, 131, 183–84
Image warping, 131
Imaging processes,
    color and black-and-white, 109–23
    three-dimensional, 157–98
    two-dimensional, 125–52
Impact strikers, 59
In-betweens, and action, 180–81
Indirect command files, 95
Industrial design, 265
Information systems, 238–41
Ink jet plotters, 71
Input devices for graphics peripherals,
    56–57, 85–86
    one-dimensional, 58–63
    three-dimensional point, 74
    two-dimensional pixel, 67
    two-dimensional point, 63–64
    user needs and, 101
    for voxels, 80
    for zels, 75–76
Input text, 212
Instancing, 172
Instruction register, 29
Instruction word, 41
Instrumentation displays, 260
Integer numbers, 5, 13
Integrated publishing, 206–7
Integrated systems, 202–3
Intensity resolution of pixels, 15
Interaction software, 84–94
Interaction techniques, 101–2
Interactive command interpreter, 39
Interactive soft copy, 57
Interactive systems, 215
    and animation, 222, 223
    two-dimensional, 235–61
Interactive video games, 255
Interfacing users and computer
    systems,
    design considerations, 100–4
    interaction software, 84–94
    producing and directing systems,
        96–100
    properties of dialogue, 94–96
Interior design, 269–73

Interpolation, and action, 181
Interpreter, 41
Inverse transformation, 170
Invoked programs, 35
I/O. *See* Input; Output
Isobars, 254

Joysticks, 64
Justification of type, 214

Kerning type, 214
Keyboard, 58–59, 85–86, 93, 212
    user needs and, 101
Key positions, and action, 181
Keys, 135–36
Kilobyte, 5
Knockouts, 135

Languages, programming, 35, 40–48
Leading, type, 213
Length, type, 213
Lens, 174
Letter spacing, 214
Life (software), 145
Light pen, 64
Lights and lighting, 185–89
Line(s), 11. *See also* Vector
    graphics peripherals to make, 54–56
    rendering, 190–91
    representation, 134
    two-dimensional continuous, 16–17
Line copy, 14
Line graph, 250
LISP (language), 45
Local action, 178
Local operators, 143–45
Logical functions, 7
Logo, (language), 45
Look-up tables, 114–15, 118, 226
Low-pass filter, 147
Luminance, 54, 114–18
Luminescence, 182–83
Luster of surfaces, 184

Machine language, 41
Machines, computer-controlled, 237,
    267
Magenta-yellow-cyan-black. *See* Pro-
    cess color
Main memory, 30
Management and management sys-
    tems, 96–97
Management decision systems, 246–55
Mapping. *See* Image mapping
Maps. *See* Cartography
Market testing, 267

Marquee, 226
Matching templates, 151
Matrix, 8
Matte, 112
Matte compositing, 135–40
Matte surface, 186–87
Megabyte, 5
Memory (computer), 4, 7, 16, 30–33
Menu, 90–91
Microprocessor chip, 29, 30
Milling machine, 76, 80
Mirror surfaces, 184
Mixing of colors, 217
Model construction, 158–66
Modem, 238
Moire pattern, 24
Monadic image processes, 126–31
Monitor and control systems, 236–38
Monitors, 101, 237–38. *See also*
    Displays
Motion blur, 181
Motion control systems, 224
Motion graphics, 224
Motion pathway, 178
Mouse, 58, 63–64
Multiple pass cinematography, 224
Multiplex holograms, 75
Multispectral images, 243
Multiuser system, 38, 39
MYCB (magenta-yellow-cyan-black).
    See Process color

NAPLPS, 241
Navigational systems, 237
Negative look-up table, 115
Networks, 48–50
Noise reduction, 148
Normal determination, 152
Normal of a surface, 18
North American Presentation Level
    Protocol Standard (NAPLPS), 241
Nuclear magnetic resonance (NMR),
    80
Number of degrees of freedom, 54
Numbers, 5, 35
Numerical control, 76, 80
    of tools, 268

Objects, 158
    actors and actions on, 177–81
    lights and lighting of, 185–89
    model construction of, 158–66
    primitive transformations of, 168–72
    rendering, 190–98
    set construction of, 166–68
    surface attributes of, 182–85

Objects of revolution, 159–60
Occultation, 191
OCR. *See* Optical character recognition
Offices, automated, 239
Offsetting objects, 168–69
Omnidirectional light, 186
One-dimensional peripherals, 58–63
Opaque surface rendering, 193
Opcode, 41
Operand, 41
Operating system (OS), 38–39
Operators of graphics systems, 104, 236
Optical character recognition (OCR), 58, 212
OS. *See* Operating system
Output devices for graphics peripherals, 56–57, 86
   one-dimensional, 58–63
   three-dimensional point, 75
   two-dimensional pixel, 71–73
   two-dimensional point, 64–67
   user needs and, 101
   for voxels, 80
   for zels, 76, 80
Overlays, 138

Package design, 274–77
Pages, on-screen, 91–92
Pagination, 219–22
Paint systems, 218–19
Palette, 114–15
Pan, 174
Pantographs, 75, 76
Parallel port, 33
Parameter table, 178
Parametric surface patches, 166
Pascal (language), 45
Patterns, 126, 183–84
Peer graph, 250
Perception, 151
Peripheral devices for graphics, 53–80
   connecting, 33
   number of degrees of freedom, 54
   one-dimensional, 58–63
   and subroutine libraries, 46
   three-dimensional, 73–80
   topologies of, 54–57
   two-dimensional, 63–73
   zero-dimensional, 58
Peripheral memory, 31–32
Perspective, 13, 172–76
   drafting, 195
Phase, and animation, 179
Photogrammetry, 152, 158
   and model construction, 162

Photography, 13, 21, 74, 118, 219
   of CRT displays, 67, 72–73
Physical simulations, 267
Pica, type, 213
Picked cursor, 85
Picture Description Instructions, 241
Pie chart, 250
Pixel, 20. *See also* Bitmaps; Voxels; Zels
   averaging, 145
   definition of, 14
   graphics peripherals to make, 54–56
   read and write, 126
   techniques of point to, 134–35
   two-dimensional discrete images, 14–16
   two-dimensional input of, 67
   two-dimensional output of, 71–73
   weighted average of, 147
Plane(s), 11
   in three-dimensional space, 18
   two-dimensional continuous, 16–17
Platen, 63, 65, 224
Plotters, 54, 58, 64–65
Point(s), 11, 14, 20
   calculating sequence of, 162–63
   digitizing, 74, 159–62
   fractals, 166
   memory storage. *See* Display list memory
   to pixel techniques, 134–35
   rendering, 190
   statistical distributions of, 163–66
   three-dimensional input of, 74
   three-dimensional output of, 75
   in three-dimensional space, 18
   two-dimensional continuous, 16–17
   two-dimensional input of, 63–64
   two-dimensional output of, 64–67
   of type, 213
Pointed cursor, 85
Point list table, 161
Point of view, 172–75
Polar coordinates, 12
Polar graph, 250
Polygon, 17, 18, 20
   memory storage. *See* Display list memory
Polygonal shading, 193–95
Polyhedra, 17–18
Ports, input and output, 30, 33
   serial and parallel, 33
Ports, on-screen, 91–92, 175–76
Posterization, 123
Potentiometers, 63, 90
Presentation graph, 250
Primitive functions, 163

Primitive transformations of solid objects, 168–72
Printers, 56–71. *See also* Dot matrix printers
Priority in two-dimensions, 13
Procedures (program), 35
Process color, 112
Process control systems, 236, 268
Process planning, 267
Production cost ratio, 100
Production scheduling and monitoring systems, 97
Production time ratio, 100
Production units, computer graphics, contracting with, 97–98
   rules of thumb concerning, 98, 100
Program counter, 29
Programs, 6–7, 34–40. *See also* Software
Prompt message, 86
   multiple, 93
Pseudocolor, 123
Pulldown menus, 92

Quantization (digitizing), 21–22
QWERTY keyboard, 59, 93, 101

Radar, 74, 76
RAM. *See* Random access memory
Random access memory (RAM), 30
Raster graphics,
   peripherals. *See* Video raster display
   subroutine libraries for, 46
Read only memory (ROM), 30–31
Read operation, 7
Real numbers, 5, 14
Reconstruction, 13, 151–52
Rectification points, 162
Red-green-blue (RGB) gamut, 110, 182
   codes for, 118
   conversions, 112
Reflections, 186–88
Refraction, 189
Refresh vector CRT displays, 32–33, 65, 218
Registers, 29
Relational data structures, 8
Rendering, 190–98
Resolution,
   color, 112, 114
   intensity, 15
   luminance, 54
   spatial, 54
   temporal, 54
Restoration techniques, 148
RGB. *See* Red-green-blue gamut
Robot arms, 75

Robotics, 58, 283
ROM. *See* Read only memory
Rotation, 128, 169–70
Run process control, 268

Sample (digitizing), 21
Scale of an axis, 11
Scalings, 128
Scan conversion, 134, 193
Scattergram, 250
Screen, 85–95
Script, 222
Scrolling, 91, 126
Scroll lock, 91
Sections, 160–61
Self-mattes. *See* Keys
Sensors, 236–37
Serial port, 33
Set construction, 166–68, 226–28
Shading, 193–95
Shadows, 188–89
Shaft encoders, 61, 63, 74, 224
Shape,
 of a matrix, 8
 of numbers, 35
 representation in models, 158–59
Sharpening filters, 147
Shear transformation, 170
Simulation,
 of action, 179–80
 analysis of product design, 266
Single user system, 38
Sizing transformation, 169
Sliders, 90
Slit-scans, 226
Softcopy graphics peripherals, 57
Software, 28, 33–40. *See also*
 Programs
 accounting, 269
 general types of, 33–40
 interaction, 84–94
 virtual applications, 92–93
Solid models, 18. *See also* Polyhedra;
 Three-dimensional graphic processes; Three-dimensional media
 applications
 actors and actions on, 177–81
 construction of, 158–66
 lights and lighting, 185–89
 primitive transformations of, 168–72
 rendering, 190–98
 set construction of, 166–68
 surface attributes of, 182–85
Solid renderings, 193
Solonoid, 58
Sonar, 74
Spatial aliasing, 23, 24

Spatial data-base managers, 239
Spatial frequency processing, 148–49
Spatial resolution, 54
 of a bitmap, 15
Specular reflections, 187
Spherical coordinates, 12–13
Spotlight, 186
Spreadsheets, 97, 249–50
Sprites, 141–43
Squashing objects, 181
Stamp sprite, 143
Static mattes, 136, 138
Status register, 29
Stepping motor, 61, 63
Stereopsis, 176
Stewards in graphics systems, 104
Storyboard, 222
Streaks, 141, 224
Stretching objects, 181
Strobes, 141, 224
Subroutine libraries, 46
Subroutines, 35
Surface attributes, 182–85
Surface net, 251
Surfaces. *See* Polyhedra
Switches, 58
Synthavision (language), 42
Systems programmers, 104

Teletext, 239, 241
Televisions. *See* Monitors; Video raster
 display
Television scanners, 67
Templates,
 graphic, 95–96
 matching, 151
Temporal aliasing, 23
Temporal resolution, 54
Tetrahedron, 18
Text,
 input/output, 58–63
 manipulation, 93–94
Textile and clothing design, 277–78
Texture of surfaces, 184–185, 187
Thermographic printers, 71
Three-dimensional digitizers, 74
Three-dimensional graphic peripherals,
 74–80
Three-dimensional graphic processes,
 6, 157–98
 actors and actions, 177–81
 animation, 226–28
 conversions, hybrid forms, zels, 20
 lights and lighting, 185–89
 model construction, 158–66
 perspective, windows, ports, 172–76
 primitive transformations, 168–72

rendering, 190–98
 set construction, 166–68
 surface attributes, 182–85
Three-dimensional media applications,
 architecture and interior design,
 269–73
 clothing and textile design, 277–78
 industrial design, 265–69
 package design, 274–77
Three-dimensional space, 12
Threshold, black-and-white, 115
Ticker, 241
Ticklers, 239
Time, 11, 177, ???
Time-sharing, 39, 41, 50
Tint color, 118, 123
Toggles, 90
Touch sensitive screen, 64
Trackball, 64
Transaction validations, 94
Transformations, of objects, 168–72,
 178–79
Translation of objects, 168–69
Transparencies, 67
Transparency of surfaces, 183
Traveling mattes, 138
Trees, data, 8
Tristimulus color gamuts, 110–12
Truncate responses, 95
Turnkey systems, 102
Two-dimensional graphic peripherals,
 63–73
Two-dimensional graphic processes, 6,
 11, 13, 125–52
 computer vision, 149–52
 continuous images. *See* Point(s),
 Line(s), Plane(s)
 conversions, hybrid forms, zels, 20
 discrete images. *See* Pixel
 dyadic processes, 135–43
 image enhancement, 147–49
 local and global operators, 143–45
 monadic image, 126–31
 point to pixel techniques, 134–35
Two-dimensional interactive systems,
 business graphics, 246–55
 cartography, 243–46
 education and training, 258–61
 information systems, 238–41
 management decision systems, 246–
 55
 monitor and control systems, 236–
 38
 video instruments and games, 254–
 58
Two-dimensional media applications,
 animation, 222–28

color correction and separation, 219
digital typography, 207–14
fine arts, 228
illustration systems, 205–19
pagination, 219–22
Two-dimensional space, 11–12
2½ dimensional system, 13
Type-ahead facility, 95
Typography, 207–14

Union operators, 166–67
Unit names, 33
Users of computer graphics systems,
236, 237, 238
ergonomic considerations, 100–4
man-machine interface, 101–2
system selection and, 102–3
systems operation and staffs, 104
Utilities programs, 38

Value rule, spreadsheet, 249
Value, spreadsheet, 249
Variable name, 7
of ports, 33
Vector, 17, 54. See also Line(s)
Vector displays. See Refresh vector
CRT display
Vector graphics, 17, 56, 190. See also
Three-dimensional graphics
processes
subroutine libraries for, 46
Vertices of a polygon, 17
Videodisc, 31, 238–39
Video games, 254–58
Video raster display, 71–72
Video synthesizers, 255
Videotex, 239, 241
Virtual applications, 92–93

Virtual environments, 260–61
Virtual memory, 31
Visual language, 110
color and black-and-white, 109–23
three-dimensional imaging, 157–98
two-dimensional imaging, 125–52
Volume, 11. See also Occultation;
Voxels
and light interaction, 189
representation in models, 158–59
Voxels, 17, 126
input peripherals for, 80
and model construction, 162
output peripherals for, 80

Wait symbol, 85, 86
Warp and weft, 277
Weighted average of pixels, 147
Window, on-screen, 91, 172–74, 175
Window/port management, 91, 175
Wipes, 138, 140
Wire frame rendering, 190–91
Word (computing unit), 4–5, 7
Word processing, 93, 212
Work station, graphics, 216–17
Write operation, 7

Xanadu (data base), 239
X axis, 11
X rays, 80

Y axis, 11

Z axis, 12
Zels, 20, 126
input/output for, 75–76, 80
and model construction, 162